Anonymous

**Liturgy**

Or, Book of Worship, for the use of the new Church signified by the new Jerusalem

Anonymous

**Liturgy**
*Or, Book of Worship, for the use of the new Church signified by the new Jerusalem*

ISBN/EAN: 9783337162252

Printed in Europe, USA, Canada, Australia, Japan

Cover: Foto ©Lupo / pixelio.de

More available books at **www.hansebooks.com**

OR

# BOOK OF WORSHIP,

FOR THE USE OF

## THE NEW CHURCH

SIGNIFIED BY THE

## NEW JERUSALEM.

REVISED AND PUBLISHED BY ORDER OF THE
GENERAL CONVENTION.

NEW YORK:
PUBLISHED BY THE GENERAL CONVENTION OF THE NEW JERUSALEM
CHURCH IN THE UNITED STATES,
AT THE OFFICE OF ITS BOARD OF PUBLICATIONS,
346 BROADWAY,
JOHN L. JEWETT, AGENT.
1860.

# ORDER OF WORSHIP.

---

While the people are assembling, a voluntary may be played upon the organ.

### INTRODUCTION.

The congregation being seated, the Minister, opening the Word, may read one or more of the following passages.

JEHOVAH is in his holy Temple; let all the earth keep silence before him. — Hab. ii. 20.

ENTER into his gates with thanksgiving, into his courts with praise: be thankful unto him, and bless his name. — Ps. c. 4.

ONE thing have I desired of JEHOVAH, that will I seek after; that I may dwell in the house of JEHOVAH all the days of my life, to behold the beauty of JEHOVAH, and to inquire in his temple. — Ps. xxvii. 4.

GIVE unto JEHOVAH, O ye kindreds of the people, give unto JEHOVAH glory and strength: give unto JEHOVAH the glory due unto his name: bring an offering, and come into his courts. O worship JEHOVAH in the beauty of holiness: fear before him, all the earth. — Ps. xcvi. 7, 8, 9.

FOR from the rising of the sun even unto the going down of the same, my name shall be great among the Gentiles; and in every place incense shall be offered unto my name, and a pure offering: for my name shall be great among the heathen, saith JEHOVAH of hosts. — Mal. i. 11.

EXALT ye JEHOVAH our GOD, and worship at his footstool; for he is holy. — Ps. xcix. 5.

HOLINESS becometh thine house, O JEHOVAH, for ever. — Ps. xciii. 5.

Here may be a short pause for silent prayer; after which, the Minister may say one of the following Collects: or, instead of the Prayer and Collect, or after them, a Selection may be sung.

## COLLECTS.

GIVE ear to my words, O JEHOVAH; consider my meditation. Hearken unto the voice of my cry, my King, and my GOD; for unto thee will I pray. My voice shalt thou hear in the morning, O JEHOVAH; in the morning will I address thee, and will look up: for thou art not a GOD that hath pleasure in wickedness; neither shall evil dwell with thee. The profane shall not stand in thy sight; thou hatest all workers of iniquity. Thou shalt destroy them that speak falsehood: JEHOVAH will abhor the man of blood and deceit. But as for me, I will come into thy house in the multitude of thy mercy: in thy fear will I worship toward thy holy temple. Lead me, O JEHOVAH, in thy righteousness, because of mine enemies; make thy way straight before my face. — Ps. v. 1-8.

HEAR my cry, O GOD; attend unto my prayer. From the end of the earth will I cry unto thee, when my heart is overwhelmed: lead me to the rock that is higher than I. For thou hast been a shelter for me, a strong tower from the enemy. I will abide in thy tabernacle for ever: I will trust in the covert of thy wings. For thou, O God, hast heard my vows: thou hast given me the heritage of those that fear thy name. — Ps. lxi. 1-5.

O GOD, thou art my GOD; early will I seek thee My soul thirsteth for thee, my flesh longeth for thee, in a dry and thirsty land, where no water is; to see thy power and thy glory, so as I have seen thee in the sanctuary. Because thy loving kindness is better than life, my lips shall praise thee. Thus will I bless thee while I live: I will lift up my hands in thy name. — Ps. lxiii. 1 – 4.

GIVE ear, O JEHOVAH, to my prayer; and attend to the voice of my supplications. In the day of my trouble I will call upon thee: for thou wilt answer me. Among the gods there is none like unto thee, O LORD; neither are there any works like unto thy works. All nations whom thou hast made shall come and worship before thee, O LORD; and shall glorify thy name. For thou art great, and doest wondrous things: thou art GOD alone. — Ps. lxxxvi. 6 – 10.

O JEHOVAH, I cry unto thee; make haste unto me: give ear unto my voice, when I cry unto thee. Let my prayer be set forth before thee as incense; and the lifting up of my hands as the evening sacrifice. — Ps. cxli. 1, 2.

Here the Minister may read two of the following passages, as collated, showing that the LORD in His DIVINE HUMANITY is

THE TRUE OBJECT OF WORSHIP.

HEAR, O Israel, JEHOVAH our God is one JEHOVAH. Deut vi. 4.

AND he was clothed with a vesture dipped in blood: and his name is called THE WORD OF GOD. And he hath on his vesture and on his thigh a name written, KING OF KINGS, AND LORD OF LORDS. — Rev. xix. 13, 16.

FOR unto us a CHILD is born, unto us a SON is given: and the government shall be upon his shoulder: and his name shall be called Wonderful, Counsellor, The mighty GOD, The EVERLASTING FATHER, The Prince of Peace. — Is. ix. 6.

AND she shall bring forth a SON, and thou shalt call

his name JESUS: for he shall save his people from their sins. Behold, a virgin shall be with child, and shall bring forth a Son, and they shall call his name Emmanuel, which being interpreted is, God with us. — Mat. i. 21, 23.

Thus saith Jehovah thy Redeemer, and he that formed thee from the womb, I am Jehovah that maketh all things; that stretcheth forth the heavens alone; that spreadeth abroad the earth by myself. — Is. xliv. 24.

In the beginning was the Word, and the Word was with God, and the Word was God. The same was in the beginning with God. All things were made by him; and without him was not any thing made that was made. And the Word was made flesh, and dwelt among us. — John i. 1, 2, 3, 14.

For thus saith Jehovah that created the heavens; God himself that formed the earth and made it; he hath established it, he created it not in vain; he formed it to be inhabited: I am Jehovah; and there is none else; there is no God else besides Me; a just God and a Savior; there is none besides Me. Look unto Me, and be ye saved, all the ends of the earth; for I am God, and there is none else. — Is. xlv. 18, 21, 22.

Come unto Me, all ye that labor and are heavy laden, and I will give you rest. Take My yoke upon you, and learn of Me; for I am meek and lowly in heart: and ye shall find rest unto your souls. — Mat. xi. 28, 29.

Thus saith Jehovah, the King of Israel, and his Redeemer, Jehovah of Hosts; I am the First, and I am the Last; and beside me there is no God. — Is. xliv. 6.

I am Alpha and Omega, the Beginning and the Ending, saith the Lord; who is, and who was, and who is to come, the Almighty. — Rev. i. 8.

BEHOLD, the LORD JEHOVAH will come with strength and his arm shall rule for him: behold, his reward is with him, and his work before him. He shall feed his flock like a SHEPHERD: he shall gather the lambs with his arm, and carry them in his bosom; and shall gently lead those that are with young. — Is. xl. 10, 11.

I AM the good SHEPHERD, and know my sheep, and am known of mine. My sheep hear my voice, and I know them, and they follow me: and I give unto them eternal life; and they shall never perish, neither shall any one pluck them out of my hand. My FATHER, who gave them me, is greater than all; and no one is able to pluck them out of my FATHER's hand. I and the FATHER are ONE. — John x. 14, 27-30.

DOUBTLESS Thou art our FATHER, though Abraham be ignorant of us, and Israel acknowledge us not: Thou, O JEHOVAH, art our FATHER, our Redeemer; thy name is from everlasting. — Is. lxiii. 16.

JESUS saith unto him, Have I been so long time with you, and yet hast thou not known ME, Philip? he that hath seen ME, hath seen the FATHER. I am in the FATHER, and the FATHER in ME. — John xiv. 9, 10.

INTRODUCTION TO PRAYER.

The Minister may then read one or more of the following passages as introductory to prayer; or one of the Invitations to Worship on pages 41, 42, and 43.

AND after six days, JESUS taketh Peter, James, and John his brother, and bringeth them up into a high mountain apart, and was transfigured before them; and his face did shine as the sun, and his raiment was white as the light. And, behold, there appeared unto them Moses and Elias talking with him. Then answered Peter, and said unto JESUS, LORD, it is good for us to be here: if thou wilt, let us make here three tabernacles; one for Thee, and one for Moses, and one for Elias. While he yet spake, behold, a bright cloud overshadowed them: and behold a voice out of the cloud, which said, This is my beloved Son, in whom I am well pleased: hear ye Him. — Mat. xvii. 1 – 5.

AGAIN I say unto you, that if two of you shall agree on earth, as touching any thing that they shall ask, it shall be done for them of my FATHER who is in heaven: for where two or three are gathered together in my name, there am I in the midst of them. Then came Peter to him, and said, LORD, how oft shall my brother sin against me, and I forgive him? till seven times? JESUS saith unto him, I say not unto thee, until seven times; but until seventy times seven. — Mat. xviii 19 – 22.

AND JESUS answering, saith unto them, Have faith of GOD. For verily I say unto you, that whosoever shall say unto this mountain, Be thou removed, and be thou cast into the sea; and shall not doubt in his heart, but shall believe that those things which he saith shall come to pass; he shall have whatsoever he saith. Therefore I say unto you, What things soever ye desire when ye pray, believe that ye receive them, and ye shall have them. And when ye stand praying, forgive, if ye have aught against any: that your FATHER also who is in heaven may forgive you your trespasses. But if ye do not forgive, neither will your FATHER who is in heaven forgive your trespasses. — Mark xi. 22 – 26.

BUT love ye your enemies, and do good, and lend, hoping for nothing again; and your reward shall be great, and ye shall be the children of the HIGHEST: for he is kind unto the unthankful and the evil. Be ye therefore merciful, as your FATHER also is merciful. — Luke vi. 35, 36.

AND I say unto you, Ask, and it shall be given you; seek, and ye shall find; knock, and it shall be opened unto you. For every one that asketh receiveth; and he that seeketh findeth; and to him that knocketh it shall be opened. If a son shall ask bread of any of you that is a father, will he give him a stone? or if a fish, will he, for a fish, give him a serpent? or if he shall ask an egg, will he offer him a scorpion? If ye then, being evil, know how to give good gifts unto your children; how much more shall the Heavenly FATHER give the Holy Spirit to them that ask him. — Luke xi. 9 – 13.

Two men went up into the temple to pray; the one a Pharisee, and the other a publican. The Pharisee stood and prayed thus with himself: GOD, I thank thee that I am not as other men, extortioners, unjust, adulterers, or even as this publican. I fast twice in the week; I give tithes of all that I possess. And the publican, standing afar off, would not lift so much as the eyes unto heaven; but smote upon his breast, saying, GOD be merciful to me a sinner. I tell you, this man went down to his house justified rather than the other: for every one that exalteth himself, shall be abased; and he that humbleth himself, shall be exalted. — Luke xviii. 10 – 14.

BUT the hour cometh, and now is, when the true worshipers shall worship the FATHER in spirit and in truth: for the FATHER seeketh such to worship him. GOD is a Spirit; and they that worship him, must worship in spirit and in truth. — John iv. 23, 24.

AND JESUS said unto them, I am the bread of life: he that cometh to me, shall never hunger; and he that believeth on me, shall never thirst. All that the FATHER giveth me, shall come to me; and him that cometh to me, I will in no wise cast out. — John vi. 35, 37.

BELIEVE me, that I am in the FATHER, and the FATHER in me; or else believe me for the very works' sake. Verily, verily, I say unto you, He that believeth on me, the works that I do shall he do also: and greater ones than these shall he do, because I go unto my FATHER. And whatsoever ye shall ask in my name, that will I do; that the FATHER may be glori fied in the SON. If ye shall ask any thing in my name, I will do it. — John xiv. 11 – 14.

I AM the true Vine, and my FATHER is the Husbandman. Every branch in me that beareth not fruit, he taketh away; and every one that beareth fruit, he purgeth it, that it may bring forth more fruit. Now ye are clean through the word which I have spoken unto you. Abide in me, and I in you. As the branch cannot bear fruit of itself, except it abide in the vine, no more can ye, except ye abide in me. — John xv. 1 – 4.

I AM the vine, ye are the branches: he that abideth in me, and I in him, the same bringeth forth much fruit: for without me ye can do nothing. If a man abide not in me, he is cast forth as a branch, and is withered; and men gather them, and cast them into the fire, and they are burned. If ye abide in me, and my words abide in you, ye shall ask what ye will, and it shall be done unto you. — John xv. 5 – 7.

HEREIN is my FATHER glorified, that ye bear much fruit; so shall ye be my disciples. As the FATHER hath loved me, so have I loved you: continue ye in my love. If ye keep my commandments, ye shall abide in my love; even as I have kept my FATHER's commandments, and abide in his love. — John xv. 8 – 10.

YE have not chosen me, but I have chosen you, and ordained you, that ye should go and bring forth fruit, and that your fruit should remain: that whatsoever ye shall ask of the FATHER in my name, he may give it you. These things I command you, that ye love one another. — John xv 16, 17.

VERILY, verily, I say unto you, Whatsoever ye shall ask the FATHER in my name, he will give it you. Hitherto have ye asked nothing in my name: ask, and ye shall receive, that your joy may be full. These things have I spoken unto you in proverbs: but the time cometh, when I shall no more speak unto you in proverbs, but I shall show you plainly of the FATHER At that day ye shall ask in my name: and I say not unto you, that I will pray the FATHER for you; for the FATHER himself loveth you, because ye have loved me, and have believed that I came out from GOD. I came forth from the FATHER, and am come into the world: again I leave the world, and go to the FATHER. — John xvi. 23 - 28.

WHEREWITH shall I come before JEHOVAH,
And bow myself before the high GOD?
Shall I come before him with burnt offerings,
With calves of a year old?
Will JEHOVAH be pleased with thousands of rams,
Or with ten thousands of rivers of oil?
Shall I give my first-born for my transgression,
The fruit of my body for the sin of my soul?
He hath showed thee, O man, what is good;
And what doth JEHOVAH require of thee,
But to do justly, and to love mercy,
And to walk humbly with thy GOD? — Mic. vi. 6 - 8.

JEHOVAH is my light and my salvation; whom shall I fear? JEHOVAH is the strength of my life; of whom shall I be afraid? When the wicked, mine enemies and my foes, came upon me to eat up my flesh, they stumbled and fell. Though an host should encamp against me, my heart shall not fear: though war should rise against me, in this will I be confident. One thing have I desired of JEHOVAH, that will I seek after; that I may dwell in the house of JEHOVAH all the days of my life, to behold the beauty of JEHOVAH, and to inquire in his temple. For in the time of trouble he shall hide me in his pavilion: in the secret of his tabernacle shall he hide me; he shall set me up upon a rock. And now shall mine head be lifted up above mine enemies round about me: therefore will I offer in his tabernacle sacrifices of joy; I will sing, yea, I will sing praises to JEHOVAH. Hear, O JEHOVAH;

I cry with my voice: have mercy also upon me, and answer me. — Ps. xxvii. 1–7.

COME and hear, all ye that fear GOD, and I will declare what he hath done for my soul. I cried unto him with my mouth, and he was extolled with my tongue. If I regard iniquity in my heart, the LORD will not hear. But verily GOD hath heard; he hath attended to the voice of my prayer. Blessed be GOD, who hath not turned away my prayer, nor his mercy from me. — Ps. lxvi. 16–20.

AND when thou prayest, thou shalt not be as the hypocrites: for they love to pray standing in the synagogues and in the corners of the streets, that they may be seen of men. Verily I say unto you, they have their reward. But thou, when thou prayest, enter into thy closet; and when thou hast shut thy door, pray to thy FATHER who is in secret: and thy FATHER who seeth in secret, shall reward thee openly. But when ye pray, use not vain repetitions, as the heathen do: for they think that they shall be heard for their much speaking. Be not ye therefore like unto them: for your FATHER knoweth what things ye have need of, before ye ask him. — Mat. vi. 5–8.

O COME, let us worship and bow down: let us kneel before the face of JEHOVAH our Maker. — Ps. xcv. 6.

Or this.

*Min.*  O COME, let us worship and bow down:

*Peo.*  Let us kneel before the face of Je | hovah | **our** | Maker.

*M.*  For he is our GOD:

*P.*  And we are the people of his pasture, and the | sheep | of his | hand

Here the Minister may repeat one or more of the following passages or prayers, or one of those on pages 44 and 45; the people saying those parts designated for them: the Minister indicating the time for kneeling, by saying, "O come, let us worship," &c.

HAVE mercy upon me, O GOD, according to thy loving-kindness: according unto the multitude of thy tender mercies, blot out my transgressions. Wash me thoroughly from mine iniquity, and cleanse me from my sin. For I acknowledge my transgressions: and my sin is ever before me. Against thee, thee only, have I sinned, and done evil in thy sight: that thou mightest be justified when thou speakest, and be clear when thou judgest. Behold, I was shapen in iniquity; and in sin did my mother conceive me. Behold, thou desirest truth in the inward parts: and in the hidden part thou shalt make me to know wisdom. Purge me with hyssop, and I shall be clean; wash me, and I shall be whiter than snow. — Ps. li. 1 – 7.

HIDE thy face from my sins, and blot out all mine iniquities. Create in me a clean heart, O GOD; and renew a right spirit within me. Cast me not away from thy presence; and take not thy Holy Spirit from me. Restore unto me the joy of thy salvation; and uphold me with thy free Spirit. Then will I teach transgressors thy ways; and sinners shall be converted unto thee. — Ps. li. 9 – 13.

O LORD, open thou my lips, and my mouth shall show forth thy praise. For thou desirest not sacrifice; else would I give it: thou delightest not in burnt-offering. The sacrifices of GOD are a broken spirit: a broken and a contrite heart. O GOD, thou wilt not despise. Do good in thy good pleasure unto Zion: build thou the walls of Jerusalem. Then shalt thou be pleased with the sacrifices of righteousness, with burnt-offering and whole burnt-offering: then shall they offer bullocks upon thine altar. — Ps. li. 15 – 19.

O JEHOVAH, thou hast searched me, and known me: thou knowest my down-sitting and my up-rising: thou understandest my thought afar off. Thou compassest my path and my lying down, and art acquainted with all my ways. For there is not a word in my tongue, but lo, O Jehovah, thou knowest it altogether. — Ps. cxxxix. 1–4.

Whither shall I go from thy Spirit? or whither shall I flee from thy presence? If I ascend up into heaven, thou art there: if I make my bed in hell, behold, thou art there. If I take the wings of the morning, and dwell in the uttermost parts of the sea; even there shall thy hand lead me, and thy right hand shall hold me. If I say, Surely the darkness shall cover me; even the night shall be light about me. Yea, the darkness hideth not from thee; but the night shineth as the day: the darkness and the light are both alike to thee. — Ps. cxxxix. 7–12.

I remember the days of old; I meditate on all thy works; I muse on the work of thy hands. I stretch forth my hands unto thee: my soul thirsteth after thee, as a thirsty land. Hear me speedily, O Jehovah; my spirit faileth: hide not thy face from me, lest I be like unto them that go down into the pit. Cause me to hear thy loving-kindness in the morning; for in thee do I trust: cause me to know the way wherein I should walk; for I lift up my soul unto thee. Deliver me, O Jehovah, from my enemies: I flee unto thee to hide me. Teach me to do thy will; for thou art my God: thy Spirit is good; lead me into the land of uprightness. — Ps. cxliii. 5–10.

Out of the depths have I cried to thee, O Jehovah: Lord, hear my voice: let thine ears be attentive to the voice of my supplications. If thou, O Jah, shouldest mark iniquities, O Lord, who shall stand? But there is forgiveness with thee, that thou mayest be feared. I wait for Jehovah, my soul doth wait, and in his word do I hope. My soul waiteth for the Lord more than they that watch for the morning: more than they that watch for the morning. Let Israel hope in Jehovah;

## ORDER OF WORSHIP. 15

for with JEHOVAH there is mercy: and with him is plenteous redemption; and he shall redeem Israel from all his iniquities. — Ps. cxxx. 1-8.

BE merciful unto me, O LORD: for I cry unto thee daily. Rejoice the soul of thy servant: for unto thee, O LORD, do I lift up my soul. For thou, LORD, art good, and ready to forgive; and plenteous in mercy unto all them that call upon thee. Give ear, O JEHOVAH, to my prayer; and attend to the voice of my supplications. In the day of my trouble I will call upon thee: for thou wilt answer me. — Ps. lxxxvi. 3-7.

O JEHOVAH God of Hosts, hear my prayer: give ear, O GOD of Jacob. Behold, O God, our shield; and look upon the face of thine anointed. For a day in thy courts is better than a thousand. I had rather be a door-keeper in the house of my GOD, than to dwell in the tents of wickedness. For JEHOVAH GOD is a sun and shield; JEHOVAH will give grace and glory: no good will he withhold from them that walk uprightly. O JEHOVAH of hosts, blessed is the man that trusteth in thee. — Ps. lxxxiv. 8-12.

THY mercy, O JEHOVAH, is in the heavens; and thy faithfulness reacheth unto the clouds. Thy righteousness is like the mountains of GOD; thy judgments are a great deep: O JEHOVAH, thou preservest man and beast. How excellent is thy loving-kindness, O GOD! therefore the children of men put their trust under the shadow of thy wings. They shall be abundantly satisfied with the fatness of thy house; and thou shalt make them drink of the river of thy pleasures. For with thee is the fountain of life: in thy light shall we see light. O continue thy loving-kindness unto them that know thee; and thy righteousness to the upright in heart. — Ps. xxxvi. 5-10.

UNTO thee, O JEHOVAH, I lift up my soul: O my GOD, I trust in thee. Let me not be ashamed; let not mine enemies triumph over me. Yea, let none that wait on thee be ashamed: let them be ashamed who transgress without cause. Show me thy ways, O Jehovah; teach me thy paths. Lead me in thy truth, and teach me · for thou art the God of my salvation; on thee do I wait all the day. Remember, O Jehovah, thy tender mercies and thy loving-kindnesses; for they have been ever of old. Remember not the sins of my youth, nor my transgressions: according to thy mercy remember thou me, for thy goodness' sake, O Jehovah. — Ps. xxv. 1 – 7.

Let my cry come near before thee, O Jehovah: give me understanding according to thy word. Let my supplication come before thee: deliver me according to thy word. My lips shall utter praise, when thou hast taught me thy statutes. My tongue shall speak of thy word: for all thy commandments are righteousness. Let thy hand help me; for I have chosen thy precepts. I have longed for thy salvation, O Jehovah; and thy law is my delight. Let my soul live, and it shall praise thee; and let thy judgments help me. I have gone astray like a lost sheep: seek thy servant; for I do not forget thy commandments. — Ps. cxix. 169 – 176.

PRAYERS.

O Jehovah God of Israel, who dwellest between the cherubims, thou art the very God, even thou alone, of all the kingdoms of the earth: thou hast made heaven and earth. Bow down thine ear, O Jehovah, and hear; open thine eyes, O Jehovah, and see. Look down from heaven, and behold from the habitation of thy holiness and of thy glory. Doubtless thou art our Father, though Abraham be ignorant of us, and Israel acknowledge us not: thou, O Jehovah, art our Father, our Redeemer; thy name is from everlasting.

We acknowledge, O Jehovah, our wickedness, and the iniquity of our fathers; for we have sinned against thee. We are all as an unclean thing; and all our righteousnesses are as filthy rags: and we all do fade as a leaf; and our iniquities, like the wind, have taken us away. But now, O Jehovah, thou art our Father: we are the clay, and thou our potter; and we all are the work of thy hand. Help us, O God of our salvation, for the glory of thy name: and deliver us, and purge away our sins, for thy name's sake. O Jehovah, lift thou up the light of thy countenance upon us. Arise for our help; and redeem us for thy mercy's sake. Show us thy mercy, O Jehovah; and grant us thy salvation. O Lord, hear; O Lord, forgive; O Lord, hearken, and do: defer not, O our God. Quicken us, and we will call upon thy name. Turn us again, O Jehovah God of hosts; cause thy face to shine, and we shall be saved.

Let all that put their trust in thee rejoice: let them shout for joy because thou defendest them: let them also that love thy name be joyful in thee. So teach us to number our days, that we may apply our hearts unto wisdom. O satisfy us early with thy mercy, that we may rejoice and be glad all our days.

God be merciful unto us, and bless us; and cause his face to shine upon us: that thy way may be known upon earth, thy saving health among all nations. Let the people praise thee, O God; let all the people praise thee. Then shall the earth yield her increase; and God, even our own God, shall bless us. Amen.

*Or this.*

O Jehovah, our Lord, how excellent is Thy name in all the earth! who hast set Thy glory above the heavens. Unto Thee, O Jehovah, do I lift up my soul; O my God, I trust in Thee: let me not be ashamed. Show me Thy ways, O Jehovah; teach me Thy paths. Lead me in Thy truth, and teach me; for Thou art the God of my salvation: on Thee do I wait all the day. O keep my soul and deliver me: let me not be ashamed; for I put my trust in Thee. Examine me, O Jehovah, and prove me; try my reins and my heart. Bow down Thine ear to me; deliver me speedily: be

Thou my strong Rock, for a house of defence to save me. For with Thee is the fountain of life: in Thy light shall we see light. O continue Thy lovingkindness unto them that know Thee, and thy righteousness to the upright in heart. I acknowledge my transgressions, and my sin is ever before me. Purge me with hyssop, and I shall be clean; wash me, and I shall be whiter than snow. Hide Thy face from my sins, and blot out all mine iniquities. Create in me a clean heart, O God; and renew a right spirit within me. Cast me not away from thy presence, and take not thy Holy Spirit from me. Restore unto me the joy of thy salvation, and uphold me with thy free spirit. Do good in thy good pleasure unto Zion; build Thou the walls of Jerusalem. For Thy mercy is great unto the heavens, and Thy truth unto the clouds. Be Thou exalted, O God, above the heavens: let Thy glory be above all the earth. All nations whom thou hast made shall come and worship before Thee, O Lord; and shall glorify Thy name: for Thou art great, and doest wondrous things; Thou art God alone. Blessed be JEHOVAH for evermore. AMEN and AMEN.

### RESPONSIVE PRAYERS.

*Min.* Praise waiteth for thee, O God, in Zion; and unto thee shall the vow be performed. O thou that hearest prayer, unto thee shall all flesh come. — Ps. lxv. 1, 2.

*Peo.* Be merciful unto me, O Lord; for I cry unto thee daily. Rejoice the soul of thy servant; for unto thee, O Lord, do I lift up my soul. — Ps. lxxxvi. 3, 4.

*M.* Thou, Lord, art good, and ready to forgive; and plenteous in mercy unto all them that call upon thee. — Ps. lxxxvi. 5.

*P.* Give ear, O JEHOVAH to my prayer; and attend to the voice of my supplications. In the day of my trouble I will call upon thee; for thou wilt answer me. — Ps. lxxxvi. 6, 7.

ORDER OF WORSHIP. 19

*M.* All nations, whom thou hast made, shall come and worship before thee, O LORD; and shall glorify thy name : for thou art great, and doest wondrous things; thou art GOD alone. — Ps. lxxxvi. 9, 10.

*P.* Teach me thy way, O JEHOVAH; I will walk in thy truth: unite my heart to fear thy name. I will praise thee, O LORD my God, with all my heart; and will glorify thy name for evermore. — Ps. lxxxvi. 11, 12.

*M.* Thou art worthy, O LORD, to receive glory, and honor, and power: for thou hast created all things; and for thy pleasure they are, and were created. — Rev. iv. 11.

*P.* Blessing, and honor, and glory, and power, be unto him that sitteth upon the throne, and unto the LAMB, for ever and ever. — Rev. v. 13.

*Min.* and *Peo.* AMEN..

Or this.

*Min.* Give ear, O Shepherd of Israel, thou that leadest Joseph like a flock; thou that dwellest between the cherubims, shine forth. Before Ephraim, and Benjamin, and Manasseh stir up thy strength, and come and save us.

*Peo.* Turn us again, O GOD, and cause thy face to shine; and we shall be saved.

*M.* O JEHOVAH GOD OF HOSTS, how long wilt thou be angry against the prayer of thy people? Thou feedest them with the bread of tears, and givest them tears to drink in great measure. Thou makest us a strife unto our neighbors; and our enemies laugh among themselves.

*P.* Turn us again, O GOD OF HOSTS, and cause thy face to shine; and we shall be saved. — Ps. lxxx. 1-7.

*M.* Return, we beseech thee, O GOD OF HOSTS, look down from heaven, and behold, and visit this vine; and the vineyard which thy right hand hath planted, and the branch that thou madest strong for thyself. — Ps. lxxx. 14, 15.

*P.* So will not we go back from thee: quicken us, and we will call upon thy name. — Ps. lxxx. 18.

*Min.* and *Peo.* Turn us again, O JEHOVAH GOD OF HOSTS; cause thy face to shine, and we shall be saved. AMEN. — Ps. lxxx. 19.

### THE LORD'S PRAYER.

OUR FATHER, who art in the heavens; Hallowed be thy name. Thy kingdom come. Thy will be done, as in heaven, so also upon the earth. Give us this day our daily bread. And forgive us our debts, as we also forgive our debtors. And lead us not into temptation; but deliver us from evil. For thine is the kingdom, and the power, and the glory, for ever: AMEN.

### INTRODUCTION TO THE LESSONS.

Here one of the following portions from the Word may be used, the Minister and People reading alternate *lines*, all standing; or the Minister may read alone, the people sitting.

1. The law of JEHOVAH is perfect, converting the soul:
The testimony of JEHOVAH is sure, making wise the simple.
2. The statutes of JEHOVAH are right, rejoicing the heart:
The commandment of JEHOVAH is pure, enlightening the eyes.
3. The fear of JEHOVAH is clean, enduring for ever:
The judgments of JEHOVAH are true, and righteous altogether.
4. More to be desired are they than gold; yea, than much fine gold:
Sweeter also than honey, and the honey-comb.
5. Moreover, by them is thy servant warned:
In keeping them there is great reward.
6. Who can understand his errors?
Cleanse thou me from secret faults.

7. Keep back thy servant also from presumptuous sins:
Let them not have dominion over me.
8. Then shall I be upright;
And I shall be innocent from great transgression.
9. \* Let the words of my mouth, and the meditation
of my heart, be acceptable in thy sight, O JEHOVAH,
my Rock, and my Redeemer.— Ps. xix. 7–14.

1. Blessed are the undefiled in the way,
Who walk in the law of JEHOVAH.
2. Blessed are they that keep his testimonies,
That seek him with the whole heart.
3. They also do no iniquity:
They walk in his ways.
4. Thou hast commanded to keep thy precepts diligently:
O that my ways were directed to keep thy statutes.
5. Then shall I not be ashamed,
When I have respect unto all thy commandments
6. I will praise thee with uprightness of heart,
When I shall have learned thy righteous judgments
7. I will keep thy statutes:
O forsake me not utterly.— Ps. cxix. 1–8.

1. Wherewith shall a young man cleanse his way?
By taking heed according to thy Word.
2. With my whole heart have I sought thee:
O let me not wander from thy commandments.
3. Thy Word have I hid in mine heart,
That I might not sin against thee.
4. Blessed art thou, O JEHOVAH:
Teach me thy statutes.
5. With my lips have I declared all the judgments of
thy mouth:
I have rejoiced in the way of thy testimonies, as
much as in all riches.

---

\* When read alternately, both Minister and People may read this verse.

6. I will meditate in thy precepts,
And have respect unto thy ways.
7. I will delight myself in thy statutes:
I will not forget thy Word. — Ps. cxix. 9 – 16.

1. For ever, O JEHOVAH, thy Word is settled in heaven :
thy faithfulness is unto all generations:
Thou hast established the earth, and it abideth.
2. They continue this day according to thy judgments :
For all are thy servants.
3. Unless thy law had been my delights,
I should then have perished in mine affliction.
4. I will never forget thy precepts:
For with them thou hast quickened me.
5. I am thine, save me :
For I have sought thy precepts.
6. The wicked have waited for me to destroy me:
But I will consider thy testimonies.
7. I have seen an end of all perfection :
But thy commandment is exceeding broad.
Ps. cxix. 89 – 96.

1. O how love I thy law:
It is my meditation all the day.
2. Thou hast made me wiser than mine enemies,
through thy commandments:
For they are ever with me.
3. I have more understanding than all my teachers :
For thy testimonies are my meditation.
4 I understand more than the ancients;
Because I keep thy precepts.
5. I have refrained my feet from every evil way,
That I might keep thy Word.
6. I have not departed from thy judgments;
For thou hast taught me.
7. How sweet are thy words unto my taste!
Sweeter than honey to my mouth.
8. Through thy precepts I get understanding:
Therefore I hate every false way. — Ps. cxix. 97 – 104

## THE FIRST LESSON.

*Here the Minister may read a Lesson from the Old Testament, the people sitting.*

*At the close of the Lesson, the Minister may say, and the choir and people chant or respond, all standing, the following*

### DOXOLOGY. (p. 212.)

*Min.* To JESUS CHRIST be glory and dominion for ever and ever.

*Peo.* He is the ALPHA | and·the O | MEGA,
The BEGINNING and the | END, the | FIRST · and the | LAST:
Who is, and who was, and who | is to | come;
The | AL | MIGH | TY. — Rev. i. 6, 8, 17.

*Here, all standing, one of the following Responsive Services may be used the Responses to be either read or sung.*

## THE TEN COMMANDMENTS.

EXODUS XX.

Now therefore hearken, O Israel, to the statutes and to the judgments, which I teach you, to do, that ye may live, and go in and possess the land which Jehovah the God of your fathers giveth you. Ye shall not add to the word which I command you, neither shall ye diminish from it, that ye may keep the commandments of Jehovah your GOD which I command you.

And GOD spake all these words, saying,

### I.

I AM JEHOVAH thy GOD, who have brought thee out of the land of Egypt, out of the house of bondage.

Thou shalt have no other gods before me. Thou shalt not make unto thee any graven image, or any likeness of any thing that is in heaven above, or that is in the earth beneath, or that is in the water under the earth: thou shalt not bow down thyself to them, nor serve them: for I JEHOVAH thy GOD am a jealous GOD visiting the iniquity of the fathers upon the children unto the third and fourth generation of them that hate me; and showing mercy unto the thousandth generation of them that love me, and keep my commandments.

Holy, holy, holy, is JE | HO·VAH of | Hosts:
The whole | earth is | full·of his | glory.

## II.

Thou shalt not take the name of JEHOVAH thy GOD in vain: for JEHOVAH will not hold him guiltless that taketh his name in vain.

He hath commanded his | cove·nant for | ever:
Holy and | rev·erend | is His | name.

## III.

Remember the Sabbath day to keep it holy. Six days shalt thou labor, and do all thy work: but the seventh day is the Sabbath of JEHOVAH thy GOD: in it thou shalt not do any work, thou, nor thy son, nor thy daughter, thy man-servant, nor thy maid-servant, nor thy cattle, nor thy stranger that is within thy gates: for in six days JEHOVAH made heaven and earth, the sea, and all that in them is, and rested the seventh day: wherefore JEHOVAH blessed the Sabbath day, and hallowed it.

JEHOVAH is in his | holy | temple:
Let all the | earth keep | si·lence be | fore him.

## IV.

Honor thy father and thy mother; that thy days

may be long upon the land which JEHOVAH thy GOD giveth thee.

Thy hands have made me, and | fashioned | me:
Make me to understand, that I may | learn | thy com | mandments.

### V.
Thou shalt not kill.

With the merciful thou wilt show thyself | merci | ful:
With an upright man thou wilt | show thy | self | upright.

### VI.
Thou shalt not commit adultery.

With the pure thou wilt | show thy·self | pure:
And with the froward thou wilt | show thy | self | froward.

### VII.
Thou shalt not steal.

Order my steps | in thy | word,
And let not any iniquity have do | minion | over | me.

### VIII.
Thou shalt not bear false witness against thy neighbor.

I have chosen the | way of | truth:
Thy judgments | have I | laid be | fore me.

### IX.
Thou shalt not covet thy neighbor's house.

Incline my heart to thy | testi | monies;
And | not to | cov·etous | ness.

### X.
Thou shalt not covet thy neighbor's wife, nor his man-servant, nor his maid-servant, nor his ox, nor his ass, nor any thing that is thy neighbor's.

All that JE | HOVAH hath | spoken,
We | will | do and | hear.

## THE TEN COMMANDMENTS.

#### DEUTERONOMY V.

Hear, O Israel, the statutes and judgments which I speak in your ears this day, that ye may learn them, and keep, and do them. Jehovah talked with you face to face in the mount, out of the midst of the fire, saying,

### I.

I am Jehovah thy God, who brought thee out of the land of Egypt, from the house of bondage. Thou shalt have none other gods before me. Thou shalt not make thee any graven image, or any likeness of any thing that is in heaven above, or that is in the earth beneath, or that is in the waters beneath the earth: thou shalt not bow down thyself to them, nor serve them: for I Jehovah thy God am a jealous God, visiting the iniquity of the fathers upon the children, unto the third and fourth generation of them that hate me; and showing mercy unto the thousandth generation of them that love me, and keep my commandments.

Holy, holy, holy, Lord | God Al | mighty;
Who was, and who | is, and who | is to | come.

### II.

Thou shalt not take the name of Jehovah thy God in vain: for Jehovah will not hold him guiltless that taketh his name in vain.

Who shall not fear | thee, O | Lord,
And glorify thy name? for | thou a | lone art | holy.

### III.

Keep the Sabbath day to sanctify it, as Jehovah thy God hath commanded thee. Six days thou shalt labor, and do all thy work: but the seventh day is the

Sabbath of JEHOVAH thy GOD: in it thou shalt not do any work, thou, nor thy son, nor thy daughter, nor thy man-servant, nor thy maid-servant, nor thine ox, nor thine ass, nor any of thy cattle, nor thy stranger that is within thy gates; that thy man-servant and thy maid-servant may rest as well as thou. And remember that thou wast a servant in the land of Egypt, and that JEHOVAH thy GOD brought thee out thence through a mighty hand and by an outstretched arm: therefore JEHOVAH thy GOD commanded thee to keep the Sabbath day.

This is the day which JE | HO.VAH hath | made:
We will re | joice · and be | glad in | it.

### IV.

Honor thy father and thy mother, as JEHOVAH thy GOD hath commanded thee; that thy days may be prolonged, and that it may go well with thee, in the land which JEHOVAH thy GOD giveth thee.

The righteous shall in | her · it the | land,
And | dwell there | in for | ever.

### V.

Thou shalt not kill.

Let thy mercies come unto me, that | I may | live;
For thy | law is | my de | light.

### VI.

Neither shalt thou commit adultery

Thy word is | very | pure:
Therefore thy | servant | loveth | it.

### VII.

Neither shalt thou steal.

Righteous art thou, | O JE | HOVAH;
And | upright | are thy | judgments.

## VIII.

Neither shalt thou bear false witness against thy neighbor.

Through thy precepts I get | under | standing:
Therefore every | false way | do I | hate.

## IX.

Neither shalt thou desire thy neighbor's wife.

I have in | clined my | heart
To perform thy statutes | always, | to the | end.

## X.

Neither shalt thou covet thy neighbor's house, his field, or his man-servant, or his maid-servant, his ox, or his ass, or any thing that is thy neighbor's.

Thou art near, | O JE | HOVAH;
And all thy com | mandments | are | truth.

## THE TWO GREAT COMMANDMENTS.

Now these are the commandments, the statutes, and the judgments, which JEHOVAH your GOD commanded to teach you, that ye might do them in the land whither ye pass over to possess it; that thou mightest fear JEHOVAH thy GOD, to keep all his statutes and his commandments, which I command thee, thou, and thy son, and thy son's son, all the days of thy life; and that thy days may be prolonged. Hear, therefore, O Israel, and observe to do; that it may be well with thee, and that ye may increase mightily, as JEHOVAH GOD of thy fathers hath promised thee, in the land that floweth with milk and honey.

## I.

The First of all the Commandments is, Hear, O Israel; the LORD our GOD is one LORD: and thou shalt love the LORD thy GOD with all thy heart, and with all thy soul, and with all thy mind, and with all thy strength. This is the First Commandment.

1. Thou art | wor·thy, O | Lord,
To receive | glo·ry, and | hon·or, and | power:
2. For thou hast cre | a·ted all | things;
And for thy pleasure they | are, and | were cre | ated.

## II.

And the Second is like unto it: Thou shalt love thy neighbor as thyself. On these Two Commandments hang all the Law and the Prophets.

1. All the paths of JEHOVAH are | mer·cy and | truth,
To those that keep his covenant | and his | testi | monies.

And these words which I command thee this day shall be in thine heart; and thou shalt teach them diligently unto thy children, and shalt talk of them when thou sittest in thine house, and when thou walkest by the way, and when thou liest down, and when thou risest up. And thou shalt bind them for a sign upon thine hand, and they shall be as frontlets between thine eyes. And thou shalt write them upon the posts of thine house, and on thy gates.

1. Behold, Je|ho·vah our | God
Hath showed us his | glory | and his | greatness:
2. And we have | heard his | voice
Out of the | midst | of the | fire:
3. We have | seen this | day,
That God doth | talk with | man, and he | liveth.
4. And Jehovah commanded us to do | all these | statutes;
To fear Jehovah our | God, for our | good | always:
5. That he might pre | serve·us a | live,
As | it | is this | day.
6. And it shall be our | righteous | ness,
If we observe to | do all | these com | mandments,
7. Before Je|ho·vah our | God,
As he | hath com | manded | us.

## THE TEN BLESSINGS.

### MATTHEW V.

AND seeing the multitudes, he went up into a mountain: and when he had sat down, his disciples came unto him. And he opened his mouth, and taught them, saying,

### I.

Blessed are the poor in spirit: for theirs is the kingdom of heaven.

JEHOVAH is nigh them that are of a | broken | heart;
And saveth such as | be · of a | contrite | spirit.

### II.

Blessed are they that mourn: for they shall be comforted.

This is my comfort in | my af | fliction;
For thy | word hath | quickened | me.

### III.

Blessed are the meek: for they shall inherit the earth.

The meek will he | guide in | judgment;
And the | meek · will he | teach his | way.

### IV.

Blessed are they that do hunger and thirst after righteousness: for they shall be filled.

He shall receive blessing | from JE|HOVAH.
And righteousness from the | GOD of | his sal | vation.

### V.

Blessed are the merciful: for they shall obtain mercy.

He that trusteth | in JE | HOVAH,
Mercy shall | compass | him a | bout.

## VI.

Blessed are the pure in heart: for they shall see GOD.

Create in me a clean | heart, O | GOD :
And renew a | right | spir·it with | in me.

## VII.

Blessed are the peacemakers: for they shall be called the children of GOD.

Behold, how good and how | pleas·ant it | is,
For brethren to dwell to | geth·er in | uni | ty.

## VIII.

Blessed are they that are persecuted for righteousness' sake: for theirs is the kingdom of heaven.

The salvation of the righteous is | of JE | HOVAH :
He is their | strength · in the | time of | trouble.

## IX.

Blessed are ye, when they shall revile you, and persecute you, and shall say all manner of evil against you falsely, for my sake.

The angel of JE | HO·VAH en | campeth
Around them that fear him, | and de | liv·ereth | them.

## X.

Rejoice and be exceeding glad; for great is your reward in heaven: for so persecuted they the prophets who were before you.

Blessed be JEHOVAH the God of | Isra | el.
From everlasting and to ever | lasting: A | men, and A | men.

## THE NEW JERUSALEM.

### I.

AND I saw a new heaven and a new earth for the first heaven and the first earth were passed away; and there was no more sea. And I, John, saw the holy city, New Jerusalem, coming down from GOD out of heaven, prepared as a bride adorned for her husband. And I heard a great voice out of heaven saying, Behold, the tabernacle of GOD is with men, and he will dwell with them, and they shall be his people, and GOD himself shall be with them, their GOD.

And GOD shall wipe away all | tears·from their | eyes;
And there shall be no more | death, neither | sor·row, nor | crying;
Neither shall there be | any·more | pain:
For the former | things are | passed a | way.

### II.

AND he that sat upon the throne said, Behold, I make all things new. I am Alpha and Omega, the Beginning and the End. I will give unto him that is athirst of the fountain of the water of life freely.

And the Spirit and the | Bride say, | Come.
And let | him that | heareth say, | Come.
And let him that | thirsteth | come.
And whosoever will, let him take the | wa·ter of | life | freely.

### III.

AND there came unto me one of the seven angels, and talked with me, saying, Come hither, I will show thee the Bride, the LAMB's wife. And he carried me away in the spirit to a great and high mountain, and showed me that great city, the holy Jerusalem, descending out of heaven from GOD, having the glory of GOD: and her light was like unto a stone most precious, even like a jasper stone, clear as crystal; and had a wall great and high, and had twelve gates, and at the gates twelve angels, and names written thereon, which are the names of the twelve tribes of the children of Israel.

And the twelve gates were | twelve | pearls;
Every several | gate·was of | one | pearl:
And the street of the city was | pure | gold,
As it | were trans | parent | glass.

## IV.

AND the wall of the city had twelve foundations, and in them the names of the twelve apostles of the LAMB. And he that talked with me had a golden reed to measure the city, and the gates thereof, and the wall thereof. And the city lieth four-square; and the length is as large as the breadth: and he measured the city with the reed, twelve thousand furlongs: the length and the breadth and the height of it are equal. And he measured the wall thereof, an hundred forty and four cubits, the measure of a man, that is, of an angel. And I saw no temple therein: for the LORD GOD Almighty and the LAMB are the temple of it.

And the city had no | need of the | sun,
Neither of the | moon, to | shine in | it·
For the glory of GOD did | lighten | it,
And the | LAMB·is the | light there | of.

## V.

AND the nations of them that are saved shall walk in the light of it: and the kings of the earth do bring their glory and honor into it. And the gates of it shall not be shut at all by day: for there shall be no night there. And they shall bring the glory and honor of the nations into it.

And there shall in no wise enter | into | it
Any | thing | that de | fileth,
Or worketh abomination, or | mak·eth a | lie:
But they that are written in the | LAMB'S | book of | life.

## VI.

AND he showed me a pure river of water of life, clear as crystal, proceeding out of the throne of GOD and of the LAMB. In the midst of the street of it, and on either side of the river, was the tree of life, which bare twelve manner of fruits, and yielded her fruit every month: and the leaves of the tree were for the healing of the nations.

And the throne of God and of the Lamb shall | be in | it;
And his | ser·vants shall | serve | him:
And they shall | see his | face;
And his | name shall | be·in their | foreheads.

## VII.

And, behold, I come quickly; and my reward is with me, to give every man according as his work shall be. I am Alpha and Omega, the Beginning and the End, the First and the Last. Blessed are they that do his commandments, that they may have right to the tree of life, and may enter in through the gates into the city. I Jesus have sent mine angel to testify unto you these things in the churches. I am the root and the offspring of David, the bright and morning Star.

He that testifieth | these | things,
Saith, | Surely | I come | quickly:
A | ····· | men.
Even | so, | come, Lord | Jesus.

### THE SECOND LESSON.

A Lesson from the New Testament may now be read, the people sitting.

Here one of the following Responsive Selections, or any other, may be used; the Minister reading the first line of each verse, and the People reading or singing the second. Or, a Selection or Hymn may be sung.

## RESPONSIVE SELECTION 1.

1. O give thanks unto Jehovah; for he is good:
For his | mercy | is for | ever.
2. Who can utter the mighty acts of Jehovah?
Who can | show·forth | all his | praise?

3. Blessed are they that keep judgment,
And he that doeth | righteous·ness | at all | times.
4. Remember me, O JEHOVAH,
With the favor that thou | bearest | to thy | people.
5. O visit me with thy salvation,
That I may | see the | good · of thy | chosen,
6. That I may rejoice in the joy of thy nation,
That I may glory with | thine in | heri | tance.
Ps. cvi. 1 – 5.

RESPONSIVE SELECTION 2.

1. Blessed be JEHOVAH,
Because he hath heard the | voice · of my | sup-pli | cations.
2. Jehovah is my strength and my shield;
My heart trusted in | him, and | I am | helped.
3. Therefore my heart rejoiceth greatly;
And with my | song | will I | praise him.
4. JEHOVAH is their strength;
And he is the saving | strength of | his an | ointed.
5. Save thy people, and bless thine inheritance:
Feed them also, and | lift them | up for | ever.
Ps. xxviii. 6 – 9.

RESPONSIVE SELECTION 3.

1. Have mercy upon me, O GOD,
According | to thy | loving | kindness.
2. According to the multitude of thy tender mercies,
Blot | out | my trans gressions.
3 Wash me thoroughly from mine iniquity,
And | cleanse me | from my | sin.
4. For I acknowledge my transgressions;
And my | sin is | ever be | fore me.
5. Against thee, thee only, have I sinned,
And done | evil | in thy | sight:
6 That thou mightest be justified when thou speakest,
And be | clear | when thou | judgest.

## RESPONSIVE SELECTION 4.

1. God be merciful unto us, and bless us;
And cause his | face to | shine up | on us:
2. That thy way may be known upon earth,
Thy saving | health a | mong all | nations.
3. Let the people praise thee, O God;
Let all the | people | praise | thee.
4. O let the nations be glad,
And | let them | sing for | joy.
5. For thou shalt judge the people righteously,
And govern the | na·tions up | on the | earth.
6. Let the people praise thee, O God;
Let all the | people | praise | thee.
7. The earth shall yield her increase:
Gód, our | own | God, shall | bless us.
8. God shall bless us;
And all the ends of the | earth shall | fear | him.
Ps. lxvii.

## RESPONSIVE SELECTION 5.

1. Teach me, O Jehovah, the way of thy statutes;
And I shall | keep it | un·to the | end.
2. Make me to understand, and I shall keep thy law;
And I shall ob | serve · it with | all the | heart.
3. Make me to go in the path of thy commandments;
For there | in do | I de | light.
4. Incline my heart unto thy testimonies,
And | not to | cove·tous | ness.
5. Turn away mine eyes from beholding vanity
Quicken | thou me | in thy | way.
6. Establish thy word to thy servant,
Who is de | voted | to thy | fear.
7. Turn away my reproach which I fear:
For thy | judgments | are | good.
8. Behold, I have longed for thy precepts:
Quicken me | in thy | righteous | ness.—Ps. cxix. 33.

## RESPONSIVE SELECTION 6.

1. Thy word is a lamp to my feet,
And a | light un | to my | path.
2. I have sworn, and I will perform,
That I will keep the | judgments | of thy | justice.
3. I am afflicted very much:
Quicken me, O Jehovah, ac | cording | to thy | word.
4. Accept, I beseech thee, the freewill offerings of my mouth, O Jehovah;
And | teach thou | me thy | statutes.
5. My soul is continually in my hand:
Yet do I | not for | get thy | law.
6. The wicked have laid a snare for me:
Yet I | erred not | from thy | precepts.
7. Thy testimonies have I taken as an heritage for ever:
For they are the re | joicing | of my | heart.
8. I have inclined my heart,
To perform thy statutes | always, | to the | end.
Ps. cxix. 105–112.

## RESPONSIVE SELECTION 7.

1. Bless Jehovah, O my soul;
And all that is within me, | bless his | holy | name.
2. Bless Jehovah, O my soul;
And forget not | all his | bene | fits:
3. Who forgiveth all thine iniquities;
Who healeth | all | thy dis | eases;
4. Who redeemeth thy life from destruction;
Who crowneth thee with | kindness | and with | mercies;
5. Who satisfieth thy mouth with good:
Thy youth is re | newed | like the | eagle's.
6. Jehovah executeth righteousness,
And judgment for | all that | are op | pressed.
7. He made known his ways to Moses,
His deeds to the | children of | Isra | el.—Ps. ciii.

## RESPONSIVE SELECTION 8.

1. Thy testimonies are wonderful;
   Therefore | doth my | soul | keep them.
2. The entrance of thy words giveth light;
   It giveth under | standing | to the | simple.
3. I opened my mouth, and panted:
   For I | longed for | thy com | mandments.
4. Look thou upon me, and be merciful unto me,
   As thou dost unto | those that | love thy | name.
5. Order my steps in thy word:
   And let not any iniquity have do | minion | over | me.
6. Deliver me from the oppression of man:
   So | will I | keep thy | precepts.
7. Make thy face to shine upon thy servant;
   And | teach thou | me thy | statutes.
8. Rivers of waters run down mine eyes,
   Because they | do not | keep thy | law.

   Ps. cxix. 129–136.

## THE SERMON.

Then the Minister, if he think proper, may repeat one of the Prayers on page 46, or such other as he sees fit; all kneeling.

An Anthem, Selection, or Hymn may now be sung; the people standing.

The Minister may then pronounce the following Benediction, or the Blessing in Num. vi. 24, 25, 26; all standing.

## BENEDICTION.

THE grace of our LORD JESUS CHRIST be with you all. AMEN.

# INVITATIONS

AND

# PRAYERS,

REFERRED TO

ON PAGES 7, 13, AND 38.

# INVITATIONS TO WORSHIP.

BELOVED BRETHREN: — We are now assembled in the presence of the LORD, to acknowledge him in his Divine Humanity as our FATHER in the heavens; to worship him in spirit and in truth; to confess before him our manifold evils; to give thanks to him for his abundant mercies; to pray that his kingdom may come, and his will be done, on the earth, as it is done in heaven; and with humble hearts to ascribe the power and glory unto him. Let us then look to the LORD for his divine blessing.

*Or this.*

Beloved Brethren: — The LORD in His love and wisdom having preserved us through another week, in this our transitory home, having given us our daily bread, and provided for our earthly wants, hath now invited and required us, on this His holy day, to come into his gates with thanksgiving and into his courts with praise. Let us then look to Him, that we may receive of that bread which cometh down from heaven, and of that water of life which satisfieth the thirst of the soul. Here let all our anxious and earthly cares be removed, and all our holy and heavenly affections awakened.

This is the day that the LORD hath made: it is the day in which the LORD arose; and it is the day in which we should also, in a more especial manner, arise from natural to spiritual affections and thoughts; —from the cares of the body, to the concerns of the soul;—from the scenes of time, to the realities of eternity. Thus will the day be to us a blessing.

And when we pray to the LORD, when we hear His Holy Word, or when we utter our rejoicings for His mercy and goodness toward us, our hearts will be warmed, our minds enlightened, our life renewed and strengthened, and our souls fed with the food on which the angels live. And in all His mercies we shall recognize the LORD as present, and the glory of the HOLY ONE beaming upon us from His opened Word.

*Or this.*

Beloved Brethren:— We are directed in the divine Word to render unto the LORD the worship of our hearts and of our lips. For he is our Creator; and we are the work of his hands: He is our Preserver; for it is in Him that we live, and move, and have our being: He is our Redeemer; for he delivers us from our evils: He is our Savior; for He saves us from our sins. He is good to all; and his tender mercies are over all his works. He maketh his sun to rise on the evil and on the good, and sendeth rain on the just and on the unjust.

Nevertheless, it is not for his own sake that the LORD requires us to worship him, but for our sake. For when we prostrate ourselves before our Heavenly FATHER, in heartfelt acknowledgment of Him; when we supplicate him for his mercies; when we praise him for his benefits, we are raised, for the time, above our selfish and worldly life; and the door is opened for the LORD to enter; to implant in our hearts and minds states of innocence, charity, and faith; and to establish within us the kingdom of heaven.

True worship, like true religion, is external as well as internal. But in order that the one may be in harmony and correspond with the other, it is proper that the silent worship of the heart should be brought forth into fulness in the open worship of the lips; and this is more abundantly effected, when the true worshipers of the LORD are assembled together to seek his presence in his holy temple. The LORD is evermore inviting us to come unto him, that we may have life: Let us comply with his gracious invitation: Let us pour out before him the feelings of sincere humiliation and repentance: Let us hearken with meekness to his holy Word, and to his Divine Commandments: Let us entreat him to breathe upon us the life-giving influences of his Holy Spirit.

# PRAYERS.

Our Father, who art in the heavens; help us, we humbly pray thee, to acknowledge and reverence thy holy name, and to worship thee in thy works, in thy Word, and in thy Divine Humanity. In thy holy Word reveal to us thy truth, enlighten us in thy way, and reign in us by thy wisdom, till we become thine image. Warm our hearts with thy love, fill our affections with the spirit of thy goodness, till our inner man is made into thy likeness. Help us, O Lord, to bring forth thy love and wisdom into our daily life: May they speak in what we say, and act in what we do; and may our earthly nature become in all things subject to thy heavenly influences. Feed our souls from the table of thy love with that spiritual food best suited to our states; and enable us to look to thee for all that is good, and all that is true. We confess our trespasses and sins before thee, and pray thee to forgive us. O Lord, remember not our iniquities against us; but as far as the east is from the west, so far remove our transgressions from us. Preserve us in all temptations and trials of soul, through which it may be our lot to pass: Suffer us not to be tempted above what we are able to bear: May all the afflictions either of body or soul incident to our progress in the regenerate life, in the denying of self, taking up the cross, and following thee, be but the means in thy merciful hands, of loosening the hold of evil upon us, and delivering us from it.

Our Heavenly FATHER, whatsoever things we have asked for ourselves, we would also ask for others: for our rulers and governors; for our nation, and all nations; and for thy Church and people throughout the world. Especially would we ask them for all who acknowledge thee in thy Divine Humanity, as the only GOD of heaven and earth.\*

For thine is the kingdom, and the power, and the glory, forever. AMEN.

Or this.

O LORD, our FATHER in heaven, we would approach Thee in love and in worship. In Thy Divine Humanity we acknowledge Thee as Creator, Redeemer, and Savior. We come to thee; we humble ourselves before Thee, confessing that we have sinned: and ask of Thy Divine mercy, that our sins may be forgiven, as we forsake them and put them away, and as we thus forgive those who trespass against us. Be thou present with us now and always. LORD, teach us to pray for all things that are good and true, and fit us to receive them at Thy hands. May our hearts and understandings ever be open before Thee, to receive Thy quickening love and heavenly wisdom; and as Thou rememberest us, so may we remember others, and ever seek to do them good. May love to our neighbor impel us to teach him, as we have learned of Thee: may the prosperity and welfare of Thy Church be always present before us; and may we ever pray for the peace of Jerusalem. May kindness to all be impressed upon our life and conduct: may the wanderer be restored to the right way, and the way-faring man preserved in the truth. May Thy blessings be multiplied upon the faithful; and Thy mercies, like the dews of heaven, descend upon them: and may we all forsake our evils, and look to Thee alone as the Sun of our spiritual firmament, and worship Thee alone for ever and ever. AMEN.

\* This prayer is designed as a paraphrase upon the Lord's Prayer, and to be used alone: but if the Lord's Prayer is used in connection, it should be inserted before the closing sentence.

ORDER OF WORSHIP.

PRAYERS AFTER THE SERMON.

Our FATHER in heaven,* who hast given us grace at this time with one accord to make our common supplications unto thee, and dost promise that when two or three are gathered together in thy name, thou wilt grant their request; fulfil now, O LORD, the desires and petitions of thy servants, as may be most expedient for them; granting us in this world knowledge of thy truth, and in the world to come life everlasting. AMEN.

Or this.

O LORD, our Heavenly FATHER, we look to thee; we worship at thy footstool; we acknowledge thee to be the author and the giver of all good things. We thank thee for the gift of thy Word, for the blessings of the Sabbath, for the ordinances of thy house, and for the wondrous things revealed to us out of thy law. Deeply impress upon our minds the truths of thy Holy Word; shed abroad thy love in our hearts, and enable us to conform our lives to thy will. Continue unto us thy favor which is life, and thy loving kindness which is better than life. Guide us by thy counsel, and afterwards receive us into glory. AMEN.

\* This is the prayer of *Chrysostom*, except that the address is changed from "Almighty God" to "Our Father in heaven."

THE

# ORDINANCE OF BAPTISM.

The Minister and *candidate* standing near the font, the service may be commenced by reading one or more of the following passages.

COMFORT ye, comfort ye my people,
Saith your GOD.
Speak ye comfortably to Jerusalem, and cry unto her,
That her warfare is accomplished,
That her iniquity is pardoned:
For she hath received of JEHOVAH's hand
Double for all her sins.
The voice of him that crieth in the wilderness,
Prepare ye the way of JEHOVAH;
Make straight in the desert a highway for our GOD.
Every valley shall be exalted,
And every mountain and hill shall be made low:
And the crooked shall be made straight,
And the rough places plain:
And the glory of JEHOVAH shall be revealed,
And all flesh shall see it together:
For the mouth of JEHOVAH hath spoken it.— Is. xl. 1-5.

BEHOLD, I will send my messenger,
And he shall prepare the way before me:
And the LORD, whom ye seek,
Shall suddenly come to his temple,
Even the Messenger of the covenant, whom ye delight
    in:
Behold, he shall come, saith JEHOVAH of hosts.
But who may abide the day of his coming?

And who shall stand when he appeareth?
For he is like a refiner's fire, and like fuller's soap.
And he shall sit as a refiner and purifier of silver:
And he shall purify the sons of Levi,
And purge them as gold and silver,
That they may offer unto JEHOVAH
An offering in righteousness.
Then shall the offering of Judah and Jerusalem
Be pleasant unto JEHOVAH,
As in the days of old,
And as in former years. — Mal. iii. 1 – 4.

In those days came John the Baptist, preaching in the wilderness of Judæa, and saying, Repent ye: for the kingdom of heaven is at hand. For this is he that was spoken of by the prophet Esaias, saying, The voice of one crying in the wilderness, Prepare ye the way of the LORD, make his paths straight.

And the same John had his raiment of camel's hair, and a leathern girdle about his loins; and his meat was locusts and wild honey.

Then went out to him Jerusalem, and all Judæa, and all the region round about the Jordan, and were baptized of him in the Jordan, confessing their sins. But when he saw many of the Pharisees and Sadducees come to his baptism, he said unto them, O generation of vipers, who hath warned you to flee from the wrath to come? Bring forth therefore fruits meet for repentance: and think not to say within yourselves, We have Abraham for father: for I say unto you, that GOD is able of these stones to raise up children unto Abraham. And now also the axe is laid unto the root of the trees: therefore every tree which bringeth not forth good fruit, is hewn down, and cast into the fire. I indeed baptize you with water unto repentance; but he that cometh after me is mightier than I, whose shoes I am not worthy to bear: he shall baptize you with the Holy Spirit, and with fire: whose fan is in his hand, and he will thoroughly purge his floor, and gather his wheat into the garner; but he will burn up the chaff with unquenchable fire.

## BAPTISM. 49

Then cometh JESUS from Galilee to the Jordan unto John, to be baptized of him. But John forbade him, saying, I have need to be baptized of thee, and comest thou to me? And JESUS answering said unto him, Suffer it to be so now; for thus it becometh us to fulfil all righteousness. Then he suffered him. And JESUS, when he was baptized, went up straightway out of the water: and, lo, the heavens were opened unto him, and he saw the Spirit of GOD descending like a dove, and lighting upon him: and lo a voice from heaven, saying, This is my beloved SON, in whom I am well pleased. — Mat. iii.

THERE was a man of the Pharisees, named Nicodemus, a ruler of the Jews: the same came to JESUS by night, and said unto him, Rabbi, we know that thou art a teacher come from GOD: for no one can do these miracles that thou doest, except GOD be with him.

JESUS answered and said unto him, Verily, verily, I say unto thee, Except a man be born again, he cannot see the kingdom of GOD.

Nicodemus saith unto him, How can a man be born when he is old? can he enter the second time into his mother's womb, and be born?

JESUS answered, Verily, verily, I say unto thee, except a man be born of water and of the Spirit, he cannot enter into the kingdom of GOD. That which is born of the flesh is flesh; and that which is born of the Spirit is spirit. Marvel not that I said unto thee, Ye must be born again. The wind bloweth where it listeth, and thou hearest the sound thereof, but canst not tell whence it cometh, and whither it goeth: so is every one that is born of the Spirit. — John iii. 1 - 8.

AND they brought young children to him, that he should touch them: and the disciples rebuked those that brought them. But when JESUS saw it, he was much displeased, and said unto them, Suffer the little children to come unto me, and forbid them not: for of such is the kingdom of GOD. Verily I say unto you, Whosoever shall not receive the kingdom of God as a little child, he shall not enter therein. And he took them up in his arms, put his hands upon them, and blessed them.— Mark x. 13-16.

AND JESUS came and spake unto them, saying, All power is given unto me in heaven and in earth. Go ye therefore, and make disciples of all nations; baptizing them into the name of the FATHER, and of the SON, and of the HOLY SPIRIT; teaching them to observe all things whatsoever I have commanded you: and lo, I am with you all the days, until the consummation of the age. Amen.— Mat. xxviii. 18-20.

Then may be read the whole or a part of the following

EXTRACTS FROM THE DOCTRINES OF THE NEW CHURCH.

" The ordinance of baptism is intended as a sign that the person baptized belongs to the church, and for a memorial that he is to be regenerated: for the washing of baptism signifies nothing else than spiritual washing, which is regeneration.

"All regeneration is effected by the LORD, through the instrumentality of the truths of faith, and of a life in accordance with them. Baptism, therefore, is a testification that the person baptized belongs to the church, and is capable of being regenerated: for it is in the church that the LORD, who alone regenerates man, is acknowledged; and there also is the Word, which contains the truths of faith by which regeneration is effected. These truths the LORD teaches in John: " Except a man be born of water and of the Spirit, he cannot enter into the kingdom of GOD."— iii. 5. Water, in the spiritual sense, here signifies the truth of faith derived from the Word; the Spirit, a life according to that truth; and being born, being regenerated thereby.

"Since every one who is regenerated also undergoes temptations, which are spiritual combats against evils and falsities, the water used in baptism likewise signifies those temptations.

"As baptism is appointed a sign and memorial of those things, man may be baptized as an infant; and if he has not been baptized in his infancy, he may be baptized as an adult.

" Let those, therefore, who are baptized, remember, that baptism itself confers neither faith nor salvation, but merely testifies that they will receive faith, and be saved, if they are regenerated.

[" Hence may be seen the import of the LORD's words in Mark : " He that believeth, and is baptized, shall be saved; but he that believeth not, shall be condemned."— xvi. 16. Here to believe signifies to acknowledge the LORD, and to receive divine truths from him by means of the Word; and to be baptized is to be regenerated by the LORD by means of those truths.] " — *H. D.* 202–208.

[" The *First Use* of baptism is, introduction into the Christian Church, and *at the same time* insertion among Christians in the spiritual world." — *T. C. R.* 677.

" The *Second Use* of baptism is, that the Christian may know and acknowledge the LORD JESUS CHRIST the Redeemer and Savior, and follow Him. — *T. C. R.* 681.

" The *Third Use* of baptism is, that man may be regenerated. — *T. C. R.* 684.

" Since these three uses follow in order, and join themselves together in the last, and thus, in the idea of the angels, cohere as one; therefore, when baptism is performed, read in the Word, and named, the angels who are present do not understand baptism, but regeneration. — *T. C. R.* 685.]

[" The baptism of John represented the cleansing of the external man; but the baptism which is at this day with Christians, represents the cleansing of the internal man, which is regeneration. — *T. C. R.* 690. By means of the baptism of John, a way was prepared, that JEHOVAH the LORD might be able to come down into the world, and perform redemption.— *T. C. R.* 688. The reason why a way was prepared by the baptism of John was, because, by means of that, they were introduced into the future church of the LORD, and in heaven were inserted among those there who expected and desired the Messiah, and thus were guarded by angels, so that devils from hell might not break forth and destroy them."] — *T. C. R.* 689.

"As soon as infants are baptized, angels are appointed over them by the LORD, to take care of them; by whom they are kept in a state of receiving faith in the LORD: and as they grow up, and come to the exercise of their own right and their own reason, the guardian angels leave them, and they associate to themselves such spirits as make one with their life and faith.— *T. C. R.* 677.

"That not only infants, but also all, are inserted by baptism among Christians in the spiritual world, is because people and nations in that world are distinguished according to their religions. Moreover, all of the same religion are arranged into societies in heaven, according to the affections of love to GOD and love towards the neighbor. In the spiritual world, by which is meant both heaven and hell, all things are most distinctly arranged, in the whole and in every part, or in general and in every particular. On this distinct arrangement there, the preservation of the whole universe depends; and this distinction cannot be effected, unless every one, after he is born, be known by some sign, indicating to what religious assembly he belongs; for, without the Christian sign, which is baptism, some Mahometan spirit, or some one of the idolaters, might apply himself to Christian infants newly born, and also to children, and infuse into them an inclination for his religion, and thus draw away their mind, and alienate them from Christianity; which would be to distort and destroy spiritual order." — *T. C. R.* 678.

"Thus baptism signifies initiation into the church, and into those things which are of the church; thus

BAPTISM. 53

it signifies regeneration, and those things which are of regeneration: not that by baptism any one is regenerated, but that it is a sign of it, which he should remember." — *A. C.* 4255.

Then the Minister may read the whole or a part of the following

INSTRUCTION.

The divine ordinance of Baptism is designed to promote the regeneration and salvation of men. It is one of the means by which we may be protected from evil influences, and prepared to receive the good influences of the LORD and his angels.

This ordinance has a spiritual signification, and denotes the cleansing of the mind. For as water is the means of cleansing the body, so truth is the means of cleansing the mind. Hence water corresponds to and denotes truth; that is, such instruction concerning our duty as we find in the literal sense of the Sacred Scriptures, and particularly in the Ten Commandments. And the application of water to the body corresponds to and denotes the work of purifying the mind by obeying and conforming to the truth. And while merely natural men see nothing but the natural sign, and understand the ordinance only according to its natural sense, spiritual men, and the angels who are associated with them, perceive the things which are signified, and so understand the ordinance in its spiritual sense. Consequently, when we are administering or receiving this ordinance, a union is effected between us and the angels, between our feelings and their feelings, between our thoughts and their thoughts, and between our efforts and their efforts: thus they unite with us in this sacred ordinance, as they afterwards unite in performing the spiritual work which is represented by it.

When we know that baptism denotes the purification of the mind and life, we can see why it is made to be the sign of introduction into the church; for it

5*

represents the whole work by which a man becomes a true member of the church.

From the spiritual signification of baptism, we can see the duty of all who have any thing to do in relation to it — *the duty of the church, the duty of parents and guardians,* and *the duty of all who receive it.*

When the ordinance is administered, it is the *duty of the members of the church* to desire and to pray that those who receive it may receive that which is denoted by it; and it is afterwards their duty to do all that they can to promote that object.

When *parents* and *guardians* present for baptism the children that have been committed to their care, they ought to desire and pray that they may be spiritually baptized; that when they come to the age of freedom and rationality, they may be regenerated, and thus prepared for the LORD's kingdom: and it thenceforth becomes their duty to endeavor to promote this object, by withdrawing them from evil and leading them to good, by implanting true ideas and cherishing good affections in their minds, and by causing them to know and acknowledge that every thing good and true in them cometh down from Him who alone is good and true — from the Source of their spiritual life — from their FATHER who is in heaven. And this duty of parents and guardians continues until their children come to maturity, and are thus transformed into brothers, and sisters, and friends.

And as children become able to understand, it is their duty to listen and conform to the instruction which is given to them, to love and to honor their parents and teachers, and to look up through them to the LORD, who is over all.

But there are some who are not baptized, until they come to maturity, and are able to understand the nature of the ordinance. When they become sensible of their evils and impurities, and desire to be cleansed and delivered from them, then it is proper for them to be baptized: for baptism represents the purification of the mind; and in coming forward to be baptized, they express the desire that they may have this spiritual work done in them, and also the desire that they may become associated with those in the spiritual world and in the natural world, who will aid them in performing the work

And when they desire to gain more knowledge of the LORD, of his Word, and of his kingdom, and more knowledge of their duty in relation to him and to one another, then it is proper for them to be baptized; for baptism is the means which the LORD has appointed for introducing them to angels of heaven, and to members of the church upon earth, who will communicate unto them their views and feelings, who will assist them by their experience, who will aid them in understanding the things which have been revealed to them — in perceiving their goodness, as well as their truth — and will thus aid them in bringing them into the life.

Here the Minister may read the following

## DOCTRINES OF THE NEW CHURCH.

1. THAT there is one GOD: that in him is a Divine Trinity called the FATHER, the SON, and the HOLY SPIRIT: that these three are distinct, and at the same time united in him, as the soul, the body, and the operation are in man: and that the one GOD is the LORD JESUS CHRIST.

2. That saving faith is to believe in him as the Redeemer, Regenerator, and Savior from sin.

3. That the Sacred Scripture is Divine Truth: that it is revealed to us as a means by which we may distinguish between good and evil; by which we may be delivered from the influence of evil spirits; and by which we may become associated with angels, and conjoined with the LORD.

4. That we must abstain from doing evil, because it is of the devil and from the devil: and that we must do good, because it is of GOD and from GOD.

5. That in abstaining from evil and in doing good we are to act as of ourselves; but we must at the same time believe and acknowledge that the will, the understanding, and the power to do so, are of the LORD alone.

*Here the Minister may address the adult candidate in the following manner.*

*Min.* You have been instructed in the signification and use of the sacred ordinance of Baptism, and you have heard what are the doctrines of the New Church: Do you now desire to come into a more full knowledge and acknowledgment of these doctrines, and to live according to them; that through faith in the LORD, and obedience to his commandments, you may receive that internal and spiritual baptism, which the outward ordinance represents? and for this end do you desire to be introduced into the LORD's New Church by the ordinance of baptism?
*Answer:* — I do.

*When adults are to be baptized, who have been adequately instructed in the doctrines of the New Church, and have given satisfactory evidence of having entered upon a corresponding life, the following questions may be used instead of the above. In the case of such persons it is not expected that the Confirmation Service will be used.*

*Min.* You have been instructed in the signification and use of the sacred ordinance of Baptism, and you have heard what are the doctrines of the New Church: Do you now declare your belief and acknowledgment of those doctrines, and by the divine mercy of the LORD are you endeavoring to live according to them; that through faith in him, and obedience to his commandments, you may receive that internal and spiritual baptism, which the outward ordinance represents? and for this end do you desire to be introduced into the LORD's New Church by the ordinance of Baptism?
*Answer:* — I do.

## BAPTISM.

*When infants or children are to be baptized, the Minister may say to the parents or guardians:*

*Min.* You have now been instructed in the signification and use of the sacred ordinance of Baptism, and you have heard what are the doctrines of the New Church: Do you desire and intend to have *this child* brought up in the knowledge and acknowledgment of these doctrines, and in a life according to them; that through faith in the LORD, and obedience to him, *he* may receive that internal and spiritual baptism, which the outward ordinance represents? and for this end do you desire to have *him* baptized into the LORD's New Church?

*Answer:* — I do.

*Here may be used the following prayer, or the LORD's Prayer, or both.*

MOST merciful LORD, who dost baptize with the Holy Spirit and with fire, and who dost invite all men to come unto thee, that they may be made heirs of thine eternal kingdom; bless, we pray thee, the administration of thy holy ordinance; graciously receive *this person* [or *this child*, or *these*, &c.,] now about to be baptized, into thy True Christian Church; insert *him* as to spirit among Christians in the spiritual world, and thus embrace *him* within the arms of thy divine protection, [and thereby preserve *him* in a state to receive faith in thee,] and bestow on *him* the blessings of thy Holy Spirit. Being enrolled by baptism in the number of those who acknowledge thee to be the only GOD of heaven and earth, the Redeemer and Savior of mankind, may *he* henceforth deny *himself*, and take up *his* cross, and follow thee. [As *he* grows in stature] May *he* grow in the knowledge and love of thee, and of thy kingdom. May *he* renounce the evils of self-love and the love of the world, engage victoriously in the spiritual conflicts necessary for *his* purification, and live a life devoted to thy will. So may *he* be cleansed from the impurities of *his* nature, be established in love to thee and charity towards *his* neighbor, and finally be raised into thy heavenly kingdom. Amen.

OUR FATHER, who art in the heavens; Hallowed be thy name. Thy kingdom come. Thy will be done, as in heaven, so also upon the earth. Give us this day our daily bread. And forgive us our debts, as we also forgive our debtors. And lead us not into temptation; but deliver us from evil. For thine is the kingdom, and the power, and the glory, for ever. Amen.

<small>Then the Minister, naming the person to be baptized, and applying the water to his forehead, shall say:</small>

A. B. { *Thou art hereby baptized* (or) *I baptize thee* } *into the name of the* FATHER, *and of the* SON, *and of the* HOLY SPIRIT: *Amen.*

JEHOVAH bless thee, and keep thee: JEHOVAH make his face to shine upon thee, and be gracious unto thee: JEHOVAH lift up his countenance upon thee, and give thee peace.

<small>Then taking the person by the right hand, the Minister may say:</small>

We receive this person, [or this child,] now baptized with water, into the LORD's Church on earth; to the end that by the baptism of repentance and regeneration, *he* may finally be received into the LORD's kingdom in heaven.

<small>The Minister may then use the following Exhortation.</small>

### TO ADULTS.

You have now been admitted by baptism into the True Christian Church, and have taken the name of a Christian of the New Jerusalem. This is the first use of baptism. But there must be a knowledge and acknowledgment of the LORD, into whose name you have been baptized, together with faith and obedience, as a means of becoming regenerated. It is the

LORD's will that these more essential uses shall follow. But this must depend upon the quality of your future life. Cultivate, therefore, with all diligence, an acquaintance with the Holy Word, and with the heavenly doctrines of the New Jerusalem. Shun all evils as sins against GOD. Renounce the love of self and the world, and learn to love the LORD with all your heart, and your neighbor as yourself. Thus will you become useful and happy in this life, and attain to an eternal inheritance in the kingdom of heaven.

#### TO THE PARENTS AND GUARDIANS OF CHILDREN.

To you as *his* earthly parents the care of *this child* is committed by *his* FATHER in heaven. Be faithful, therefore, to the trust. It is the will of the LORD that *this child* shall be trained for heaven; and he has appointed you to the discharge of this sacred duty. Endeavor to educate *him* with continual reference to the end for which *he* was created. Form aright *his* mind and life, while under your immediate control: " For what doth it profit a man, if he gain the whole world, and lose his own soul?" Let *him* be initiated into the worship and acknowledgment of the LORD, according to the Heavenly Doctrines of the New Jerusalem. Let *him* learn by heart the LORD's Prayer, the Ten Commandments, and the " Doctrines of the New Church." Teach *him* to shun all evils as sins against GOD, and to love the LORD with all *his* heart, and *his* neighbor as *himself.* Thus will *he* be prepared for a useful and happy life in this world and for eternal usefulness and happiness in heaven.

Instead of the above exhortation, or after it, one or more of the following passages from the Word may be read.

JOHN did baptize in the wilderness, and preach the baptism of repentance for the remission of sins. . . . . And he preached, saying, There cometh one mightier than I after me, the latchet of whose shoes I am not worthy to stoop down and unloose. I indeed have baptized you with water; but he shall baptize you with the Holy Spirit. — Mark i. 4, 7, 8.

Jesus answered, Verily, verily, I say unto thee, Except a man be born of water and of the Spirit, he cannot enter into the kingdom of God. That which is born of the flesh is flesh; and that which is born of the Spirit is spirit. Marvel not that I said unto thee, Ye must be born again. — John iii. 5 – 7.

Not every one that saith unto me, Lord, Lord, shall enter into the kingdom of heaven; but he that doeth the will of my Father who is in heaven. — Mat. vii. 21.

If any one will come after me, let him deny himself, and take up his cross, and follow me. For whosoever will save his life, shall lose it: and whosoever will lose his life for my sake, shall find it. — Mat. xvi. 24, 25.

I am the good shepherd, and know my sheep, and am known of mine. As the Father knoweth me, even so know I the Father: and I lay down my life for the sheep. And other sheep I have, which are not of this fold: them also I must bring, and they shall hear my voice; and there shall be one fold, one shepherd. Therefore doth my Father love me, because I lay down my life, that I might take it again. No one taketh it from me, but I lay it down of myself. I have power to lay it down, and I have power to take it again. This commandment have I received of my Father. — John x. 14 – 18.

My sheep hear my voice, and I know them, and they follow me: and I give unto them eternal life; and they shall never perish, neither shall any one pluck them out of my hand. My Father, who gave them me, is greater than all; and no one is able to pluck them out of my Father's hand. I and the Father are one. — John x. 27 – 30.

And, behold, one came and said unto him, Good Master, what good thing shall I do, that I may have

BAPTISM. 61

eternal life? And he said unto him, ..... If thou wilt enter into life, keep the commandments. — Mat. xix. 16, 17.

THE first of all the commandments is, Hear, O Israel; the LORD our GOD is one LORD: And thou shalt love the LORD thy GOD with all thy heart, and with all thy soul, and with all thy mind, and with all thy strength. This is the first commandment. And the second is like unto it: Thou shalt love thy neighbor as thyself. There is none other commandment greater than these. — Mark xii. 29 – 31.

THEREFORE all things whatsoever ye would that men should do to you, do ye even so to them: for this is the law and the prophets. — Mat. vii. 12.

AND these words, which I command thee, shall be in thine heart: and thou shalt teach them diligently unto thy children; and shalt talk of them when thou sittest in thine house, and when thou walkest by the way, and when thou liest down, and when thou risest up. — Deut. vi. 6. 7.

Here a suitable Selection, or Hymn, may be sung, if convenient.

BENEDICTION.

The grace of our LORD JESUS CHRIST be with you all: Amen.

# CONFIRMATION.

[There are two Sacraments in the church, Baptism, and the Holy Supper. Baptism represents the removal of evils and falsities by means of truth; and the Holy Supper represents the reception of goods and truths from the LORD. Besides these there are no divinely appointed Sacraments.

It is proper, however, that those persons who were baptized in infancy or childhood, should, when they come to adult age — and those adults who are baptized before they come to a full knowledge and acknowledgment of the doctrines of the New Jerusalem, should, after a suitable time, make a full acknowledgment of the doctrines, and of their desire and effort to live according to them. For this purpose the following service is prepared.]

*The Minister may commence the service by reading one or more of the following passages.*

THERE was a man sent from GOD, whose name was John. The same came for a witness, to bear witness of the Light, that all through him might believe. He was not that Light, but was sent to bear witness of that Light. That was the true Light, which enlighteneth every man that cometh into the world. He was in the world, and the world was made by him, and the world knew him not. He came unto his own, and his own received him not. But as many as received him, to them gave he power to become children of GOD, even to them that believe on his name: Who were born, not of blood, nor of the will of the flesh, nor of the will of man, but of GOD. — John i. 6-13.

Jesus answered, Verily, verily, I say unto thee, Except a man be born of water and of the Spirit, he cannot enter into the kingdom of God. That which is born of the flesh is flesh; and that which is born of the Spirit is spirit. Marvel not that I said unto thee, Ye must be born again. The wind bloweth where it listeth, and thou hearest the sound thereof; but canst not tell whence it cometh, and whither it goeth: so is every one that is born of the Spirit. — John iii. 5 – 8.

Verily, verily, I say unto you, I am the door of the sheep. All that ever came before me are thieves and robbers: but the sheep did not hear them. I am the door: by me if any one enter in, he shall be saved, and shall go in and out, and find pasture. The thief cometh not, but for to steal, and to kill, and to destroy: I am come that they might have life, and that they might have it more abundantly. I am the good shepherd: the good shepherd giveth his life for the sheep. — John x. 7 – 11.

I am the good shepherd, and know my sheep, and am known of mine. As the Father knoweth me, even so know I the Father: and I lay down my life for the sheep. And other sheep I have, which are not of this fold: them also I must bring, and they shall hear my voice; and there shall be one fold, one shepherd. Therefore doth my Father love me, because I lay down my life, that I might take it again. No one taketh it from me, but I lay it down of myself. I have power to lay it down, and I have power to take it again. This commandment have I received of my Father. — John x. 14 – 18.

My sheep hear my voice, and I know them, and they follow me: and I give unto them eternal life; and they shall never perish, neither shall any one pluck them out of my hand. My Father, who gave them me, is greater than all; and no one is able to pluck them out of my Father's hand. I and the Father are one. — John x. 27 – 30.

I am the way, the truth, and the life: no one cometh unto the FATHER but by me. If ye had known me, ye would have known my FATHER also: and from henceforth ye know him, and have seen him. Philip saith unto him, LORD, show us the FATHER, and it sufficeth us. JESUS saith unto him, Have I been so long time with you, and yet hast thou not known me, Philip? he that hath seen me, hath seen the FATHER; and how sayest thou, Show us the FATHER? Believest thou not that I am in the FATHER, and the FATHER in me? The words that I speak unto you I speak not of myself: but the FATHER that dwelleth in me, he doeth the works. Believe me, that I am in the FATHER, and the FATHER in me: or else believe me for the very works' sake. Verily, verily, I say unto you, He that believeth on me, the works that I do shall he do also: and greater ones than these shall he do, because I go unto my FATHER. And whatsoever ye shall ask in my name, that will I do; that the FATHER may be glorified in the SON. If ye shall ask any thing in my name, I will do it. — John xiv. 6-14.

IF ye abide in me, and my words abide in you, ye shall ask what ye will, and it shall be done unto you. Herein is my FATHER glorified, that ye bear much fruit: so shall ye be my disciples. As the FATHER hath loved me, so have I loved you: continue ye in my love. If ye keep my commandments, ye shall abide in my love; even as I have kept my FATHER's commandments, and abide in his love. These things have I spoken unto you, that my joy might remain in you, and that your joy might be full. — John xv. 7-11.

THIS is my commandment, That ye love one another, as I have loved you. Greater love hath no one than this, that one lay down his life for his friends. Ye are my friends, if ye do whatsoever I command you. Henceforth I call you not servants; for the servant knoweth not what his lord doeth: but I have called you friends; for all things that I have heard of my FATHER, I have made known unto you. Ye have not chosen me, but I have chosen you, and ordained you, that ye should go and bring forth fruit, and that your fruit should remain; that whatsoever ye shall ask of the FATHER in my name, he may give it you. These things I command you, that ye love one another. — John xv. 12–17.

Then may be read the following

## INSTRUCTION.

" The two Sacraments, Baptism and the Holy Supper, are, as it were, TWO GATES to eternal life. Every Christian man, by baptism, which is the FIRST GATE, is admitted and introduced into the things which the church teaches from the Word concerning another life; which all are means by which man may be prepared for and led to heaven. The OTHER GATE is the Holy Supper, through which every man, who has suffered himself to be prepared and led by the LORD, is admitted and introduced into heaven. There are no more universal gates.

"After the FIRST GATE there is a PLAIN, over which he must run; and the other is the GOAL, where is the prize, to which he directed his course: for the palm is not given till after the contest, nor the reward till after the combat. — *T. C. R.* 721.

" These Sacraments may also be compared to a double temple, one of which is below, and the other above; and in the lower of which the gospel concerning the new advent of the LORD is preached, and also concerning regeneration and thence salvation by Him. From this temple, around the altar, there is an ascent into the upper temple, in which the Holy Supper is celebrated; and thence a passage into heaven, where the LORD receives them.

" They may also be compared to the tabernacle; in which, behind the entrance, appeared the table upon which the bread of faces was arranged in order; and also the golden altar of incense; and in the midst, the candlestick with the lamps lighted, by which all those things come into view; and at length, for those who suffer themselves to be illuminated, the veil is opened to the Holy of Holies: where, in the place of the ark, in which the decalogue had been, the Word is laid up, over which was the propitiatory, with cherubs of gold." — *T. C. R.* 669

ADDRESS TO THOSE WHO WERE BAPTIZED IN INFANCY OR CHILDHOOD.

You were baptized in the New Church during your infancy [or childhood]. While you were unable to do any thing for your*self*, the LORD provided that your parents [or guardians] should take care of you. They have been led to do such things as were conducive both to your spiritual and your natural welfare. They have taken care of your *body*, and prepared you for living in this world; and, at the same time, they have taken care of your *mind*, and endeavored to prepare you to live in the spiritual world.

By bringing you to the ordinance of baptism in the New Church, they have not only introduced you into the Church, but they have brought you under the care of the angels of the New Heaven. These angels have constantly attended upon you, and watched over you for your good. They have endeavored to protect you from evil influences, and to cause you to receive good influences. While the LORD has by his Spirit and Providence caused your parents to operate upon you in a natural and visible manner, he has led your angels to operate upon you in a spiritual and invisible manner. While he has caused your parents to love you, to give you spiritual instruction, and to lead you in the way that you should go, he has through his angels inspired you with a love for your parents, and a disposition to listen to them; he has given you an affection for the truths of his Word and the doctrines of his Church, and a desire to live according to them.

Many, very many things have been done for you,

while you have been unable to coöperate, while you did not even know that any one was taking thought for your welfare, and consequently while you did not know how much you had to be thankful for. Others labored, and ye have entered into their labors. But those who labored for you are blessed. It is happiness to them to see you enjoying the fruits of their labors; and they will be still more blessed, when they begin to see you enjoying the happiness of doing for others what they have done for you.

But you have been coming forward; your faculties have been gradually unfolding; you have therefore been able to coöperate more and more with those who have been working for you. You have been able to act more and more voluntarily, and as of your*self*, in conforming to the instruction which you have received. We trust that you have in some degree been enabled to coöperate with the influence of the LORD and his angels, in contending against your natural, selfish, and worldly inclinations; and that you have consequently, in some degree, become receptive of the loves which come down from heaven — of love to the LORD and love to the neighbor. We trust that you have begun to do that which is, in the spiritual sense, denoted by eating of his flesh and drinking his blood; and that you are, therefore, prepared to come to the ordinance of the Holy Supper.

As you have now arrived at adult age, and as your faculties of freedom and rationality are unfolded, the duty henceforth devolves upon you, to cultivate, to regulate, and to use those faculties. Your natural parents [or guardians] will no longer think that they ought to control you, but will desire that you should be *a free and rational being*. They apparently leave you to your*self;* but you are not really left to your*self:* you are not *an orphan:* you are not without a father and a mother. And we trust that as you have been coming to maturity, you have been coming out of a natural into a spiritual state of mind. We trust that you have acquired some knowledge of, and have learned to love, the spiritual influences which have been operating, and are now operating, upon you; so that now, when you are coming out from under the government of your natural parents [or guardians], you do voluntarily come under the government of your spiritual Parents — of the LORD, and of his Church. We trust that you will look unto Him as your FA-THER, and to the holy city, the New Jerusalem, as your Mother.

ADDRESS TO ADULTS WHO WERE BAPTIZED BEFORE PROFESSING THEIR BELIEF IN THE DOCTRINES.

You have been introduced by Baptism into the New Church; and by the same means you have been brought more fully under the influence of the angels of the New Heaven. Under these influences and in these circumstances you have been studying the Doctrines of the New Jerusalem; and as you have proceeded, your understanding of them has been continually growing clearer, your faith in them firmer, and your affection for them stronger. Spiritual darkness has been dissipated; spiritual clouds have been dispelled or illuminated; and the coldness of your natural state has been yielding before the warmth of the spiritual Sun. You are now, therefore, beginning to feel established in these Doctrines, and to feel at home in the Holy City that is coming down from GOD out of heaven.

You have also been doing some of the spiritual works which are denoted by baptism: you have been abstaining from the evils which are forbidden in the Commandments, as sins against GOD; and you have been contending in your own mind against the evil affections and inclinations which would lead to those sins. And in doing these things, you have not been imagining that you were acting of your*self*, and by your own power; but you have believed and acknowledged that you were acting from the LORD, and by the power which he is continually giving you through the influence of the Holy Spirit. And in consequence of shunning evils internally as well as externally, you have in some degree overcome the love of them; and in the same degree you have begun to receive a love for the opposite goods: as the love of self and the love of the world have in some degree been brought into subordination, so in the same degree the heavens have been opened to you, and the Holy Spirit has come down upon you; that is, the internals of your mind have been opened, and love to the LORD and love to the neighbor have begun to flow down into the externals: thus a holy, a sanctifying influence has begun to descend, and to be diffused throughout the whole man. You have thus begun to do internally that which is denoted by receiving the Holy Supper: for you have begun to receive into your will that which is denoted by the bread, and into your understanding that which is denoted by the wine; and you are therefore prepared to come to that ordinance externally.

Here the Minister may read the following

DOCTRINES OF THE NEW CHURCH.

1. THAT there is one GOD; that in him is a Divine Trinity called the FATHER, the SON, and the HOLY SPIRIT; that these three are distinct, and at the same time united in him, as the soul, the body, and the operation are in man; and that the one GOD is the LORD JESUS CHRIST.

2. That saving faith is to believe in him as the Redeemer, Regenerator, and Savior from sin.

3. That the Sacred Scripture is Divine Truth; that it is revealed to us as a means by which we may distinguish between good and evil, by which we may be delivered from the influence of evil spirits, and by which we may become associated with angels and conjoined with the LORD.

4. That we must abstain from doing evil, because it is of the devil and from the devil: and that we must do good, because it is of GOD and from GOD.

5. That in abstaining from evil and doing good we are to act as of ourselves; but we must at the same time believe and acknowledge that the will, the understanding, and the power to do so, are of the LORD alone.

*Min.* Do you acknowledge and receive these doctrines?
*Answer:* — I do.
*Min.* Do you desire and intend, by the divine mercy of the LORD, to live according to them?
*Answer:* — I do.
*Min.* You have been baptized with water, which represents the truths that are contained in the literal sense of the Scriptures: May you also be baptized with the Holy Spirit and with fire; that is, with the Divine Wisdom and the Divine Love which are contained in the spiritual sense.

You have been baptized into the name of the FATHER, and of the SON, and of the HOLY SPIRIT: May you have this baptism spiritually fulfilled in you: May you receive into your mind and life that which is denoted by the FATHER, that which is denoted by the SON, and that which is denoted by the HOLY SPIRIT. May the LORD JESUS CHRIST abide in you, and you in him; so that you may be brought into his image and likeness, and so that you may from him bring forth the fruits of righteousness.

*Then may be said the Lord's Prayer, all kneeling.*

OUR FATHER, who art in the heavens; Hallowed be thy name. Thy kingdom come. Thy will be done, as in heaven, so also upon the earth. Give us this day our daily bread. And forgive us our debts, as we also forgive our debtors. And lead us not into temptation; but deliver us from evil. For thine is the kingdom, and the power, and the glory, for ever: Amen.

The candidate then kneels, or continues kneeling; and the Minister, laying his hands on his head, may repeat one or both of the following blessings.

BLESSED are they that do His commandments, that they may have right to the tree of life, and may enter in through the gates into the city. — Rev. xxii. 14.

JEHOVAH bless thee, and keep thee: JEHOVAH make His face to shine upon thee, and be gracious unto thee: JEHOVAH lift up His countenance upon thee, and give thee peace. — Num. vi. 24 - 26.

The service may be concluded by singing an Anthem, Selection, or Hymn; and by the Benediction, if no services follow.

## BENEDICTION.

THE grace of our LORD JESUS CHRIST be with you all. AMEN.

THE

# SACRAMENT OF THE HOLY SUPPER.

[Persons who have been introduced into the New Church by Baptism, and who have arrived at maturity, (which with males is at the age of twenty-one, and with females at the age of eighteen years,) who have made a full acknowledgment of their faith in the doctrines of the church, and declared their desire and intention to live according to them, and who are in a state of charity and peace with their brethren, are regarded as proper persons to receive the sacrament of the Holy Supper.]

The service may be commenced by singing an appropriate Selection or Hymn. The Minister may then read the following.

"THE INSTITUTION OF THE HOLY SUPPER BY THE LORD.

"JESUS kept the Passover with his disciples: and when the evening was come, he sat down with them. 'And as they did eat, JESUS took BREAD, and blessed, and brake, and gave to his disciples, and said, Take, eat; this is MY BODY. And he took the CUP; and when he had given thanks, he gave it to them, saying, Drink ye all of it; for this is MY BLOOD of the New Covenant, which is shed for many.'— Mat. xxvi. 20 - 28; Mark xiv. 22 – 24; Luke xxii. 19, 20.

"THE DOCTRINE OF THE LORD CONCERNING HIS FLESH AND BLOOD AND CONCERNING THE BREAD AND WINE.

"'LABOR not for the meat which perisheth, but for that meat which endureth unto everlasting life, which the SON OF MAN will give unto you. Verily, verily, I say unto you, Moses gave you not that bread from heaven, but my FATHER giveth you the true bread from heaven: for the bread of GOD is he that cometh down from heaven, and giveth life to the world. I am the bread of life: he that cometh unto me shall never hunger, and he that believeth on me shall never thirst. I am the bread which came down from heaven. Verily, verily, I say unto you, He that believeth on me hath everlasting life: I am that bread of life. Your fathers did eat the manna in the wilderness, and are dead. This is the bread which cometh down from heaven, that one may eat thereof, and not die. I am the living bread which came down from heaven; if any one eat of this bread, he shall live for ever: and the bread that I will give is my flesh, which I will give for the life of the world. Verily, verily, I say unto you, Except ye eat the flesh of the SON OF MAN, and drink his blood, ye have no life in you. Whoso eateth my flesh, and drinketh my blood, hath eternal life; and I will raise him up at the last day: for my flesh is meat indeed, and my blood is drink indeed. He that eateth my flesh, and drinketh my blood, dwelleth in me, and I in him.'—John vi. 27, 32, 33, 35, 41, 47–51, 53–56."— *T. C. R.* 703.

"The Holy Supper was instituted by the LORD, to be a means whereby the church may have conjunction with heaven, and thus with the LORD: it is, therefore, the holiest solemnity of divine worship.

"The manner in which such conjunction is effected by the Holy Supper, is not understood by those who are unacquainted with the internal or spiritual sense of the Word; since they do not think beyond the external sense, which is that of the letter. It is only from the internal or spiritual sense of the Word, that it can be known what is signified by the LORD's body and blood, and by the bread and the wine; and also what is signified by eating.

"In the spiritual sense, the LORD's body or flesh, and the bread, signifies the good of love; the LORD's blood and the wine, the good of faith; and eating, appropriation and conjunction. In no other sense do the angels, who are attendant on man when he receives the sacrament of the Supper, understand these things; for they perceive all things spiritually. Hence it is, that, on such occasions, a holy principle of love and of faith flows into man from the angels, thus through heaven from the LORD; and hence conjunction is effected.

"From these considerations it is evident, that when man partakes of the bread, which is the body, he is conjoined to the LORD by the good of love, directed to Him and derived from Him; and that when he partakes of the wine, which is the blood, he is conjoined to the LORD by the good of faith, directed to Him and derived from Him. But it must be particularly observed, that conjunction with the LORD by means of the sacrament of the Holy Supper, is effected with those alone who are influenced by the good of love to Him, and of faith in Him and from Him. With these there is conjunction by means of this most holy ordinance: with others there is indeed the LORD's presence, but no conjunction with Him.

"Besides, the Holy Supper includes and comprehends the whole of the divine worship instituted in the Israelitish Church; for the burnt offerings and sacrifices, in which the worship of that church principally consisted, were denominated by the single term BREAD: hence, also, the Holy Supper is the completion or fulness of that representative worship."—*H. D.* 210–214.

Then may be read the following

INSTRUCTION.

The LORD has given to the Church two external representative ordinances, Baptism, and the Holy Supper. These ordinances have spiritual significations; and in their spiritual sense they involve all we have to do in preparation for heaven. Baptism, or the washing of the body with water, denotes the purification of the mind, and the removal of every thing that is evil and false; and the Holy Supper denotes the reception and implantation of what is good and true: thus the two ordinances represent the whole work of regeneration — the whole work by which we come out of a natural state into a spiritual one — the work of rejecting the influence of evil spirits, and yielding to the influence of the LORD and his angels — the work of resisting the love of self and the love of the world, until they are brought into subordination to the love of the LORD and the love of the neighbor.

It is made our duty to receive Baptism before we receive the Holy Supper, because the spiritual works which are represented by Baptism precede and prepare the way for those which are represented by the Holy Supper: for the evils and falsities which come up from beneath are opposite to the goods and truths which come down from above; so opposite and contrary, that we cannot be under the influence of both at the same time: consequently we must be successively delivered from the former, before we can receive the latter; and in the degree that we resist and put away what is evil and false, in that degree are we able to receive what is good and true; or, in other words, in the degree that we perform the spiritual works represented by Baptism, in that degree are we prepared to receive the Holy Supper, and the things represented by it.

[While we are performing the duties which are represented by Baptism; that is, while we are abstaining from those things which are forbidden by the Commandments, and are resisting our natural inclinations to do those things, then we think of the LORD, of his government, and his laws, only in natural light; for our evil inclinations prevent spiritual light from coming down out of heaven into our minds: consequently, we then think of him as an Almighty Being who acts from such principles as natural men act from, who acts from a love of his own glory and happiness, and who therefore loves and rewards those who love and obey him, and hates and punishes those who hate and disobey him.

But as we conform to his precepts, our views of him

change; the more we conform, the more plainly do we see that it is good for us to conform, and the more happiness do we enjoy while we are conforming; at the same time our desire to do the things which are forbidden is continually diminishing; our love for ourselves and for the world is by degrees overcome and made subordinate; and as this is done, love towards our neighbor is insinuated, which makes us love the Commandments; that is, it makes us love to do what they require, and unwilling to do what they forbid: and together with love to our neighbors there is insinuated into our minds a spiritual light, by which the Commandments are lifted up and glorified; their interior spirit and life are gradually unfolded, and we are continually able to see more and more wonderful things in them.

And as our views of the Divine Laws change, so our views of the LORD himself change: when we find that they are good for us, we begin to think that he gave them for that reason. Thus we are led to review all our opinions concerning him. We did suppose that in governing us and giving us laws, he acted from a love of governing, and a regard to his own glory; but now we begin to think that he acts from love towards us, that he governs from love, and that he gives laws from love. We also begin to see that he does not love us because we have been loving him, and that he does not do good unto us because we have been doing good unto him; but that he loves us because he is infinitely good, and that he does good unto us because he loves to do good. We become sensible that while we were buried in sin, while we were opposing and hating him and every thing that is good, he was loving us; and that from love he took upon himself our nature, and came down to save us; to deliver us from the evils of our will, and from the falsities of our understandings, and instead of them to fill our minds with wisdom and goodness. For this purpose he purified and glorified the human nature which he assumed; he delivered it from the evil and false propensities which it inherited from its mo-

ther, and filled it with his own Love and Wisdom.
By doing this, he showed us what we have to do, and
he gave us power to do it. While he was doing this,
he gave us all the knowledge of himself that we are
capable of receiving; and by the manner in which he
glorified his Humanity and made it Divine, he showed
how we may be regenerated and made spiritual.]

While we are reading the Scriptures, which give an
account of what the LORD did while he dwelt in the
world, we see him in two aspects; we see him as a
*good* Being, and a *wise* Being; and we see that all
the works and words that proceeded from him, proceeded from his Love and Wisdom united. These
two attributes are what are denoted by his flesh and
his blood, which he says we must eat and drink that
we may have eternal life; and they are also what
are denoted by the bread and the wine of the Holy
Supper. His flesh and the bread denote his Love or
Goodness, and his blood and the wine denote his
Wisdom or Truth. As bread and wine are appropriated to us, and made to enter into the composition
of our bodies, by our eating and drinking them; so
there is such a thing as spiritual eating and drinking,
by means of which the LORD's Goodness and Truth
may be received and appropriated by our minds. We
spiritually eat, when we meditate upon and love his
Goodness, and desire to have such goodness in our
own minds; and we spiritually drink, when we meditate upon the instruction which he gave, and when
we endeavor to receive it into our minds, so that we
may think and act according to it.

For example, when we consider the feelings which
the LORD manifested toward all men, even toward
those who hated him, then we can form an idea of
his Goodness; we can form an idea of the nature of
his Love. If we take delight in such Love, if we
love it, and desire to receive it into our minds so as
to act from it, then we eat spiritual food; we receive
that goodness into our minds: while we are loving it,
it flows from the LORD into our spirits; it nourishes
them, and gives them eternal life: for to feel such

love, and to act from it, is eternal life; that is, such life as the angels live.

So when we listen to him while he is teaching us to love our enemies, and to do good, and lend, hoping for nothing in return, that we may be like our FATHER who is in heaven, who is kind unto the unthankful and the evil; if we love this instruction, and desire to receive it into our minds, and to live according to it, then we spiritually drink; we receive spiritual wine into our spirits; and it enters into them and nourishes and strengthens them. Whence it may be seen that by wine is denoted spiritual truth.

[Now there are various kinds of goodness and truth which the LORD manifested and taught while he dwelt among us performing a work of redemption. All of these are presented to us, that we may receive them into our spirits, and be nourished by them: for he says, "As the living FATHER hath sent me, and I live by the FATHER; so he that eateth me, even he shall live by me." He was, as to his Humanity, continually obtaining knowledge of the goodness and the truth of his internal Divinity: then by loving that goodness and truth, by receiving them into his Humanity, and bringing them into life, his Humanity also was made Divine, and was united with his Essential Divinity. So, if we do that which is denoted by eating him; that is, if we love, receive, and appropriate the grace and truth which came by him, we shall become likenesses of him, shall live by him, and shall thus have eternal life.

But we must not imagine that we fully understand his goodness and truth the first time we think of them, or that we love them enough the first time that we feel any affection for them: for although he has in his mercy brought them down, so that even our senses can perceive them, and so that even the natural man can form an idea of them, yet in themselves they are infinite; and they will for ever continue to unfold themselves to our view, as our minds unfold themselves to receive them. When we are beginning to understand and to love them, we are beginning a new life; we are beginning to partake of the food which he has brought down from heaven — the food of which we shall eat for ever, and by means of which we shall live for ever And the reason why this spiritual food will continue to nourish us for ever is, because it is the infinite goodness and wisdom of the LORD himself, which he gives without measure; and because the more we receive of it, and the longer we live upon it, the better shall we understand it, and the more shall we be able to receive of it.]

From the spiritual signification of the Holy Supper, we can see what we ought to be doing spiritually, while we are partaking of it naturally; and that is, while we are eating the bread and drinking the wine, we ought to be meditating upon, and loving, and receiving into our minds the Divine Goodness and Wisdom which are denoted by them. And in order that we may be prepared to do this, two things are necessary. In the first place, we must have arrived at adult age: for if we have not, we shall not be free and rational beings; and the works which we do will not be entirely our own, but will in part proceed from those who have control over us. Secondly, we must have been baptized, and must have begun to do the spiritual works which are denoted by that ordinance; that is, we must have begun to abstain from evils as sins, and we must have begun to fight against and to overcome our inclinations to them: for until we have begun to do this, we can have no genuine affection for the things which are represented by the bread and wine; and if we have any affection for them, it will be for our own sake, and not for their sake. But when we have overcome the love of any evil, we shall receive from the LORD a love for the opposite good; and when we have overcome the love of any falsity, we shall receive a love for the opposite truth: thus are we prepared to come to the Holy Supper; thus are we prepared to partake of it internally, as well as externally — to receive the bread and wine, and at the same time to receive something of the goodness and truth which are represented by them.

[When the LORD dwelt among us, he turned water into wine; and he also did the spiritual work which is denoted by it: that is, he transformed the prohibitory commandments into doctrines of love. The commandments in relation to himself, which forbid our having other gods before him, our taking his name in vain, and our violating his holy day, are transformed into the doctrine that we should love him with all the heart; and he presented himself to us in such a manner that we could do it. So the commandments in relation to our neighbors, which forbid our doing or desiring to do any evil to them, were transformed into the doctrine that we should love them as ourselves.

But it was at a marriage that he turned the water into wine: so it is at a spiritual marriage that he transforms the commandments into doctrines of love; it is when he can produce the marriage of goodness and truth in our minds; when evil loves are overcome in us, and we begin to receive good loves in place of them. With these loves all his commandments can be united in marriage; and when they are thus united, we obey without any hope of reward: we can do good, and lend, hoping for nothing again; for it is our meat and our drink to do his will.]

Here one or more of the following passages from the Word may be read.

AND in this mountain shall JEHOVAH of hosts make
  unto all people
A feast of fat things, a feast of wines on the lees,
Of fat things full of marrow,
Of wines on the lees well refined.
And he will destroy in this mountain
The face of the covering cast over all people,
And the vail that is spread over all nations.
He will swallow up death in victory;
And the LORD JEHOVIH will wipe away tears from off
  all faces;
And the rebuke of his people shall he take away from
  off all the earth :

For JEHOVAH hath spoken it.
And it shall be said in that day,
Lo, this is our GOD;
We have waited for him, and he will save us:
This is JEHOVAH;
We have waited for him,
We will be glad and rejoice in his salvation.
               Is. xxv. 6 – 9.

AND, thou son of man, thus saith the LORD JEHO-
VIH: Speak unto every feathered fowl, and to every
beast of the field,
  Assemble yourselves, and come;
Gather yourselves on every side,
To my sacrifice that I do sacrifice for you,
A great sacrifice upon the mountains of Israel,
That ye may eat flesh, and drink blood.
Ye shall eat the flesh of the mighty,
And drink the blood of the princes of the earth,
Of rams, of lambs, and of goats, of bullocks,
All of them fatlings of Bashan.
And ye shall eat fat till ye be full,
And drink blood till ye be drunken,
Of my sacrifice which I have sacrificed for you.
Thus ye shall be filled at my table with horses and
     chariots,
With mighty men, and with all men of war,
Saith the LORD JEHOVIH. — Ezek. xxxix. 17 – 20.

AND I heard as it were the voice of a great multitude, and as the voice of many waters, and as the
voice of mighty thunderings, saying, Alleluia : for the
LORD GOD Omnipotent reigneth. Let us be glad
and rejoice, and give the glory unto him: for the
marriage of the LAMB is come, and his Wife hath
made herself ready. And to her was granted that she
should be arrayed in fine linen, bright and clean : for
the fine linen is the righteousness of the saints. And
he saith unto me, Write, Blessed are they that are
called unto the marriage supper of the LAMB. — Rev
xix. 6 – 9.

AND I saw an angel standing in the sun; and he cried with a loud voice, saying to all the fowls that fly in the midst of heaven, Come and gather yourselves together unto the supper of the great GOD; that ye may eat the flesh of kings, and the flesh of captains, and the flesh of the mighty, and the flesh of horses, and of them that sit upon them, and the flesh of all, both free and bond, and small and great.— Rev. xix. 17, 18.

BEHOLD, I stand at the door, and knock: if any one hear my voice, and open the door, I will come in unto him, and will sup with him, and he with me. To him that overcometh will I grant to sit with me in my throne, even as I also overcame, and sat down with my FATHER in his throne. He that hath an ear, let him hear what the Spirit saith unto the churches.— Rev. iii. 20 – 22.

THEREFORE if thou bring thy gift to the altar, and there rememberest that thy brother hath aught against thee; leave there thy gift before the altar, and go thy way: first be reconciled to thy brother, and then come and offer thy gift.— Mat. v. 23, 24.

THEN came the day of unleavened bread, when the passover must be killed. And he sent Peter and John, saying, Go and prepare us the passover, that we may eat. And they said unto him, Where wilt thou that we prepare? And he said unto them, Behold, when ye are entered into the city, there shall a man meet you, bearing a pitcher of water; follow him into the house where he entereth in. And ye shall say unto the goodman of the house, The Master saith unto thee, Where is the guestchamber, where I shall eat the passover with my disciples? And he shall show you a large upper room furnished: there make ready. And they went, and found as he had said unto them: and they made ready the passover.— Luke xxii. 7 – 13.

Now when the evening was come, he sat down with

the twelve. And as they did eat, he said, Verily I say unto you, that one of you shall betray me. And they were exceedingly sorrowful, and began every one of them to say unto him, LORD, is it I? And he answered and said, He that dippeth his hand with me in the dish, the same shall betray me. The SON OF MAN goeth as it is written of him: but wo unto that man by whom the SON OF MAN is betrayed! it had been good for that man if he had not been born. Then Judas, who betrayed him, answered and said, Master, is it I? He said unto him, Thou hast said.

And as they were eating, JESUS took the Bread, and blessed, and brake, and gave to the disciples, and said, Take, eat; this is my Body. And he took the Cup, and gave thanks, and gave to them, saying, Drink ye all of it; for this is my Blood of the New Covenant, which is shed for many for the remission of sins. But I say unto you, I will not drink henceforth of this fruit of the vine, until that day when I drink it new with you in my FATHER'S kingdom. And when they had sung an hymn, they went out into the Mount of Olives. — Mat. xxvi. 20 – 30.

Here the Minister, uncovering the Bread, may repeat the following prayer, or the LORD'S Prayer, or both, all kneeling.

O LORD our Redeemer and Savior, thou who art the Bread of life, draw near, and bless us, while we engage in this holiest act of worship. We confess before thee, O LORD, that of ourselves we are only evil, and all unworthy of thy great goodness, and of the manifold blessings we daily receive at thy hands. Yet, trusting in thy Divine mercy, and encouraged by thy gracious invitations, we come, with humble and penitent hearts, to present ourselves before thee, and, in the way of thine appointment, seek conjunction with thee. Prepare our hearts and minds, we entreat thee, for such heavenly communion. May every evil affection and false suggestion be removed, and may love to thee and charity towards our neighbor be implanted in their stead; so that while our bodies are nourished by the bread and wine, our souls may be strengthened and refreshed by angels' food — by love to thee and to one another. And may we thus realize that in thy Holy Supper thou art present with all the benefits of thy redemption. May it be a signing, sealing, and testifying that we are thy children, opening to us the mansions of heaven, and conjoining us more closely with thee for evermore. Amen.

OUR FATHER, who art in the heavens; Hallowed be thy name. Thy kingdom come. Thy will be done, as in heaven, so also upon the earth. Give us this day our daily bread. And forgive us our debts, as we also forgive our debtors. And lead us not into temptation; but deliver us from evil. For thine is the kingdom, and the power, and the glory, for ever. AMEN.

Then shall the Minister repeat one of the following passages.

JESUS took the Bread, and blessed, and brake, and gave to the disciples, and said, Take, eat; this is my Body. — Mat. xxvi. 26.

JESUS took Bread, and blessed, and brake, and gave to them, and said, Take, eat; this is my Body. — Mark xiv. 22.

AND he took Bread, and gave thanks, and brake, and gave unto them, saying, This is my Body which is given for you: this do in remembrance of me. — Luke xxii. 19.

Here shall he break and distribute the Bread.

Then shall he take the Cup, and repeat one of the following passages.

AND he took the Cup, and gave thanks, and gave to them, saying, Drink ye all of it; for this is my Blood of the New Covenant, which is shed for many for the remission of sins. — Mat. xxvi. 27, 28.

AND he took the Cup, and when he had given thanks, he gave to them: and they all drank of it. And he said unto them, This is my Blood of the New Covenant, which is shed for many. — Mark xiv. 23, 24.

LIKEWISE also the Cup after supper, saying, This cup is the New Covenant in my Blood, which is shed for you. — Luke xxii. 20.

Then shall he present the Wine to the communicants.

When all have partaken, one or more of the following passages may be read.

IF ye love me, keep my commandments. And I will pray the FATHER, and he shall give you another Comforter, that he may abide with you for ever: the Spirit of truth; whom the world cannot receive, because it seeth him not, neither knoweth him: but ye know him; for he dwelleth with you, and shall be in you. I will not leave you comfortless: I will come to you. Yet a little while, and the world seeth me no more; but ye see me: because I live, ye shall live also. At that day ye shall know that I am in my FATHER, and ye in me, and I in you. He that hath my commandments, and keepeth them, he it is that loveth me: and he that loveth me, shall be loved of my FATHER; and I will love him, and will manifest myself to him.

Judas saith unto him, not Iscariot, LORD, how is it that thou wilt manifest thyself unto us, and not unto the world?

JESUS answered and said unto him, If a man love me, he will keep my words: and my FATHER will love him; and we will come unto him, and make our abode with him. He that loveth me not, keepeth not my sayings: and the word which ye hear is not mine, but the FATHER'S who sent me. These things have I spoken unto you, being present with you. But the Comforter, the Holy Spirit, whom the FATHER will send in my name, he shall teach you all things, and bring all things to your remembrance, whatsoever I have said unto you. — John xiv. 15 – 26.

PEACE I leave with you; my peace I give unto you: not as the world giveth, give I unto you. Let not your heart be troubled, neither let it be afraid. Ye have heard how I said unto you, I go away, and come unto you. If ye loved me, ye would rejoice, because I said, I go unto the FATHER: for my FATHER is greater than I. And now I have told you before it come to pass, that, when it is come to pass, ye might believe. Hereafter I will not talk much with you: for the prince of this world cometh, and hath nothing in me. But that the world may know that I love the FATHER: and as the FATHER gave me commandment, even so I do. Arise, let us go hence. — John xiv. 27 – 31.

THIS is my commandment, That ye love one another, as I have loved you. Greater love hath no one than this, that one lay down his life for his friends. Ye are my friends, if ye do whatsoever I command you. Henceforth I call you not servants; for the servant knoweth not what his lord doeth: but I have called you friends; for all things that I have heard of my FATHER, I have made known unto you. Ye have not chosen me, but I have chosen you, and ordained you, that ye should go and bring forth fruit, and that your fruit should remain; that whatsoever ye shall ask of the FATHER in my name, he may give it you. These things I command you, that ye love one another. — John xv. 12 – 17.

THESE words spake JESUS, and lifted up his eyes to heaven, and said, FATHER, the hour is come; glorify thy SON, that thy SON also may glorify thee: as thou hast given him power over all flesh, that he should give eternal life to as many as thou hast given him. And this is life eternal, that they might know thee the only true GOD, and JESUS CHRIST, whom thou hast sent. I have glorified thee on the earth: I have finished the work which thou gavest me to do. And now, O FATHER, glorify thou me with thine own self, with the glory which I had with thee before the world was.

I have manifested thy name unto the men whom thou gavest me out of the world: thine they were, and thou gavest them me; and they have kept thy word. Now they have known that all things whatsoever thou hast given me are of thee: for I have given unto them the words which thou gavest me; and they have received them, and have known surely that I came out from thee, and they have believed that thou didst send me. I pray for them: I pray not for the world, but for them whom thou hast given me; for they are thine. And all mine are thine, and thine are mine; and I am glorified in them. And now I am no more in the world; but these are in the world, and I come to thee. Holy FATHER, keep through thine own name those whom thou hast given me, that they may be one, as we are. While I was with them in the world, I kept them in thy name: those that thou gavest me I have kept, and none of them is lost, but the son of perdition; that the scripture might be fulfilled. And now come I to thee; and these things I speak in the world, that they might have my joy fulfilled in themselves.

I have given them thy word; and the world hath hated them, because they are not of the world, even as I am not of the world. I pray not that thou shouldst take them out of the world, but that thou shouldst keep them from the evil. They are not of the world, even as I am not of the world. Sanctify them through thy truth: thy word is truth. As thou hast sent me into the world, even so have I also sent them into the world: and for their sakes I sanctify myself, that they also might be sanctified through the truth. Neither pray I for these alone, but for them also who shall believe on me through their word: that they all may be one; as thou, FATHER, art in me, and I in thee, that they also may be one in us: that the world may believe that thou hast sent me. And the glory which thou gavest me I have given them; that they may be one, even as we are one: I in them, and thou in me, that they may be made perfect in one; and that the world may know that thou hast sent me, and hast loved them as thou hast loved me.

FATHER, I will that they also, whom thou hast given me, be with me where I am; that they may behold my glory, which thou hast given me: for thou lovedst me before the foundation of the world. O righteous FATHER, the world hath not known thee: but I have known thee, and these have known that thou hast sent me. And I have declared unto them thy name, and will declare it; that the love wherewith thou hast loved me may be in them, and I in them.—John xvii.

JESUS saith to Simon Peter, Simon, son of Jonas, lovest thou me more than these? He saith unto him, Yea, LORD; thou knowest that I love thee. He saith unto him, Feed my lambs. He saith to him again the second time, Simon, son of Jonas, lovest thou me? He saith unto him, Yea, LORD; thou knowest that I love thee. He saith unto him, Feed my sheep. He saith unto him the third time, Simon, son of Jonas, lovest thou me? Peter was grieved because he said unto him the third time, Lovest thou me? and he said unto him, LORD, thou knowest all things; thou knowest that I love thee. JESUS saith unto him, Feed my sheep. — John xxi. 15 – 17.

Then a Selection, Anthem, or Hymn may be sung.

## BENEDICTION.

THE grace of our LORD JESUS CHRIST be with you all. AMEN.

# MARRIAGE.

*The persons about to be married having presented themselves before the Minister, the Bride standing on the right hand of the Bridegroom, the following instruction may be given.*

WE are now assembled in the presence of our Heavenly FATHER, to witness and confirm the marriage of A B and C D: Let us therefore hear the declarations of the Divine Word concerning the institution of Marriage.

And JEHOVAH GOD said, It is not good that the man should be alone; I will make him a help meet for him. . . . . And JEHOVAH GOD brought the woman unto the man. And the man said, This is now bone of my bones, and flesh of my flesh. Therefore shall a man leave his father and his mother, and shall cleave unto his wife: and they shall be one flesh. — Gen. ii. 18, 22 – 24.

JESUS said, He who made them at the beginning, made them male and female; and said, For this cause shall a man leave father and mother, and shall cleave to his wife: and they twain shall be one flesh. Wherefore they are no more twain, but one flesh, What therefore GOD hath joined together, let not man put asunder. — Mat. xix. 4 – 6

THE Heavenly Doctrines of the New Jerusalem teach us that marriage is the union of one man and one woman in the bonds of genuine conjugial love. Love truly conjugial descends from heaven; and in its origin it is the union of the Divine Love and the Divine Wisdom, the Divine Goodness and the Divine Truth, in the LORD. Hence the union of goodness and truth in heaven is from the LORD; and this union is the essence of the heavenly marriage, and the source of conjugial love on earth. In the Divine Word, the LORD is called the Bridegroom and Husband; and the Church, the Bride and Wife: and heaven itself is compared to a Marriage.

When a pair is united in love truly conjugial, each one loves the interior affections and thoughts, as well as the outward form and conduct, of the other. Thus each one loves to think, to will, and to act as the other does; and in this manner to be united to the other, and to become as one man; according to the LORD's words, "They twain shall be one flesh."

Whatever is performed under the influence of conjugial love, is done from a principle of freedom on both sides; for each party is in the enjoyment of freedom, when each one loves what the other thinks, and what the other wills. But the desire of exercising dominion in marriage destroys genuine love, and takes away its freedom, and also its delight.

Marriage is a holy state; and to enjoy its blessedness, we must be delivered from the love of self, and become principled in supreme love to the LORD, and in mutual love to each other. For, when the husband and the wife are engrossed in the love of self, they become disjoined and separated, first in their interior affections and thoughts, and then in their outward transactions. But when they are principled in love to the LORD and to one another, they become more and more conjoined and united, first in their affections and thoughts, and then in the ultimate conduct of life.

In the primeval ages, conjugial love prevailed, and its nature was well known; but as man declined into evil, the knowledge of it became obscured: and as its state in man always runs parallel with the state of the church in him, genuine conjugial love, in these latter ages, has become almost a stranger on the earth. But we are assured that in the New Jerusalem it will be restored, and will be among the chief of the blessings made accessible to those who worship the LORD JESUS CHRIST alone, and keep his commandments.

## MARRIAGE.

### THE LORD'S PRAYER.

*By the Minister alone.*

OUR FATHER, who art in the heavens; Hallowed be thy name. Thy kingdom come. Thy will be done, as in heaven, so also upon the earth. Give us this day our daily bread. And forgive us our debts, as we also forgive our debtors. And lead us not into temptation; but deliver us from evil. For thine is the kingdom, and the power, and the glory, for ever. Amen.

The parties standing, the Minister shall say, A B and C D: The bonds of marriage are holy and inviolable in the sight of heaven; and you have come before the LORD to enter into the conjugial covenant. Let me therefore ask: Do you, trusting in the LORD, propose to enter into this covenant from a sincere desire of promoting the welfare of each other, for time and for eternity?
*Each will answer:* — I do.

### To the Man.

*Min.* A B: Do you desire to have this woman for your wife?
*Answer:* — I do.

### To the Woman.

*Min.* C D: Are you willing to have this man for your husband?
*Answer:* — I am.

### To both.

*Min.* Do you promise before the LORD, to live together in love; to be faithful to each other through life; and to perform your respective duties, in the holy state into which you are about to enter, according to the divine laws of the marriage covenant?
*Answer by each:* — I do.

When no ring is used, the words, "In giving this ring," and 'In taking this ring," are to be omitted; and the hands are to be joined.

### To the Man.

*Min.* In giving this ring, do you, in the name of the LORD, espouse this woman as your wife?
*Answer:* — I do.

### To the Woman.

*Min.* In taking this ring, do you, in the name of the LORD, receive this man as your husband?
*Answer:* — I do.

When a ring is used, the hands are to be joined here; and the Minister shall proceed to say:

*Min.* Ye are now Husband and Wife. Ye are no more twain, but one flesh. "What, therefore, GOD hath joined together, let not man put asunder."

Then the following prayer may be used by the Minister, all kneeling.

O LORD our Redeemer and Savior, in thee the Divine Love and the Divine Wisdom are joined in One. Thou art the fountain of life, and the source of conjugial love in Heaven and in the Church. Thou art the Creator of human pairs, its recipients on earth Crown, we beseech thee, with thy blessing, thy servant and handmaid now joined together in the marriage covenant. Unite their hearts in supreme love to thee, and in mutual love to each other. Open their eyes upon the relations and duties of the conjugial state: sustain them in the trials of life: diminish their sorrows: increase their joys: and confirm them more and more in every good word and work. Inspire them with true conjugial love: give them one heart, one mind, and one way: lead them in the paths of righteousness and peace: and when they have finished their course on earth, receive them into the celestial marriage — a life of eternal usefulness and happiness in heaven: Amen.

## MARRIAGE.

*The parties still kneeling, the Minister shall rise, and laying his hands, one upon the head of each, shall pronounce one of the following Blessings.*

JEHOVAH bless you, and keep you: JEHOVAH make his face to shine upon you, and be gracious unto you: JEHOVAH lift up his countenance upon you, and give you peace.

THE blessing of JEHOVAH be upon you: We bless you in the name of JEHOVAH.

MAY the blessing of the LORD JESUS CHRIST rest upon you: May His peace descend upon you: May the influence of His Holy Spirit draw you nearer and nearer towards Himself, and into more and more union of spirit with each other; thus rendering your union happy here, and by means of it preparing you to live hereafter in his more immediate presence in blessedness for ever.

*An Anthem, Selection, or Hymn may then be sung.*

## BENEDICTION.

THE grace of our LORD JESUS CHRIST be with you all: AMEN.

# FUNERAL SERVICE FOR ADULTS.

*The service may be commenced by reading one or more of the following passages.*

WHAT man liveth, and shall not see death? Shall he deliver his soul from the hand of the grave? — Ps. lxxxix. 48.

I will ransom them from the hand of the grave: I will redeem them from death. O death, I will be thy plagues: O grave, I will be thy destruction. — Hos. xiii. 14.

O JEHOVAH, make me to know mine end,
And the measure of my days, what it is;
That I may know how frail I am.
Behold, thou hast made my days as an handbreadth;
And mine age is as nothing before thee:
Verily every man at his best state is altogether vanity.
Ps. xxxix. 4, 5.

HEAR my prayer, O JEHOVAH,
And give ear unto my cry:
Hold not thy peace at my tears:
For I am a stranger with thee,
A sojourner, as all my fathers were.
O spare me, that I may recover strength,
Before I go hence, and be no more. — Ps. xxxix. 12, 13.

LORD, thou hast been our dwelling place,
In generation and generation.
Before the mountains were brought forth,

Or ever thou hadst formed the earth and the world,
Even from everlasting to everlasting, thou art God.
Thou turnest man to destruction;
And sayest, Return, ye children of men.
For a thousand years in thy sight
Are as yesterday when it is past,
And as a watch in the night.
Thou carriest them away as with a flood;
They are as a sleep:
In the morning they are like grass which groweth up.
In the morning it flourisheth, and groweth up;
In the evening it is cut down, and withereth. . . .
The days of our years are threescore years and ten;
And if by reason of strength they be fourscore years,
Yet is their strength labor and sorrow:
For it is soon cut off, and we fly away. . . .
So teach us to number our days,
That we may apply our hearts unto wisdom.
Ps. xc. 1 – 6; 10, 12.

Like as a father pitieth his children,
So Jehovah pitieth them that fear him.
For he knoweth our frame;
He remembereth that we are dust.
As for man, his days are as grass:
As a flower of the field, so he flourisheth.
For the wind passeth over it, and it is not;
And the place thereof shall know it no more.
But the mercy of Jehovah is from everlasting to everlasting upon them that fear him,
And his righteousness unto children's children;
To such as keep his covenant,
And to those that remember his commandments to do them. — Ps. ciii. 13 – 18.

Wilt thou show wonders to the dead?
Shall the dead arise and praise thee?
Ps. lxxxviii. 10

Now that the dead are raised, even Moses showed at the bush, when he called the Lord the God of

Abraham, and the God of Isaac, and the God of Jacob. For he is not a God of the dead, but of the living: for to him all are living. — Luke xx. 37, 38.

WHY seek ye the living among the dead? He is not here, but is risen. — Luke xxiv. 5, 6.

JESUS said, I am the Resurrection, and the Life. He that believeth in me, though he were dead, yet shall he live: and whosoever liveth and believeth in me, shall never die. — John xi. 25, 26.

THEN shall the kingdom of heaven be likened unto ten virgins, who took their lamps, and went forth to meet the bridegroom. And five of them were wise, and five were foolish. They that were foolish took their lamps, and took no oil with them: but the wise took oil in their vessels with their lamps. While the bridegroom tarried, they all slumbered and slept. And at midnight there was a cry made, Behold, the bridegroom cometh; go ye out to meet him. Then all those virgins arose, and trimmed their lamps. And the foolish said unto the wise, Give us of your oil; for our lamps are gone out. But the wise answered, saying, Not so; lest there be not enough for us and you: but go ye rather to them that sell, and buy for yourselves. And while they went to buy, the bridegroom came; and they that were ready went in with him to the marriage: and the door was shut. Afterward came also the other virgins, saying, Lord, Lord, open to us. But he answered and said, Verily I say unto you, I know you not. Watch therefore, for ye know neither the day nor the hour wherein the SON OF MAN cometh. — Mat. xxv. 1 – 13.

TAKE ye heed, watch and pray: for ye know not when the time is. For the SON OF MAN is as a man taking a far journey, who left his house, and gave authority to his servants, and to every one his work, and commanded the porter to watch. Watch ye therefore; for ye know not when the master of the house cometh, at evening, or at midnight, or at the cock-crowing, or in the morning: lest coming suddenly he find you sleeping. And what I say unto you I say unto all, Watch. — Mark xiii. 33 – 37.

AND I say unto you, my friends, Be not afraid of them that kill the body, and after that have no more that they can do. But I will forewarn you whom ye shall fear: Fear him who after he hath killed hath power to cast into hell; yea, I say unto you, fear him. Are not five sparrows sold for two farthings? and not one of them is forgotten before GOD. But even the very hairs of your head are all numbered. Fear not therefore: ye are of more value than many sparrows. — Luke xii. 4 – 7.

LAY not up for yourselves treasures upon earth, where moth and rust doth corrupt, and where thieves break through and steal; but lay up for yourselves treasures in heaven, where neither moth nor rust doth corrupt, and where thieves do not break through nor steal: for where your treasure is, there will your heart be also. — Mat. vi. 19 – 21.

AND seek not ye what ye shall eat, or what ye shall drink, neither be ye of doubtful mind. For all these things do the nations of the world seek after: and your FATHER knoweth that ye have need of these things. But rather seek ye the kingdom of GOD; and all these things shall be added unto you. Fear not, little flock; for it is your FATHER's good pleasure to give you the kingdom. Sell what ye have, and give alms; provide yourselves bags which wax not old, a treasure in the heavens that faileth not, where no thief approacheth, neither moth corrupteth. For where your treasure is, there will your heart be also.
Let your loins be girded about, and your lights burning; and ye yourselves like unto men that wait for their lord, when he will return from the wedding; that when he cometh and knocketh, they may open

unto him immediately. Blessed are those servants, whom the Lord when he cometh shall find watching: verily I say unto you, that he shall gird himself, and make them to sit down to meat, and will come forth and serve them. And if he shall come in the second watch, or come in the third watch, and find them so, blessed are those servants. And this know, that if the master of the house had known what hour the thief would come, he would have watched, and not have suffered his house to be broken through. Be ye therefore ready also: for the SON of MAN cometh at an hour when ye think not. — Luke xii. 29–40.

LET not your heart be troubled: ye believe in GOD, believe also in me. In my FATHER's house are many mansions; if not, I would have told you: I go to prepare a place for you. And if I go and prepare a place for you, I will come again, and receive you unto myself; that where I am, ye may be also. — John xiv. 1–3.

AND I heard a voice from heaven saying unto me, Write, Blessed are the dead who die in the LORD from henceforth. Yea, saith the Spirit, that they may rest from their labors; and their works do follow with them. — Rev. xiv. 13.

HE that is unjust, let him be unjust still: and he that is filthy, let him be filthy still: and he that is righteous, let him be righteous still: and he that is holy, let him be holy still. Behold, I come quickly: and my reward is with me, to give every one according as his work shall be. I am the ALPHA and the OMEGA, the BEGINNING and the END, the FIRST and the LAST. Blessed are they that do his commandments; that they may have right to the tree of life, and may enter in through the gates into the city. — Rev. xxii. 11–14.

Then a Selection or Hymn may be sung, if convenient.

Such parts of the following Instruction may then be read as the person officiating thinks proper.

He who seeth our substance yet being imperfect, and in whose book all our days are written — He who seeth the end from the beginning, who knoweth what is in man, by whom the very hairs of our heads are all numbered, and before whom stand always present and together in their order the most minute things of our life from the commencement of our existence to eternity — He who is Love itself, and who hath all power in heaven and in earth, has permitted the removal of our *friend* and *brother* from this world of nature to the world of spirits. By His permission, he has changed *his* state of existence; *he* has thrown off *his* material covering adapted to the duties and the uses of this material world, and which is therefore now no longer needed, and is rising in *his* spiritual body, which is adapted to the duties and the uses of the spiritual world. " The dust returns to the earth as it was, and the spirit is returning to God who gave it."

Of this great change, all that is visible to our eyes, or perceivable by any of our organs of sense, is the work of destruction and of death. Being themselves formed from the substances of this world, these organs can perceive only the substances of this world. They can perceive therefore only the body which has been left. And in looking upon this body, we behold the eyes closed and lifeless. The tongue is silent; and the whole form is motionless and cold. We therefore call this change death; and that part of our minds which is in immediate connection with these senses, dwells only upon the picture of what is material in it. Thus our merely natural affections feel an aching void; and our natural thoughts are filled with the idea of a total separation from the object of our affection, and dwell upon the acts and sufferings of the body put off — upon what it once was, and what it now is.

But to the eyes of angels and of spirits, all that is visible is the work of creation and of life. For they see nothing of the body that is left, but behold only a human being awakening into life. They are witnessing a resurrection; they are greeting a new companion, and welcoming a spirit newly born into their world. And all that in us which is in common with the angels, and makes one with their state — all those affections which have the LORD and His kingdom for their objects, and all those thoughts which delight to soar into eternity and to behold the things of eternal life — all that affection for *him* that has left us, which regards chiefly *his* spiritual welfare instead of our own gratification, and thus makes one with *his* state — all that in us which "seeks first the kingdom of GOD and his righteousness" — all this looks upon the event as angels do; for it sees it from the same point of position with them, viewing it from the other side of the grave. All spiritual affection sees with the eye of faith. It loves to dwell upon the freed spirit, rejoices in its welfare, and delights to accompany it in its resurrection to the mansions of eternal life.

And in order that these spiritual realities may prevail over the natural appearances with men, and that spiritual affections may rule within their natural affections and make them to be living, the LORD Himself teaches distinctly in His Word, that the dead are raised — that the GOD of Abraham, the GOD of Isaac, and the GOD of Jacob, is not the GOD of the dead, but of the living — that He is not the GOD of shapeless phantoms, but of human beings. He rose Himself also from the sepulchre on the third day, and ascended into heaven; thus actually exhibiting what we call death as it really is in itself, as it was with Him, and hence as it is with all those who live from Him according to his commandments, a resurrection into a higher and more interior state of existence. He also reveals in His Word, that man's permanent state of existence is not in this world, and that it is of divine order that all should pass from their preparatory state here to their home in the spiritual world. For He says therein in relation to Himself, "The hour is come that the SON OF MAN should be glorified. Verily, verily, I say unto you, Except a corn of wheat fall into the ground and die, it abideth alone: but if it die, it bringeth forth much fruit:" [thus teaching that in all spiritual and natural growth, it is necessary for that which is external or lower to be put off, in order that what is internal or higher may come forth and flourish. And from this we may learn in relation to ourselves, that what is external with us is given for the sake of what is internal; that what is worldly and temporal is given for the sake of what is spiritual and eternal; and that when the former has performed its use towards the formation and development of the latter, it must pass away, that what is living may come forth from within, and may grow and act in freedom. Our material bodies are given to envelop and protect the soul or spirit within, during its formation and growth, during the period of its preparation for living separate and of itself to eternity. Natural life envelops and protects spiritual life while it is yet in its germ. Natural affections surround and protect spiritual affections while they are yet in embryo, and give them support and nourishment during their effort to be born and to come forth into independent existence; as the seed covers and protects the germ, and gives it support and nourishment during the period of its first starting and rising above the ground into the light of day. But when this use is performed, it is of divine order that natural life, the life in this world, should cease to be man's actual life; that is, should as it were come to its end; as the external of the seed is cast off after the germ has come forth. Indeed, all progress to eternity, even the perpetual advancement of angels, consists in laying aside the lower and more external things of their life, as higher or more internal things are received, and by their means have become formed within them. The things which are of self, which partake of their own proper life, are for ever passing away, as things from the LORD are for ever being received and coming to maturity in them. For men were created to be images and likenesses of Him who is a Spirit, to enjoy the interior blessedness of spiritual existence in the light of

His countenance, to breathe the purer and living atmosphere of heaven, to rejoice in the light of interior wisdom, and be blessed with the life of heavenly love. They were created to live with life unchanged and unperverted from the Fountain of life — with life which is truly such, and therefore never-ending — with life which finds its constant delight in acts of more elevated and interior and extensive usefulness. They were created to be ministers of Him who made them, doing the pleasure of Him who is always doing mercy. They were not created for this world, but this world for them; as it is written in John, " They are not of the world, even as I am not of the world." And they begin their existence here, and remain here for a brief period, merely that they may be prepared for their eternal home — that the lower or more external principles of their minds may be drawn into exercise by the things of the world, may become formed and developed by worldly uses, by doing the LORD's will on earth, and thus be prepared as foundations on which the higher and more internal principles, which are to come into use and exercise hereafter, may stand firmly fixed, and thus that their life here may become a suitable basis on which their higher and eternal life hereafter may for ever securely rest. This is the divine purpose with regard to men; this is the order of the Divine Providence of the LORD, the order of His infinite wisdom and of His infinitely pure and ardent love in relation to them. Even with respect to those who choose while here to live contrary to the divine purpose, to do their own wills, and to live according to their own natural inclinations, and thus prepare for themselves the foundations of an unhappy and more interiorly evil life hereafter for ever, even with regard to these, it is still better for them and for all that they should live among their like, and come more fully and freely into the kind of life which they have chosen. There is in the hearts of all men, both good and evil, a deep and secret yearning for more freedom and fulness of the kind of life which they have chosen to be their life — for a more full and free exercise of that kind of delight which they have chosen to be their delight. But with regard to those, who, by denying themselves, by ceasing to do their own wills, and compelling themselves to do the LORD's will, and to act while here according to His precepts, it must surely be, that they can be unspeakably more blessed by coming into the more immediate presence and perception of Him whom they have chosen to be their GOD, and whom they in reality and above all else love; it must surely be, that they can more fully and truly live by drawing more near to Him who, they know and feel, is Life itself. Indeed the great object of the Divine Love, which is a heaven of human beings whom He can fill with blessedness to eternity, cannot be accomplished unless they are removed hence to fill their appointed place in heaven — to occupy their permanent and provided mansion in the FATHER's house. It is thus the divine order with all men, that they should leave this world — that their connection with that body which is of the substance of this world, and which is of no other use than to enable them to act in this world, should be severed — that their spirits should break forth from their material covering in order to come into a more elevated or more interior state of existence, as the germ breaks forth in the planted seed and casts off its outward covering, before it can rise above the ground, and grow up towards heaven in the light of day.]

But notwithstanding it is thus revealed in the Word that this is the divine order in relation to all men, notwithstanding the Gospel makes known a resurrection and a life beyond the grave, a divinely appointed and permanent home, yet such is the state of men, and such the power with them of sensual appearances, that the life in the spiritual world seems phantomlike and unreal. In order, therefore, that men may be raised above these appearances to the senses, and may come to realize and be interested in their spiritual, their real, and eternal state of existence, the LORD in His mercy has in these latter days caused His Word to be opened, and the seven seals of His

Book to be loosed. He has caused the interior things of it to be revealed, whereby spiritual realities are made manifest. He has caused light to break forth from within, its interior light to shine forth, in which light alone the interior things of His creation can be seen and understood; and thus the spiritual world, which is an interior world, and therefore the real and eternal world, is brought forth to view. The doctrine of the resurrection, which in its general is contained in the letter of the Word, is now unfolded as to the particulars contained within it. It is now made possible for us with the eyes of our understandings to view death as angels do, who see it from the other side of the grave; that while we are viewing with our natural eyes that side of this event which is turned towards the earth, unilluminated, cold, and dark, we may with the eyes of our spirits also behold that side which is turned towards the Sun of heaven, warmed by the love or mercy and brightened with the wisdom of his rays.

From the revelations now made, we learn, that as soon as the life has departed from the inmost fibres, and the spirit has become entirely separated from its most intricate connections with the body, which generally takes place on the third day after the heart has ceased to beat, the spirit rises free in the world of spirits. This resurrection is effected by the LORD through the ministry of angels, who in a manner most wonderful, with love ineffable and gentleness indescribable, disengage every part and portion of the spirit, not only from all its connections with the more external parts of the body, but also from its most secret and delicate intertwinings with the inmost fibrils of it. For the angels are recipients and thus communicators of the divine love and mercy, which with its living and powerful attraction draws forth every thing living about the man, so that nothing vital can remain behind. And when he is raised up fully, and into the freedom of life in that world, his attending angels do not leave him — do not separate themselves from him and go away; for angels love every one, and desire nothing more than to do him service, to instruct, and convey him to heaven. But the man himself, whose state as to goodness of life is not such, or is not as yet such, as to enjoy a long continuance in association with those who are in states so elevated, dissociates himself from them. At first, then, after leaving his attending angels, he comes into the society of good spirits; and if he chooses not to remain with these, then into society with those whose state is less elevated, until he finds associates so far resembling himself, that he can have delight and receive advantage from continuing with them during this his first state in the spiritual world. Thus he rises a man as before, and is seen by the inhabitants of that world, and they are seen by him, in human form, as the inhabitants of this world are seen by each other. He rises indeed with a spiritual body, a body formed not of material but spiritual substances, a body therefore invisible to our material eyes, but yet seen and known by spirits in all respects as fully as men in this world are seen and known by men. The spirit thus raised enters that world with the same prevailing character, with affections and thoughts essentially the same with those which marked him while here, and consequently he is as properly an object of our interest and affection as he was while here. Indeed he comes actually into company, into manifest association, with those spirits who were secretly in connection with him while he was in this world, and through whom he received those affections and thoughts which made him while here to be what he was. He thus comes at first among those who are of the same character with himself, who love what he loves, and think as he thinks; and, therefore, among those who seem, and indeed are, entirely familiar to him, and with whom he feels at home.

But as he is now in a spiritual world, a more living world, his mind becomes more and more developed. He comes more and more into his real character. The things within, in the secret recesses of the heart, begin to come forth. All the more external things of the spirit which are inconsistent with these are put away. The whole man comes into a state of consistency with himself. What in this world was secret, there at length comes to light; what was hidden in the heart is there known and comes abroad: the secret ends and purposes become there open and manifest ones; the inmost desires show themselves in speech and act, and the great objects of the love are openly sought by all the powers and faculties of the man. If it was the sincere desire and purpose of his heart, if it was his end, while here, to do the Lord's will and to be prepared for His kingdom in the heavens, all more external or inferior desires which thwarted his great or inward purpose, and obstructed his path to heaven in which he was endeavoring to walk — all views of things which here appeared to him to be true, but yet were false and opposed to heaven, are there seen to be what they are, and are cheerfully renounced; and thus the angel-man within comes forth and breathes and acts in freedom, and makes him an angel-man without, fitted for the blessedness of eternal consociation with angels of a similar character in heaven. But if his great end and hidden ruling purpose while here was only the good of himself, and of those whom he regarded as parts of himself, if his heart sought first the things which belong to this world, then this inward character and ruling love comes forth there, and all appearances of goodness and of truth, all his more external affections which here may have seemed so kind and so good, all his thoughts and conversation which here may have seemed so brilliant and so true, are there renounced as mere obstructions in his path: the evil spirit within shows himself to be an evil spirit without; and he becomes fitted for eternal association with those who are like himself, with them to enter into their appropriate abodes in hell.

To him, therefore, who views this event in this spiritual light which shines forth from the Word now opened by the Lord, it cannot but be seen either as the work or the permission of the Divine Mercy. For this light is the light of the Divine Love or Mercy; and it cannot but reveal and make manifest the mercy which always secretly rules in every event. Hence, at the departure of those who have loved the LORD and His Word, and have sought first while in this world the kingdom of GOD and His righteousness, the spiritual man rejoices; because they are about to enter upon a higher and purer, a more blessed and happy state of life; because they can render to those who remain here more efficient, more constant, and far more important service — a service which has heaven for its object, eternity for its end; and because the whole heaven, the whole kingdom of the LORD, becomes more perfect at the reception of every new inhabitant. And at the departure of the evil he cannot lastingly mourn; for he knows that they have been removed at the moment most favorable to their eternal condition, at the lightest possible degree of the life which they had chosen, at the earliest point therein at which they could be made willing to stop, before they had laid the foundations of a deeper state of condemnation. It is only as our affections and thoughts rest upon earth, that clouds and darkness surround this event of the Divine Providence, and we are enveloped with the gloom of funereal sadness: but as our interests rise towards heavenly things, mourning vanishes; as we ascend above the clouds, there is nothing to obstruct the pure sunshine of heaven.

But all that proceeds from the LORD, all his operations, and all his permissions, are infinite and eternal, and hence universal. They are not limited to one, but affect all, and open new duties in all and towards all. He has permitted *our brother* to be removed, not only as a means of good to *him* and to all in that world to which *he* has gone, but to all in this world also, more especially to those who have been closely associated with *him*, yet in some degree to every one of us who are here present this day. This event has been permitted, to enable us more fully to realize the existence of the world to which *he* has gone, that it may be more present to us, and be more regarded by us; that by *his* being carried upwards, all the feelings and thoughts in us which are connected with *him* may be carried upwards with *him;* that our grasp upon this world may be loosened, our love for the things of it may be made subservient to a love for the things of the eternal world — to lessen our anxiety respecting "what we shall eat, or what we shall drink, or wherewithal we shall be clothed," and thus enable us to "seek first the kingdom of God and His righteousness."

And in particular with regard to those of us who are bound to *him* that has gone with the bonds of strong affection, *his* natural connection with us has been permitted to be severed, not that this affection may be in any degree lessened, but that it may be changed; not that any thing of it may be lost, but that it may be renewed; that it may become the love of *his* eternal welfare; that by our hearts following *him* to *his* appointed mansion in the Father's house, to the home of *his* eternal use in heaven, it may become a love of that good, which it is *his* eternal delight to contribute towards the happiness and prosperity of the universal kingdom of the Lord. The infirm body of our love for *him,* the impure natural part of our affection for *him,* indeed dies; for this body is from ourselves. But with regard to all that is pure and disinterested, with regard to all that is spiritual and living, all that is from the Lord in it, not a hair of the head shall perish; but it rises again stronger and purer than before.

Thus in relation to every one of us, the death and resurrection of *our brother* is intended to produce a change in our minds corresponding with that through which *he* is now passing. It is intended to produce death and resurrection there — a death of what is gross, external, corporeal, and earthly in our affections, and a resurrection into fuller life and freer activity of all that is pure, internal, spiritual, and immortal in them. So that every death that occurs around us is intended to lift us up one step at least towards heaven — to advance us one step at least in our preparation for our own full and final departure hence. For by perpetual deaths and resurrections of this spiritual kind, even the angels are perpetually advancing. They are perpetually dying as to themselves, and living again as to the LORD. They are perpetually leaving what is finite, impure, and imperfect, and rising again towards what is infinite and pure and perfect. Their advancement for ever into more and more interior states, and hence into more and more fulness of that degree of life which they are able to receive, and thus their advancement in purity and blessedness for ever, is by their continually applying and appropriating, by their continually living, the heavenly meaning of these words of the LORD, as they at first became angels by living out their natural meaning while on earth: " He that loveth father or mother more than me, is not worthy of me: and he that loveth son or daughter more than me, is not worthy of me: and he that taketh not his cross, and followeth after me, is not worthy of me. He that findeth his life shall lose it; and he that loseth his life for my sake shall find it."

Then the following prayer, or the Lord's Prayer, or both, may be used.

O LORD GOD of our fathers, most merciful LORD JESUS CHRIST, in whose presence the living and the dead are standing together, to whom all are alive, and with whom there is no death, through whose tender mercy, in these latter times, the day-spring from on high hath visited us, to give light to them that sit in darkness and the shadow of death, to guide our feet in the way of peace; give us to see in this as in all the dispensations of thy wisdom, the bright footsteps of an all-merciful providence, which in every act of apparent destruction, doth but further the progress of an eternal creation, and through the death of this life, doth bestow the life of a heavenly kingdom. O cause, we beseech thee, that this solemn visitation may deeply impress us with the uncertainty of our own perishable state, and the necessity of preparing for the concerns of an eternal world ; and seeing that the axe is laid unto the root of the trees, may we, without delay, strive to bring forth fruits worthy of repentance. Grant, O LORD, that we may watch as becometh those who know not the hour in which the SON OF MAN cometh; and that following thee in the regeneration, when the cry shall be made at midnight, "Behold, the bridegroom cometh, go ye out to meet him," being ready, with our lamps trimmed and filled with oil, we may enter with him to the marriage. We ask this, O LORD, in thine own name, and for thy divine mercy's sake. Amen.

OUR FATHER, who art in the heavens; Hallowed be thy name. Thy kingdom come. Thy will be done, as in heaven, so also upon the earth. Give us this day our daily bread. And forgive us our debts, as we also forgive our debtors. And lead us not into temptation; but deliver us from evil. For thine is the kingdom, and the power, and the glory, for ever: AMEN.

A suitable Selection or Hymn may now be sung, if convenient.

BENEDICTION.

The grace of our LORD JESUS CHRIST be with you all: Amen.

If any service is desired at the grave, the following, after the coffin is lowered, may be used.

WE now commit *his* body to the tomb. That which was formed of the dust of the ground, and into which the breath of life is no longer breathed, is again returned to the ground whence it was taken — earth to earth, ashes to ashes, dust to dust. As *he* has taken *his* final leave, so let us now take our final leave of this *his* earthly tenement, never again to be occupied by *him*. As " he is not here, but is risen," let us in our thoughts and feelings no longer tarry here, nor henceforth seek *him* here: but let all that in us, by which *he* was bound to us in love, rise upwards with *him*, and accompany *him* to the " green pastures " and the " still waters," whither the LORD leadeth all those who have walked " in the paths of righteousness for His name's sake." And as all the duties of merely natural affection, all earthly duties, towards *him*, now close while the grave closes upon *his* body, may all the duties of spiritual affection, all spiritual duties, towards *him*, enjoy a resurrection with him, be opened into more freedom and fulness of action, and be unfolded, in blessings to *him* and to us, with perpetual newness of life for ever.

And I heard a voice from heaven, saying unto me, Write, Blessed are the dead who die in the LORD from henceforth. Yea, saith the Spirit, that they may rest from their labors; and their works do follow with them. — Rev. xiv. 13.

BENEDICTION.

THE grace of our LORD JESUS CHRIST be witn you all. AMEN.

# FUNERAL SERVICE FOR INFANTS AND LITTLE CHILDREN.

The service may be commenced by reading such passages of the Word from the Funeral Service for Adults as the person officiating shall think proper, together with one or more of the following passages.

AND they brought unto him also infants, that he would touch them: but when his disciples saw it, they rebuked them. But JESUS called them, and said, Suffer little children to come unto me, and forbid them not: for of such is the kingdom of GOD. Verily I say unto you, Whosoever shall not receive the kingdom of GOD as a little child, shall in no wise enter therein. — Luke xviii. 15 – 17.

AT the same time came the disciples unto JESUS, saying, Who is the greatest in the kingdom of heaven? And JESUS called a little child unto him, and set him in the midst of them, and said, Verily I say unto you, Except ye be converted, and become as little children, ye shall not enter into the kingdom of heaven. Whosoever, therefore, shall humble himself as this little child, the same is greatest in the kingdom of heaven. And whoso shall receive one such little child in my name, receiveth me. — Mat. xviii. 1 – 5.

TAKE heed that ye despise not one of these little ones; for I say unto you, that their angels in heaven do always behold the face of my FATHER who is in heaven.
Even so it is not the will of your FATHER who is in heaven, that one of these little ones should perish. — Mat. xviii. 10, 14.

A Selection or Hymn may now be sung, if convenient.

Then may be read a part or the whole of the following Instruction.

We are told in the Sacred Scripture, that not a sparrow falls to the ground, without the notice of our Heavenly Father; and that even the very hairs of our heads are all numbered. From this it is plain that the Divine Providence of the LORD watches over every human being, from the first moment of his life to the last; and nothing happens to him by chance, but every thing that takes place is by the providence or permission of the LORD. Every event of life is so ordered by infinite love and wisdom, that, if rightly improved by man, it will contribute to human happiness and human salvation. Certainly, then, such an event as the removal of a person from the natural to the spiritual world, can take place only under the divine providence of the LORD — can take place only because divine love provides or permits this, and divine wisdom foresees that it will be for the everlasting good of that person.

This is a consoling thought, especially in relation to the removal of infants and little children to the spiritual world. Their removal is indeed the severing of a tender tie between them and the little circle in which they moved. The feelings which bind us to them are of a peculiarly tender and delicate nature. Their smiles, their artless manners, the tones of their voices, the sweet expression of their faces, their dawning minds, all take a deep hold of the human heart. They awaken affections in the mind of the parent analogous to the paternal love of the LORD, and develop some of the most vigorous germs of pure and disinterested affection. Thus parents seem to live for their children, and children for their parents. There is a mutual interchange of happiness between them — a circle of heavenly affections, innocence, and delights. And thus it is hard for our natural feelings to sever the natural connection between us and our children.

But in the doctrines of the New Jerusalem we have much consoling instruction given us concerning death and the state of infants and children in the other life. We are taught that death itself is not the loss of life: it is only passing from life in this world to life in the spiritual world. The soul or spirit of man is the real man, and this never dies; for it derives immortality from the capacity of knowing, loving, and serving the Lord. When therefore the material body dies, the spirit goes immediately to live in the spiritual world, in a spiritual body.

Hence we learn concerning the resurrection, that immediately after the death of the body, man rises into the spiritual world; that he loses nothing, and leaves nothing behind, which constituted any part of the real man. We learn that he continues to live hereafter a human being, enjoying all the means of happiness which he possessed in the natural world. He there has a body, and every sense which he had in this world. The body, however, in which he rises after death, is a spiritual body; because the world in which he is henceforth to live, is a spiritual world. And the life, too, which he there lives, is human life, purified and happy, or depraved and miserable, according to the character of the ruling love which influenced him on earth, and the quality of the life which he lived here.

But it is manifest that those who die in infancy and childhood have not adopted either good or evil loves as their ruling loves, have not confirmed themselves in either a good or an evil life. It is true, indeed, that they inherited from their parents an hereditary nature, in which there are tendencies, dispositions, and propensities to all kinds of evils. But inasmuch as they have not confirmed themselves by their life in these evil inclinations and propensities, have not committed sin with a full knowledge of the nature and consequences of sin, therefore, through the mercy of the Lord, they attain to salvation.

That those who die in infancy and childhood are received into heaven, may be inferred from what is said in the Sacred Scriptures. When the LORD was here upon earth, he said, " Suffer little children to come unto me, and forbid them not; *for of such is the kingdom of* GOD. Verily I say unto you, whosoever shall not receive the kingdom of GOD as a little child, he shall in no wise enter therein." And again, speaking of little children, he says, " Their angels in heaven do always behold the face of my FATHER who is in heaven."

It has been supposed by some, that infants will remain infants, and children remain children, in the spiritual world; while by others it has been supposed that they will at once become perfect angels. Neither the one nor the other of these views is correct. But infants and little children are born into the heavenly world in the same state in which they leave this world; and they gradually grow up there, as they would have grown up here. If they had continued to live on earth, we know that their bodies would gradually have grown up, their minds would have become active, they would have increased in knowledge, and all their faculties would have become developed to manhood or to womanhood. So in the spiritual world they will gradually grow in wisdom and in stature, their minds will gradually come to maturity, and their bodily appearance will change as their minds advance, till they are seen by their associates and companions as men and women. For in that world the outward appearance corresponds to the inward state and character. The growth of the mind goes on there as well as here, but in a more regular and orderly manner; because those who have the care and education of children in that world are far better fitted for their employment than parents and teachers and nurses on earth are, and also because there the means of instruction are far more perfect.

Infants, as soon as they come into the heavenly world, are committed to the care of those guardian angels, who are peculiarly qualified to take care of and educate children. These guardian angels instruct them step after step in the lessons of heavenly wisdom and life; they train them to the performance of those duties and uses to which they are afterwards to be appointed by the Lord; they initiate them into the delights of heaven, and introduce them to the companionship of those who are like themselves in age and qualities of mind. The angels to whose care infants are committed, are those who, when they lived in the natural world, loved little children from a real desire to do good and be useful to them, and at the same time loved God. These angels have as many children given to them as they desire, and are able to bring up in a proper manner.

Those who have the care of little children in heaven, act the part of mothers to them; and they take the place of their natural mothers. To them the children look up as to their mothers; and they love, respect, and are obedient to them. But they are especially and constantly initiated into this state, to know no other father, and afterwards to acknowledge no other, but the Lord; and that they have life from him. They are taught that He is their Father in heaven; and that they must look to him, and acknowledge him, as their only Father.

Thus we may see that they are not made unhappy from the want of their earthly parents. They do not ever feel as if they were strangers there. They feel at home where they are. They have every means around them that can contribute to their happiness and their future usefulness. They have the Lord for their Father. They have one who receives them, and treats them, and loves them, as their own mother. They have brothers, and sisters, and companions, and playmates. They have schools, and teachers who instruct them in those things which have a tendency to make them grow wise and good. They have beautiful gardens in which they can walk, and lawns and fields in which they enjoy their childish sports. Every thing which they see around them appears to be alive. The very atmosphere in which they live, and which they breathe, sparkles with brilliancy and with life.

When we think of our children that have gone to

live in the heavenly world, we ought to think of them under the light and influence of the New Jerusalem. We ought to think of them as now living in a blissful state above; think of them as happy, and as having every thing done for them that they want or need to have done; much more than we could do for them, if they were with us here on earth. We ought to think of them as growing in knowledge and in usefulness; as improving in mind, increasing in stature, and preparing to become angels. We ought not to think of them in any manner as dead, but as gone to live in another better and happier state of existence.

If we look in this manner at the removal of children to the heavenly world, and their state of life there, we shall cease to mourn, or to indulge in any inordinate grief, at their departure from us. We shall try to yield up any selfish desires that we may have to keep them with us, and be willing to have them go when the Lord calls them. We shall remember what he says, " Suffer little children to come unto me, and forbid them not." We shall endeavor to let our minds rise, as they are rising; that when we go into the world whither they have gone, we may be better prepared to enjoy such society as theirs.

When we look at the state of infants and little children in heaven, and see the advantages of nurture and education there over those on earth, we are led to see and feel that it is well with our children who have gone there. We ought not, indeed, to desire to have our children taken from us; on the other hand, we ought to do what we can to preserve their life and health in this world; for this corresponds to the desire to do what we can for their spiritual and eternal life; and Divine Providence has clothed this love of their spiritual life with the love of their natural life. But when the Lord has taken them from us, when He sees it to be best for their good and for ours that they should live no longer with us in this world, and when we are inclined to feel sad on account of our loss, we ought to think how well it is with our children; and if we truly love them, we shall learn to be resigned to what is for their everlasting happiness. We ought to take a living, elevated view of their state, and even rejoice that they are where they can be so much more happy than we could have made them here on earth. In obedience to his commands, when the LORD calls them, we should suffer them to go unto him, and forbid them not. We should not let our natural feelings prevail so far as to oppose what He sees to be best for them.

From a knowledge of the education and state of children in the spiritual world, we are led to see how important and responsible are the duties of parents towards their children on earth. The LORD has shown us the states of those in heaven, that we may learn to make earth itself more heavenly; that we may make the home and family and education on earth more like those in heaven.

It is our first and most important duty as parents, to give the children committed to us a religious education; to instruct them in the truths of the Sacred Scriptures; to bring them up under the sphere and influence of the Church; to teach them to live in love towards one another, and to learn and keep the commandments of the LORD. Especially is it our duty to withdraw our children as much as possible from evil influences and evil spheres, and prevent them from cherishing hatred and revenge, or any evil feelings: for by the indulgence of such affections, mutual love and innocence are extinguished in the youthful mind; and thus our children are excluded from the sphere and influence of heaven, where nothing but mutual love prevails.

It is well known that infants and little children in this world are subjects of peculiar influences from the heavenly world. The LORD himself teaches this, when he says, "*Their angels in heaven,*"—that is, the angels who watch over, guard, and protect little children, "do always behold the face of my FATHER who is in heaven." The heavenly influences, too, that come down to us through infants and children, are some of the most saving and redeeming influences.

## FUNERAL SERVICE FOR INFANTS AND CHILDREN. 119

They are powerful for good. Infants have always formed a sphere of heaven upon earth. How important that this sphere of innocence and childlike humility should be preserved in the church, in society, in our families, and in our own hearts.

The LORD says to his disciples, " Verily I say unto you, Except ye be converted, and become as little children, ye shall not enter the kingdom of heaven."

*Then the following prayer, or the LORD's Prayer, or both, may be used.*

O BLESSED and ever-living LORD GOD and SAVIOR Almighty, thou who art the resurrection and the life, who hast now been pleased to call the departed [little one, or child, or dear one] from this transitory stage of being; give us to see in this, as in all the dispensations of thy wisdom, the bright footsteps of an all-merciful providence, which in every act of apparent destruction, doth but further the progress of an eternal creation, and through the death of this life, doth bestow the life of a heavenly kingdom. O cause, we beseech thee, that this solemn visitation may deeply impress us, who remain, with the uncertainty of our continuance here, and the necessity of making timely preparation for that hereafter in which the state of our life will be fixed for ever. Seeing the frailty of all things below, may we fix our hearts entirely on the substantial reality of the things that are above. May this dispensation be sanctified to the spiritual and eternal good of us all, and especially to the afflicted family and friends. In mercy comfort them with thy presence, and strengthen them by the influences of thy Holy Spirit, so that with sincere and humble hearts they may feel it good to say, " Thy will be done." May they, and all of us who are here present this day, receive and use so wisely all the dispensations of thy providence, that the messenger of natural death shall be to us the herald of everlasting life. May our removal from earth be an admission into heaven; and may our separation from friends according to the flesh, be our consociation with spiritual kindred in the world of bliss. Receive us, O Heavenly Father, when we go hence, into thy more immediate presence, to be fed by thee at the fountain of living waters, where pain and sorrow shall cease for ever, where we shall again meet the dear ones who have gone before us, and where thou thyself wilt wipe away all tears from our eyes. Amen.

Our Father, who art in the heavens; Hallowed be thy name. Thy kingdom come. Thy will be done, as in heaven, so also upon the earth. Give us this day our daily bread. And forgive us our debts, as we also forgive our debtors. And lead us not into temptation; but deliver us from evil. For thine is the kingdom, and the power, and the glory, for ever. Amen.

A Selection or Hymn may now be sung, if convenient.

BENEDICTION.

The grace of our Lord Jesus Christ be with you all. Amen.

If any service is desired at the grave, Selection 17 may be sung, or read: after which the Minister may read the following passages

At the same time came the disciples unto Jesus, saying, Who is the greatest in the kingdom of heaven? And Jesus called a little child unto him, and set him in the midst of them, and said, Verily I say unto you, Except ye be converted, and become as little children, ye shall not enter into the kingdom of heaven. Whosoever, therefore, shall humble himself as this little child, the same is greatest in the kingdom of heaven. — Matt. xviii. 1-4.

Take heed that ye despise not one of these little ones; for I say unto you, that their angels in heaven do always behold the face of my FATHER who is in heaven.— Mat. xviii. 10.

JESUS said, Suffer little children, and forbid them not, to come unto me: for of such is the kingdom of heaven. — Mat. xix. 14.

*When the coffin is lowered into the grave, the Minister may say,*

FORASMUCH as it hath pleased the LORD, in his wise and good Providence, to remove this child to the spiritual world, we do therefore commit the body to the grave, earth to earth, ashes to ashes, dust to dust; with the confident assurance that *he* will live for ever in a state of happiness and of active usefulness in the heavenly world.

And I heard a voice from heaven saying unto me, Write, Blessed are the dead who die in the LORD from henceforth.— Rev. xiv. 13.

*Then may be said the LORD's Prayer, or the prayer on page 119.*

BENEDICTION.

THE grace of our LORD JESUS CHRIST be with you all: AMEN.

# ORDINATION.

The whole or a part of the following Service may be used, to be commenced by singing a suitable Selection or Hymn, all standing. The Minister may then read the following passage:

AND JESUS went about all the cities and villages, teaching in their synagogues, and preaching the gospel of the kingdom, and healing every sickness and every disease among the people. But when he saw the multitudes, he was moved with compassion on them, because they fainted, and were scattered abroad, as sheep having no shepherd. Then saith he unto his disciples, The harvest truly is plenteous, but the laborers are few; pray ye therefore the Lord of the harvest that he will send forth laborers into his harvest. — Mat. ix. 35 – 38.

Then may be read one or more of the following chapters:

Exodus XXVIII.; Isaiah XI.; XLII. 1–16; LII.; LXI.; LXII.; Mat. x.; John x. 1 – 16.

The Ordaining Minister may then deliver the following

## ADDRESS.

DIVINE order requires that Ministers should be appointed to administer the ordinances of the church, and to officiate in the public worship of the LORD; to teach men the way to heaven, and to lead them therein. Wherefore it is necessary that proper persons should be called and set apart to that office, in a manner becoming the sacred nature of the duties they are to discharge.

Be it known, therefore, to all present, that A B has been duly recommended and approved as a person properly qualified to be introduced into the Ministry of the New Jerusalem.

The ordination of Ministers is effected by the imposition of hands, because this signifies the communication of spiritual life from the LORD, and of illumination, and of the power of instruction, which particularly belong to the ministerial office.

The doctrines of the New Church teach that "The common good consists of the following things: that in a society or kingdom there be

I. What is Divine among the people:
II. That there be Justice among them:
III. That there be Morality." — Doc. Char. 65.

They also teach that "what is Divine exists there through the Ministry; Justice, through the magistrates and judges; and Morality, through what is Divine and what is Just." — Doc. Char. 66.

That "the clergy, because they are to teach doctrine from the Word, concerning the LORD, and concerning redemption and salvation from Him, are to be inaugurated by the covenant, promise, or pledge of the Holy Spirit, and by the representation of its transmission; but that it is received by the clergy according to the faith of their life." — Can. p. 30.

We are also taught, that "By the touch of the hand, is signified communication, transmission, and reception." — A. C. 10,130.

And that "To put the hand on the head, is representative that blessing is communicated to the understanding and to the will, thus to the man himself." — A. C. 6292.

"That Divine virtue, which, among the clergy, is meant by the operation of the Holy Spirit, is, in particular, illustration, and instruction; but to these may be added two intermediate virtues, which are, perception and disposition: there are, therefore, among the clergy, four successive operations, following each other in this order, — *Illustration, Perception, Disposition*, and *Instruction*. ILLUSTRATION is from the LORD alone. PERCEPTION has place in a man according to the state of his mind as formed by doctrines: and where those doctrines are true, the perception is rendered clear by the light of illustration; but where they are false, the perception is rendered obscure, yet so as to have the appearance of clearness, arising from the reasonings and arguments which have been used for their confirmation. Such apparent clearness is, however, only a consequence of that false and delusive light, which, in the eye of the merely natural man, appears like the light of truth. DISPOSITION arises from the affection of the love of the will; and it is the delight springing from that love, which effects it. If this delight spring from the love of evil and its attendant falsity, it gives birth to a zeal which is outwardly sharp, harsh, furious, fiery, and inwardly full of anger, rage, and unmercifulness: but if it spring from the love of good and its attendant truth, it then gives birth to a zeal which is outwardly soft and smooth, yet loud and burning, and inwardly full of charity, kindness, and mercy. INSTRUCTION follows as an effect produced by the former. Thus illustration, which is from the LORD, is changed into various lights and colors in every individual, according to the state of his mind." — T. C. R. 155.

"With respect to the priests, they ought to teach men the way to heaven, and also to lead them: they ought to teach them according to the doctrine of their church derived from the Word, and they ought to lead them to live according to it. Priests who teach truths, and thereby lead to good of life, and so to the LORD, are the good shepherds of the sheep; but they who only teach, and do not lead to good of life, and so to the LORD, are the evil shepherds.

"Priests ought not to claim to themselves any power over the souls of men, inasmuch as they do not know in what state the interiors of a man are; still less ought they to claim the power of opening and shutting heaven, since that power belongs to the LORD alone.

"Dignity and honor ought to be paid to priests, on account of the sanctity of their office; but they who are wise give the honor to the LORD, from whom all sanctity is derived, and not to themselves; whilst they who are not wise attribute the honor to themselves, whereby they take it from the LORD. They who attribute honor to themselves, on account of the sanctity of their office, prefer honor and gain to the salvation of souls, which they ought to provide for; but they who give the honor to the LORD, and not to themselves, prefer the salvation of souls to honor and gain. The honor of any employment is not in the person, but is adjoined to him according to the dignity of the thing which he administers; and what is adjoined does not belong to the person himself, and is also separated from him with the employment. All personal honor is the honor of wisdom and the fear of the LORD.

" Priests ought to teach the people, and to lead them by means of truths to good of life; but still they ought to force no one, since no one can be forced to believe contrary to what he thinks from his heart to be truth. He who believes otherwise than the priest, and makes no disturbance, ought to be left in peace; but he who makes disturbance ought to be separated; for this also is agreeable to order, for the sake of which the priesthood is established."—H. D. 315-318.

" *Charity in the Priest.* When he looks to the LORD and shuns evils as sins, and does the appointed work of his ministry sincerely, justly, and faithfully, he does the good of use continually, and becomes a charity in form. And he does the good of use, or the work of his ministry, sincerely, justly, and faithfully, when he feels affected for the salvation of souls: and in proportion as this is the case, he is affected by truths; for truths are the means of leading souls to heaven: and when he leads them to the LORD, it is then he is leading them by means of truths to heaven. And he has then also an earnest love of teaching truths from the Word; for in teaching them from the Word, he teaches them from the LORD; for the LORD is *the Word*:

and furthermore, He is *the Way, the Truth, and the Life*, as He himself says, John xiv. 5; and He is *the Door*, John x. 9. He, therefore, who enters the fold by the LORD as the door, is a *good shepherd;* but he who does not, is a *bad shepherd*, who is called *a thief and a robber.* John x. 1–9."— Doct. Char. 86.

Ministers are representatives of the LORD. Their official duties are representatives of his Divine operations. He is present with all men, and operating upon all. In his Divine Humanity he is with us, and his Spirit is always operating upon us. Without him we can do nothing. But he is invisible, and his operations are invisible. He has therefore provided that there should be ministers to represent him among men, — ministers to teach in an external manner doctrines which correspond to what he teaches in an internal manner, and to do externally things which correspond with what he does internally. Thus he is by his internal influence endeavoring to enlighten men, so that they may know what is good and true; but this influence would have no effect upon them, if he did not also provide that they should receive some external instruction, into which his influence might fall, and in which it might be embodied. He has therefore given the Sacred Scriptures; and has provided that there should be ministers to explain them, and to teach the doctrines which are contained in them.

So, too, he is continually endeavoring to baptize men with the Holy Spirit and with fire; that is, to regenerate them by the influence of his Love and Wisdom: and as a means of preparing us to be operated upon in this manner, he has provided that there should be ministers to baptize with water, and to teach men the necessity of regeneration, and the manner in which the work is to be accomplished.

So, again, he is constantly endeavoring to give spiritual life unto men, and to cherish and increase it. This spiritual life is his Goodness and Truth. His Goodness is the life of our wills, and his Truth is the life of our understandings. But he cannot give us these things, merely by flowing into our minds, and operating upon them in an internal manner. He cannot give them to us in such a manner that we can receive them, without in the first place giving us a knowledge of them : and this must be given in an external way; that is, through the senses. He has therefore revealed his Goodness and Truth in the Sacred Scriptures: he has also instituted the Holy Supper; in which the bread is an emblem of his Goodness, the wine an emblem of his Truth, and the eating of the bread and drinking of the wine represent the reception and appropriation of his Goodness and Truth: he has provided that there should be ministers to explain the Scriptures, so as to make the Goodness and Truth of them manifest and intelligible; also to administer the ordinance of the Holy Supper, to unfold the spiritual meaning of it, to show us how we may be prepared for it, and thus enable us to receive it internally as well as externally, — to receive the Goodness into our wills, and the Truth into our understandings, as well as to receive the bread and wine into our bodies.

And with regard to the work of Redemption, ministers should be representatives of the LORD. When the power of evil spirits was becoming predominant upon earth, he took upon himself our nature, and thus came down into our state and circumstances, so that he might overcome the obstacles which lay in the way of our salvation — that he might do such works as men could not do, but which needed to be done that they might be saved. Inasmuch as he took upon himself our nature, he took upon himself also the hereditary tendencies and propensities of it; so that he could have such feelings and thoughts arise in his Humanity, as arise in the minds of unregenerate men. Evil spirits could operate upon his Humanity, as they operate upon men; except that in relation to men they are often successful, whereas in relation to him they were always unsuccessful. And as by means of his Humanity, before it was glorified, evil spirits could have access to him, so by the same means he could have access to them. As the evil spirits could inspire evil feelings and false thoughts into his Humanity, so he could, from the Divine Love and Wisdom of his internal Divinity, bring down into his Humanity the good feelings and the true thoughts which were necessary to overcome them. He thus caused his Humanity to have Divine human feelings and thoughts, in relation to every evil and false thing which the evil spirits could suggest. By this means he purified and glorified his Humanity, so that it could be no more tempted: and by this means he at the same time overcame all kinds of evil spirits; for he caused them to see themselves, and every thing that proceeded from them, as he saw them in the divine light of heaven, in the presence of which they could not abide for a moment.

It was on account of his Infinite Love towards men, that he took upon himself their nature, and came down into their circumstances, and performed these works of salvation. This Infinite Love is eternal. It operates as powerfully now, as it did then. His Divine Humanity is also eternal; and it has the same power of saving men from the influence of evil spirits now, that it had then. And as it was then, so it is now; his power is manifest in none but those who love him and believe in him. Those who love him and believe in him, do by this means receive him into their minds; so that they love, think, and act from him. Accordingly, when any thing evil and false is suggested to them, they think and feel in relation to it from his Divine Humanity; they think and feel as he leads them to think and feel; they think and feel in relation to it, as he felt and thought when in the world. And the evil spirits do not regard them as mere men; for they perceive that the LORD as to his Divine Humanity is in them, and that his Divine Power operates through them: consequently they relinquish the combat, turn their backs upon him, and flee from his presence.

Now it is the effort of the LORD that all men should

receive of the Love from which he performed, and is now performing, these works of redemption and salvation; and when we receive it, we are all led by it to perform works corresponding to his works,—corresponding as the finite corresponds with the Infinite—as imperfect human things correspond with the perfect Divine. When we receive his Divine Love, it leads us all to have compassion upon one another when we are in states of suffering, especially spiritual suffering; or when we are in danger of it. It leads us to come spiritually near to one another, and to enter into one another's states of mind, that we may afford one another assistance and protection.

Thus the influence of the Divine Love, when it is received into the mind, has a tendency to make all men perform works which more or less correspond with the work of Redemption; but when it is received by ministers, it leads them to do works which correspond more perfectly, because it is their office and duty to coöperate with the LORD in saving men.

One great part of the duty of a minister, and one great means of usefulness, is for him to learn to put himself in the place of his people; that is, to suppose himself to be in their states and circumstances, and then to consider what would be good for himself, if he were there. If he loves them, and desires to be useful to them, he will be constantly going to them in this manner; for this is the means by which he can adapt any thing to their states: for when he goes into their states, he loses nothing of the goodness, or wisdom, or spiritual power, that properly belongs to him; but, on the contrary, he acquires the additional power of being able to adapt all that he has to their benefit; for when he spiritually goes to them, or enters into their states, he can perceive how they think and feel; he can for the time think and feel as they do; and when this is the case, he can see how he could be made to think and feel differently;—how he could be lifted up out of his present state;—he can see what kind of treatment would be suited to him;—he can see what kind of instruction he would need, and how it should be expressed that he might understand it and be affected by it. And when he sees what would be good for himself, he can see what will be good for those whom he is endeavoring to assist.

If a minister proceed in this manner, he will not act with harshness and severity, for he will not act from his natural man; but he will act and speak with gentleness and kindness, for he will act and speak from the spiritual man; he will act and speak from the Love and Wisdom which have flowed into his mind from the LORD; he will treat others as the LORD has treated him; he will treat others as he would have others treat him: for before he acts, he puts himself in their places, and ascertains what would be good for himself; or, in other words, what he would have others do for him.

Every one has the power of doing this in some degree, but the power is enlarged by practice and experience: it increases, as the love of doing good increases; till at length one acquires the habit of entering into the states of others, and learning what is good for them, without effort. His love is with them, his feelings are with them, he is with them; and consequently he knows by intuition what is good for them.

This power which is given to ministers to enter into the states of their people, is a most important means of usefulness: without it they might perhaps be ministers of the law that was given through Moses, but not of the grace and truth that came by JESUS CHRIST. But there is a reciprocal power given to the people, which is equally important; and that is, the power of entering into the states of their ministers. They are generally employed in the various uses of life, so that they cannot, like ministers, make it their principal business to acquire and communicate spiritual knowledge. But when, from a love of performing spiritual uses, their ministers enter into their states of mind, and adapt heavenly things to them, they can, from a love of receiving spiritual uses, enter into the states of their ministers, and then in a greater or less degree understand and feel as they do. For on the Sabbath and other suitable occasions, they leave their usual employments, they cease to do their own ways, to find their own pleasure, to exercise their own affections, to think their own thoughts, or to speak their own words; and they come unto their minister as to a representative of the LORD, that they may delight themselves in the LORD, and in the holy things that proceed from him; that they may be spiritually lifted up; that they may ride upon the high places of the earth; and that they may perceive and feed upon the food of angels — the living bread which the LORD himself brought down from heaven: for it is a minister's duty to show his people what this bread is, and how they may come into possession of it; it is his duty to bring it down to their states and capacities, so that they may have a perception of it, and an affection for it. And while he is endeavoring to do this, they also have something to do; while he is endeavoring to bring down the Divine truth to meet their states, they should endeavor to go up as far as they can to meet it. When this is the case, if he endeavors to explain any thing, they will endeavor to understand it; and if he shows them what feelings we ought to have upon any subject, they will endeavor to come under the influence of such feelings: thus, by means of his efforts united with their efforts, they are lifted up, so that they can see as he sees, and feel as he feels. He is then performing the use for which he is appointed and ordained. He is a medium of Divine Blessings. Freely he receives from the LORD, and freely gives to his people. He is not acting of himself, nor for himself; he is not seeking his own pleasure, nor doing his own ways, nor speaking his own words; but he is delighting himself in the LORD, and in receiving and communicating the things which are from the LORD: and when his people coöperate with him, when they enter into his states — into his feelings and thoughts, they also will delight in the LORD, and will receive the Holy Spirit that proceeds from Him.

*After the Address, the Ordaining Minister shall then ask the candidate the following questions:*

*Ord. Min.*— Do you sincerely believe that it is of the Divine Providence of the LORD, that you are called to the office of a minister in the New Jerusalem?
*Answer.*— I do.
*Ord. Min.*— Do you now, in the presence of the LORD, and of this assembly, declare your faith in the Divine Word, and in the Heavenly Doctrines of the New Jerusalem, as unfolded in the writings of Emanuel Swedenborg?
*Answer.*— I do.
*Ord. Min.*— Do you now desire to be ordained as a minister, that you may perform the duties of that office, in teaching and leading men according to those doctrines?
*Answer.*— I do.

*Then shall the Ordaining Minister read the following passages:*

AND JESUS came and spake unto them, saying, All power is given unto me in heaven and in earth. Go ye, therefore, and make disciples of all nations, baptizing them into the name of the FATHER, and of the SON, and of the HOLY SPIRIT; teaching them to do all things whatsoever I have commanded you: and lo, I am with you all the days, until the consummation of the age. Amen.— Matt. xxviii. 18-20.

And as ye go, preach, saying, The kingdom of heaven is at hand.

Behold, I send you forth as sheep in the midst of wolves: be ye therefore wise as serpents, and harmless as doves.

He that receiveth you, receiveth me; and he that receiveth me, receiveth him that sent me.— Matt. x. 7, 16, 40.

Ye have not chosen me, but I have chosen you, and ordained you, that ye should go and bring forth fruit; and that your fruit should remain: that whatsoever ye shall ask of the FATHER in my name, he may give it you.— John xv. 16.

Peace be unto you: as the FATHER hath sent me, I also send you. And when he had said this, he breathed on them, and saith unto them, Receive ye the Holy Spirit.—John xx. 21, 22.

Here, the candidate kneeling, the Ordaining Minister shall lay his hands upon his head, and say:

*Ord. Min.* — You are hereby ordained to be a minister of the New Jerusalem, and are set apart to the performance of the duties pertaining to the first grade of that sacred office. To you is given the authority and power to teach and preach the Heavenly Doctrines of the New Jerusalem: to lead in the public worship of the LORD: to administer the ordinance of Baptism, the rite of Confirmation, and the sacrament of the Holy Supper: to consecrate marriages, and officiate at funerals; and thus, as a minister of the LORD, to instruct the people, and lead them in the way of life.

*[And as you have been invited by ———— society to become their pastor, and have accepted their invitation, you are also hereby introduced into the pastorate of *this* society: you are authorized to preside at its ecclesiastical meetings: to lead its worship: to officiate in receiving members into it: to watch over them: to administer to them the ordinances of the church: to instruct them in its doctrines; and to lead them in the way of eternal life.]

JEHOVAH bless thee, and keep thee: JEHOVAH make his face to shine upon thee, and be gracious unto thee: JEHOVAH lift up his countenance upon thee, and give thee peace.

The candidate will then rise, and the Ordaining Minister will address him thus:

*Ord. Min.* — The LORD in his Divine Providence

* This paragraph is not to be used, except when a minister is settled as pastor of a society at the time of his ordination.

has chosen and ordained you to be a minister in his New Jerusalem.

*And placing a copy of the Holy Scriptures in the right hand of the candidate, he shall say:*

Receive, therefore, the WORD OF THE LORD, the Fountain and Source of all goodness and truth to angels and men.

*And placing in his left hand a copy of the True Christian Religion, he shall say:*

Receive, also, the "True Christian Religion," wherein is contained the Universal Theology of the New Church — the Heavenly Doctrines of the New Jerusalem.

From this WORD, according to these Doctrines, may you ever teach the people, and lead them in the way of life. Be ever mindful of the sanctity of your office. Conduct yourself on all occasions as becomes your calling, with humility, meekness, and kindness. "Let your light so shine before men, that they may see your good works, and glorify your FATHER who is in the heavens." Be faithful to the charge committed to your trust. And may the LORD JESUS CHRIST be with you always. May He open your understanding, so that you may perceive in all the Scriptures the things concerning Himself. May you receive of His fulness, and grace for grace. And may He ever enable you freely to give, as you have freely received.

*Then an Anthem, Selection, or Hymn may be sung.*

## BENEDICTION.

THE grace of our LORD JESUS CHRIST be with you all. AMEN.

# INSTALLATION.

[When a Minister has been invited by a Society to become its Pastor, and has accepted the invitation, it seems to be good and useful to both pastor and people, that he be inducted into office by appropriate religious services. The whole or a part of the following may be used.]

So much as may seem proper of the service for Ordination preceding the questions to the candidate, may be used. Then the Ordaining Minister will proceed as follows:

*Ord. Min.* — A B: You have already been ordained as a Minister, and have been authorized to perform the duties which belong to the first grade in the ministry. The New Jerusalem Society in this place has invited you to become its pastor, and you have accepted the invitation; and we are now assembled to perform the religious services by which you are to be inducted into that office.

Do you now, therefore, in the presence of the LORD, and of this assembly, declare that you desire to be introduced into this office, in order that you may teach and lead this people according to the Heavenly Doctrines of the New Jerusalem, as unfolded from the LORD's Holy Word, in the writings of Emanuel Swedenborg?

*Answer.* — I do.

The candidate will then kneel, and the Ordaining Minister will lay his hands upon his head, and address him as follows:

*Ord. Min.* — You are hereby introduced into the office of pastor of this society. You are authorized to preside at its ecclesiastical meetings; to officiate in receiving members into it; to watch over them; to administer unto them the ordinances of the church; to instruct them in its doctrines, and lead them in the way of life eternal.

And while you are performing these duties, may you know and acknowledge Him who standeth in the midst of us: may you be under the influence and guidance of Him who baptizeth with the Holy Spirit and with fire: may the Lord Jesus Christ be with you always: may He open your understanding, so that you may perceive in all the Scriptures things concerning himself: may you receive of his fulness, and grace for grace: and may he enable you freely to give, as you have freely received.

Jehovah bless thee, and keep thee: Jehovah make his face to shine upon thee, and be gracious unto thee: Jehovah lift up his countenance upon thee, and give thee peace.

Here an Anthem, Selection, or Hymn may be sung.

## BENEDICTION.

The grace of our Lord Jesus Christ be with you all: Amen.

# CONSECRATION.

So much as may be proper of that part of the Ordination Service which precedes the questions to the candidate, may here be used; after which, the service will proceed as follows:

WHEN a person is about to enter upon an office of dignity and honor, it is important for him to examine himself, that he may see what his motives are, and what affections are prevailing in his mind.

It is of Divine Order, and of the Divine Providence, that there should be governments in the church and in the state: for without government, evils could not be prevented in a community; without government, the good of the whole could not be provided for; without government, men cannot be brought into their proper relations to one another, so that they may work together — so that many men may become as one man — so that the power of every part may contribute to the security, the welfare, and the happiness of every other part.

And as there must be governments in the church and in the state, so there must be offices, both ecclesiastical and civil; and there must be various grades among the offices, that the rulers themselves may be superintended, that each one may perform his own duty, and that the true relations among them may be preserved.

Thus it may be seen that all offices are designed for uses; and that all persons who properly fill offices, are employed, not in making others do good unto them, but in themselves doing good unto others: the higher the office, the less does any one do for himself, and the more for others.

And as offices are designed for uses, and as those who fill them must be employed in performing uses so it is of Divine Order that offices should be desired from a love of uses, and filled with a love of uses. This is the case with angels and spiritual men. The ruling love with all of them is love towards others; and the love from which they act in their offices is the love of performing uses to their neighbors. This characteristic they derive from Him who fills the highest office, and who rules over all in the heavens. He does not act from the love of governing, from a love of glory, nor from a love of having his subjects worship, honor, and serve him; but from a love of doing good unto them. And when he came into the world, not to be ministered unto, but to minister unto others, he manifested his true character, and showed the nature of the love from which he always acts.

Whence it is manifest, that, if we would be in his kingdom, and would be conjoined with him, we must act from a similar love; that those in his kingdom who are nearest to him, are most like him; that those who are most elevated, are the most humble; and that those who fill the highest offices, are the least under the influence of self-love, and most under the influence of love towards others: accordingly, when he had, by a life of usefulness, showed the nature of his own love, then, in order that we might become like him, he said unto the disciples, "Whosoever will be great among you, let him be your minister; and whosoever will be chief among you, let him be your servant."

*The Ordaining Minister will here address the candidate as fol.ows:*

*Ord. Min.*— You have already been ordained as a Minister of the New Jerusalem, and have been authorized to perform the duties which belong to the first grade in the ministry. Application has been made to the proper authorities, that you be introduced into the second grade, and the request has been granted.

Do you now, in the presence of the LORD, and of

this assembly, declare that you desire to be introduced into this grade of the ministry, in order that you may perform the duties of it?
*Answer.* — I do.

Then shall the Ordaining Minister read the following passages:

AND JESUS came and spake unto them, saying, All power is given unto me in heaven and in earth. Go ye, therefore, and make disciples of all nations, baptizing them into the name of the FATHER, and of the SON, and of the HOLY SPIRIT; teaching them to do all things whatsoever I have commanded you: and, lo, I am with you all the days, until the consummation of the age. Amen. — Matt. xxviii. 18–20.

And as ye go, preach, saying, The kingdom of heaven is at hand.

Behold, I send you forth as sheep in the midst of wolves: be ye therefore wise as serpents, and harmless as doves.

He that receiveth you, receiveth me; and he that receiveth me, receiveth him that sent me. — Matt. x. 7, 16, 40.

Ye have not chosen me, but I have chosen you, and ordained you, that ye should go and bring forth fruit, and that your fruit should remain: that whatsoever ye shall ask of the FATHER in my name, he may give it you. — John xv. 16.

Peace be unto you: as the FATHER hath sent me, I also send you. And when he had said this, he breathed on them, and saith unto them, Receive ye the Holy Spirit. — John xx. 21 22.

Here, the candidate kneeling, the Ordaining Minister shall lay his hands upon his head, and say:

*Ord. Min.* — You are hereby introduced into the second grade of the ministry. You are authorized to institute Societies and Associations: to grant licenses, and to ordain ministers, according to the Constitution of the General Convention: to counsel them, and to watch over them: to officiate at the installation of pastors: to preside at the ecclesiastical meetings of the Convention, and of Associations, when invited to do so: and to administer the Holy Supper on those occasions. And that you may be able to perform these uses, may the LORD JESUS CHRIST be with you always: may he breathe upon you, and cause you to receive his Holy Spirit: may he fill you with the love which he feels towards men; and may he cause you to receive of his fulness, and grace for grace.

JEHOVAH bless thee, and keep thee: JEHOVAH make his face to shine upon thee, and be gracious unto thee: JEHOVAH lift up his countenance upon thee, and give thee peace.

Then an Anthem, Selection, or Hymn may be sung.

BENEDICTION.

The grace of our LORD JESUS CHRIST be with you all: AMEN.

# DEDICATION.

*The Minister shall place the Word, open, upon the desk, to denote that its internal sense is now revealed.*

The "Order of Worship" may be followed to the close of the Prayer: then may succeed the following passage from the Word, the Minister reading the first line, and the people reading or singing the second line, of each verse; or the whole may be read by the Minister.

1. O JEHOVAH, remember David,
 And | all | his af | flictions:
2. How he sware unto JEHOVAH,
 And vowed unto the | MIGHTY | ONE of | Jacob;
3. Surely I will not come into the tabernacle of my house,
 Nor go | up in | to my | bed;
4. I will not give sleep to mine eyes,
 Or | slumber | to mine | eyelids;
5. Until I find out a place for JEHOVAH,
 Habitations for the | MIGHTY | ONE of | Jacob.
6. Lo, we heard of it at Ephratah:
 We found it | in the | fields · of the | wood.
7. We will go into his tabernacles:
 We will | worship | at his | footstool.
8. Arise, O JEHOVAH, into thy rest;
 Thou, and the | ark | of thy | strength.
9. Let thy priests be clothed with righteousness;
 And let thy | saints | shout for | joy. . . . .

10. For Jehovah hath chosen Zion;
 He hath desired it | for his | habi | tation.
11. This is my rest for ever:
 Here will I dwell; for I | have de | sired | it.
12. I will abundantly bless her provision:
 Her poor will I | satis | fy with | bread.
13. I will also clothe her priests with salvation:
 And her saints shall | shout a | loud for | joy

The Minister may then read 1 Kings VIII. 1–63.

The Doxology in the Order of Worship, p. 23, may follow.

Here may be read the Ten Commandments.

Then may be read a Lesson from the New Testament: John II. 13–25; or some other suitable portion.

Here may be read the following

## ADDRESS.

We are assembled together in this place, for the purpose of setting apart this house from all ordinary and secular uses, and dedicating it to the more immediate service of the Lord, and to the performance of the uses of divine worship and religious instruction.

Though, indeed, the heaven, and heaven of heavens, cannot contain the Lord, much less this house that is built with men's hands; yet may he have respect unto the prayers which we offer up unto him this day, and grant that his name may be placed here. He hath said, " Where two or three are gathered together in my name, there am I in the midst of them." May he be thus present with us, and be in the midst of us.

We hope and trust that this house has been built

from the desire to promote the advancement of the Lord's kingdom upon the earth. It is henceforth to be set apart from all worldly and secular uses, and to be exclusively appropriated to the worship and service of the Lord Jesus Christ. It is to be consecrated to the uses of that worship, and to instruction in the Heavenly Doctrines of the New Jerusalem. This altar, this pulpit, these seats, and all things belonging to this house, are to be consecrated to the uses of religious worship and instruction.

The Doctrines of the New Jerusalem have been revealed from the Lord out of heaven. In this house we desire to be instructed in these Heavenly Doctrines. Here may we, and our children, and our children's children, and whosoever will, come and drink of the waters of life. Here may we receive the Bread that cometh down from heaven, and giveth life unto the world. Here may the tabernacle of God be with men, and may he dwell with them, and they be his people, and God himself be with them, and be their God.

Here we place the Sacred Scriptures. And when the ministers of the Lord here endeavor to expound these Scriptures, and perform the other duties of their office, may they remember that they stand in his presence, and that they are his ambassadors and representatives. May they know and acknowledge him, and act under his guidance and influence. May their understandings be opened, so that they may see, and be enabled to show, in all the Scriptures, things concerning him.

And when the Lord's people draw near in spirit unto him in this place, when they hold communion with him in prayer, when they express their affections in songs of praise, and thanksgiving, and glorification, and when they read and listen to his holy Word, may the influences of the Lord's grace, mercy, and peace be given unto them in rich abundance.

When the ordinance of Baptism is administered here, may those who receive it be afterward baptized with the Holy Spirit and with fire.

When the table of the LORD is spread in this house, may his children come to this holy ordinance in faith and charity: may they eat and drink worthily, and thus receive truly human life from him.

And whenever the worshipers of the LORD shall come up to this house, to perform any of the duties that are enjoined upon them in the Sacred Scriptures and the Doctrines of the New Jerusalem, may they have grace given them to worship him in spirit and in truth; and, coming before him with clean hands and a pure heart, may the services which they shall perform here be always acceptable to him. And may the grace of the LORD JESUS CHRIST be always with them. Amen.

Then the New Jerusalem Service may be used, or a Selection or Hymn may be sung, all standing.

THE SERMON.

An Anthem, Selection, or Hymn may be sung

BENEDICTION.

THE grace of our LORD JESUS CHRIST be with you all. AMEN.

# INSTITUTION OF SOCIETIES.

[When receivers of the Heavenly Doctrines desire to come into the form of a Society of the LORD's New Church, it is desirable that this be done after some orderly manner, that will conduce to the end for which brethren should be thus associated ; namely, the more full acknowledgment and worship of the LORD, and the performance of the uses of mutual charity. The following order of exercises for such an occasion may be used.

If any of those who are to constitute the Society, have not previously been introduced into the New Church by baptism, and have not made an acknowledgment of their faith in the doctrines, and of their desire and intention to live according to them, this should be done before proceeding with the services.]

The Minister may commence the service by reading one or more of the following passages:

I WAS glad when they said unto me,
Let us go into the house of JEHOVAH.
Our feet shall stand within thy gates, O Jerusalem :
Jerusalem is built as a city that is compact together.
Whither the tribes go up, the tribes of JAH,
A testimony to Israel,
To give thanks to the name of JEHOVAH.
For there are set thrones of judgment,
The thrones of the house of David.
Pray for the peace of Jerusalem :
They shall prosper that love thee.
Peace be within thy walls,
Prosperity within thy palaces.
For my brethren and companions' sakes,
I will now say, Peace be within thee.
For the sake of the house of JEHOVAH our GOD,
I will seek good to thee. — Ps. cxxii.

BEHOLD, how good and how pleasant it is,
For brethren to dwell together in unity.
It is like the precious ointment upon the head,
That ran down upon the beard, Aaron's beard,
That went down to the skirts of his garments:
Like the dew of Hermon,
That descended upon the mountains of Zion:
For there JEHOVAH commanded the blessing,
Life forevermore.— Ps. cxxxiii.

IF thy brother shall trespass against thee, go and tell him his fault between thee and him alone: if he shall hear thee, thou hast gained thy brother. But if he will not hear, take with thee one or two more, that in the mouth of two or three witnesses every word may be established. And if he shall neglect to hear them, tell it unto the church: but if he neg'ect to hear the church, let him be unto thee as an heathen man and a publican. Verily I say unto you, Whatsoever ye shall bind on earth, shall be bound in heaven; and whatsoever ye shall loose on earth, shall be loosed in heaven. Again I say unto you, That if two of you shall agree on earth as touching any thing that they shall ask, it shall be done for them of my FATHER who is in heaven: for where two or three are gathered together in my name, there am I in the midst of them.— Mat. xviii. 15-20.

A NEW commandment I give unto you, That ye love one another; as I have loved you, that ye also love one another. By this shall all know that ye are my disciples, if ye have love one to another.— John xiii. 34, 35.

THESE things I command you, that ye love one another. If the world hate you, ye know that it hated me before it hated you. If ye were of the world, the world would love its own: but because ye are not of the world, but I have chosen you out of the world, therefore the world hateth you.— John xv. 17-19.

Then the Minister may read the following

## ADDRESS.

We are not required to form ourselves into societies, or churches, because such a requirement is not necessary. It is not necessary that we should be required to do things which we love to do, but things which we do not love to do, and at the same time need to do. It is true that while we are in a natural state of mind, we have no disposition to form ourselves into churches, and to perform the duties of members; and it is equally true, that while we are in that state, we ought not to form ourselves into churches. But we are required to do things which will bring us into a suitable state — which will bring us out of a natural state into a spiritual one; that is, out of a state in which natural loves rule, into one in which spiritual loves rule. We are required to abstain from evils, because they are sins against God: and as far as we conform to this requirement, so far the love of doing evils will be overcome, together with the love of self and the world, in which all evil affections originate; and as far as these evil loves are overcome and removed, so far will good loves flow in, and will prevail in us: as the power of love to self and to the world diminishes, the power of love to the Lord and love to the neighbor increases.

Now the spiritual labors by which we resist evil loves, are what is denoted by the ordinance of Baptism; and the reception and exercise of the good loves which flow in after evil loves are overcome, are what is denoted by the Holy Supper. Hence we may see why it was, at the time when he was instituting this ordinance, that the Lord announced to his disciples that he gave them a new commandment, which was, that they should love one another.

When we come under this new commandment, or become filled with this new love, we shall be churches in the least form; and the same principle will lead us to do good unto others, to unite with them, and thus to become churches in a larger form. We shall regard those who have affections similar to ours, as our nearest relatives. We shall constantly remember that their good affections, and our good affections, flow down from the same source — from the Fountain of our spiritual life — from our FATHER who is in the heavens: we shall consequently be sensible that we are brethren; and we shall perceive how good and how pleasant it is for brethren to dwell together in unity.

It is good, and it is pleasant. It gratifies our new wills and our new understandings. It is in the highest degree both useful and agreeable. Hence we find, in the revelations which have been made to the New Church concerning the spiritual world, that heaven consists of innumerable societies, that the angels are adapted to one another by their various capacities, and are united by loving and doing good to one another.

The LORD has provided that these same principles may be implanted in us while we live in this world; and as soon as they are implanted, they will lead us to begin to act in a similar manner. They will make us love one another, and make us desire to live together, and act together.

The uses of living in this manner are various, and in the highest degree important. It gives us spiritual freedom. It gives us an opportunity to bring forth all the genuine New Church affections and thoughts that are conceived within us. It places us in circumstances that are most favorable for obedience to the new commandment; for love to one another is in its most active and delightful state, it enjoys and rejoices most, and it appears in its truest forms, and puts on its most beautiful ornaments, when it meets with those who act upon the same principle, when it can see the likeness of its heavenly FATHER in those who are around it, so that when it is doing good unto them, it can perceive that it is doing good unto Him. When we do ourselves act from love to one another, and are associated with those who act from similar love, then we can bear one another's burdens, can protect one another from evil, can aid one another in seeing and removing the evils which still adhere to us, and can receive, welcome, and cherish the good things which come down from heaven, when the way is thus prepared.

When we are united in this manner, we are a society of the church, and can perform the uses of a church in the world. It is our duty to provide for having the ordinances administered in a proper manner. It is our duty to have social worship ; to unite in prayer, in thanksgiving, and in praise : to magnify the Lord, and to exalt his name together : for it is the duty of us all ; and in doing it together, we aid one another, and unite love to the Lord with love to the neighbor. It is our duty to receive spiritual instruction together ; for brotherly love is the feeling into which spiritual truth can be received, and brotherly life is the form in which it is brought into effect. When we are united by this feeling, we coöperate, and aid one another in receiving the truth, and in practising it.

And while we are thus earnestly engaged in performing our own duties, we shall be doing the greatest possible service to our children, and to those who are looking to us for spiritual instruction ; for we shall then be giving that instruction in the most intelligible, the most attractive, and the most effective manner. We give it, not as a curious subject of speculation, of criticism, and debate ; but we present it in a living form, as it is when doing its work. In this case, it is attended by a sanctity that affects the hearts, and a power that carries it into the lives, of all who are prepared to receive it. The instruction which is given in this manner, comes down like the holy oil and the heavenly dew ; it has a vivifying and saving influence, wherever it goes : for in it the Lord conveys his blessing, life forevermore.

Those who are to constitute the Society, sitting conveniently together, should rise as their names are here read by the Minister; who may then address them as follows:

*Min.* — You have been introduced into the New Church by baptism; you have declared your faith in the Heavenly Doctrines of the New Jerusalem, and your desire and intention to live according to them: Do you now wish to become united into a society for that purpose?

*Answer.* — We do.

*Min.* — You are therefore hereby acknowledged as a regularly instituted society, under the name of ——————————; and are commended to the fellowship of all other societies of the New Jerusalem.

They should then sign their names to the Articles of Charity and Faith, or Doctrines of the New Church, in a book provided for that purpose; after which the Holy Supper may be administered.

# ADMISSION OF MEMBERS INTO SOCIETIES.

The *candidates* should rise as their names are called by the Minister; and then he should ask *them* the following question:

*Min.* — You have been introduced into the New Church by baptism; you have also declared your faith in the Heavenly Doctrines of the New Jerusalem, and your desire to live according to them: Do you now desire to become *members* of this Society for that purpose?

*Answer.* — I do.

Then the Society should rise, and the Minister should take the *candidates* by the hand, and address *them* as follows:

*Min.* — We therefore freely receive you into our communion; we acknowledge you as *members* of this Society, and as having a right to all the privileges which we enjoy.

They should then sign their names to the Articles of Charity and Faith, or the Doctrines of the New Church, in the book of the Society.

# INSTITUTION OF ASSOCIATIONS.

[When several Societies in the New Church desire to come into the form of an Association, the following order of services may be used.]

The delegates or representatives of the Societies which are to constitute the Association being seated near each other, the Minister may read the passages and address in the order of services for the Institution of Societies, and then proceed as follows:

AND as individuals become more useful to one another, and to the world, by being formed into Societies; so Societies become more useful to one another, and to the world, by being formed into Associations. As all the parts of the body are different, and as all these differences qualify the parts to perform different uses, and make the whole a complete system of uses; so it is with individuals and societies. Every part does, either directly or indirectly, contribute to the welfare of the whole; and the whole does, either directly or indirectly, contribute to the welfare of every part. The LORD himself loves the whole, and all the parts; and he is continually endeavoring to do good unto them: so, as they become recipients of his love, they learn to love one another, and to do good to one another.

Here the delegates will rise, as the Minister reads their names; when he shall address them as follows:

*Min.* — Do you now, as the representatives of \_ \_\_
_____ \_ Societies in the New Jerusalem, speaking and acting in their behalf, wish to be united

into an Association, as a means of enabling you more fully to perform the uses of mutual charity?
*Answer.*— We do.

*Min.*— You are therefore hereby acknowledged as a regularly instituted Association, under the name of ———————————— ; and are commended to the fellowship of all other Associations in the New Jerusalem.

They should then sign the Articles of Charity and Faith, or the Doctrines of the New Church, in a book provided for that purpose.

Then may the Holy Supper be administered.

# FAMILY WORSHIP.

## MORNING AND EVENING PRAYER.

Once, or more, on each day, at some regular hour, all the members of the household should assemble themselves together for the worship of the LORD; when a portion of the Holy Word should be read; after which, all kneeling, the head of the family, or some other suitable person, should lead in the use of the LORD's Prayer: or any of the prayers in the Order of Worship may be used, or such other as may be desired. After prayer, a Selection, Anthem, or Hymn may be sung, if convenient.

## ACKNOWLEDGMENT OF THE LORD AT MEALS.

*These may be said, or read.*

OUR FATHER, who art in the heavens, . . . Give us this day our daily bread: . . . Amen.— Mat. vi. 9, 11, 13.

JEHOVAH is my Shepherd; I shall not want. He maketh me to lie down in green pastures; he leadeth me beside the still waters. — Ps. xxiii. 1, 2. O give thanks unto JEHOVAH, for he is good; for his mercy endureth forever. Amen.— Ps. cxviii. 1.

BLESS JEHOVAH, O my soul, and forget not all his benefits: Who forgiveth all thine iniquities; who healeth all thy diseases: . . . Who satisfieth thy mouth with good: thy youth is renewed like the eagle's. Amen.— Ps. ciii. 2, 3, 5.

I will extol thee, my GOD, O King; and I will bless thy name for ever and ever. . . . The eyes of all wait upon thee; and thou givest them their meat in due season. Thou openest thine hand, and satisfiest the desire of every living thing. . . . My mouth shall speak the praise of JEHOVAH; and let all flesh bless his holy name for ever and ever: Amen.— Ps. cxlv. 1, 15, 16, 21.

O GIVE thanks unto JEHOVAH, for he is good; for his mercy endureth for ever. . . . For he satisfieth the longing soul, and filleth the hungry soul with goodness. Amen.— Ps. cvii. 1, 9.

O JEHOVAH, how manifold are thy works: in wisdom hast thou made them all: the earth is full of thy riches. Amen.— Ps. civ. 24.

How excellent is thy loving-kindness, O GOD: therefore the children of men put their trust under the shadow of thy wings. They shall be abundantly satisfied with the fatness of thy house; and thou shalt make them drink of the river of thy pleasures: for with thee is the fountain of life. Amen.— Ps. xxxvi. 7 - 9.

The following may also be used.

| Ps. xxxvi. 10. | Ps. lxxxvi. 11, 12. | Ps. cvii. 8. |
| lxviii. 19, 20. | ciii. 1 - 5. | cxvii. 1, 2. |
| lxxx. 14, 15. | cvii. 1. | cxlv. 1, 2. |

OUR FATHER in heaven, may we be thankful for thy daily mercies, and constantly look to thee for the bread of life which cometh down from heaven. Amen.

BLESS to our use, O LORD, what thy bounty has provided; and give us thankful hearts. Amen.

WE praise thy name, O LORD, for these manifestations of thy goodness. Feed our souls with the bread of life, and give us grateful hearts, for thy mercy's sake. Amen.

OUR FATHER who art in the heavens, for all thy blessings we pray thee to make us truly thankful. Amen.

# SELECTIONS AND CHANTS.

### CHANT 1.

### SELECTION 1.

That the man who does not live ill, is regenerated by the Word of the Lord, 1—5; but that he who lives ill, perishes at the day of judgment, 6, 7; because the Lord knows every one, 8.

1. Blessed | is the | man,
That walketh not in the | counsel | of · the un|godly,
2. Nor standeth in the | way of | sinners,
Nor sitteth in the | seat | of the | scornful.
3. But his delight is in the | law · of JE|HOVAH ;
And in his law doth he | medi·tate | day and | night.
4 And he shall be like a tree planted by the | riv·ers of | waters,
That bringeth forth his | fruit | in his | season :
5. His leaf also | shall not | wither ;
And whatsoever he | doeth | shall | prosper.
6. The ungodly | are not | so :
But are like the chaff which the | wind doth | drive a|way.
7. Therefore the ungodly shall not | stand · in the | judgment,
Nor sinners in the congre|gation | of the | righteous.
8 For JEHOVAH knoweth the | way · of the | righteous ;
But the way of the un|godly | shall | perish.     Ps. i

▲

## CHANT 2.

[musical notation]

## SELECTION 2.

*The prayers of the church, that in mercy their sins may be remitted, 1—4; that thus they have good and conjunction, 5—7.*

1. Good and upright | is Je|hovah;
   Therefore will he teach | sinners | in the | way.
2. The meek will he | guide in | judgment:
   And the meek | will he | teach his | way.
3. All the paths of Jehovah are | mer·cy and | truth,
   To those that keep his covenant | and his | testi|monies
4. For thy name's sake, | O Je|hovah,
   Pardon mine in|i·quity, | for · it is | great.
5. What man is he that | fear·eth Je|hovah?
   Him shall he teach in the | way that | he shall | choose.
6. His soul shall | dwell in | good;
   And his seed | shall in|her·it the | earth.
7. The secret of Jehovah is with | them that | fear him;
   And he will make them to | know his | cove|nant.

Ps. xxv. 8.

## CHANT 3.

[musical notation]

## SELECTION 3.

*Concerning the Lord when he was in temptations, and subjugated the hells; and then in a state of humiliation, in which he prayed to the Father, 1—9.*

1. O Jehovah, how are they increased that | trouble | me:
   Many are they that | rise | up a|gainst me.
2. Many there be who | say · of my | soul,
   There is no | help for | him in | God.
3. But thou, O Jehovah, art a | shield for | me;
   My glory, and the | lifter | up · of mine | head.

## SELECTIONS AND CHANTS. 3

4. I cried unto Jehovah | with my | voice,
And he heard me from the mountain | of his | holi|ness.
5 I laid me | down and | slept :
I awaked ; for Je|hovah | did sus|tain me.
6. I will not be afraid of ten | thou · sands of | people,
That have set themselves a|gainst me | round a|bout.
7. Arise, | O Je|hovah ;
Save | me, | O my | God :
8. For thou hast smitten all my enemies up|on the | cheek ;
Thou hast broken the | teeth of | the un|godly.
9 Salvation belongeth |· to Je|hovah :
Thy blessing | is up|on thy | people.  Ps. iii.

### Chant 4.

### SELECTION 4.

Concerning the Lord when in great temptations, 1—3 : that they should fear him, because he has protection from the Father, 4 : an exhortation to repentance, 5—9

1. Hear me | when I | call,
O | God · of my | righteous|ness.
2. Thou hast enlarged me when | in dis|tress ;
Have mercy up|on · me, and | hear my | prayer.
3. O ye sons of men, how long shall my glory | be for | shame ?
How long will ye love vanity, and | seek | after | lying ?
4. But know that Jehovah hath set apart the godly | for him|self :
Jehovah will hear me | when I | call unto | him.
5 Stand in awe, | and sin | not :
Commune with your own heart up|on your | bed, and be | still
6 Offer the sacrifices of | righteous|ness,
And put your | trust | in Je|hovah.
7. There be many that say, Who will | show us | good ?
O Jehovah, lift up the light of thy | counte|nance up·|on us.
8. Thou hast put gladness | in my | heart,
More than in the time their | corn · and their | wine in|creased
9. I will both lay me down in | peace, and | sleep ;
For thou only, O Jehovah, dost | make me | dwell in | safety.
Ps. iv.

## CHANT 5. DOUBLE.

## SELECTION 5.

*Prayer of the Lord to the Father that he would assist, 1—3, 7. 8: against the evil, false speakers, and hypocrites, 4—6.*

1. Give ear to my words, | O Je|hovah ;
Con|sider | my com|plaint.
2. Hearken to the voice of my cry, my | King · and my | God ;
For to | thee | will I | pray.
3. My voice shalt thou hear in the morning, | O Je|hovah ;
In the morning will I ad|dress thee, | and look | up.
4. For thou art not a God that hath pleasure in | wicked|ness ;
Neither shall | evil | dwell with | thee.
5. The profane shall not | stand · in thy | sight :
Thou hatest all workers | of in|iqui|ty.
6. Thou shalt destroy | them · that speak | falsehood :
Jehovah will abhor the |man of | blood · and de|ceit.
7. But as for me, I will come into thy house in the greatness |
of thy | mercy :
In thy fear will I worship | toward · thy | holy | temple.
8. Lead me, O Jehovah, in thy righteousness, because of mine |
ene|mies :
Make thy way | straight be|fore my | face.        Ps. v. 1–8.

## SELECTION 6.

*That the Lord fulfilled the law or the Word from the first things of it to the last, and that he was therefore hated, and suffered temptations, and that thus he united the Humanity to his Divinity, 1—8.*

1. Thy hands have made me and | fashioned | me :        [ments.
Make me to understand, that I may | learn | thy com|mand-

2. They that fear thee will be | glad · when they | see me,
Because I have | hoped | in thy | word.
3. I know, O JEHOVAH, that thy | judg·ments are | justice ;
And that thou in faithfulness | hast af|flicted | me.
4. Let, I pray thee, thy mercy | be · for my | comfort,
According to thy | word | to thy | servant.
5 Let thy tender mercies come unto me, that | I may | live;
For thy | law is | my de|light.
6 Let the proud be ashamed; for they dealt perversely with me with|out a | cause:
I will | medi·tate | in thy | precepts.
7 Let those that fear thee | turn to | me,
And those that | know thy | testi|monies.
8. Let my heart be | sound · in thy | statutes,
That I |may not | be a|shamed.   Ps. cxix. 73.

CHANT 6.

SELECTION 7.

Concerning the state of the Lord's grief and perturbation from temptations, with his confidence from the Divinity, 1—8.

1. As the hart panteth for the | brooks of | water,
So panteth my | soul for | thee, O | GOD.
2. My soul thirsteth for GOD, for the | living | GOD:
When shall I come and ap|pear be|fore | GOD?
3 My tears have been my meat | day and | night;
While they continually say unto me, | Where | is thy | GOD?
4. When I re|member · these | things,
I pour | out my | soul with|in me.
5. For I had gone with the | multi|tude ;
I went with them | to the | house of | GOD,
6. With the voice of | joy and | praise,
With a multitude that | kept a | festi|val.
7. Why art thou bowed down, | O my | soul?
And why art thou dis|quiet|ed with|in me?
8. Hope thou in GOD, for I | shall yet | praise him,
For the , help · of his | counte|nance.   Ps. xlii.

### CHANT 7. DOUBLE.

## SELECTION 8.

*Prayer of the Lord to the Father when he was in the last state of temptations, which state is despair, 1—7; and that being aided he repressed the hells, 8—10.*

1. O JEHOVAH, rebuke me not | in thine | anger,
   Neither chasten me | in thy | hot dis|pleasure.
2. Have mercy upon me, O JEHOVAH; for | I am | weak:
   O JEHOVAH, heal me; | for my | bones are | vexed.
3. My soul is also | sorely | vexed:
   But thou, O JE|HOVAH, | how | long?
4. Return, O JEHOVAH, de|liv·er my | soul:
   O save me | for thy | mercies' | sake.
5. For·in death there is no re|mem·brance of | thee:
   In the grave | who shall | give thee | thanks?
6. I am weary | with my | groaning;
   All the night make I my bed to swim; I | water my | couch with my | tears.
7. Mine eye is consumed be|cause of | grief;
   It waxeth old because of | all mine | ene|mies.
8. Depart from me, all ye workers of in|iqui|ty:
   For JEHOVAH hath | heard the | voice · of my | weeping.
9. JEHOVAH hath heard my | suppli|cation;
   JEHOVAH | will re|ceive my | prayer.
10. Let all mine enemies be ashamed and | sorely | vexed:
    Let them return and be | sudden|ly a|shamed.   Ps. vi

SELECTIONS AND CHANTS. 7

CHANT 8. DOUBLE.

SELECTION 9.

Thanksgiving and joy of the Lord, that the evil are judged and destroyed, 1—8; that the good are delivered, 9, 10.

1. I will praise thee, O JEHOVAH, with | all the | heart;
   I will declare | all thy | won·derful | works.
2. I will be glad and re|joice in | thee:
   I will sing praise to thy | name, O | thou Most | High.
3. When mine enemies are | turned | back,
   They shall fall and | perish | at thy | presence.
4. For thou hast maintained my | right·and my | cause;
   Thou sattest in the | throne | judging | right.
5. Thou hast rebuked the heathen, thou hast de|stroyed the | wicked,
   Thou hast put out their | name for|ev·er and | ever.
6. The enemy, they have come to per|pet·ual | ruins:
   And thou hast destroyed cities; their re|mem·brance is | perished | with them.
7. But JEHOVAH shall en|dure for|ever:
   He hath pre|pared his | throne for | judgment;
8. And he shall judge the world in | righteous|ness,
   He shall minister judgment to the | peo·ple in | upright|ness
9. JEHOVAH also will be a refuge | for ·the op|pressed,
   A | ref·uge in | times of | trouble.
10. And they that know thy name will | trust in | thee:
    For thou, O JEHOVAH, hast not for|saken | them that | seek thee.          Ps. ix 1--10

## Chant 9.

## SELECTION 10.

That divine truth will go forth on all sides, 1—4: that this will proceed from the Lord, from the first to the last things of heaven and the church, 5, 6.

1. The heavens declare the | glory of | God;
And the firmament showeth the | work | of his | hands.
2. Day unto day | utter·eth | speech,
And night unto | night | showeth | knowledge.
3. There is no | speech nor | language,
Where their | voice | is not | heard.
4. Their line is gone out into | all the | earth,
And their words to the | end | of the | world.
5. In them hath he set a tabernacle | for the | sun,
¹Which, as a bridegroom coming | out·of his | chamber,
Rejoiceth as a strong | man to | run a | race.
6. His going forth is from the | end·of the | heavens,
¹And his circuit unto the | ends of | it;
And there is nothing | hid·from the | heat there|of.

Ps. xix, 1—6

## Chant 10.

## SELECTION 11.

Celebration of the Father by the Lord, that he would regard his innocence, and assist against the hells, 1—3, 9: the state of the Lord's humiliation is described, 4, 6; and the state of his glorification, 6—8.

1. O Jehovah, our Lord, how excellent is thy name in | all the |
Who hast set thy | glo·ry a|bove the | heavens.    [earth!
2. Out of the mouth of babes and sucklings hast thou ordained
   strength because of thine | ene|mies,
To put to silence the | en·emy | and·the a|venger.

SELECTIONS AND CHANTS.  9

3. When I behold thy heavens, the | work · of thy | fingers,
   The moon and the | stars which | thou · hast or|dained;
4. What is man, that thou art | mindful | of him ?
   And the son of man, that | thou dost | visit | him ?
5. For thou madest him a little lower | than the | angels,
   And hast crowned him with | glory | and with | honor.
6. Thou hast made him to rule over the | works · of thy | hands;
   Thou hast put | all things | un·der his | feet:
7. All | sheep and | oxen,
   And also the | beasts | of the | field:
8. Fowls of the air, and fishes | of the | sea,
   And whatever passeth | through the | paths · of the | seas.
9. O JEHOVAH, | our | LORD,
   How excellent is thy | name in | all the | earth !   Ps. viii.

CHANT 11.

SELECTION 12.

The prayers of the church to the Lord that they may be preserved from the hells, 1—3; that they may be instructed in truth, 4—6; that in mercy their sins may be remitted, 7, 8.

1. Unto thee, O JEHOVAH, do I lift | up my | soul:
   O my | GOD, I | trust in | thee:
2. Let me not | be a|shamed:
   Let not mine enemies | triumph | over | me.
3. Yea, let none that wait for thee | be a|shamed:
   Let them be ashamed who trans|gress with|out a | cause.
4. Make me to | know thy | ways,
   O JEHOVAH, | teach thou | me thy | paths.
5. Lead me in thy | truth, and | teach me:
   For thou art the GOD of my salvation : on thee do I | wait |
      all the | day.
6. Remember, O JEHOVAH, thy | tender | mercies
   And thy kindnesses, for they | are from | ever|lasting.
7. Remember not the | sins · of | my | youth,
   Nor | my trans|gres|sions.
8. According to thy mercy re|mem·ber thou | me,
   For thy goodness' | sake, | O JE|HOVAH.   Ps. xxv

## CHANT 12.

## SELECTION 13.

A prayer of the Lord to the Father that he would assist, and he shall prevail, 1-4. that those who are in the truths and goods of the church may be saved, 5.

1. Blessed | be JE|HOVAH,
   Because he hath heard the | voice · of my | suppli|cations.
2. JEHOVAH is my | strength, and my | shield ;
   My heart trusted in | him, and | I am | helped.
3. Therefore my heart re|joiceth | greatly ;
   And with my | song | will I | praise him.
4. JEHOVAH | is their | strength,
   And he is the saving | strength of | his an|ointed.
5. Save thy people, and bless thine in|heri|tance :
   Feed them also, and | lift them | up for|ever.   Ps. xxviii. 6.

## CHANT 13.

## SELECTION 14.

That there will be a new church, which will acknowledge and worship the Lord, 1-4 : celebration of him by that church on account of redemption, 5—11.

1. Thou hast de|livered | me
   From the | strivings | of the | people :
2. Thou hast made me the | head · of the | nations :
   A people whom I | have not | known shall | serve me.
3. As soon as they hear of me, they | shall o|bey me :
   The sons of the stranger shall sub|mit them|selves unto | me.
4. The sons of the stranger shall | fade a|way,
   And shall be afraid | out of | their close | places

SELECTIONS AND CHANTS.   11

5. JEHOVAH liveth, and blessed | be my | Rock ;
And let the GOD of my sal|vation | be ex|alted.
6. It is GOD that a|vengeth | me,
And subdueth the | people | under | me.
7. He delivereth me from mine | ene|mies ;
Yea, thou liftest me up above| those that | rise · up a|gainst
8. Thou hast de|livered | me                                [me.
From the | man of | vio|lence.
9 Therefore will I give thanks unto thee, O JEHOVAH, a|mong
the | nations,
And sing | praises | un·to thy | name.
10. Great deliverance giveth | he · to his | king ;
And showeth mercy | unto | his an|ointed ;
11. Unto | Da|vid,
And to his | seed for | ever|more.        Ps. xviii. 43.

CHANT 14.

SELECTION 15.

Prayer of the church to the Lord, and, in the supreme sense, a prayer of the Lord to the Father, that because he alone fights against the hells, he would assist, 1—6; that he has integrity, 7; and thus redemption, 8.

1. Mine eyes are ever | toward · JE|HOVAH ;
For he shall bring forth my | feet out | of the | net.
2. Turn thee unto me, and have | mer·cy up|on me :
For I am | deso·late | and af|flicted.
3 The troubles of my | heart · are en|larged :
O bring thou me | out of | my dis|tresses.
4 Look upon mine affliction | and my | pain ;
And for|give | all my | sins.
5. Consider mine enemies, for | they are | many ;
And they | hate · me with | cruel | hatred.
6. O keep my soul, and de|liver | me :
Let me not be ashamed, | for I | trust in | thee.
7. Let integrity and uprightness pre|serve | me ;
For | I do | wait on | thee.
8. Redeem | Isra|el,
O GOD, | out of | all his | troubles     Ps. xxv. 15–22

### CHANT 15.

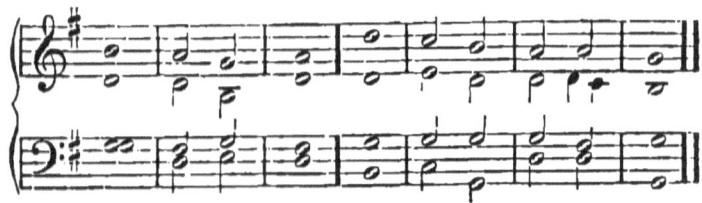

### SELECTION 16.

Prayer of the Lord to the Father, that after the judgment executed upon the evil, a new church may be instituted, 1—7.

1. Thou hast been favorable, O Jehovah, | to thy | land ;
   Thou hast brought back the cap|tivi|ty of | Jacob.
2. Thou hast forgiven the iniquity | of thy | people ;
   Thou hast | covered | all their | sin.
3. Thou hast taken away | all thy | wrath ;
   Thou hast turned away from the | heat | of thine | anger.
4. Restore us, O God of | our sal|vation,
   And turn a|way thine | anger | from us.
5. Wilt thou be angry with | us for|ever ?
   Wilt thou prolong thine anger to | all | gener|ations?
6. Wilt thou not re|vive · us a|gain,
   That thy people | may re|joice in | thee ?
7. Make us to see thy mercy, | O Je|hovah,
   And | grant us | thy sal|vation.     Ps. lxxxv.

### CHANT 16.

### SELECTION 17.

Concerning the Lord, that he teaches and leads to the truths and goods of heaven and the church, 1—3 : hence there is no fear of the hells, because he preserves, and gives good and truth in abundance, 4—7; in heaven with the Lord to eternity, 8, 9.

1. Jehovah | is my | Shepherd ;
   I | shall | not | want.
2. He maketh me to lie | down · in green | pastures ;
   He leadeth me be|side the | still | waters.

SELECTIONS AND CHANTS. 13

3. He re|stor·eth my | soul;  [sake.
He leadeth me in the paths of righteousness | for his | name's |
4. Yea, though I walk through the valley of the | shad·ow of |
I | will | fear no | evil:  [death,
5. For | thou art | with me;
Thy rod and thy | staff they | comfort | me.
6. Thou preparest a | table be|fore me
In the presence | of mine | ene|mies:
7 Thou anointest my | head with | oil;
My | cup | runneth | over.
8 Surely goodness and mercy shall | follow | me
All the | days | of my | life;
9 And | I shall | dwell
In the house of Je|hovah | for|ever.  Ps. xxiii.

CHANT 17.

SELECTION 18.

That from the unition of the Divinity and the Humanity in the Lord, there will be a church which will be in all truths from the Lord, and safe from infestation by falsities, 1—8.

1. Thou dost visit the earth, and | water | it;
Thou greatly enrichest it with the river of | God, which is | full of | water.
2. Thou dost pre|pare them | corn,
When thou hast | so pro|vided | for it.
3. Thou waterest the ridges thereof a|bundant|ly;
Thou | set·tlest the | fur·rows there|of.
4 Thou makest it | soft with | showers;
Thou | bless·est the | spring·ing there|of.
5 Thou crownest the | year · with thy | goodness;
And thy | paths | drop | fatness:
6. They drop upon the pastures of the | wilder|ness;
And the little hills re|joice on | every | side.
7. The pastures are | clothed with | flocks:
The valleys also are | covered | o·ver with | corn:
8. They | shout for | joy:
They | do ' also | sing.  Ps. lxv. 9

## CHANT 18. DOUBLE.

## SELECTION 19.

The confidence of the Lord from his Divinity against the hells, 1–3. 6, 7: his combats with them, 4–7: that in his zeal he subjugated and overthrew them. 8–11.

1. I will love thee, O JE|HO·VAH, my | strength.
   JEHOVAH is my rock, and my fortress, and | my de|liver|er ;
2. My GOD, my rock, in | him · I will | trust ;
   My buckler, and the horn of my sal|vation, | my high | tower.
3. I will call upon JEHOVAH, who | is·to be | praised ;
   'So shall I be | saved · from mine | ene|mies.
4. The sorrows of death | compassed | me,
   And the floods of ungodly | men made | me a|fraid.
5. The sorrows of hell compassed | me a|bout :
   The snares of | death pre|vented | me.
6. In my distress I called up|on JE|HOVAH,
   And | cried un|to my | GOD :
7. He heard my voice | out · of his | temple,
   And my cry came be|fore him, | in·to his | ears.
8. Then the earth | shook and | trembled ;
   The foundations of the hills moved and were | sha·ken be·cause · he was | wroth.
9. There went up a smoke | out · of his | nostrils,       [by it
   And fire out of his mouth devoured : | coals were | kindled |
10. He bowed the heavens also, | and came | down :
    And there was | darkness | un·der his | feet.
11. And he rode upon a cherub, | and did | fly :
    Yea, he did fly up|on the | wings · of the | wind.   Ps. xviii.

## CHANT 19. DOUBLE.

## SELECTION 20.

*That the Lord fights from his Divinity, 1—6: and subjugates the hells 7–10: that they have no savior, 11: wherefore they will be destroyed, 12.*

1. It is God that girdeth | me with | strength,
   And | maketh | my way | perfect.
2. He maketh my | feet like | hinds',
   And setteth me up|on my | high | places.
3. He teacheth my | hands to | war,
   So that a bow of steel is | broken | by mine | **arms**.
4. Thou hast also | given | me
   The | shield of | thy sal|vation:
5. And thy right hand hath | held me | up;
   And thy gentleness | hath | made me | **great**.
6. Thou hast enlarged my | steps under | me,
   That my | feet | did not | slip.
7. I have pursued mine enemies, and over|taken | them:
   Neither did I turn again | till they | were con|sumed.
8. I have wounded them that they were not | a ble to | rise:
   They are | fallen | under my | feet.
9. For thou hast girded me with | strength to the | battle:
   Thou hast subdued under me | those that | rose a|gainst me
10. Thou hast also given me the necks of mine | ene|mies;
    That I might de|stroy | them that | hate me.
11. They cried, but there was | none to | save;
    Unto Jehovah, but he | did not | answer | them.
12. Then did I beat them small as the dust be fore the | wind
    I did cast them | out as the | dirt in the  streets.

*Ps. xviii. 32*

16 SELECTIONS AND CHANTS.

CHANT 20. DOUBLE.

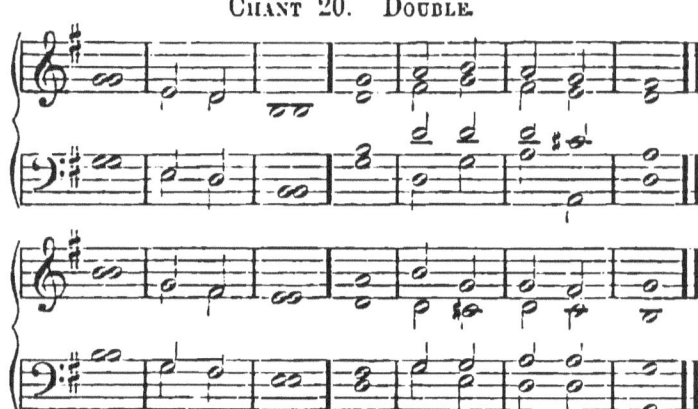

SELECTION 21.

*That the Lord had integrity, 1—8, 11; and divine truth, 9, 10; and is the only God, 12.*

1. JEHOVAH rewarded me according to my | righteous|ness;
   According to the cleanness of my hands | hath he | recom
   pensed | me :
2. For I have kept the | ways of JE|hovah,
   And have not wickedly de|parted | from my | GOD.
3. For all his judgments | were be|fore me,
   And I did not put a|way his | statutes | from me.
4. I was also | upright | with him,
   And I kept myself from | mine in|iqui|ty.
5. Therefore hath JEHOVAH recompensed me according to my | righteous|ness.
   According to the cleanness of my | hands be|fore his | eyes.
6. With the merciful thou wilt show thyself | merci|ful;
   With an upright man thou wilt | show thy|self | upright.
7. With the pure thou wilt | show thy·self | pure ;
   And with the froward thou wilt | show thy|self | froward.
8. For thou wilt save the af|flicted | people;
   But wilt | bring down | lofty | eyes.
9. For thou wilt | light my | lamp :
   JEHOVAH my GOD | will en|light·en my | darkness.
10. For by thee I have run | through a | troop ;
    And by my GOD have I | leaped | o·ver a | wall.
11. GOD, his way is perfect: the word of JE|ho·vah is | tried:
    He is a buckler to all | those that | trust in | him.
12. For who is GOD | save JE|hovah?
    Or who is a | rock | save our | GOD?   Ps. xviii. 20.

### CHANT 21. DOUBLE.

## SELECTION 22.

That the Lord in his zeal subjugated and overthrew the hells, 1—4: that thus divine truth appears, 5, 6: that from his Divinity he prevailed over them, 7—10.

1. He made darkness his | secret | place;
   His pavilion around him was dark waters, thick | clouds | of the | skies.
2. At the brightness that | was be|fore him,
   His thick clouds passed, | hail and ! coals of | fire.
3. JEHOVAH also thundered | in the | heavens,
   And the Highest gave his voice; | hail and | coals of | fire.
4. Yea, he sent out his arrows, and | scattered | them;
   And he shot out lightnings, | and dis|com·fited | them.
5. Then the channels of | waters were | seen,
   And the foundations of the | world | were dis|covered,
6. At thy rebuke, | O JEHOVAH,
   At the blast of the | breath | of thy | nostrils.
7. He sent from a|bove, he | took me,
   He drew me | out of | many | waters.
8. He delivered me from my strong | ene|my,
   And from them that hated me: for they | were too | strong for | me.
9. They prevented me in the day of my ca|lami|ty:
   But JE|HOVAH | was my | stay.
10. He brought me forth also into a | large | place:
    He delivered me, because | he de|lighted | in me.

Ps. xviii. 11.

## CHANT 22.

## SELECTION 23.

Concerning the state of the Lord's temptations, and the grievous insurrection of the infernals against him, 1—5: that he is confident of victory, 6, 7.

1. How long wilt thou forget me, O JEHOVAH? | for|ever?
   How long wilt thou | hide thy | face from | me?
2. How long shall I take counsel | in my | soul,
   Having sorrow | daily | in my | heart?
3. How long shall mine | ene|my
   Be ex|alted | over | me?
4. Consider and hear me, O JE|HO·VAH my | GOD:
   Enlighten mine eyes, lest I | sleep the | sleep of | death;
5. Lest mine enemy say, I have pre|vailed a|gainst him;
   And those that trouble me re|joice when | I am | moved.
6. But I have trusted | in thy | mercy;
   My heart shall re|joice in | thy sal|vation.
7. I will sing | un·to JE|HOVAH,
   Because he hath dealt | bounti|fully | with me.   Ps. xiii.

## CHANT 23.

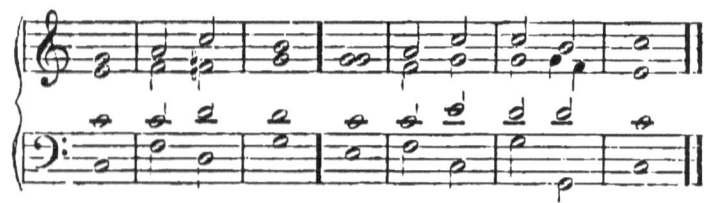

## SELECTION 24.

Celebration of the Lord because he sustains the church, 1—4: that salvation is from him, 5—7, 10: that those are saved who trust in him, and that those perish who trust in themselves, 8, 9.

1. JEHOVAH hear thee in the | day of | trouble;
   The name of the | GOD of | Ja·cob de|fend thee.
2. Send thee help from the | sanctu|ary,
   And sus|tain thee | out of | Zion.

3. Remember all thy | offer|ings,
   And accept thy | burnt | sacri|fice.
4. Grant thee according to | thine own | heart,
   And ful|fil | all thy | counsel.
5. We will rejoice in | thy sal|vation,
   And in the name of our | GOD · we will | set up | banners.
6. JEHOVAH fulfil | all · thy pe|titions.
   Now know I that JEHOVAH | saveth | his an|ointed :
7. He will hear him from his | holy | heaven,
   With the saving | strength of | his right | hand.
8  Some trust in chariots, and | some in | horses :
   But we will remember the name of JE|HOVAH | our | GOD.
9. They are brought | down and | fallen :
   But we are | risen, and | stand | upright.
10. Save, | O JE|HOVAH!
    Let the King | hear us | when we | call.          Ps. xx.

### CHANT 24.

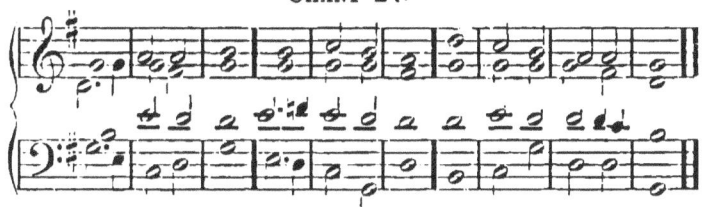

### SELECTION 25.

*That those who love their neighbor and God, will be of the Lord's church, 1—5.*

1. O JEHOVAH, |who · shall a|bide
   In thy | taber|nacle ?
   Who shall dwell in the mountain | of thy | holi|ness ?
2  He that walketh | upright|ly,
   And worketh | righteous|ness,
   And speaketh the | truth | in his | heart.
3  He that slandereth | not · with his | tongue,
   Nor doeth evil to | his com|panion,
   Nor bringeth re|proach up|on his | neighbor.
4. In whose eyes a vile person | is con|temned :
   But he honoreth them that | fear JE|HOVAH.
   He that sweareth to his com|pan·ion, and | changeth | not.
5. He that putteth not out his money to | usu|ry,
   Nor taketh reward against the | inno|cent :
   He that doeth these | things shall | nev·er be | moved.
                                                  Ps. xv

CHANT 25.

SELECTION 26.

[The first 21 verses of this Psalm treat of the Lord's passion.] That thence there will be a church, 1, 2, 5: that the Lord endured from the power of his Divinity, 3, 4: that thereby there will be a church, which will be gathered from all parts, which will worship him, 6—12.

1. I will declare thy | name · to my | brethren :
   In the midst of the congre|gation | will I | praise thee.
2. Ye that fear JEHOVAH, | praise | him ;
   ¹All ye the seed of Jacob, | glori·fy | him ;
   And fear him, all ye the | seed of | Isra|el.
3. For he hath not des|pised · nor ab|horred
   The af|fliction | of · the af|flicted :
4. Neither hath he hid his | face from | him ;
   But when he | cried unto | him, he | heard.
5. My praise shall be of thee in the | great congre|gation :
   I will pay my vows be|fore | them that | fear him.
6. The meek shall eat and be | satis|fied :
   ¹They shall praise JEHOVAH that | seek | him :
   Your | heart shall | live for|ever.
7. All the | ends · of the | earth
   Shall remember and | turn un|to JE|HOVAH :
8. And all the kindreds | of the | nations
   Shall | wor·ship be|fore thy | face.
9. For the kingdom | is JE|HOVAH'S :
   And he is the | ru·ler a|mong the | nations.
10. All they that be fat upon earth shall | eat and | worship :
    ¹All they that go down to the dust shall | bow be|fore him :
    And none can | keep a|live · his own | soul.
11. A seed shall | serve | him ;
    It shall be accounted to the | LORD · for a | gener|ation.
12. They shall come, and declare his | righteous|ness
    To a people that shall be born, that | he hath | done | this.
                                        Ps. xxii. 22.

SELECTIONS AND CHANTS.  21

### CHANT 26. PECULIAR.

Use 2d and 3d divisions alternately.

### SELECTION 27.

That the divine truth perfects man, because it is wisdom, 1—9: that there will be no pride, 10—12: that thus it will be pure and accepted, 13, 14.

1. The law of JE|HOVAH is | perfect,
   Con|vert·ing the | soul :
2. The testimony of JE|HOVAH is | sure,
   Making | wise the | simple.
3. The precepts of JE|HOVAH are | right,
   Re|joic·ing the | heart :
4. The commandment of JE|HOVAH is | pure,
   En|light·ening the | eyes.
5. The fear of JE|HOVAH is | clean,
   En|dur·ing for|ever :
6. The judgments of JE|HOVAH are | truth ;
   They are righteous | alto|gether.
7. More desirable | are they·than | gold ;
   Yea, than | much fine | gold ;
8. Sweeter | also than | honey,
   And the | honey-|comb.

9. Moreover, by them is thy | servant | warned :
   In keeping them is | great re|ward.
10. Who can under|stand his | errors ?
    Cleanse thou me from | secret | faults.
11. Keep back thy servant also from pre|sump·tuous | sins ;
    Let them not rule | over | me.
12. Then shall | I be | upright,
    And I shall be innocent from | great trans|gression.

13. Let the | words·of my | mouth,
    And the meditation | of my | heart,
14. Be acceptable | in thy | sight,
    O JEHOVAH, my rock, and | my re|deemer.

Ps. xix. 7—14.

### Chant 27.

## SELECTION 28.

*A prayer of the Lord to the Father that he would assist and show his power, 1–6*

1. O God, my | heart is | fixed :
   I will sing and give | praise even | with my | glory.
2. Awake, | psalte·ry and | harp :
   I will a|wake | with the | dawn.
3. I will praise thee, O Jehovah, a|mong the | people ;
   And I will sing praises to | thee a|mong the | nations.
4. For thy mercy is great a|bove the | heavens ;
   And thy truth | reacheth | un·to the | clouds.
5. Be thou exalted, O God, a|bove the | heavens ;
   And thy glory a|bove | all the | earth.
6. That thy beloved may | be de|livered ;
   Save with thy right | hand, and | answer | me.    Ps. cviii.

### Chant 28.

## SELECTION 29.

*That they have no spiritual nourishment, which however they will have through the Word, 2—7.*

1. O give thanks to Jehovah ; for | he is | good :
   For his | mercy | is for | ever . . . . .
2. Fools, from the way of | their trans|gression,
   And from their in|i·quities | are af|flicted.
3. Their soul doth ab|hor all | food ;
   And they draw | near·to the | gates of | death.

SELECTIONS AND CHANTS.  23

4. Then they cry unto JEHOVAH | in their | trouble:
   He saveth them | out of | their dis|tresses.
5. He sent his word, and | healed | them;
   And delivered | them from | their de|structions.
6. Let them confess to Je|hovah his | mercy,
   And his wonderful | works·to the | chil·dren of | men.
7. And let them sacrifice sacrifices of | thanksgiv|ing,
   And declare his | works | with re|joicing.   Ps. cvii. 17-22.

CHANT 29.   DOUBLE.

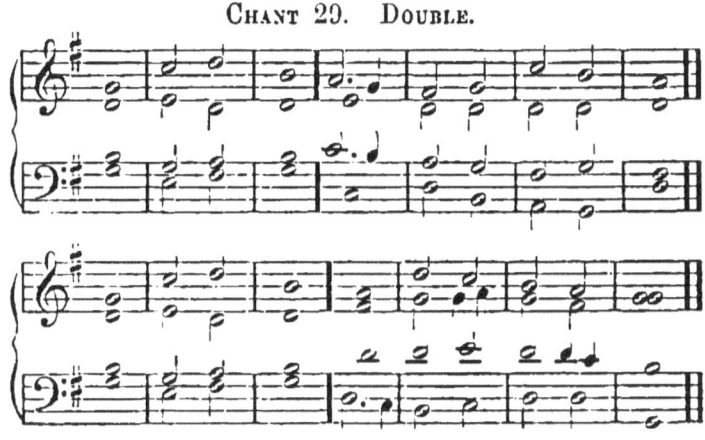

SELECTION 30.

That the Divinity and divine power are the Lord's, 1—4: that his Humanity, being glorified, will rise again, 5—8.

1. JEHOVAH is the portion of my part and | of my | cup:
   Thou | dost main|tain my | lot.
2. The lines are fallen to me in | pleasant | places;
   Yea, I have a | goodly | heri|tage.
3. I will bless JEHOVAH, who hath | given me | counsel:
   My reins also in|struct me | in the | nights.
4. I have set JEHOVAH | always be|fore me:
   Because he is at my right | hand, I shall | not be | moved.
5. Therefore my heart is glad, and my | glory re|joiceth:
   My flesh shall | also | rest in | hope.
6. For thou wilt not leave my | soul in | hell:
   Neither wilt thou suffer thine Holy | One to | see cor|ruption
7. Thou wilt show me the | path of |life:
   In thy | pres·ence is | ful·ness of |joy;
8. At | thy right | hand
   Are | pleas·ures for'ever'more.          Ps. xvi. 5

### CHANT 30.

### SELECTION 31.

*A prayer of the Lord to the Father to assist, that he may see the church established, 1—6.*

1. Praise ye Jah : O give thanks to Jehovah, for | he is | good ;
For his | mercy | is for | ever.
2. Who can utter the mighty | acts · of Je|hovah ?
Who can | show forth | all his | praise ?
3. Blessed are they that | keep | judgment,
And he that doeth | righteous·ness | at all | times.
4. Remember me, | O Je|hovah,
With the favor that thou | bearest | to thy | people.
5. O visit me with | thy sal|vation ;
That I may | see the | good · of thy | chosen ;
6. That I may rejoice in the | joy · of thy | nation ;
That I may glory with | thine in|heri|tance.   Ps. cvi.

### CHANT 31.

### SELECTION 32.

*Celebration of the Lord on account of his mercy, 1, 2 ; that all in the heavens will confess him, 3—5 ; because his kingdom is eternal, 6*

1. Jehovah is gracious, and | full · of com|passion ;
Slow to | an·ger, and | great in | mercy.
2. Jehovah is | good to | all ;
And his mercies are | over | all his | works
3. All thy works shall praise thee, | O Je|hovah ;
And thy | saints shall | bless | thee.
4. They shall speak of the glory | of thy | kingdom,
And | talk | of thy | might.

SELECTIONS AND CHANTS.

5. To make known to the sons of men his | mighty | acts,
And the glorious | maj·esty | of his | kingdom.
6. Thy kingdom is an ever|lasting | kingdom;
And thy dominion through|out all | gener|ations.

Ps. cxlv. 8

CHANT 32. DOUBLE.

SELECTION 33.

Concerning the Lord, that from his Divinity he possesses all good and truth, thus honor and glory, 1—7; that those who are with him will be made glad through his power, 8.

1. The king shall joy in thy strength, | O Je|hovah;
And in thy salvation how | great·ly shall | he re|joice!
2. Thou hast given him his | heart's de|sire,
And hast not with|held · the re|quest · of his | lips.
3 For thou preventest him with the | bless·ings of | goodness:
Thou hast set a crown of pure | gold up|on his | head.
4. He asked life of thee, thou | gavest it | him,
Length of | days for|ev·er and | ever.
5 His glory is great in | thy sal|vation :
Honor and majesty | hast thou | laid up|on him.
6. For thou hast made him most | bless·ed for|ever:
Thou hast made him glad with the | joy · of thy | counte|nance.
7 For the king trusteth | in Je|hovah,
And through the mercy of the Most | High · he shall | not be | moved.
8 Be thou exalted, O Jehovah, in | thine own | strength:
So will we | sing and | praise thy | power.

Ps. xxi. 1—7, 13

C

### Chant 33.

### SELECTION 34.

*Celebration of the Lord for redemption and reformation, 1—7.*

1. Bless Jehovah, | O my | soul;
   And all that is within me, | bless his | holy | **name.**
2. Bless Jehovah, | O my | soul;
   And forget not | all his | bene|fits.
3. Who forgiveth all thine in|iqui|ties;
   Who | healeth | all · thy dis|eases;
4. Who redeemeth thy | life · from de|struction;
   Who crowneth thee with | kindness | and with | **mercies;**
5. Who satisfieth thy | mouth with | good:
   Thy youth is re|newed | like the | eagle's.
6. Jehovah doeth | righteous|ness,
   And judgment for | all that | are op|pressed.
7. He made known his | ways unto | Moses,
   His deeds unto the | chil·dren of | Isra|el.      Ps. ciii

### Chant 34.

### SELECTION 35.

*Prayer to the Father that he would assist against those that wish to destroy him, 1—3; that he will assist against them, and that they will perish, 4, 5; celebration for assistance, 6, 7.*

1. Save me, O | God, by thy | name;
   And | judge me | by thy | strength.
2. Hear my | prayer, O | God;
   Give ear to the | words | of my | mouth.

SELECTIONS AND CHANTS. 27

3. For strangers are risen up against me, and oppressors | seek·
They have | not set | GOD be|fore them.   [for my | soul :
4. Behold, | GOD · is mine | helper :
The LORD is with | them · that up|hold my | soul.
5. He shall reward evil unto mine | ene|mies :
Cut them | off | in thy | truth.
6. I will freely sacrifice | unto | thee :
I will praise thy name, O JE|HOVAH ; | for · it is | good.
7. For he hath delivered me | out · of all | trouble :
And mine eye hath looked up|on mine | ene|mies.    Ps. liv

CHANT 35.

SELECTION 36.

Celebration of the Lord, because he delivers those who trust in him from all evil, 1—10.

1. I will bless JEHOVAH | at all | times :
Continually shall his | praise be | in my | mouth.
2 My soul shall make her | boast · in JE|HOVAH :
The humble shall | hear, | and be | glad.
3. O magnify JE|HOVAH | with me,
And let us ex|alt his | name to|gether.
4. I sought JEHOVAH, | and he | heard me,
And delivered | me from | all my | fears.
5. They looked unto him, and | were en|lightened :
And their | faces were | not a|shamed.
6. This poor man cried, and JE|HOVAH | heard ;
And saved him | out of | all his | troubles.
7. The angel of JE|HO·VAH en|campeth
Around them that fear him, | and de|liv·ereth | them.
8. O taste and see that JE|HOVAH is | good :
Blessed is the | man that | trust·eth in | him.
9. O fear JEHOVAH, | ye his | saints ;
For there is no | want to | them that | fear him.
10. The young lions do lack, and | suffer | hunger :
But they that seek JEHOVAH shall | not want | any | good.
                                            Ps. xxxiv

### Chant 36.

## SELECTION 37.

That the heavens and the earths are the Lord's, that therefore he is to be celebrated, 1—5.

1. Jehovah hath prepared his | throne · in the | heavens;
And his kingdom | ruleth | over | all.
2. Bless | ye Je|hovah,
His angels, | that ex|cel in | strength:
3. That | do his | word,
By hearkening to the | voice | of his | word.
4. Bless ye Jehovah, | all his | hosts;
Ye ministers of | his that | do his | pleasure.
5. Bless Jehovah, all his works, in all places of | his do|minion:
Bless Je|hovah, | O my | soul.     Ps. ciii. 19—22.

### Chant 37.

## SELECTION 38.

Concerning the church which is from the Lord through the Word, 1—3, that those will be in it who are not in falsities and evils, 4—6: that they will receive the Lord, who has overcome the hells, and glorified his humanity, 7—10.

1. The earth is Jehovah's, and the | fulness there|of;
The world, and | they that | dwell there|in.
2. For he hath founded it up|on the | seas,
And established | it up|on the | streams.
3. Who shall ascend into the mountain | of Je|hovah?
Or who shall | stand · in his | holy | place?

## Chant 38.

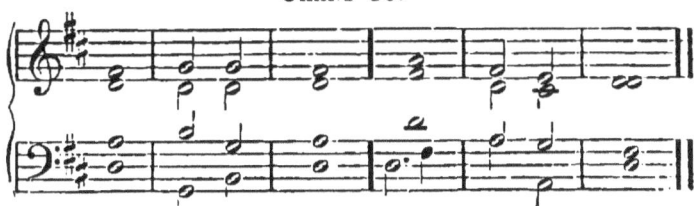

4. He that is clean of hands, and | pure in | heart;
   Who hath not lifted up his soul to vanity, nor sworn de|ceit-
   ful|ly.
5. He shall receive blessing | from Je|hovah,
   And righteousness from the God of | his sal|vation.
6. This is the generation of | them that | seek him,
   That seek thy | face, O | Jacob.

## Chant 39. Ternary.

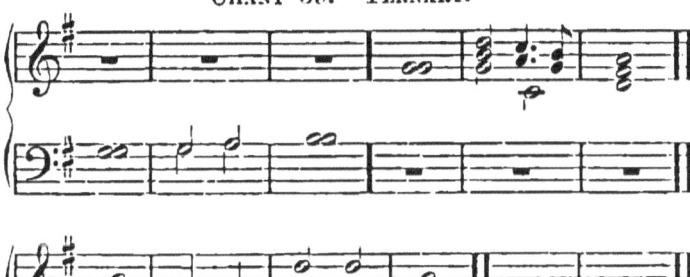

7. Lift up your heads, ♦ O ye | gates;
   And be ye lifted up, ye ever|lasting | doors;
   And the King of | glory | shall come | in.
8. Who is this | King of | glory?
   Jehovah | strong and | mighty,
   Je|hovah | migh·ty in | battle.
9. Lift up your heads, | O ye | gates;
   Even lift up, ye ever|lasting | doors;
   And the King of | glory | shall come | in.
10. Who is this | King of | glory?
    Je|ho·vah of | Hosts,
    He | is the | King of | glory.

Ps. xxiv.

### CHANT 40. DOUBLE.

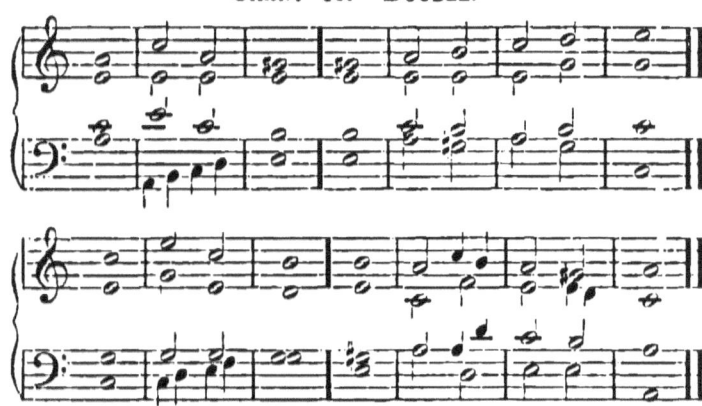

### SELECTION 39.

That the Lord has integrity, purity, and innocence, 1—7, 12: that he has the divine love of saving, 8, 9: that he is in combats with the malicious, 10, 11: that redemption comes when he conquers, 12, 13.

1. Judge me, | O Je|hovah ;
For I have walked in | mine in|tegri|ty :
2. I have trusted also | in Je|hovah ;
I | shall | not | slide.
3. Examine me, O Jehovah, and | prove | me ;
Try my | reins | and my | heart.
4. For thy kindness is be|fore mine | eyes :
And I have | walked | in thy | truth.
5. I have not sat with | vain | persons,
Neither will | I go | in · with dis|semblers.
6. I have hated the congregation of | evil|doers ;
And | will not | sit · with the | wicked.
7. I will wash mine hands in | inno|cence :
So will I compass thine | altar, | O Je|hovah :
8. That I may publish with the voice of | thanksgiv|ing,
And tell of | all thy | wondrous | works.
9. O Jehovah, I have loved the habitation | of thy | house,
⁴And the place | where thine | honor | dwelleth.
10. Gather not my | soul with | sinners,
Nor my | life with | men of | blood :
11. In whose | hands is | mischief,
And their right | hand is | full of | bribes.
12. But as for me, I will walk in mine in|tegri|ty :
Redeem me, and be | merciful | unto | me.
13. My foot standeth in an | even ⁚ place :
In the congregations | will I | bless Je|hovah.    Ps. xxvi.

### CHANT 41. DOUBLE.

### SELECTION 40.

Address of the Lord to the Father, that he does not fear the hells which fight against him, 1—4; concerning his union with the Father, 5—10.

1. Jehovah | is my | light
   And my sal|vation ; | whom · shall I | fear?
2. Jehovah is the | strength · of my | life ;
   Of | whom · shall I | be a|fraid?
3. When the wicked, mine enemies | and my | foes,
   Came upon me to eat up my | flesh, they | stum·bled and | fell.
4. Though an host encamp against me, my | heart · shall not | fear :
   Though war rise against me, in this will | I be | confi|dent.
5. One thing have I desired of Jehovah, | that · will I | seek ;
   That I may dwell in the house of Jehovah | all the | days · of my | life,
6. To behold the beauty | of Je|hovah,
   And to in|quire | in his | temple.
7. For in the | day of | trouble
   He shall | hide · me in | his pa|vilion :
8. In the secret of his tabernacle | shall he | hide me ;
   He shall set me | up up|on a | rock.
9. And now shall mine head be | lifted | up
   Above mine | ene·mies | round a|bout me :
10. Therefore will I offer in his tabernacle sacri|fices of | joy ;
    I will sing, yea, I will sing | praises | to Je|hovah.

Ps. xxvii. 1.—6

### Chant 42. Double.

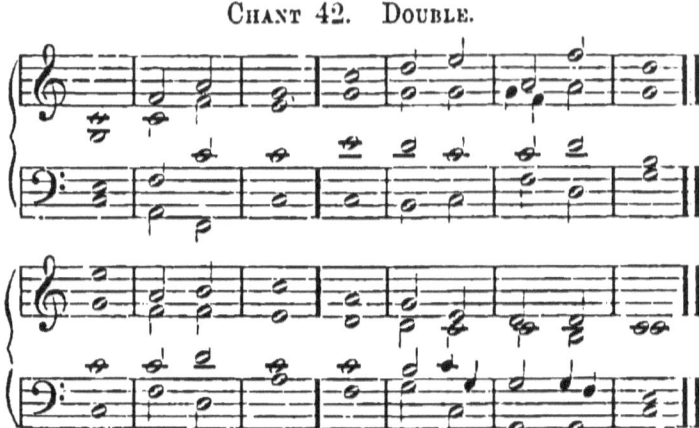

### SELECTION 41.

*That those who are in truths from the Word will adore the Lord, who is the Word, 1—4: concerning the power of divine truth from the Word, 5—12.*

1. Give unto Jehovah, O ye | sons of | God ;
   Give unto Je|hovah | glory and | strength :
2. Give unto Jehovah the glory | of his | name :
   Worship Jehovah in the | beau·ty of | holi|ness.
3. The voice of Jehovah is up|on the | waters :
   The God of glory thundereth : Jehovah | is u] ·on | many | waters.
4. The voice of Jehovah is | power|ful :
   The voice of Jehovah is | full of | majes|ty.
5. The voice of Jehovah | break·eth the | cedars ;
   Yea, Jehovah breaketh the | ce·dars of | Leba|non.
6. He maketh them also to | skip · like a | calf ;
   Lebanon and Sirion like a | young | uni|corn.
7. The voice | of Je|hovah
   Di|vid·eth the | flames of | fire.
8. The voice of Jehovah shaketh the | wilder|ness :
   Jehovah shaketh the | wilder|ness of | Kadesh.
9. The voice of Jehovah maketh the | hinds to | calve,
   And dis|cover|eth the | forests.
10. And | in his | temple
    Doth every one | speak | of his | glory.
11. Jehovah sitteth up|on the | flood ;
    Yea, Jehovah | sitteth | King for | ever.
12. Jehovah will give | strength · to his | people :
    Jehovah will | bless his | peo·ple with | peace     Ps. xxix

SELECTIONS AND CHANTS.     32

## Chant 43. Double.

## SELECTION 42.

*A prayer of the Lord to the Father that he would protect against those who devise evil, 1—5: and who wish to kill him, 6: that hence he has grief of heart, 7—10.*

1. In thee, O Jehovah, do I | put my | trust :
   Let me | never | be a|shamed.
2. Deliver me in thy | righteous|ness :
   Bow down thine ear to me ; de|liv·er me | spee·di|ly.
3. Be thou to me a | rock of | strength,
   For an | house · of de|fence to | save me :
4. For thou art my | rock · and my | fortress ;
   Therefore for thy name's sake | lead · me and | guide | me.
5. Pull me out of the net that they have privily | laid for | me ;
   For | thou | art my | strength.
6. Into thine hand I com|mit my | spirit :
   Thou hast redeemed me, O Je|hovah, | God of | truth.
7. I have hated them that regard lying | vani|ties ;
   But I have | trusted | in Je|hovah.
8. I will be glad and re|joice · in thy | mercy :
   For thou | hast con|sid·ered my | trouble :
9. Thou hast known my soul in ad|versi|ties :
   And | hast not | shut me | up
10. Into the hand of the | ene|my :
    Thou hast set my | foot · in a | large | place.     Ps. xxxi.

Dox. O bless our | God, ye | people,
   And make the | voice · of his | praise · to be | heard
   Who holdeth our | soul in | life,
   And suff·reth | not our | feet · to be | moved.

## Chant 44.

## SELECTION 43.

*That the Lord through trust in the Father is delivered, 1—5: in despair thinking himself deserted, but he is not, 6, 7: trust should be in the Lord, 8—10.*

1. How great | is thy | goodness,
   Which thou hast laid | up for | them that | fear thee;
2. Which thou hast | wrought for | them,
   That trust in thee be|fore the | sons of | men.
3. Thou shalt hide them in the secret | of thy | presence,
   From the | pride | of | man
4. Thou shalt secrete them | in · a pa|vilion,
   From the | strife | of | tongues.
5. Blessed | be Je|hovah;
   For he hath showed me his marvellous | kindness | in a · strong | city.
6. For I | said · in my | haste,
   I am cut | off · from be|fore thine | eyes.
7. But thou heardest the voice of my | suppli|cations,
   When I | cried | unto | thee.
8. O | love Je|hovah,
   All | ye his | godly | ones.
9. Jehovah pre|serv·eth the | faithful,
   And plentifully re|ward·eth the | proud | doer.
10. Be of good courage, and he shall | strength·en your | heart,
    All ye that | hope | in Je|hovah.      Ps. xxxi. 19.

Dox. O give thanks to Jehovah, for | he is | good;
    For his | mercy | is for|ever.      Ps. cxviii. 29.

## CHANT 45.

## SELECTION 44.

Celebration of the Lord, because the church is from him through the Word, 1–9: howsoever the evil may oppose, nevertheless it will be, 10, 11.

1. Rejoice in JEHOVAH, | O ye | righteous;
Praise is | comely| for the | upright.
2. Praise JEHOVAH | with the | harp :
Sing unto him with the| psal·tery | of ten | strings.
3. Sing unto | him a · new | song :
Play skilfully | with a | loud | noise.
4. For the word of JE|HOVAH is | right ;
And all his | works are | done in | truth.
5. He loveth | jus·tice and | judgment :
The earth is full of the | goodness | of JE|HOVAH.
6. By the word of JEHOVAH were the | heavens | made,
And all the host of them by the | breath | of his | mouth.
7. He gathereth the waters of the sea together | as an | heap :
He layeth up the | deep in | storehous|es.
8 Let all the earth | fear JE|HOVAH :
Let all the inhabitants of the world | stand in | awe of | him
9. For he | spake, and it | was :
He commanded, | and it | stood | fast.
10. JEHOVAH bringeth the counsel of the | na·tions to | nought:
He maketh the devices of the | peo·ple of | none ef,fect.
11. The counsel of JEHOVAH | stand·eth for|ever ;
The thoughts of his | heart to | all · gener|ations.
12. Blessed is the nation whose | GOD · is JE|HOVAH ;
The people he hath chosen for his | own in!heri|tance.

Ps. xxxiii

CHANT 46.

## SELECTION 45.

Blessed are those who are of the church, 1—4: that man's own intelligence will effect nothing, 5, 6: that those are saved who trust in the Lord, 7—11.

1. Blessed is the nation whose | God · is Je|hovah ;
   The people he hath chosen for his | own in|heri|tance.
2. Jehovah looketh | from the | heavens :
   He beholdeth | all the | sons of | men.
3. From the place of his | habi|tation,
   He looketh upon all the in|habi·tants | of the | earth.
4. He fashioneth their | hearts a|like ;
   He con|sid ereth | all their | works.

5. There is no king saved by the multitude | of an | host :
   A mighty man is not de|livered | by much | strength.
6. An horse is a vain | thing for | safety :
   Neither shall he de|liv·er by | his great | strength.

7. Behold the eye of Jehovah is upon | them that | fear him,
   Upon them that | hope | in his | mercy.
8. To deliver their | soul from | death,
   And to | keep · them a|live in | famine.
9. Our soul waiteth | for Je|hovah :
   He is our | help | and our | shield.
10. For our heart shall re|joice in | him ;
    Because we have trusted | in his | holy | name.
11. Let thy mercy, O Je|hovah, | be up|on us,
    According | as we | hope in | thee.  Ps. xxxiii. 12.

## CHANT 47.

## SELECTION 46.

*That the Lord preserves the good, and that the evil perish, 1—12.*

1. Come, ye children, hearken | unto | me :
I will teach | you the | fear · of Je|hovah.
2. What man de|sireth | life,
And loveth | days, that he | may see | good?
3. Keep thy | tongue from | evil,
And thy | lips from | speaking | guile.
4. Depart from evil, | and do | good;
Seek | peace, | and pur|sue it.
5. The eyes of Jehovah are up|on the | righteous,
And his ears are | open | to their | cry.
6. The face of Jehovah is against | them that · do | evil,
To cut off the remembrance | of them | from the | earth.
7. The righteous cry, and Je|hovah | heareth ;
And delivereth them | out of | all their | troubles.
8. Jehovah is nigh unto the | broken in | heart ;
And saveth such as | be · of a | contrite | spirit.
9. Many are the afflictions | of the | righteous :
But Jehovah doth de|liver him | from them | all.
10. He keepeth | all his | bones :
Not | one of | them is | broken.
11. Evil shall | slay the | wicked ;
And they that hate the | righteous | shall be | guilty.
12. Jehovah redeemeth the | soul · of his | servants ;
And none of them that | trust in | him · shall be | guilty.

Ps. xxxiv. 11

## CHANT 48.

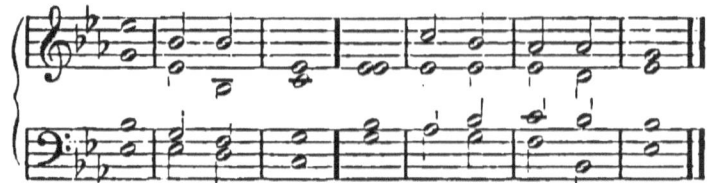

## SELECTION 47.

That it is to be acknowledged that all good and truth are from the Lord, 1—7; that good and truth are with those who acknowledge the Lord, 8: that the Lord protects from evil, and that the evil perish, 9, 10.

1. Thy mercy, O JEHOVAH, is | in the | heavens:
Thy faithfulness | reacheth | un·to the | clouds.
2. Thy righteousness is like the | moun·tains of | GOD;
Thy judgments | are a | great | deep:
3. O JEHOVAH, thou preservest | man and | beast:
How precious is thy | loving | kindness, O | GOD.
4. Therefore the children of men | put their | trust
Under the | shadow | of thy | wings.
5. They shall be abundantly | satis|fied
With the | fatness | of thy | house;
6. And thou shalt | make them | drink
Of the | river | of thy | pleasures.
7. For with thee is the | foun·tain of | life :
In thy | light shall | we see | light.
8. O continue thy kindness unto | them that | know thee;
And thy righteousness | to the | up·right in | heart.

9. Let not the foot of pride | come a|gainst me;
And let not the hand of the | wicked | thrust me | out.
10. There are the workers of in|i·quity | fallen :
They are cast down, and shall | not be | a·ble to | rise.

Ps. xxxvi. 5

## CHANT 49.

## SELECTION 48.

*A comparison between the lot of the evil and the good: that the evil, though they flourish for a short time, finally perish and are cast down into hell, 1, 2. 9—11, 13—17: that the good are saved by the Lord, and are taken up into heaven, 3—8, 12, 18.*

1. Fret not thyself because of | evil|doers,
   Neither be thou envious against the workers | of in|iqui|ty.
2. For they shall soon be cut down | like the | grass,
   And shall | wither | as the green | herb.
3. Trust in JEHOVAH, | and do | good;
   Thou shalt dwell in the land, and in | faith·fulness | shalt be | fed.
4. Delight thyself also | in JE|HOVAH;
   And he shall give thee the de|sires | of thine | heart.
5. Commit thy way | unto JE|HOVAH;
   Trust also in him; and | he shall | bring to | pass.
6. And he shall bring forth thy righteousness | as the | light,
   And thy | judgment | as the | noonday.

7. Rest | in JE|HOVAH,
   And wait | patient|ly for | him.
8. Fret not thyself because of him who prospereth | in his | way,
   Because of the man who bringeth | wick·ed de|vi·ces to | pass.
9. Cease from anger, and for|sake | wrath:
   Fret not thyself in | any | wise· to do | evil.
10. For evildoers shall | be cut | off:
    But those that wait on JEHOVAH, they | shall in|her·it the | earth.
11. For yet a little while, and the | wicked is | not: [not.
    Yea, thou shalt diligently consider his | place, and | it is |
12. But the meek shall in|herit the | earth;
    And shall delight themselves | in · the a|bun·dance of | peace.

13. The wicked plotteth a|gainst the | just,
    And gnasheth up|on him | with his | teeth.
14. The LORD shall | laugh at | him;
    For he seeth | that his | day is | coming.
15. The wicked have drawn | out the | sword,
    And | they have | bent their | bow,
16. To cast down the | poor and | needy,
    To slay such as be of | upright | conver|sation.
17. Their sword shall enter into | their own | heart,
    And their | bows | shall be | broken.
18. A little that a | righteous man | hath
    Is better than the | rich·es of | many | wicked.   Ps. xxxvii.

40 SELECTIONS AND CHANTS.

CHANT 50.

## SELECTION 49.

*A comparison between the lot of the evil and the good: that the evil, although they flourish for a short time, finally perish, and are cast down into hell, 2, 5—7: that the good are saved by the Lord, and are taken up into heaven, 1, 3, 4, 7—18.*

1. A little that a | righteous man | hath,
   Is better than the | rich·es of | many | wicked.
2. For the arms of the wicked | shall be | broken :
   But JEHOVAH | doth up|hold the | righteous.
3. JEHOVAH knoweth the | days · of the | upright :
   And their inheri|tance shall | be for | ever.
4. They shall not be ashamed in the | evil | time :
   And in the days of famine they | shall be | satis|fied.

5. But the wicked | shall | perish,
   And the enemies of JEHOVAH shall be | as the | fat of | lambs·
6. They | shall con|sume ;
   Into smoke shall | they con|sume a|way.

7. The wicked borroweth, and payeth | not a|gain :
   But the righteous | showeth | mer·cy, and | giveth.
8. For such as be blessed of him shall in|her·it the | earth ;
   And they that be cursed of | him shall | be cut | off.
9. The steps of a good man are ordered | by JE|HOVAH,
   And he de|lighteth | in his | way.
10. Though he fall, he shall not be | wholly cast | down ;
    For JEHOVAH doth up|hold him | with his | hand.
11. I have been young, and | now am | old ;
    Yet have I not seen the righteous forsaken, | nor his | seed begging | bread.
12. He is gracious all the | day, and | lendeth ;
    And | his | seed is | blessed.

13. Depart from evil, | and do | good ;
    And | dwell for|ever|more.
14. For JEHOVAH | loveth | judgment,
    And for|saketh | not his | saints.

SELECTIONS AND CHANTS.    41

15. They are pre|served for|ever:
    But the seed of the | wick·ed shall | be cut | off.
16. The righteous shall in|her·it the | land,
    And | dwell there|in for|ever.
17. The mouth of the righteous | speaketh | wisdom,
    And his | tongue doth | talk of | judgment.
18. The law of his GOD is | in his | heart;
    None | of his | steps shall | slide.     Ps. xxxvii. 16–31

CHANT 51.

SELECTION 50.

That the evil, although they flourish for a short time, finally perish, and are cast down into hell, 1, 4—6, 8: that the good are saved by the Lord, and are taken up into heaven, 2, 3, 7, 9—11.

1. The wicked doth | watch the | righteous,
   And | seek to | slay | him.
2. JEHOVAH will not leave him | in his | hand,
   Nor con|demn him | when·he is | judged.
3. Wait on JEHOVAH, and | keep his | way;
   And he shall exalt thee | to in|her·it the | land.
4. When the wicked | are cut | off,
   Thou | shalt | see | it.
5. I have seen the wicked | in great | power,
   And spreading himself | like a | green | bay-tree.
6. Yet he passed away, and, | lo, he was | not;
   Yea, I sought him, but | he could | not be | found.
7. Mark the perfect man, and be|hold the | upright;
   For the | end ·of that | man is | peace.
8. But the transgressors shall be de|stroyed to|gether:
   The end of the | wick·ed shall | be cut | off.
9. But the salvation of the righteous is | of JE|HOVAH:
   He is their | strength · in the | time of | trouble.
10. And JEHOVAH shall | help | them,
    And | shall de|liver | them.
11. He shall deliver them | from the | wicked:
    And save them, be|cause they | trust in | him.

                                           Ps. xxxvii. 32

## CHANT 52.

## SELECTION 51.

*Thanksgiving and celebration of the Father, because he hath helped him, 1—7.*

1. I waited patiently | for JE|HOVAH ;
   And he inclined unto | me, and | heard my | cry.
2. He brought me up also out of an | hor·rible | pit,
   Out | of the | miry | clay,
3. And set my feet up|on a | rock,
   And es|tablished | my | goings.
4. And he hath put a new | song ·in my | mouth,
   Even | praise un|to our | GOD :
5. Many shall | see, and | fear,
   And shall | trust | in JE|HOVAH.
6. Blessed | is that | man,
   That maketh JE|HO|VAH his | trust ;
7. And respecteth | not the | proud,
   Nor such as | turn a|side to | lies.     Ps. xl. 1—4.

## SELECTION 52.

*Thanksgiving and celebration of the Lord to the Father, because He hath helped him, 1—5: that he came into the world, as it is written in the Word, that he might do the will of the Father, 6—8: that he also preached the kingdom of God, and taught, 9, 10.*

1. Many, O JE|HO·VAH, my | GOD,
   Are thy wonderful | works which | thou hast | done :
2. And thy thoughts which are | to·ward | us,
   They cannot be reckoned up in | order | unto | thee.
3. If I would declare and ¦ speak of | them,
   They are | more than | can be | numbered.
4. Sacrifice and offering thou didst | not de|sire :
   Mine | ears | hast thou | opened.
5. Burnt-offering and sin-|offer|ing
   Hast | thou | not re|quired.
6. Then said I, | lo, I | come :
   In the volume of the | book · it is ¦ writ·ten of | me,

SELECTIONS AND CHANTS.   43

7. I delight to do thy will, | O my | God :
Yea, thy | law · is with|in my | heart.
8. I have preached righteousness in the | great congre|gation :
Lo, I have not refrained my lips, | O Je|ho·vah, thou | know-
9. Thy righteousness have I not hid with|in my | heart :   [est.
Thy faithfulness and thy sal|va·tion have | I de|clared.
10. I have not concealed thy kindness | and thy | truth,
From the | great | congre|gation.   Ps. xl. 5.

CHANT 53.

SELECTION 53.

The Lord's confidence from His Divinity as to those that seek to kill him. 1--7, 10, 11: and let those rejoice in the Lord who worship him, 8, 9.

1. Withhold not thou thy mercies from me, | O Je|hovah :
Let thy kindness and thy truth con|tin·ual|ly pre|serve me.
2. For innumerable evils have compassed | me a|bout :
My iniquities have taken hold of me, so that I am not | able | to
3. They are more than the | hairs · of my | head :   [look | up.
Therefore my | heart for|saketh | me.
4. Be pleased, O Jehovah, to de|liver | me ;
O Jehovah, make | haste to | help | me.
5. Let them be ashamed and con|found·ed to|gether,
That seek after my | soul | to de|stroy it.
6. Let them be | driven | backward,
And put to | shame, that | wish me | evil.
7. Let them be desolate for a re|ward · of their | shame,
That say unto | me, A|ha, A|ha.
8. Let all | those that | seek thee,
Re|joice · and be | glad in | thee :
9. Let such as love | thy sal|vation
Say continually, Je|ho·vah be | magni|fied.
10 But I am | poor and | needy :
Yet the Lord | thinketh | upon | me.
11 Thou art my help and my de|liver|er ;
Make no | tar·rying, | O my | God.   Ps. xl. 11

### CHANT 54.

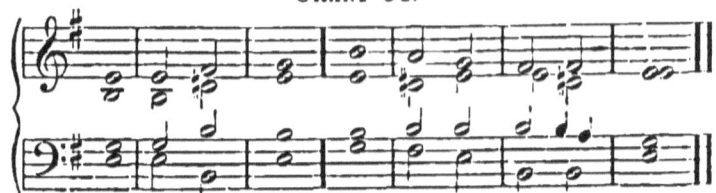

### SELECTION 54.

**The Lord, concerning the integrity of his life.**

1. Hear the right, | O Je|hovah ;
At|tend un|to my | cry.
2. Give ear | un·to my | prayer,
Which goeth not | out of | feigned | lips.
3. Let my sentence come | forth · from thy | presence :
Let thine eyes be|hold the | things · that are | equal.
4. Thou hast | proved mine | heart :
Thou hast | vis·ited | me · in the | night.
5. Thou hast tried me, and | shalt find | nothing :
I am purposed that my | mouth shall | not trans|gress.
6. Concerning the works of man, by the | word · of thy | lips
I have kept from the | paths of | the de|stroyer.
7. Hold my goings | in thy | paths,
That my | footsteps | do not | slip.     Ps. xvii. 1—5

### CHANT 55.

### SELECTION 55.

**Prayer of the Lord to the Father, that he would hear, who is true and just, 1—3; lest he fall in temptations, 4—6: that he desires the ancient state of the church.**

1. Hear my prayer, | O Je|hovah :
Give ear | un·to my | suppli|cations.
2. In thy faithfulness | answer | me,
And | in thy | righteous|ness.
3. And enter not into judgment | with thy | servant :
For in thy sight shall no man | liv·ing be | justi|fied.

SELECTIONS AND CHANTS.  45

4. For the enemy hath perse|cu·ted my | soul :
He hath smitten my | life | down·to the | ground.
5. He hath made me to | dwell in | darkness,
As those that | have been | long | dead.
6. Therefore is my spirit over|whelmed with|in me :
My heart with|in·me is | deso|late.
7. I remember the days of old : I meditate on | all thy | works ;
I muse upon the | work | of thy | hands.
8. I stretch forth my | hands unto | thee :
My soul thirsteth after thee, | as a | thirsty | land.

Ps cxliii.

CHANT 56.

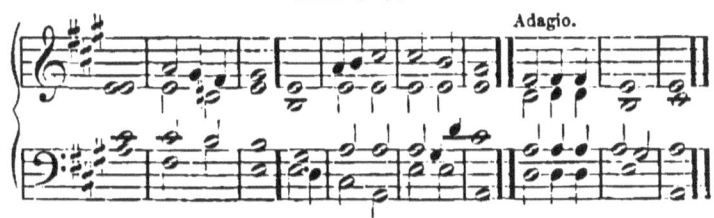

Adagio.

SELECTION 56.

That he who is in temptation, and thence in affliction, is always supported, and thereby vivified, 1—5: that the hells will not succeed, and that they are to be destroyed, 6: that the Lord has integrity, 7, 8.

1. Blessed is he that doth con|sid·er the | poor :
Jehovah will deliver him | in the | day of | evil.
2. Jehovah will pre|serve | him,
And will | keep | him a|live.
3. He shall be blessed up|on the | earth :
And thou wilt not deliver him to the | will of · his | ene|mies.
4. Jehovah will strengthen him upon the bed of | languish'ing :
Thou wilt make | all his | bed · in his | sickness.
5 I said, O Jehovah, be merciful | unto | me :
Heal my soul, for | I have | sinned a|gainst thee.....
6. By this I know that thou | fa·vorest | me,
Because mine enemy doth not | triumph | over | me.
7. And as for me, thou upholdest me in mine in|tegri|ty ;
And settest me be|fore thy | face for | ever.
8. Blessed be Jehovah, God of | Isra'el,
From everlasting | and to | ever|lasting :
A·men and | A|men.        Ps. xli. 1—4, 11—13

## CHANT 57.

### SELECTION 57.

*The grievousness of the Lord's temptations even to despair, 1—4: his prayer to the Father that divine truth may comfort him, 5—8: his consolation, 9, 10.*

1. Judge me, O God, and | plead my | cause,
Against | an un|godly | nation.
2. O de|liver | me
From the man of de|ceit · and in|iqui|ty.
3. For thou art the | God · of my | strength :
Why | dost thou | cast me | off?
4. Why | go I | mourning,
Because of the oppression | of the | ene|my?

5. O send | out thy | light,
And thy | truth; | let them | lead me :
6. Let them bring me unto thy | holy | hill,
And | to thy | taber|nacles.
7. Then will I go unto the | al·tar of | God ;
Unto God the | gladness | of my | joy :
8. And I will | praise | thee
Upon the | harp, O | God, my | God.

9. Why art thou bowed down, | O my | soul?
And why art thou dis|quiet|ed with|in me?
10. Hope in God, for I | yet shall | praise him ;
Who is the health of my | count·enance, | and my | God.
Ps. xliii.

## CHANT 58.

## SELECTION 58.

*That there will be protection from the Lord, when the last judgment comes, and while it lasts, 1—3, 6, 7: that those who are of the church, and in the doctrine of truth, will be saved by the Lord, when he comes, 4, 5: that they will have no fear of the hells, and of infestations thence, 8—10: that this is of the Lord, 10, 11.*

1. God is our | ref·uge and | strength;
   A very | present | help in | trouble.
2. Therefore will not we fear though the | earth · be re|moved,
   And though the mountains be cast | in·to the | midst · of the |
3. Though the waters thereof | roar · and be | troubled,    [seas:
   Though the mountains | shake · with the | swell·ing there|of.
4. There is a river whose streams shall make glad the | cit·y of |
       God,
   The holy place of the tabernacles | of the | Most | High.
5. God is in the midst of her, she shall | not be | moved ;
   God shall help her at the ap|proach | of the | morning.
6. The heathen raged, the | king·doms were | moved :
   He uttered his | voice, the | earth did | melt.
7. Jehovah of | Hosts is | with us ;
   The God of | Jacob | is our | refuge.
8. Come, behold the | works · of Je|hovah ;
   What desolations | he hath | made · in the | earth.
9. He maketh wars to cease to the | end · of the | earth :
   ¹He breaketh the bow, and cutteth the | spear in | sunder :
   He burneth the | char·iots | in the | fire.
10. Be still, and know that | I am | God :
    I will be ex|alt·ed a|mong the | nations ;
    ²I will be ex|alted | in the | earth.
11. Jehovah of | Hosts is | with us ;
    The God of | Jacob | is our | refuge.        Ps. xlvi

## SELECTION 59.

*The Lord's temptations, in which his trust is fixed in the Father, 1, 2: celebration for protection, 3—5.*

1. In God will I | praise his | word ;
   In Jehovah | will I | praise his | word.
2. In God will I | put my | trust :
   I will not fear what | man can | do unto | me.
3. Thy vows are up|on me. O | God :
   I will render | praises | unto | thee.
4. For thou hast delivered my | soul from | death :
   Wilt not thou de|liv·er my | feet from | falling ?
5. That I may | walk be·fore | God
   In the | light | of the | living.        Ps. lvi 10—13

### CHANT 59. DOUBLE.

## SELECTION 60.

Concerning the Lord's kingdom. Celebration of the Lord because he reigns over the church, 1, 2: that he will remove falsities and evils, 3: that he will restore the church, 4, 5: that therefore he will be celebrated, 6: because his kingdom is over all the church, 7, 8: and over the heavens, 9, 10.

1. O clap your hands, | all ye | people ;
   Shout unto | God · with the | voice of | triumph.
2. For JEHOVAH Most | High is | terrible ;
   A great | king·over | all the | earth.
3. He shall subdue the people | under | us,
   And the | nations | un·der our | feet.
4. He shall choose for us our in|heri|tance,
   The excellency of | Jacob | whom he | loved.
5. God is gone | up · with a | shout,
   JEHOVAH with the | sound | of a | trumpet.
6. Sing praises to | God, sing | praises :
   Sing praises | to our | King, sing | praises.
7. For God is the King of | all the | earth :
   Sing ye | prais·es with | under|standing.
8. God reigneth | o·ver the | nations :
   God sitteth upon the | throne · of his | holi|ness.
9. The princes of the people are | gath·ered to|gether,
   The people of the | God of | Abra|ham.
10. For the shields of the earth be|long unto | God ;
    He is | great|ly ex|alted.

Ps. xlvii

SELECTIONS AND CHANTS. 49

### Chant 60. Double.

## SELECTION 61.

Concerning the Lord's spiritual kingdom, how it is to be admired, 1—4, 9, 10: that he dissipates all falsities, 5—8: that the Divine Humanity doeth this, 11, 12.

1. Great | is JE|HOVAH,
   And | greatly | to be | praised,
2. In the city | of our | GOD,
   In the mountain | of his | holi|ness.
3. Beautiful for | situ|ation,
   The joy of all the | earth is | mount | Zion;
4. On the sides of the north, the city of the | great | King:
   GOD is known in her | pal·aces | for a | refuge.
5. For, lo, the kings | were as|sembled;
   They | passed | by to|gether.
6. They saw, and | so they | marvelled;
   They were | trou·bled, and | hast·ed a|way.
7. Fear took hold up|on them | there,
   And pain, as | of a | wo·man in | travail.
8. Thou breakest the | ships of | Tarshish
   With | an | east | wind.
9. As we have heard, so | have we | seen,
   In the city | of JE|HOVAH of | Hosts,
10. In the city | of our | GOD;
    GOD will es|tablish | it for|ever.
11. We have thought of thy | kindness, O | GOD,
    In the | midst | of thy | temple.
12. According to thy | name, O | GOD,
    So is thy praise unto the | ends | of the | earth.    Ps. xlviii.

E

## CHANT 61.

## SELECTION 62.

That the Lord's Divine Humanity dissipates all falsities, 1—3: that thence are all things of heaven and the church, 3—7: because there the Lord reigns, 8.

1. We have thought of thy | kindness, O | God,
   In the | midst | of thy | temple.
2. According to thy | name, O | God,
   So is thy praise unto the | ends | of the | earth.
3. Thy right hand is full of | righteous|ness:
   Mount | Zion | shall re|joice,
4. The daughters of Judah | shall be | glad,
   Be|cause | of thy | judgments.
5. Walk about Zion, and go | round a|bout her:
   Number | ye the | tow·ers there|of:
6. Mark ye | well her | bulwarks;
   Con|sid·er her | pala|ces:
7. That | ye may | tell it
   To the gener|ation | follow|ing:
8. For this God is our God for|ever and | ever:
   He will be our | guide | unto | death.  Ps. xlviii. 9.

## SELECTION 63.

That the Lord will come to those who are of the church, to judgment, 1—6.

1. The mighty God, Jehovah, hath spoken, and | called the earth,
   From the rising of the sun to the | going | down there|of.
2. Out of Zion, the perfection of beauty, | God hath | shined
   Our God shall | come, and shall | not keep | silence.
3. A fire shall de|vour be|fore him;
   And it shall be very tem|pest·uous | round a|bout him.
4. He shall call to the heavens | from a|bove;
   And to the earth, that | he may | judge his | people.
5. Gather my saints together | unto | me;
   Those that have made a covenant with | me by | sacri|fice.

SELECTIONS AND CHANTS. 51

6. And the heavens shall declare his | righteous|ness :
For | GOD is | judge him|self.                    Ps. l.

CHANT 62.   DOUBLE.

SELECTION 64.

The grievousness of the Lord's temptations, in which he prays to the Father, 1—6:
that he wishes to desist from combats on account of their grievousness, 7—9.

1. Give ear to my | prayer, O | GOD ;
   And hide not thy|self · from my | suppli|cation.
2. Attend unto | me, and | hear me :
   I mourn in my com|plaint, and | make a | noise :
3. Because of the voice of the | ene|my ;
   Because of the op|pression | of the | wicked :
4. For they cast upon me in|iqui|ty ;
   And in | anger | do they | hate me.
5. My heart is sorely | pained with|in me :
   And the terrors of | death are | fall·en up|on me.
6 Fearfulness and trembling are | come up|on me ;
   And horror hath | over|whelmed | me.
7 And I said, O that I had | wings · like a | dove ;
   I would fly a|way and | be at | rest.
8. Lo, I would wander | far a|way,
   And re|main · in the | wilder|ness.
9. I would hasten | my es|cape
   From the | windy | storm and | tempest.
10. O that I had | wings · like a | dove ;
    I would fly a|way and | be at | rest.       Ps. lv

## CHANT 63.

## SELECTION 65.

*Prayer of the Lord that he may be purified from the infirmities from the mother, 1—7: that if he is purified from them he will be pure, 8—11.*

1. Have mercy up|on me, O | God,
   According | to thy | loving | kindness.
2. According to the multitude | of thy | mercies,
   Blot | out | my trans|gressions.
3. Wash me thoroughly from mine in|iqui|ties,
   And | cleanse me | from my | sin.
4. For I acknowledge | my trans|gressions;
   And my | sin is | ev·er be|fore me.
5. Against thee, thee only, | have I | sinned,
   And done | evil | in thy | sight.
6. That thou mightest be justified | when thou | speakest,
   And be | clear | when thou | judgest.
7. Behold, I was shapen in in|iqui|ty;
   And in sin | did my | moth·er con|ceive me.
8. Behold, thou desirest truth in the | inward | parts;
   And in the hidden part thou shalt | make·me to | know | wisdom.
9. Purge me with hyssop, and I | shall be | clean:
   Wash me, and I | shall be | whit·er than | snow.
10. Make me to hear | joy and | gladness,
    That the bones which thou hast | broken | may re|joice.
11. Hide thy face | from my | sins,
    And blot out all | mine in|iqui|ties.           Ps. li.

## SELECTION 66.

*A prayer of the new church to the Lord, that he would come and lead them, 1; because of their affliction, 2—5.*

1. Turn us a|gain, O | God;
   And cause thy face to | shine; and | we·shall be | saved.
2. O Jehovah, | God of | Hosts,
   How long wilt thou be angry a|gainst the | prayer·of thy | people?

SELECTIONS AND CHANTS.   53

3. Thou feedest them with the | bread of | tears ;
And givest them tears to | drink in | great | measure.
4. Thou makest us a | strife · to our | neighbors :
And our enemies | laugh a|mong them|selves.
5. Turn us again, O | GOD of | Hosts ;
And cause thy face to | shine ; and | we · shall be | saved.

Ps. lxxx. 3.

CHANT 64.

SELECTION 67.

That if he is purified from the infirmities from the mother, he will be pure, 1 ; and be holy, 2, 3 : that thus he will teach divine truths, 4—6 : not external worship, but internal, 7, 8 : that he will institute a church, in which there will be worship from good, 9—11.

1. Create in me a clean | heart, O | GOD ;
And renew a right spirit | in the | midst of | me.
2. Cast me not a|way · from thy | presence ;
And take not thy | Holy | Spirit | from me.
3. Restore unto me the joy of | thy sal|vation ;
And let a free | spirit | hold me | up.
4 I will teach trans|gress·ors thy | way ;
And sinners shall be con|verted | unto | thee.
5 Deliver me from blood, O GOD, thou GOD of | my sal|vation :
My tongue shall sing a|loud · of thy | righteous|ness.
6. O LORD, open | thou my | lips ;
And my mouth | shall show | forth thy | praise.
7. For thou desirest not sacrifice, | else · would I | give :
Thou delightest not | in burnt-|offer|ing.
8. The sacrifices of GOD are a | broken | spirit :
A broken and contrite heart, O GOD, | thou wilt | not des-|
9. Do good in thy good pleasure | unto | Zion :   [pise.
Build thou the | walls · of Je|rusa|lem.
10. Then shalt | thou be | pleased
With the sacri|fi·ces of | righteous|ness.
11. With burnt-offering and whole burnt-|offer|ing :
Then shall they offer | bul·locks up|on thine | altar.

Ps. li 10.

E*

## SELECTIONS AND CHANTS.

### CHANT 65. DOUBLE.

### SELECTION 68.

Celebration of the Father by the Lord on account of help, 1—5: and on account of union, 6—8.

1. Hear my cry, O God; at|tend · to my | prayer :
   From the end of the earth will I | cry | unto | thee :
2. When mine heart is | over|whelmed,
   Lead me to the | Rock · that is | high·er than | I.
3. For thou hast been a | shelter | for me,
   A strong tower | from the | ene|my.
4. I will abide for ever in thy | taber|nacle :
   I will trust in the | covert | of thy | wings.
5. For thou, O God, hast | heard my | vows :
   Thou hast given me the heritage of | those that | fear thy |
6. Thou wilt add days to the | days · of the | king ;    [name.
   His years as gener|a·tion and | gener|ation.
7. He shall abide before | God for | ever :
   O prepare mercy and | truth ; let | them pre|serve him.
8. So will I sing praise unto thy | name for | ever,
   That I may | dai·ly per|form my | vows.        Ps. lxi

### SELECTION 69.

Confession that the Divine alone has power, and that succor is therefrom, 1—6.

1. My soul, wait thou only | upon | God ;
   For my expec|tation | is from | him.
2. He only is my rock and | my sal|vation ;
   My defence ; | I shall | not be | moved.

SELECTIONS AND CHANTS. 55

3. In GOD is my salvation | and my | glory:
The rock of my strength; my | refuge | is in | GOD.
4. Trust in him at all | times, ye | people;
Pour out your heart before him: GOD | is a | refuge | for us.
5. GOD hath spoken onee: twiee have | I heard | this;
That power be|longeth | unto | GOD.
6. Also unto thee, O LORD, be|longeth | merey:
For thou renderest to man ae|eording | to his | work.

Ps. lxii.

CHANT 66.

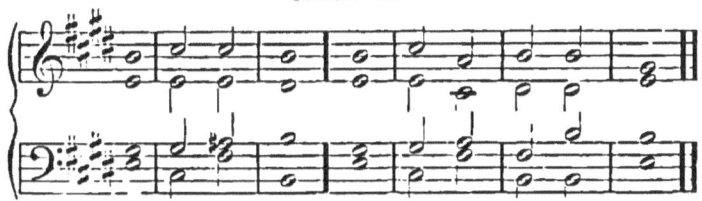

SELECTION 70.

That from the unition of the Divinity and Humanity in the Lord, there will be a a church, which will be in all truth from him, and safe from infestation of falsities.

1. Praise waiteth for thee, O | GOD, in | Zion;
And unto thee shall the | vow | be per|formed.
2. O thou that | hearest | prayer,
Unto | thee shall | all flesh | come.
3. Iniquities pre|vail a|gainst me:
Our transgressions, thou shalt | purge | them a|way.
4. Blessed is the man whom | thou dost | choose,
And cause to approach, that | he may | dwell·in thy | courts.
5 We shall be satisfied with the goodness | of thy | house,
With the | ho·liness | of thy | temple.
6. By terrible things in | righteous|ness,
Wilt thou answer us, O | GOD of | our sal|vation:
7 The confidence of all the | ends·of the | earth,
And of them that are afar | off up|on the | sea.
8 Who by his strength setteth | fast the | mountains,
Being | girded | with | power.
9. Who stilleth the | noise·of the | seas,
The noise of their waves, and the | tumult | of the | people
10. They also that dwell in the uttermost parts are a|fraid·at
thy | tokens;
Thou makest the outgoings of the morning and | evening |
to re|joice. Ps. lxv.

## CHANT 67. DOUBLE.

## SELECTION 71.

That the Lord by grievous temptations was united to his Divinity, 1—4: that thus divine truth from the Lord would be with men, 5—9: that this was effected by his integrity, 10—12.

1. Thou, O | God, hast | proved us;
Thou hast | tried · us as | sil·ver is | tried.
2. Thou broughtest us | in·to the | net;
Thou laidst af|flic·tion up|on our | loins.
3. Thou hast caused men to ride | o·ver our | heads:
We went through | fire | and through | water.
4. But thou hast | brought us | out
In|to a | wealthy | place.
5. I will go into thy house | with burnt-|offerings;
I will | pay to | thee my | vows,
6. Which my | lips have | uttered,
And my mouth hath spoken, | when I ·| was in | trouble.
7. I will offer unto thee burnt sacrifices of fatlings, with | in·cense of | rams;
I will | offer | bullocks with | goats.
8. Come and hear, all ye that | fear | God;
And I will declare what | he hath | done · for my | soul.
9. I cried unto him | with my | mouth,
And he was ex|tolled | with my | tongue.
10. If I regard iniquity | in my | heart,
The | Lord | will not | hear.
11. But verily | God hath | heard;
He hath attended | to the | voice ·of my | prayer.

12. Blessed be God, who hath not turned a|way my | prayer,
Nor his | mercy | from | me.          Ps. lxvi. 10

### Chant 68.

### SELECTION 72.

That the Lord is in his church: there is protection there against falsities and evils, 1—4: that in the Jewish church there is no longer any truth, 5, 6: that the Lord is about to execute a judgment, by which the evil will perish, and the good will be saved, 7—10, 12: let the Lord be worshipped, 11.

1. In Judah | is God | known;
His name is | great in | Isra|el.
2. In Salem also is his | taber|nacle,
And his | dwelling | place in | Zion.
3. There brake he the arrows | of the | bow,
The shield, and the | sword, | and the | battle.
4. Thou art more glorious and | excel|lent,
Than the | mountains | of | prey.
5. The stouthearted are spoiled; they have | slept their | sleep:
And none of the men of | might have | found their | hands.
6. At thy rebuke, O | God of | Jacob,
Both chariot and horse are cast | in·to a | deep | sleep.
7. Thou, even thou, | art·to be | feared:
And who may stand in thy | sight when | thou art | angry.
8. Thou didst cause judgment to be | heard from | heaven;
The earth | feared, | and was | still:
9. When God a|rose to | judgment,
To save | all the | meek·of the | earth.
10. Surely the wrath of | man shall | praise thee:
The remainder of | wrath shalt | thou re|strain
11. Vow, and pay unto Je|ho·vah your | God:
Let all that be around him bring a present to | him that
is·to be | feared.
12. He shall cut off the | spir·it of | princes:
He is terrible | to the | kings·of the | earth.     Ps. lxxvi.

## SELECTIONS AND CHANTS.

### CHANT 69.

### SELECTION 73.

That the new church is from the Lord, and all the goods and truths therein, 1–4.

1. Behold the man whose | name · is The | BRANCH;
And he shall grow | up out | of his | place:
2. And he shall build the temple | of JE|HOVAH;
Even he shall build the | temple | of JE|HOVAH:
3. And he shall | bear the | glory;
And shall sit and | rule up|on his | throne;
4. And he shall be a priest up|on his | throne;
And the counsel of peace shall | be be|tween them | both.
Zech. vi. 12.

### CHANT 70.

### SELECTION 74.

That when He is liberated the gospel will be preached, 1, 2: because then those of the church are to be saved who will worship him, 3–8.

1. I will praise the name of GOD | with a | song,
And will magnify | him with | thanksgiv|ing.
2. This also shall | please JE|HOVAH,
Better than an ox or bullock | that hath | horns and | hoofs
3. The humble shall | see, and be | glad:
And your heart shall | live that | seek | GOD:
4. For JEHOVAH | heareth the | poor,
And despiseth | not his | prison|ers.
5. Let the heavens and earth | praise | him,
The seas, and | all that | moveth there|in:

SELECTIONS AND CHANTS.  59

6. For God will | save | Zion,
And will | build the | cities of | Judah :
7. That they may | dwell there|in,
And | have it | in pos|session.
8. The seed also of his servants shall in|herit | it :
And they that love his | name shall | dwell there|in.

Ps. lxix. 30.

CHANT 71.  DOUBLE.

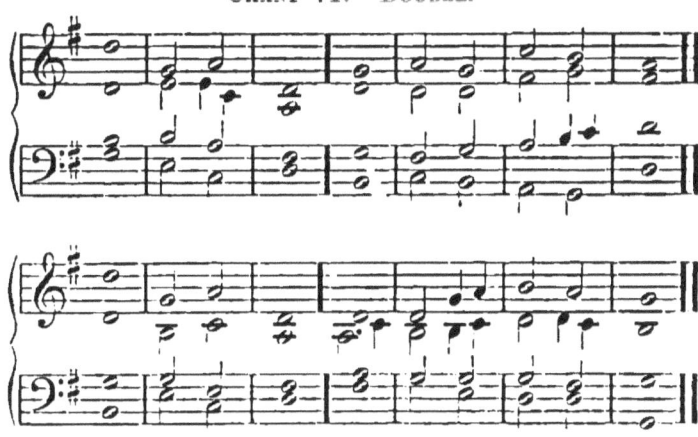

SELECTION 75.

That the universal church will acknowledge and worship the Lord from joy of heart, 1—6, 8 : also every thing of the church, 7.

1. God be merciful unto | us, and | bless us,
And cause his | face to | shine up|on us ;
2. That thy way may be | known upon | earth,
Thy saving | health a|mong all | nations.
3. Let the people praise | thee, O | God ;
Let all the | people | praise | thee.
4. O let the | na tions be | glad,
And | let them | sing for | joy :
5. For thou shalt judge the people | righteous|ly,
And govern the | nations up|on the | earth.
6. Let the people praise | thee, O | God ;
Let all the | people | praise | thee.
7. The earth shall | yield her | increase :
God, | our own | God, shall | bless us.
8. God shall | bless | us,
And all the ends of the | earth shall | fear | him.   Ps. lxvii

## SELECTIONS AND CHANTS.

### CHANT 72. DOUBLE.

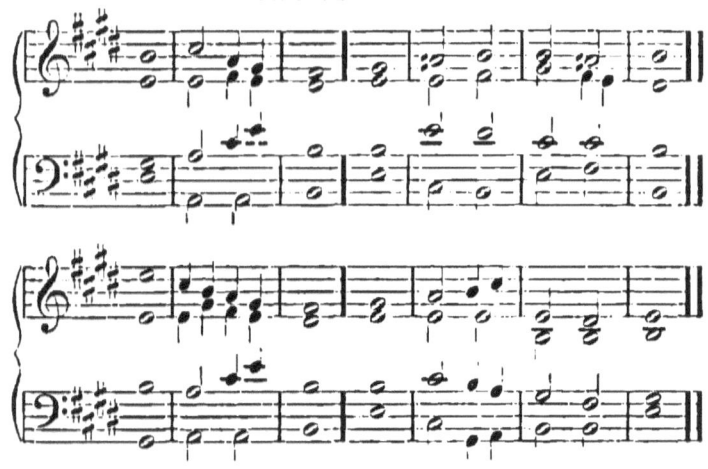

### SELECTION 76.

Concerning the Lord's kingdom, 1, 2, 4; the blessed state of those who are of his kingdom, 3, 6, 7; the worship of him from love and faith from eternity, and afterwards, 5; the greatness and extent of his dominion, 8—12.

1. Give the king thy | judg·ments, O | GOD ;
   And the king's | son thy | righteous|ness.
2. He shall judge thy people with | righteous|ness,
   And | thy | poor with | judgment.
3. The mountains shall bring | peace · to the | people,
   And the little | hills by | righteous|ness.
4. He shall judge the | poor · of the | people,          [pressor.
   And save the children of the | need·y, and | crush · the op-|
5. They shall fear thee while sun and | moon en|dure,
   Through|out all | gener|ations.
6. He shall come down like rain up|on the · mown | grass ;
   As | show·ers that | wa·ter the | earth.
7. In his days shall the | righteous | flourish,
   And abundance of | peace · till the | moon · be no | more.
8. He shall have dominion also from | sea to | sea ;
   And from the river | to the | ends · of the | earth.
9. They that dwell in the wilderness shall | bow be|fore him ;
   And his enemies | shall | lick the | dust.           [sents :
10. The kings of Tarshish and of the isles | shall bring | pre-
    The kings of Sheba and | Se·ba shall | offer | gifts.
11. Yea, all kings shall bow | down to | him ;
    All | na·tions shall | serve | him :
12. For he shall deliver the needy | when he | crieth ;
    The poor also, and | him that | hath no | helper.   Ps. lxxii

SELECTIONS AND CHANTS. 61

CHANT 73.

## SELECTION 77.

The desire and love of the Lord that he may be united to his Divinity, 1—9: that those will perish by the falsities of evil, who lay snares for him, 10, 11: that then there will be salvation from the Lord, and rejection of the evil, 12, 13.

1. O GOD thou | art my | GOD;
    Early | will I | seek | thee.
2. My soul thirsteth for thee, my flesh | longeth for | thee,
    In a dry and thirsty land, | where no | water | is:
3. To see thy power | and thy | glory,
    So as I have seen thee | in the | sanctu|ary.
4. Because thy kindness is | better than | life,
    My | lips shall | praise | thee.
5. Thus will I bless thee | while I | live :
    I will lift | up my | hands · in thy | name.
6. My soul shall be satisfied as with | marrow and | fatness;
    And my mouth shall | praise · thee with | joyful | lips.

7. When I remember thee up|on my | bed,
    And meditate | on thee | in the | watches;
8. Because thou hast | been my | help,
    Therefore in the shadow of thy | wings will | I re|joice.
9. My soul followeth | hard after | thee :
    Thy right | hand up|holdeth | me.
10. But those that seek my | soul, to de|stroy it,
    Shall go into the | lower | parts · of the | earth.
11. They shall | fall · by the | sword :
    They shall | be a | por·tion for | foxes.
12. But the king shall re|joice in | GOD;
    Every one that | sweareth by | him shall | glory :
13. But the | mouth of | them
    That | speak lies | shall be | stopped.     Ps. lxiii.

Dox. Salvation belongeth | to JE|HOVAH;
    Thy blessing | is up|on thy | people.     Ps. iii. 8.

F

## CHANT 74. PECULIAR.

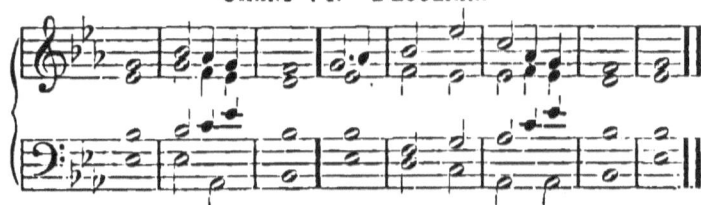

## SELECTION 78.

The greatness and extent of the Lord's dominion, 1, 2 : protection and redemption, 2—4 : the blessed state of those who are of his kingdom, 5—8 : that they acknowledged the Divine Humanity from eternity, in which is all salvation, 9, 10 : celebration of him, 11, 12.

1. Yea, all kings shall bow | down to | him;
   All | nations | shall | serve | him :
2. For he shall deliver the needy | when he | crieth ;
   The poor also, and | him that | hath no | help|er.
3. He shall spare the | poor and | needy,
   And shall | save the | souls · of the | need|y.
4. He shall redeem their soul from deceit and | vio|lence :
   And precious | shall their | blood be | in his | sight.
5. And | he shall | live ;
   And to him shall be given | of the | gold of | She|ba :
6. Prayer also shall be made for him con|tin·ual|ly ;
   And | daily | shall he | be | praised.
7. There shall be an handful of | corn · in the | earth,
   Up|on the | top · of the | moun|tains :
8. The fruit thereof shall shake like | Leba|non ;
   And they of the city shall | flourish | like the | grass · of
9. His name shall en|dure for|ever :                [the | earth
   His name shall | be con|tin·ued as | long · as the | sun :
10. And they shall be | blessed in | him ;
    All nations | shall | call him | bless|ed.
11. Blessed be JEHOVAH GOD, the GOD of | Isra|el,
    Who | only | doeth | wondrous | things :
12. And blessed be his glorious | name for|ever ;
    And let the whole | earth be | filled · with his | glo|ry.

A·men and | A|men.

Ps. lxxii. 11

SELECTIONS AND CHANTS. 65

### CHANT 75. DOUBLE.

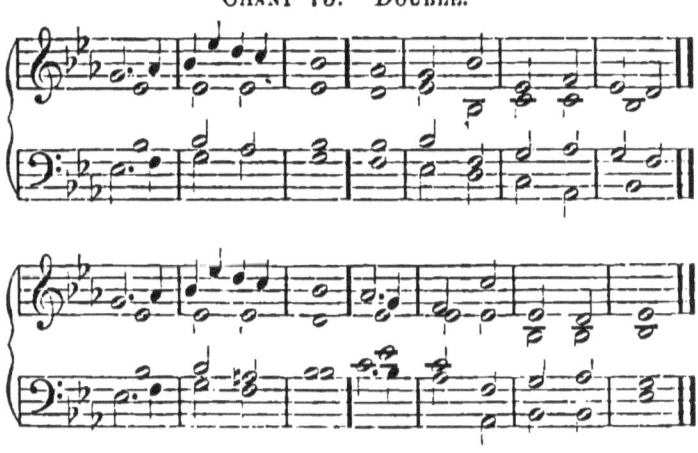

### SELECTION 79.

Unition of the Lord to the Father: that thus there will be no insurrection from the hells, nor against the church, 1, 2: that thus heaven will serve him, 3, 4: that there will then be no fear of the hells when the Divinity is united to the Humanity, 5—10.

1. Because thou hast made Je|hovah my | refuge,
   The Most | High, thy | habi|tation;
2. There shall no | evil be|fall thee,
   Neither shall any | plague come | nigh thy | dwelling.
3. For he shall give his angels | charge over | thee,
   To keep | thee in | all thy | ways.
4. They shall bear thee | up·in their | hands,
   Lest thou dash thy | foot a|gainst a | stone.
5. Thou shalt tread upon the | lion and | adder:
   The young lion and the dragon shalt thou | trample | un- der | feet.
6. Because he hath set his | love up|on me,
   Therefore will | I de|liver | him:
7. I will | set him·on | high,
   Because | he hath | known my | name.
8. He shall | call up|on me,
   And | I will | answer | him:
9. I will be | with him·in | trouble;
   I will deliver | him, and | honor | him.
10. With length of days will I | satis·fy | him,
    And will | show him | my sal|vation.   Ps. xci. 9.

## CHANT 76.

## SELECTION 80.

Concerning the Lord's love and desire towards the church and heaven, 1—5; that the church from trust in the Lord increases in truths and goods, 6—8; that its blessedness arises from trust in the Lord, 9—15.

1. How lovely are thy | taber|nacles,
   O Je|ho|vah of | hosts.
2. My soul longeth, yea, even fainteth for the | courts · of Je|hovah :
   My heart and my flesh crieth | out · for the | living | God.
3. Yea, the sparrow hath | found an | house,
   And the swallow a | nest | for her|self;
4. Where she may | lay her | young;
   Thine altars, O Jehovah of Hosts, my | King | and my |
5. Blessed are they that | dwell · in thy | house :   [God.
   They will | still be | praising | thee.
6. Blessed is the man whose | strength · is in | thee,
   In whose | heart | are the | ways.
7. Who passing through the vale of weeping | make · it a | well :
   The early rain also doth | cover | it with | blessings.
8. They go from | strength to | strength ;
   Every one appeareth be|fore | God in | Zion.
9. O Jehovah, God of Hosts, | hear my | prayer :
   Give | ear, O | God of | Jacob.
10. Behold, O | God, our | shield ;
    And look upon the | face of | thine an|ointed.
11. For a day | in thy | courts
    Is | better | than a | thousand.
12. I had rather sit at the threshold of the | house · of my | God,
    Than to dwell in the | tents of | wicked|ness.
13. For Jehovah God is a | sun and | shield :
    Jehovah | will give | grace and | glory.
14. No good will | he with|hold
    From them that | walk | upright|ly.
15. O Je|ho·vah of | Hosts,
    Blessed is the | man that | trust·eth in | thee. Ps. lxxxiv

SELECTIONS AND CHANTS.

### CHANT 77.

### SELECTION 81.

Prayer of the new church to the Lord, that he would come and lead them, 1: that the Lord instituted the church, and that he reformed it by truths from the Word, 2—5: and yet that falsities begin to destroy it, 6, 7: that the Lord would come and restore it, and that thus it will be vivified, 8—13.

1. Turn us again, O | God of | Hosts;
And cause thy face to | shine; and | we · shall be | saved.
2. Thou hast brought a | vine · out of | Egypt:
Thou hast cast out the | hea·then, and | planted | it.
3. Thou preparedst | room be|fore it,
And didst cause it to take deep | root, and it | filled the | land.
4. The hills were covered with the | shadow | of it,
And the boughs thereof were | like the | ce·dars of | God.
5. It sent out its boughs | un·to the | sea,
And its | branches | un·to the | river.
6. Why hast thou broken | down its | hedges,
So that all they who | pass · by the | way do | pluck it?
7. The boar out of the | wood doth | waste it,
And the wild beast of the | field de|voureth | it.
8. Return, we beseech thee, O | God of | hosts.
Look down from heaven, and be|hold, and | visit this | vine
9. And the vineyard which thy right | hand hath | planted,
And the branch that thou | madest | strong · for thy|self.
10. It is burned with fire, it | is cut | down:
They perish at the re|buke · of thy | counte|nance.
11. Let thy hand be upon the man of | thy right | hand,
Upon the son of man thou | madest | strong · for thy;self.
12. So will not we go | back from | thee:
Quicken us, and we will | call up|on thy | name.
13. Turn us again, O Jehovah | God of | Hosts;
Cause thy face to | shine; and | we · shall be | saved.

Ps. lxxx. 7.

F*

66 SELECTIONS AND CHANTS.

CHANT 78. DOUBLE.

SELECTION 82.

Prayer of the Lord to the Father, that he would assist in temptations, 1—8: because thus there will be worship of the Lord, and confession of him, 9—12.

1. Bow down thine ear, | O Je|hovah ;
  Hear me, for | I am | poor and | needy.
2. Preserve my soul, for | I am | godly :
  O thou my God, save thy servant | that doth | trust in | thee.
3. Be merciful unto | me, O | Lord ;
  For I cry unto | thee | all the | day.
4. Rejoice the | soul · of thy | servant :
  For unto thee, O Lord, do | I lift | up my | soul.
5. For thou, O Lord, art good, and ready | to for|give ;
  And plenteous in mercy to | all that | call up|on thee.
6. Give ear, O Jehovah, | to my | prayer ;
  And attend to the | voice · of my | suppli|cations.
7. In the day of my trouble I will | call up|on thee ;
  For | thou wilt | answer | me.
8. Among the gods there is none like unto | thee, O | Lord :
  Neither are there any | works like | unto thy | works.
9. All nations whom | thou hast | made,
  Shall come and worship be|fore thy | face, O | Lord :
10. And shall glorify thy name : for | thou art | great,
  And doest wondrous things : | thou art | God a|lone.
11. Teach me thy way, O Jehovah ; I will | walk · in thy | truth :
  Unite my | heart to | fear thy | name.
12. I will praise thee, O Lord my God, with | all my | heart :
  And I will glorify thy | name for | ever|more.  Ps. lxxxvi

## SELECTIONS AND CHANTS. 67

### CHANT 79. TERNARY.

### SELECTION 83.

Worship of the Lord, and confession of him, 1, 2: that the hells rise up, 3, 4: that they will be overthrown through assistance, 5—7.

1. Teach me thy way, | O JE|HOVAH;
   I will | walk · in thy | truth :
   Unite my | heart to | fear thy | name.
2. I will praise thee, O | LORD my | GOD,
   With | all my | heart;
   And I will glorify thy | name for | ever | more.
3. For great is thy mercy | toward | me :
   And thou | hast de|livered
   My | soul · from the | lowest | hell.
4. O GOD, the proud are risen | up a|gainst me,
   And the assemblies of the violent have | sought my | soul;
   And have | not set | thee be|fore them.
5. But | thou, O | LORD,
   Art a GOD full of com|pas·sion and | gracious,
   Long suffering, and plenteous in | mercy | and in | truth.
6. O turn unto me, and have | mercy up|on me :
   Give thy strength ' un·to thy | servant,
   And save the | son of | thine | handmaid.
7. Show me a ' to·ken for | good,
   That those who hate me may see, and | be a|shamed :
   For thou, O JEHOVAH, hast | helped · me, and | com · forted
   | me.                                          Ps. lxxxvi. 11

### CHANT 80. DOUBLE.

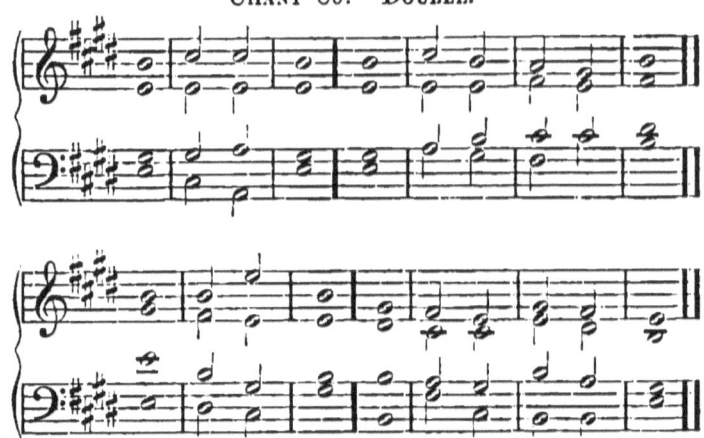

### SELECTION 84.

That all divine truth is from the Lord, 1, 2; that unition is with the Divine Humanity; wherefore from him is divine truth, 3—5; that thus the Lord has all power, 6—10.

1. I will sing of the mercies of Je|ho·vah for | ever:
With my mouth will I make known thy faithfulness to | all | gener|ations.
2. For I have said, Mercy shall be built | up for | ever:
Thy faithfulness shalt thou establish | in the | very | heavens.
3. I have made a covenant | with my | chosen ;
I have | sworn to | David my | servant:
4. Thy seed will I es|tablish for | ever,
And build up thy | throne to | all gener|ations.
5. And the heavens shall praise thy wonders, | O Je|hovah!
Thy faithfulness also in the congre|gation | of the | saints:
6. For who in heaven can be compared | to Je|hovah?
Who among the sons of God | likened | to Je|hovah?
7. God is greatly to be feared in the assembly | of the | saints,
And to be reverenced by | all that | are a|bout him.
8. O Jehovah, God of Hosts, who is like unto thee, | mighty | Jah?
Or to thy | faith·fulness | round a|bout thee?
9. Thou rulest the raging | of the | sea:
When the waves thereof a|rise, thou | stillest | them.
10. Thou hast broken Rahab in pieces as | one that·is | slain ;
Thou hast scattered thine enemies | with the | arm·of thy | strength.           Ps. lxxxix

SELECTIONS AND CHANTS. 69

CHANT 81. DOUBLE.

SELECTION 85.

That the all of heaven and the church is from the Lord, 1, 2, 4: that he has all power, 3: blessed is he that trusts in the Lord, 5—8.

1. The heavens are thine, the earth is | also | thine :
   The world and the fulness thereof, | thou hast | founded | them.
2. The north and the south, thou hast cre|ated | them :
   Tabor and Hermon shall re|joice | in thy | name.
3. Thou hast a | mighty | arm :
   Strong is thy hand, | high is | thy right | hand.
4. Justice and judgment are the sup|port · of thy | throne :
   Mercy and truth shall | go be|fore thy | face.
5. Blessed is the people that know the | joyful | sound :
   They shall walk, O JEHOVAH, in the | light · of thy | counte-|
6. In thy name shall they re|joice · all the | day ;   [nance.
   And in thy righteousness | shall they | be ex|alted.
7. For thou art the glory | of their | strength :
   And in thy favor our | horn shall | be ex|alted.
8. For JEHOVAH is | our de|fence ;
   And the HOLY ONE of | Isra|el our | King.  Ps. lxxxix. 11.

SELECTION 86.

Celebration of the Father by the Lord for assistance in temptations.

1. O praise JEHOVAH, | all ye | nations;
   Praise | ye him, | all ye | people :
2. For his kindness is | great · toward | us :
   And the truth of JEHOVAH is for|ever. | Praise ye | JAH.
   Ps. cxvii

CHANT 82.

SELECTION 87.

The Father speaking to the Lord, or the Divinity to his Humanity: that by unition with him he will have omnipotence against the hells, 1—8: that there will be an eternal union with him, 9—12: that though they of the church should fall off, yet there will be an eternal union with him, 13—20.

1. Then thou | spak·est in | vision,
   To thine | HOLY | ONE, and | saidst,
2. I have laid help upon | one ·that is | mighty;
   I have exalted one | chosen | out of · the | people.
3. I have found | Da·vid my | servant:
   With my holy oil have | I an|ointed | him.
4. With whom my hand shall | be es|tablished;
   Also mine | arm shall | strengthen | him.
5. The enemy shall not ex|act up|on him,
   Nor the son of | wicked|ness af|flict him.
6. And I will beat down his foes be|fore his | face,
   And will | plague | them that | hate him.
7. But my faithfulness and my mercy | shall be | with him:
   And in my name his | horn shall | be ex|alted.
8. I will set his hand also | in the | sea,
   And his | right hand | in the | rivers.
9. He shall cry unto me, Thou | art my | FATHER,
   My GOD, and the | Rock of | my sal|vation.
10. Also I will make | him my | firstborn,
    Higher than the | kings | of the | earth.
11. My mercy will I keep for him for ' ever | more;
    And my covenant | shall stand | fast with | him.
12. His seed also will I make to en|dure for | ever,
    And his throne | as the | days of | heaven.
13. If his children for|sake my | law,
    And | walk not | in my | judgments;
14. If they pro|fane my | statutes,
    And | keep not | my com|mandments;
15. Then will I visit their transgression | with the | rod,
    And their in|iqui|ty with | stripes.

SELECTIONS AND CHANTS.    71

16. Yet my kindness will I not make | void from | him,
    Nor suffer my | faithful|ness to | fail.
17. My covenant will | I not | break,
    Nor alter the thing that | is gone | out of · my | lips.
18. Once have I sworn by my | holi|ness,
    That I will | not lie | unto | David.
19. His seed shall en|dure for | ever,
    And his | throne · as the | sun be|fore me.
20  It shall be established for ever | as the | moon,
    And a | faithful | witness in | heaven.    Ps. lxxxix. 19.

CHANT 83.

SELECTION 88.

Prayer of the Lord to the Father that he may not fail in temptations, 1, 2; that he has confidence that he shall be delivered from the hells, which greatly assault him, 3—9.

1. Hear me | speedi|ly,
   O Je|ho·vah, my | spirit | faileth.
2. Hide not thy | face from | me,
   Lest I be like them that go | down in|to the | pit.
3. Cause me to hear thy kindness | in the | morning ;
   For in | thee | do I | trust.
4. Cause me to know the way wherein | I should | walk ;
   For I lift up my | soul | unto | thee.
5  Deliver me. O Jehovah, from mine | ene|mies :
   I flee unto | thee to | hide | me.
6  Teach me to | do thy | will ;
   For | thou | art my | God.
7. Thy | Spir·it is | good :
   Lead me into the | land of | upright|ness.
8. Quicken me, O Jehovah, for thy | name's | sake :
   For thy righteousness' sake bring my | soul | out of | trouble.
9. And of thy mercy cut off mine | ene|mies ;
   And destroy them that afflict my | soul ; for I | am thy
        servant.                                Ps. cxliii. 7

CHANT 84. DOUBLE.

## SELECTION 89.

Concerning the unition of the Lord's Divinity with his Humanity, which is the Sabbath: celebration on account of the Father's coöperation with him, 1—5: that the evil do not understand this, 6: that though they flourish, they still perish, 7—9; that thus there will be divine omnipotence against the insurgents, 10—12: that the church thence will flourish, 13—15: and will celebrate the Lord, 16.

1. It is a good thing to give | thanks · to Je|hovah,
   And to sing praises unto thy | name, O | thou Most | High;
2. To show forth thy loving kindness | in the | morning,
   And thy | faith·fulness | in the | night:
3. Upon an instrument of ten strings, and upon the | psalte|ry;
   Upon the | harp with | solemn | sound.
4. For thou, O Jehovah, hast made me glad | through thy ¦ work;
   I will triumph in the | works | of thy | hands.
5. O Jehovah, how | great · are thy | works,
   And thy | thoughts are | very | deep.
6. A brutish man | knoweth | not;
   Neither doth a | fool | under·stand | this.
7. When the wicked | spring · as the | grass,
   And when all the workers of in|iqui|ty do | flourish;
8. It is that they shall be de|stroyed for | ever:
   But thou, O Jehovah, art | high for | ever | more.
9. For, lo, thine enemies, O Jehovah, for, lo, thine enemies shall be | lost;
   All the workers of in|i·quity | shall be | scattered.
10. But my horn shalt thou exalt like an | uni|corn's:
    I shall be an|ointed | with fresh | oil.

SELECTIONS AND CHANTS. 73

11. Mine eyes | al·so shall | see
My desire | on mine | ene|mies :
12. Mine | ears shall | hear
My desire of the wicked | that rise | up a|gainst me.
13. The righteous shall flourish | like the | palm-tree :
He shall grow like a | ce·dar in | Leba|non.
14. Those that be planted in the | house·of Je|hovah,
Shall flourish in the | courts | of our | God.
15. They shall still bring forth | fruit·in old | age ;
They shall be | fat and | flourish|ing :
16. To show that Je|ho·vah is | upright ;
My rock, and there is no un|righteous|ness in | him.
Ps. xcii.

CHANT 85.

SELECTION 90.

That by the unition of the Divinity and the Humanity in the Lord, heaven and the church will endure to eternity, 1—4 : the joy of those who are in divine truths thence, 5, 6 : the Word established in the church, 7

1. Je|hovah | reigneth ;
He is | clothed with | majes|ty.
2. Jehovah is | clothed with | strength ;
He hath | girded | him|self.
3. The world also | is es|tablished,
That | it can|not be | moved.
4. Thy throne is es|tablished of | old :
Thou | art from | ever|lasting.
5. The floods have lifted up, | O Je|hovah,
¹The floods have lifted | up their | voice ;
The floods | shall lift | up their | waves.
6. Than the voices of | many | waters,
¹Than the mighty | waves·of the | sea,
Mightier | is Je|ho·vah on | high.
7. Thy testimonies are | very | sure :
Holiness becometh thine house, O Je|hovah, | for | ever.
Ps. xciii

## Chant 86.

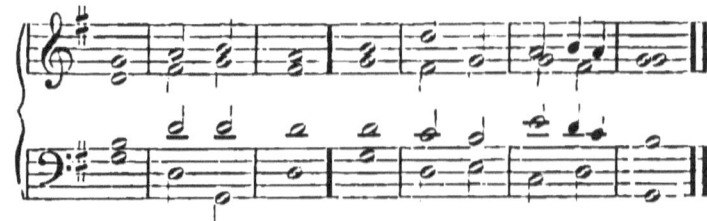

### SELECTION 91.

Perception of the Lord from his Divinity, that a church will exist and flourish, which will acknowledge him, walking in truths, 1—7.

1. I will hear what Jehovah | God will | speak :
 For he will speak | peace un|to his | people,
2. And | to his | saints :
 But let them not | turn a|gain to | folly.
3. Surely his salvation is near | them that | fear him ;
 That glory may | dwell | in our | land.
4. Mercy and truth are | met to|gether ;
 Righteousness and | peace have | kissed each | other.
5. Truth shall spring | out · of the | earth ;
 And righteousness | shall look | down · from the | heavens.
6. Yea, Jehovah | shall give | good ;
 And our | land shall | yield her | increase.
7. Righteousness shall | go be|fore him
 And shall set us | in the | way · of his | steps.   Ps. lxxxv. 8.

## Chant 87.

### SELECTION 92.

[For the spiritual sense, see Selection 6.]

1. Righteous art thou, | O Je|hovah ;
 And | upright | are thy | judgments.
2. Thy testimonies, that thou | hast com|manded,
 Are | right·eous and | very | faithful.

3. My zeal hath con|sumed | me,
Because mine enemies | have for|gotten thy | words.
4. Thy word is | very | pure;
Therefore thy | servant | loveth | it.
5. I am | small·and des|pised :
I do | not for|get thy | precepts.
6. Thy righteousness is an everlasting | righteous|ness;
And thy | law | is the | truth.
7. Trouble and anguish have taken | hold on | me :
Yet thy com|mand·ments are | my de|lights.
8. The righteousness of thy testimonies is | ever|lasting :
Make me to under|stand, and | I shall | live.    Ps. cxix. 137.

## Chant 88.

## SELECTION 93.

*Celebration of the Father by the Lord, who is to be united to him, 1 : that thus there will be protection from every assault, 2—6 : that thus there will be no insurrection from the hells, 7, 8.*

1. He that dwelleth in the secret place | of the·Most | High,
Shall abide under the | shadow | of·the Al|mighty.
2. I will say of Jehovah, He is my refuge | and my | fortress;
My God, in | him | will I | trust.
3. Surely he shall deliver thee from the | snare·of the | fowler,
And from the | noisome | pesti|lence.
4. He shall cover thee with his feathers, and under his | wings·
    shalt thou | trust :
His truth shall | be thy | shield and | buckler.
5. Thou shalt not be afraid for the | terror by | night;
Nor for the | ar·row that | fli·eth by | day;
6. Nor for the pestilence that | walketh in | darkness;
Nor for the destruction | that doth | waste at | noonday.
7. A thousand shall fall at thy side, and ten thousand at | thy
    right | hand;
But it | shall not | come nigh | thee.
8. Only with thine eyes shalt | thou be|hold,
And see the re·ward | of the | wicked.    Ps. xci

### CHANT 89. DOUBLE.

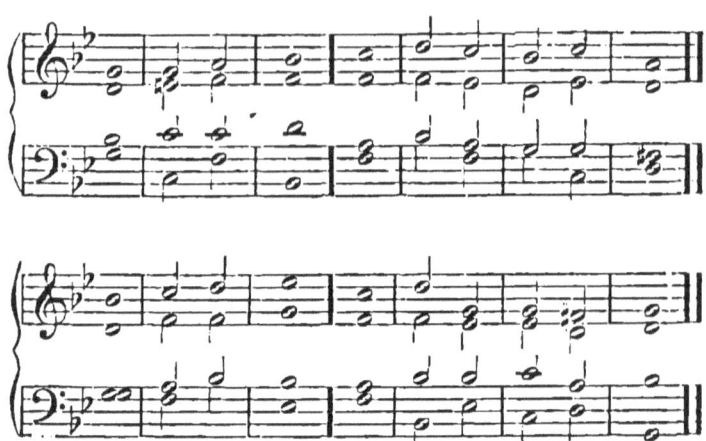

### SELECTION 94.

That the Lord, for the sake of the church, will come to judge, 1—4: that his Divinity will assist against the evil, and in temptation, 5—8: that the evil rise up, and wish to kill, 9, 10; but by help from his Divinity they will perish, 11, 12.

1. Blessed is the man whom thou dost | chasten, O | JAH;
And dost | teach him | out · of thy | law:
2. That thou mayest give him rest from the | days of | evil,
Until the | pit be | digged · for the | wicked.
3. For JEHOVAH will not cast | off his | people,
Neither will he for|sake · his in|heri|tance.
4. But judgment shall return unto | righteous|ness;
And all the upright in | heart shall | follow | it.

5. Who will rise up for me against the | evil|doers?
Who will stand up for me against the workers | of in|iqui|ty?
6. Unless JEHOVAH had | been my | help,
My soul had | almost | dwelt in | silence.
7. When I said, my | foot was | slipping,
Thy mercy, O JE|HOVAH, | held me | up.
8. In the multitude of | my | thoughts with|in me,
Thy comforts | do de|light my | soul.

9. Shall the throne of iniquity be | joined to | thee,
Which frameth | mischief | by a | law?
10. They gather themselves together against the | soul · of the righteous,
And con|demn the | inno·cent | blood.

SELECTIONS AND CHANTS. 77

11. But JEHOVAH is | my de|fence ;
    And my GOD is the | rock | of my | refuge :
12. And he shall bring upon them their own in|iqui|ty,
    And shall cut them off in their own wickedness : JEHOVAH
    our | GOD shall | cut them | off.  Ps. xciv. 12.

CHANT 90.

SELECTION 95.

Concerning the coming of the Lord, and concerning the glorification of his Humanity, that then he will have power, 1, 2: that thence is salvation, 3: that the predictions must be fulfilled, 4, 5: celebration of him, and joy therefor, 6—10: that he comes to judgment, 11, 12.

1. O sing unto JEHOVAH a | new | song ;
   For he | hath done | mar·vellous | things :
2. His right hand, and his | holy | arm,
   Hath gotten | him the | victo|ry.
3. JEHOVAH hath made known | his sal|vation :
   His righteousness hath he openly | showed · in the | sight · of
     the | nations.
4. He hath remembered his mercy | and his | truth
   Toward the | house of | Isra|el.
5. All the | ends · of the | earth
   Have seen the sal|vation | of our | GOD.
6. Make a joyful noise unto JEHOVAH, | all the | earth ;
   Make a loud noise, and re|joice, and | sing | praise.
7. Sing unto JEHOVAH | with the | harp,
   With the | harp, and the | voice · of a | psalm.
8. With trumpets and | sound of | cornet,
   Make a joyful noise be|fore the | King JE|HOVAH.
9. Let the sea roar, and the | ful·ness there|of ;
   The world, and | they that | dwell there|in.
10. Let the floods | clap their | hands :
    Let the | moun·tains be | joy·ful to|gether.
11. In the presence | of JE|HOVAH ;
    For he | com·eth to | judge the | earth.
12. He shall judge the world in | righteous|ness,
    And the | peo·ple in | upright|ness.  Ps. xcviii.

G*

## SELECTIONS AND CHANTS.

### CHANT 91. DOUBLE.

### SELECTION 96.

Celebration of the Lord by his church, that it is he alone who has power and glory, 1—9: that he will come to judgment, so that heaven and the church may worship him from joy of heart, 10—13: that he will come to judgment, 14, 15.

1. O sing unto Je|hovah a | new | song:
   Sing unto Je|hovah | all the | earth.
2. Sing unto Jehovah, | bless his | name:
   Proclaim his sal|va·tion from | day to | day.
3. Declare his glory a|mong the | nations,
   His wonders a|mong | all the | people.
4. For Jehovah is great, and greatly | to be | praised;
   He is to be | feared a|bove all | gods.
5. For all the gods of the people are | vani|ties:
   But Je|hovah | made the | heavens.
6. Honor and majesty are be|fore his | face;
   Strength and beauty are | in his | sanctu|ary.
7. Give unto Jehovah, O ye kindreds | of the | people,
   Give unto Je|hovah | glo·ry and | strength.
8. Give unto Jehovah the glory | of his | name:
   Bring an offering, and | come in|to his | courts.
9. [3]O worship Jehovah in the beauty of | holi|ness:
   Tremble be|fore him, | all the | earth.
10. Say among the nations, Je|hovah | reigneth:
    The world | al·so shall | be es|tablished,
11. That it can|not be | moved:
    He shall judge the | people | righteous|ly.

SELECTIONS AND CHANTS.   79

12. Let the heavens rejoice, and let the | earth be | glad :
    Let the sea | roar, and the | ful·ness there|of.
13. Let the field be joyful, and all that | is there|in :
    Then shall all the | trees · of the | wood re|joice.
14. In the presence of JEHOVAH ; | for he | cometh,
    For he |com·eth to | judge the | earth.
15. He shall judge the world with | righteous|ness,
    And the | people | with his | truth.           Ps. xcvi.

CHANT 92.

SELECTION 97.

Celebration of the Lord, who is the Word, and the God of the church, 1, 2: that he is to be worshipped, 3, 5, 10 : because he has power and justice, 4: that the Word is from him, 6, 7 : that he is the redeemer, 8, 9.

1. JEHOVAH reigneth, let the | people | tremble:
   He sitteth above the cherubim, | let the | earth be | moved.
2. JEHOVAH is | great in | Zion ;
   And he is | high a|bove · all the | people.
3. Let them praise thy great and terrible name, for | it is | holy :
   The king's strength | also | loveth | judgment.
4. Thou shalt establish | equi|ty ;
   Thou executest judgment and | righteous|ness in | Jacob.
5. Exalt ye JE|HO·VAH our | GOD,
   And worship at his | foot·stool ; for | he is | holy.
6. Moses and Aaron a|mong his | priests,
   And Samuel among them that | call up|on his | name.
7. They called upon JEHOVAH, and he | answered | them :
   He spake unto them | in the | cloudy | pillar.
8. They kept his testimonies, and the ordinance | that he | gave them :
   Thou answeredst them, | O JE|HO·VAH our | GOD :
9. Thou wast a GOD that for|gavest | them,
   Though thou tookest | ven·geance of | their in|ventions.
10. Exalt JEHOVAH our GOD, and worship at his | holy | moun-tain ;
    For JE|HO·VAH our | GOD is | holy.         Ps. xcix.

## CHANT 93. DOUBLE.

## SELECTION 98.

**Prayer of the Lord when in temptations even to despair, 1: that those who are out of the church expect mercy, that they may become a church, 2—8: that he hears and pities them, and that of them a church will be formed, 9—12.**

1. My days are like a shadow | that de|clineth,
   And I am | withered | like the | grass.
2. But thou, O Jehovah, shalt en|dure for | ever;
   And thy remembrance to gener|a·tion and | gener|ation.
3. Thou shalt arise, and have | mer·cy on | Zion:
   For the time to favor her, yea, the | set | time is | come
4. For thy servants take pleasure | in her | stones,
   And | fa·vor the | dust there|of.
5. And the nations shall fear the | name · of Je|hovah,
   And all the | kings · of the | earth thy | glory.
6. When Jehovah shall | build up | Zion,
   He shall ap|pear | in his | glory.
7. He will regard the prayer of the | desti|tute,
   And | not des|pise their | prayer.
8. This shall be written for the gener|a·tion to | come;
   And the people which shall be cre|ated | shall praise | Jah.
9. For he hath looked down from the height of his | sanctu|ary:
   From heaven did Je|ho·vah be|hold the | earth.
10. To hear the groaning of the | prison|er;
    To re|lease the | sons of | death;
11. To declare the name of Je|ho·vah in | Zion,
    And his | praise · in Je|rusa|lem;

SELECTIONS AND CHANTS.    81

12. When the people are | gath·ered to|gether.
    And the | king·doms to | serve JE|HOVAH      Ps cii. 11.

CHANT 94.  DOUBLE.

SELECTION 99.

That when they are in knowledges, they will be admitted into temptations, and be preserved, 2—10.

1. O give thanks unto JEHOVAH ; for | he is | good :
   For his | mercy | is for | ever.
2. They that go down to the | sea in | ships,
   That do | business | in great | waters ;
3. These see the | works · of JE|HOVAH,
   And his | wonders | in the | deep.
4. For he commandeth, and raiseth the | stormy | wind,
   Which lifteth | up the | waves there|of.
5. They mount up to heaven, they go down again | to the | deep :
   Their soul is | melt·ed be|cause of | trouble.
6. They reel and stagger like a | drunken | man ;
   And all their | wis·dom is | swallowed | up.
7. Then they cry unto JEHOVAH | in their | trouble,
   And he bringeth them | out of | their dis|tresses.
8. He maketh the | storm a | calm,
   And the | waves there|of are | still.
9. Then are they glad be|cause · they are | quiet ;
   And he bringeth them unto the | ha·ven of | their de|sire.
10. Let them confess to JE|HO·VAH his | mercy,
    And his wonderful | works · to the | chil·dren of | men.
                                   Ps. cvii. 1, 23—31

### CHANT 95.

### SELECTION 100.

*That all are taught from the literal sense of the Word, each according to the states of his intelligence, 1—15.*

1. He sendeth forth | springs into | brooks :
   They | run a|mong the | mountains.
2. They give drink to every | beast · of the | field :
   The wild | asses | quench their | thirst.
3. By them shall the fowls of the | heavens | dwell :
   They shall | sing a|mong the | branches.
4. He watereth the mountains | from his | chambers :
   The earth is | filled · with the | fruit · of thy | works.
5. He causeth the grass to | grow · for the | cattle,
   And herb | for the | ser·vice of | man :
6. That he may bring forth food | out · of the | earth ;
   And wine that maketh | glad the | heart of | man :
7. With oil to make his | face to | shine,
   And bread which doth sus|tain the | heart of | man.
8. The trees of Je|ho·vah are | full ;
   The cedars of | Leba·non, | which he | planted.
9. Where the birds | make their | nests :
   As for the stork, the | fir-trees | are her | house.
10. The high mountains are a refuge | for the · wild | goats ;
    And the | rocks | for the | conies.
11. He made the moon for ap|pointed | seasons :
    The sun doth | know his | going | down.
12. Thou makest darkness, and | it is | night ;
    Wherein all the beasts of the | forest | creep | forth.
13. The young lions | roar for | prey,
    And | seek their | food from | God.
14. The sun riseth, they gather them|selves to|gether,
    And | lay them | down · in their | dens.
15. Man goeth | forth · to his | work,
    And to his | labor | until | evening.

SELECTIONS AND CHANTS.  83

16. Bless thou Je|hovah, | O my | soul :
  Halle|lujah : | Praise ye | Jah.   Ps. civ. 10—23, 35.

CHANT 96.

SELECTION 101.

Celebration of the Lord, 1, 2; that he has omnipotence, 3—5; that he is to be worshipped, 6, 7: that they should not be like the nation from Jacob, who alienated themselves from the Lord, 8—10; with whom therefore there was no conjunction at all, 11.

1. O come, let us | sing · to Je|hovah ;
  Let us make a joyful noise to the | Rock of | our sal|vation.
2. Let us come before his presence with | thanksgiv|ing,
  And make a joyful | noise unto | him with | psalms.
3. For a great God | is Je|hovah,
  And a great | King a|bove all | gods.
4. In his hand are the | depths · of the | earth ;
  And the | heights · of the | moun·tains are | his.
5. The sea is his, | and he | made it ;
  And his | hands did | form · the dry | land.
6. O come, let us worship | and bow | down ;
  Let us kneel before the | face · of Je|ho·vah our | Maker.
7. For he | is our | God ;
  And we are the people of his pasture, | and the | sheep · of his | hand.
8. To-day if ye will hear his voice, harden | not your | heart,
  As in the provocation, in the day of temptation | in the | wilder|ness :
9. When your fathers | tempted | me,
  Proved | me, and | saw my | work.
10. Forty years was I grieved with this gener|ation, and | said,
  It is a people that do err in their heart, and they | have not | known my | ways.
11. Unto whom I | sware · in my | wrath,
  That they should not | enter | in·to my | rest.   Ps. xcv

### CHANT 97. DOUBLE.

## SELECTION 102.

*That the church is in ignorance and want of truth, 1—8.*

1. O give thanks to JEHOVAH; for | he is | good :
   For his | mercy | is for | ever.
2. Those that sit in darkness and the | shad·ow of | death,
   Being bound in af|fliction | and in | iron :
3. Because they rebelled against the | words of | GOD,
   And contemned the | counsel | of the · MOST | HIGH :
4. Therefore he brought down their | heart with | labor;
   They fell down, and | there was | none to | help.
5. Then they cried unto JEHOVAH | in their | trouble :
   He saved them | out of | their dis|tresses.
6. He brought them out of darkness and the | shad·ow of | death;
   And he | brake their | bands a|sunder.
7. Let them confess to JE|HO·VAH his | mercy,
   And his wonderful | works · to the | chil·dren of | men.
8. For he hath broken the | gates of | brass,
   And cut the | bars of | i'ron a|sunder.

Ps. cvii. 1, 10—16.

## SELECTION 103.

*Concerning the new church which the Lord redeemed, 1—3: that it is in the falsities of ignorance, 4—9.*

1. O give thanks to JEHOVAH; for | he is | good :
   ⁴For his | mercy | is for | ever.
2. Thus shall the redeemed of JE|HOVAH | say,
   Whom he hath redeemed from the | hand · of the | ene|my ;

SELECTIONS AND CHANTS. 85

3. And hath gathered them | out·of the | lands,
From the east, and from the west, from the | north, and from the ·| south.
4. They wandered in the wilderness in a | des·olate | way:
They found no | cit·y of | habi|tation.
5. They were | hung·ry and | thirsty,
And their | soul did | faint with|in them.
6. Then they cried unto JEHOVAH | in their | trouble:
He delivered them | out of | their dis|tresses.
7. And he led them forth in a | straight | way,
To go to a | cit·y of | habi|tation.
8. Let them confess to JE|HO·VAH his | mercy,
And his wonderful | works · to the | chil·dren of | men.
9. For he satisfieth the | thirsty | soul,
And filleth the | hungry | soul with | good.  Ps. cvii.

CHANT 98.

SELECTION 104.

Prayer of the Lord, that he may not fail in temptations, 1, 2: that the church and heaven may not perish, but be established, 3—7.

1. He weakened my | strength · in the | way;
He | shortened | my | days.
2. I said, O my GOD, take me not away in the | midst·of my | days:
Thy years are to gener|a·tions of | gener|ations.
3. Of old hast thou laid the foundation | of the | earth;
And the heavens | are the | work·of thy | hands.
4. They shall perish, but | thou shalt | stand:
Yea, all of them | shall wax | old · like a | garment.
5. As a vesture | shalt thou | change them,
And | they | shall be | changed.
6. But thou | art the | same,
And thy | years shall | have no | end.
7 The children of thy servants | shall con|tinue,
And their seed shall be es|tab·lished be|fore thy | face.
Ps. cii. 23—28

### Chant 99. Ternary.

### SELECTION 105.

*That a new church is to be established, which will acknowledge the Lord.*

1. Come, and let us re|turn · to Je|hovah :
For he hath torn, and | he will | heal us ;
He hath smitten, and | he will | bind us | up.
2. After two days will | he re|vive us :
In the third day he will | raise us | up ;
And we shall | live | in his | sight.
3. Then | shall we | know,
³If we follow | on to | know Je|hovah.
4. His going forth is prepared | as the | morning :
And he shall come unto us | as the | rain ;
As the latter and former | rain un|to the | earth.   Hos. vi

### Chant 100.

### SELECTION 106.

*Concerning the church established by the Lord from the gentiles, 1, 2: that its falsities are removed, and that the goods of love and charity succeed, 3–6: because the church is from the Lord, who will instruct those that are in ignorance, 7, 8.*

1. When Israel went | out of | Egypt,
The house of Jacob from a | peo·ple of | strange | language,
2. Judah was his | sanctu|ary,
Is|rael | his do|minion.
3. The sea | saw, and | fled :
The | Jordan | was turned | back.

SELECTIONS AND CHANTS.  87

4. The mountains | skipped like | rams,
   The hills | like the | young of the | flock.
5. What ailed thee, O thou sea, | that thou | fleddest?
   Thou Jordan, that | thou wast | turned | back?
6. Ye mountains, that ye | skipped like | rams?
   Ye hills | like the | young of the | flock?
7. Tremble, thou earth, at the presence | of the | Lord,
   At the presence | of the | God of | Jacob;
8. Who turned the rock into a | pool of | waters,
   The flint | in to a | foun tain of | waters.            Ps. cxiv

CHANT 101.

SELECTION 107.

Joy that there is a new church, which will trust in the Lord, 1—5; who will preserve it from evils, 6—8: that the Lord by grievous temptations was united to his Divinity, 9, 10.

1. Make a joyful noise unto God, | all the | earth :
   Sing forth the | honor | of his | name;
2. Make his praise | glori|ous :
   Say unto God, How | ter rible | are thy | works.
3. Through the greatness | of thy | power,
   Shall thine enemies sub|mit them|selves unto | thee.
4. All the earth shall worship thee, and | sing unto | thee :
   They shall | sing un|to thy | name.
5. Come and see the | works of | God :
   He is terrible in his doing | toward the | chil dren of | men.
6. He turned the sea into | dry | land :
   They went | through the | flood on | foot :
7. There did we re|joice in | him :
   He ruleth | by his | power for|ever :
8. His eyes be|hold the | nations :
   Let not the re|bel lious ex|alt them|selves.
9. O bless our | God, ye | people :
   And make the | voice of his | praise to be | heard :
10. Who holdeth our | soul in | life ;
    And suffereth | not our | feet to be | moved.       Ps. lxvi

## CHANT 102.

## SELECTION 108.

The joy of the church concerning the coming of the Lord, with whom is divine truth, 1—6: that all who are in falsities will be removed, 7: joy that the Lord is the God of heaven and the church, 8, 9: that he will protect those that are in truths from him, 10—13.

1. JEHOVAH reigneth, let the | earth re|joice ;
    Let the | many | isles be | glad.
2. Clouds and darkness are | round a|bout him :
    Justice and judgment are the found|ation | of his | throne.
3. A fire goeth be|fore his | face,
    And burneth up his | ene·mies | round a|bout.
4. His lightnings en|lightened the|world :
    The | earth did | see and | tremble.                        [VAH,
5. The mountains melted like wax at the presence | of JE|HO-
    At the presence of the | LORD of | all the | earth.
6. The heavens declare his | righteous|ness ;
    And all the | people | see his | glory.

7. Confounded be all they that serve graven | imag|es,
    That boast themselves of idols : | worship | him, all | gods.
8. Zion heard, and was glad ; and the daughters of | Judah re|joiced,
    Because of thy | judgments, | O JE|HOVAH.
9. For thou, O JEHOVAH, art high above | all the | earth ;
    Thou art exalted | far a|bove all | gods.
10. Ye that love JE|HOVAH, hate | evil :
    He pre|serveth the | souls · of his | saints.
11. He de|liver·eth | them
    Out | of the | hand · of the | wicked.
12. Light is sown | for the | righteous,
    And gladness | for the | up·right in | heart.
13. Rejoice in JEHOVAH, | O ye | righteous ;
    And give thanks at the remembrance | of his | holi|ness.

Ps. xcvii

SELECTIONS AND CHANTS. 89

### Chant 103.

Last verse.

### SELECTION 109.

*That from the literal sense of the Word are the knowledges of truth and good, from which is spiritual nourishment, 1—8: that the good may be saved, and the evil perish, 9—14.*

1. How manifold are thy works, | O Je|hovah !
   In wisdom | hast thou | made them | all.
2. The earth is | full · of thy | riches ;
   So is this | great and | wide | sea :
3. Wherein are creeping | things · without | number ;
   Both | small and | great | beasts.
4. There go the ships, and that le|via|than,
   Which thou hast | made to | play there|in.

5. These wait | all upon | thee,
   That thou mayest | give their | food · in its | season.
6. Thou givest them ; | they do | gather :
   Thou openest thine hand ; | they are | filled with | good.
7. Thou hidest thy face ; | they are | troubled :
   Thou takest away their breath ; they | die, and re|turn · to
      their | dust.
8. Thou sendest forth thy spirit ; they | are cre|ated :
   And thou dost re|new the | face · of the | ground.

9. The glory of Jehovah shall en|dure for | ever :
   Jehovah | shall re|joice · in his | works.
10. He looketh on the | earth, and it | trembleth :
    He toucheth the | mountains, | and they | smoke.
11. I will sing to Jehovah as | long · as I | live :
    I will sing praise to my God | while I | have my | being.
12. My meditation of him | shall be | sweet :
    I will be | glad · in Je'ho|vah.
13. Let the sinners be consumed | out · of the | earth ;
    And let the | wicked | be no | more.

14. Bless thou Jehovah, | O my | soul ;
    Halle|lujah : | Praise ye | Jah.    Ps. civ 21—35

## CHANT 104.

## SELECTION 110.

*That the Lord has mercy, because he knows the infirmities of man, 1—11.*

1. Jehovah is full of com|pas·sion and | gracious ;
   Slow to | an·ger, and | great in | mercy.
2. He will not | always | chide ;
   Neither will he | keep his | an·ger for | ever.
3. He hath not dealt with us according | to our | sins ;
   Nor rewarded us according to | our in|iqui|ties.
4. For as the heaven is high a|bove the | earth,
   So great is his mercy | to·ward | them that | fear him.
5. As far as the east is | from the | west,
   So far hath he removed | our trans|gressions | from us.
6. Like as a father | pit·ieth his | children,
   So Jehovah | pit·ieth | them that | fear him.
7. For he | know·eth our | frame ;
   He remembereth | that | we are | dust.
8. As for man, his | days · are as | grass :
   As a flower of the field, | so he | flourish|eth.
9. For the wind passeth over it, and | it is | not ;
   And the place there|of shall | know·it no | more.
10. But the mercy of Jehovah is from everlasting to everlasting upon | them that | fear him,
    And his righteousness | unto | children's | children :
11. To such as keep his | cove|nant,
    And to those that remember | his com|mand·ments to | do them.        Ps. ciii. 8.

## SELECTION 111.

*Concerning the Lord's union with the Father*

1. Hear, O Jehovah ; I | cry·with my | voice :
   Have mercy also up|on·me, and | answer | me.
2. When thou saidst, Seek | ye my | face ;
   My heart said unto thee, Thy face, O Je|hovah, | will I | seek.

SELECTIONS AND CHANTS.    91

3. Hide not thy | face from | me;
   Put not thy | ser·vant a|way in | anger.
4. Thou hast been my help; | leave me | not,
   Neither forsake me, O | GOD of | my sal|vation.
5. When my father and | moth·er for|sake me,
   Then JE|HO·VAH will | take me | up.
6. Teach me thy way, | O JE|HOVAH;
   And lead me | in a | path of | plainness.    Ps. xxvii. 7.

CHANT 105.

SELECTION 112.

Concerning some judgment by the Lord, that he is to be celebrated, 1: his integrity, and that he loves the upright, 2-4, 7-9: that he rejects the evil and the haughty, 6, 6: that the evil will perish when he comes, 10.

1. I will sing of | mer·cy and | judgment :
   Unto thee, O JE|HOVAH, | will I | sing.
2. I will behave myself wisely in a | perfect | way :
   O when wilt thou | come | unto | me?
3. I will walk within my house with a | perfect | heart :
   I will set no wicked | thing be|fore mine | eyes.
4. I hate the work of them that | turn a|side ;
   It shall | not cleave | unto | me.
5. A froward heart shall de|part from | me :
   I will not | know a | wicked | person.
6. Whoso privily slandereth his neighbor, him will | I cut | off :
   Him that hath a high look and a proud | heart will | not I | suffer.
7. Thine eyes shall be upon the faithful | of the | land,
   That | they may | dwell with | me.
8. He that walketh in a | perfect | way,
   He | shall | serve | me.
9. He that worketh deceit shall not dwell with|in my | house :
   He that telleth lies shall not | tarry | in my | sight.
10. I will early destroy all the wicked | of the | land ;
    That I may cut off all wicked doers from the | city | of
    JE|HOVAH.                                              Ps. ci

### CHANT 106. DOUBLE.

### SELECTION 113.

*Celebration of the Lord on account of his works for the establishment of the church, 1—8.*

1. O give thanks unto JEHOVAH ; call up|on his | name :
    Make known his | deeds a|mong the | people.
2. Sing unto him, sing | psalms unto | him :
    Talk ye of | all his | wondrous | works.
3. Glory ye in his | holy | name :
    Let the heart of them re|joice that | seek JE|HOVAH.
4. Seek JEHOVAH, | and his | strength :
    Seek his | face for | ever | more.
5. Remember his marvellous works that | he hath | done ;
    His wonders, and the | judgments | of his | mouth ;
6. O ye seed of Abra|ham his | servant,
    Ye children of | Jacob | his | chosen.
7 He is JE|HO·VAH our | GOD :
    His judgments | are in | all the | earth.
8 He hath remembered his cove|nant for | ever ;
    The word he commanded, to a | thousand | gener|ations.

Ps. cv.

### SELECTION 114.

*That the Lord came, and that they afflicted him, 1, 2 ; but that he became the God of heaven and earth, 3—6.*

1. He sent a man be|fore them, | Joseph,
    Who was | sold | for a | servant :
2. Whose feet they | hurt with | fetters :
    He | was | laid in | iron :

SELECTIONS AND CHANTS.    93

3. Until the time that his | word | came :
   The word of Je|hovah | tried | him.
4. The king sent and | loosed | him ;
   The ruler of the people, and | let him | go | free.
5. He made him | lord · of his | house,
   And | rul·er of | all his | substance :
6. To bind his princes | at his | pleasure ;
   And to | teach his | sen·ators | wisdom.    Ps. cv. 17.

Chant 107.

SELECTION 115.

Celebration of the Lord, that from him are divine truths, or the Word, 1—5: concerning the literal sense of the Word, upon which the church is founded, 6—10.

1. Bless Jehovah, | O my | soul :
   O Jehovah my | God, thou art | very | great.
2. Thou art clothed with honor and | majes|ty :
   Who coverest thyself with | light as | with a | garment :
3. Who stretchest out the heavens | like a | curtain :
   Who layeth the beams of his | chambers | in the | waters :
4. Who maketh the clouds his | chari|ot :
   Who walketh upon the | wings | of the | wind :
5. Who maketh | spir·its his | angels,
   The flaming | fire his | minis|ters.
6 He hath founded the earth up|on its | bases :
   That it should not | be re|moved for | ever.
7 Thou coveredst it with the | deep · as a | garment :
   The waters | stood a|bove the | mountains.
8. At thy re|buke they | fled :
   At the voice of thy thunder | did they | haste a|way.
9 They go up the mountains, they go | down the | valleys,
   Unto the place which | thou hast | founded | for them.
10. Thou hast set a bound which they | may not | pass ;
    That they may not re|turn to | cov·er the | earth.
11 Bless thou Jehovah, | O my | soul :
   Halle|lujah : | Praise ye | Jah.    Ps. civ. 1—9, 35

### CHANT 108. DOUBLE.

### SELECTION 116.

Celebration of the Lord, because those who were of the vastated church are rejected, 1—3. 8, 9; and those of the new church accepted, with whom truths and goods will be multiplied, 4—7, 10—12.

1. Let them exalt him in the congregation | of the | people,
And praise him in the as|sembly | of the | elders.
2. He turneth rivers into a | wilder|ness,
Springs of | water | into dry | ground;
3. A fruitful land into | barren|ness,
For the wickedness of | them that | dwell there|in.
4. He turneth the wilderness into a | pool of | waters,
And dry land | into | springs of | waters :
5. And there he maketh the | hun·gry to | dwell,
That they may prepare a | ci·ty for | habi|tation ;
6. And sow the fields, and | plant | vineyards,
Which may | yield the | fruits of | increase.
7. He blesseth them also, and they are | multi·plied | greatly;
And he suffereth not their | cattle | to de|crease.
8. Again, they are minished and | brought | low,
Through op|pres·sion, af|flic·tion, and | sorrow.
9. He poureth con|tempt upon , princes,
And causeth them to wander | in a | pathless | waste.
10. Yet setteth he the poor on | high · from af|fliction,
And maketh him | fam·ilies | like a | flock.
11. The righteous shall see, and | shall re|joice ;
And all iniquity | shall | stop her | mouth.
12. Whoso is wise, and will ob|serve these | things,
Even they shall understand the | kindness | of Je|hovah

Ps. cvii. 32

### Chant 109. Double.

## SELECTION 117.

Celebration of the Father by the Lord, that he succored him in grievous temptations, 1—9.

1. I | love Je|hovah,
   Because he hath heard my | voice, my | suppli|cations.
2. Because he hath inclined his | ear unto | me,
   Therefore will I call up|on · him as | long · as I | live.
3. The sorrows of death | compassed | me;
   And the pains of hell gat hold upon me; I | found dis|tress
       and | sorrow.
4. Then called I upon the | name · of Je|hovah:
   O Jehovah, I be|seech · thee, de|liv·er my | soul.
5. Gracious is Je|ho·vah, and | righteous;
   Yea, our | God is | merci|ful.
6. Jehovah pre|serv·eth the | simple:
   I was brought | low, and he | helped | me.
7. Return unto thy rest, | O my | soul;
   For Jehovah hath dealt | bounti|fully | with thee.
8. For thou hast delivered my | soul from | death,
   Mine eyes from | tears, my | feet from | falling.
9. [3] I will walk be|fore Je|hovah
   In the | land | of the | living.    Ps. cxvi

Dox. O bless our | God, ye | people,
   And make the | voice · of his | praise · to be | heard;
   Who holdeth our | soul in | life,
   And suffereth | not our | feet · to be | moved.

## Chant 110.

Praise ye Jah.

## Selection 118.

Celebration and confession of the Lord, 1—4: that he has redeemed men, and that he saves them to eternity, 5—9: that to worship him is wisdom, 10.

1. Praise ye | Jah.
   I will praise Jeho vah with | all the | heart,
   In the assembly of the upright, and | in the | congre|gation.
2. The works of Je|ho·vah are | great,
   Sought out by all | them · that have | plea·sure there|in.
3. His work is honorable and | glori|ous ;
   And his righteousness | doth en|dure for | ever.
4. He hath made his wonderful works to | be re|membered :
   Jehovah is | gra·cious and | full · of com|passion.
5. He hath given meat unto | them that | fear him :
   He will remember his | cove|nant for|ever.
6. He hath showed his people the power | of his | works,
   That he may give them the | heri|tage · of the | nations.
7. The works of his hands are | truth and | judgment :
   All his com|mandments | are | sure.
8. They stand fast for | ev·er and | ever,
   Done in | truth and | upright|ness.
9. He sent redemption | un·to his | people :
   ¹He hath commanded his cove|nant for | ever :
   Holy and | reve·rend | is his | name.
10. The fear of Jehovah is the be|gin·ning of | wisdom :
    ¹A good understanding have all | they that | do them :
    His praise en|dureth | for | ever.

Ps. cxi

SELECTIONS AND CHANTS. 97

### CHANT 111.

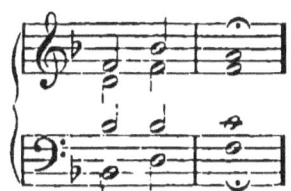

### SELECTION 119.

That he who trusts in the Lord and lives well, will be saved, 1—7, 9: he will not be afraid of the hells, howsoever they may rise up against him, 8, 10, 11.

1. Praise ye | Jah.
 Blessed is the man that | fear·eth Je|hovah,
 That delighteth | great·ly in | his com|mandments.
2. Mighty upon earth shall | be his | seed :
 The generation of the | upright | shall be | blessed.
3. Wealth and riches shall be | in his | house ;
 And his righteousness | doth en|dure for | ever.
4. Unto the upright there ariseth | light · in the | darkness :
 He is gracious, and | full · of com|pas·sion, and | righteous
5. A good man showeth | fa·vor and | lendeth :
 He will | guide · his af|fairs with | judgment.
6. Surely he shall not be | moved for | ever :
 The righteous shall be in | ever|last·ing re|membran
7. He shall not be afraid of an | e·vil re|port :
 His heart is fixed, | trust·ing | in Je|hovah.
8. His heart is established, he shall | not · be a|fraid,
 Until he see his desire up|on his | ene|mies.
9. He hath distributed, he hath given | to the | poor ;
 His righteousness | doth en|dure for | ever :
10. His horn shall be ex|alt·ed with | honor :
 The wicked shall | see it, | and be | grieved :
11. He shall gnash with his teeth, and | melt a·way :
 The desire of the | wicked | shall be | lost.

Ps cxii.

I

98  SELECTIONS AND CHANTS.

CHANT 112.

SELECTION 120.

Celebration of the Father by the Lord for the church, 1—4; that he succored him in distress, 5—9.

1. O give thanks unto JEHOVAH; for | he is | good:
For his | mercy | is for | ever.
2. Let Israel | now | say,
That his | mercy | is for | ever.
3. Let the house of | Aaron now | say,
That his | mercy | is for | ever.
4. Let them now that fear JE|HOVAH | say,
That his | mercy | is for | ever.
5. I called upon JAH | out · of dis|tress:
JAH answered me | in a | large | place.
6. JEHOVAH is for me; I | will not | fear:
What can | man do | unto | me?
7. JEHOVAH taketh my part with | them that | help me:
Therefore shall I see my de|sire upon | them that | hate me.
8. It is better to | trust · in JE|HOVAH,
Than to put | confi|dence in | man.
9. It is better to | trust · in JE|HOVAH,
Than to put | confi|dence in | princes.
10. O give thanks unto JEHOVAH; for | he is | good:
For his | mercy | is for | ever.   Ps. cxviii. 1—9, 29.

SELECTION 121.

That the evil assaulted him, but that he was succored by the Divinity, 2--6. Joy that there is divine power through his Humanity, 7, 8: that divine truth is from him, 9: that it is he by whom is all salvation, 10.

1. O give thanks unto JEHOVAH; for | he is | good:
For his | mercy | is for | ever.
2. All nations compassed | me a|bout:
But in the name of JEHOVAH | will I | cut them | off.
3. They compassed me about; yea, they compassed | me a|bout:
But in the name of JEHOVAH | will I | cut them | off.

4. They compassed me about like bees; they are quenched
   as the | fire of | thorns :
   For in the name of JEHOVAH | will I | cut them | off.
5. Thou hast thrust sore at me that | I might | fall :
   But JE|HOVAH | helped | me.
6. JAH is my | strength and | song,
   And he is be|come | my sal|vation.
7. The voice of rejoicing and salvation is in the tabernacles
   | of the | righteous :
   The right hand of JEHOVAH | doeth | valiant|ly.
8. The right hand of JEHOVAH | is ex|alted :
   The right hand of JEHOVAH | doeth | valiant|ly.
9. I shall not | die, but | live,
   And declare the | works | of JE|HOVAH.
10. JEHOVAH hath | chastened me | sore ;
    But he hath not given me | over | unto | death.
11. O give thanks unto JEHOVAH ; for | he is | good :
    For his | mercy | is for | ever.
    Ps. cxviii. 1, 10—18, 29.

CHANT 113.

SELECTION 122.

That good itself is the conjunction of good and truth, 1 ; for the good of love will flow into the truth of the external or natural man, 2, 3 : that the truth of good is from heaven upon those who are of the church, in which is salvation, 4, 5.

1 Behold, how good and how | pleas·ant it | is,
  For brethren to dwell to|geth·er in | uni|ty.
2. It is like the precious ointment up|on the | head,
   That ran | down up|on the | beard ;
3. Even | Aaron's | beard,
   That went down to the | skirts | of his | garments.
4. It is like the | dew of | Hermon,
   That descended up|on the | moun·tains of | Zion :
5. For there JEHOVAH com|mand·ed the | blessing,
   Even | life for | ever | more.        Ps. cxxxiii.

### CHANT 114. DOUBLE.

## SELECTION 123.

That the Lord fulfilled the law, or the Word, from the first things of it to the last, and that he was therefore hated, and suffered temptations; and that thus he united the Humanity to the Divinity.

1. Blessed are the perfect | in the | way,
Who walk in the | law | of Je|hovah.
2. Blessed are they that keep his | testi|monies,
That seek | him with | all the | heart.
3. They also do no in|iqui|ty:
They | walk | in his | ways.
4. Thou | hast com|manded
To keep thy | precepts | dili·gent|ly.
5. O | that my | ways
Were di|rect·ed to | keep thy | statutes.
6. Then shall I | not · be a|shamed,
When I have re|spect unto | all · thy com|mandments.
7. I will praise thee with upright|ness of | heart,
When I shall have learned the | judgments | of thy | justice.
8. I will | keep thy | statutes:
O do not for|sake me | utter|ly.         Ps. cxix

## SELECTION 124.

For the internal sense, see Selection 123.

1. For ever, | O Je|hovah,
Thy word is es|tablished | in the | heavens.
2. Thy faithfulness is unto | all · gener|ations:
Thou hast established the | earth, and | it a|bideth.

SELECTIONS AND CHANTS.   101

3. They continue this day according | to thy | judgments;
   For | all | are thy | servants.
4. Unless thy law had been | my de|lights,
   I should then have | per·ished in | mine af|fliction.
5. I will never for|get thy | precepts;
   For with them | thou hast | quickened | me.
6. I am | thine, O | save me;
   For | I have | sought thy | precepts.
7 The wicked have waited for me | to de|stroy me:
   I will con|sid·er thy | testi|monies.
8 I have seen an end of | all per|fection:
   Thy commandment | is ex|ceeding | broad.   Ps. cxix. 89.

CHANT 115.

SELECTION 125.

That the Lord raises up sinners, and leads them into truths, that they may live,
1—3: that it is divine, 4: that he saves those who believe in him, and that those
who believe not perish, 5—7: that he is to be worshipped, 8.

1. JEHOVAH upholdeth | all that | fall,
   And raiseth up | all the | bowed | down.
2. The eyes of all | wait on | thee;
   And thou givest them their | meat | in its | season.
3. Thou dost | open thine | hand,
   And satisfy the desire of | ev·ery | living | thing.
4 JEHOVAH is righteous in | all his | ways,
   And merciful | in | all his | works.
5 JEHOVAH is nigh unto all that | call upon | him,
   To all that | call upon | him in | truth.
6 He will fulfil the desire of | them that | fear him:
   He also will | hear their | cry, and will | save them.
7. JEHOVAH preserveth | all that | love him;
   But all the | wick·ed will | he de|stroy.
8. My mouth shall speak the | praise · of JEHOVAH:
   And let all flesh bless his holy | name for | ever and | ever.
   
   Ps. cxlv. 14

### CHANT 116.

### SELECTION 126.

*The coming of the Lord foretold, and the joy of those who shall come to him, who before lived in ignorance, 1–5.*

1. Sing a new song | unto Je|hovah,
   His praise | from the | end · of the | earth ;
2. Ye that go down to the sea, and all that | is there|in ;
   The isles, and the in|habi|tants there|of.
3. Let the wilderness and the cities there|of lift | up,
   The villages that | Kedar | doth in|habit.
4. Let the inhabitants of the | rock | sing,
   Let them | shout · from the | top · of the | mountains.
5. Let them give glory | unto Je|hovah,
   And de|clare his | praise · in the | islands.   Is. xlii. 10.

### CHANT 117.

### SELECTION 127.

*For the internal sense, see Selection 123.*

1. Deal bountifully | with thy | servant,
   That I may | live, and | keep thy | word.
2. Open | thou mine | eyes,
   That I may behold wondrous | things out | of thy | law.
3. I am a stranger | in the | earth :
   Hide not | thy com|mandments | from me.
4. My soul breaketh | for the | longing,
   That it hath unto thy | judgments | at all | times.

SELECTIONS AND CHANTS.    103

5. Thou hast rebuked the | proud · that are | cursed,
   Who do | err from | thy com|mandments.
6. Remove from me re|proach · and con|tempt;
   For I have | kept thy | testi|monies.
7. Princes also did sit and | speak a|gainst me:
   Thy servant did | medi·tate | in thy | statutes.
8. Thy testimonies also are | my de|light,
   And | my | counsel|lors.        Ps. cxix. 17.

CHANT 118.  DOUBLE.

SELECTION 128.

For the internal sense, see Selection 123.

1. Wherewith shall a young man | cleanse his | way?
   By taking heed ac|cording | to thy | word.
2. With my whole heart have I | sought | thee:
   O let me not | wander from | thy com|mandments.
3. Thy word have I | hid · in mine | heart,
   That I might not | sin a|gainst | thee.
4  Blessed art thou, | O Je|hovah:
   O | teach thou | me thy | statutes.
5  With my lips have | I de|clared
   All the | judgments | of thy | mouth.
6. I have rejoiced in the way of thy | testi|monies,
   As | much as | in all | riches.
7. I will meditate | in thy | precepts,
   And have res|pect un|to thy | ways.
8. I will delight myself | in thy | statutes:
   I will | not for|get thy | word.        Ps. cxix. 9.

### Chant 119.

The Treble and Tenor may change parts.

### SELECTION 129.

*That the Lord is to be worshiped from the Word, wherein is divine truth, 1—5.*

1. I will praise thee with | all the | heart :
   Before the gods will I sing | praise | unto | thee.
2. I will worship toward thy | holy | temple,
   And praise thy name for thy | mercy | and thy | truth :
   ²For thou hast magnified thy | word above | all thy | name.
3. In the day when I cried, thou didst | answer | me :
   Thou strengthenedst me with | strength | in my | soul.
4. All the kings of the earth shall praise thee, | O Je|hovah,
   When they | hear the | words · of thy | mouth.
5. Yea, they shall sing in the | ways · of Je|hovah :
   For great is the | glory | of Je|hovah.   Ps. cxxxviii.

### Chant 120.

### SELECTION 130.

*For the internal sense, see Selection 123.*

1. My soul cleaveth | unto the | dust :
   Quicken thou me ac|cording | to thy | word.
2. I have declared my ways, and | thou hast | heard me :
   O | teach thou | me thy | statutes.
3. Make me to understand the | way · of thy | precepts :
   So shall I | talk · of thy | wondrous | works.
4. My soul doth | melt for | grief :
   Strengthen thou me ac|cording | to thy | word.

SELECTIONS AND CHANTS.     105

5. Remove from me the | way of | lying;
   And grant me thy | law | gracious|ly.
6. I have chosen the | way of | truth :
   Thy judgments | have I | laid be|fore me.
7. I have cleaved unto thy | testi|monies:
   O Jehovah. | put me | not to | shame.
8. I will run the way of | thy com|mandments,
   When thou | shalt en|large my | heart.     Ps. cxix. 25

CHANT 121.   DOUBLE.

SELECTION 131.
For the internal sense, see Selection 123.

1. Remember the word | unto thy | servant,
   Upon which thou hast | caused | me to | hope.
2. This is my comfort in | mine af|fliction ;
   For thy | word hath | quickened | me.
3. The proud have had me greatly | in de|rision :
   I have not de|clined | from thy | law.
4. I remembered thy judgments of old, | O Je|hovah ;
   And have | comfort|ed my|self.
5. Horror hath taken | hold up|on me,
   Because of the wicked | that for|sake thy | law.
6. Thy statutes have | been my | songs
   In the | house of my | pilgrim|age.
7. I have remembered thy name, O Jehovah, | in the | night ;
   And | I have | kept thy | law.
8. This | did I | have,
   Be|cause I | kept thy | precepts.     Ps. cxix. 49

## Chant 122. Double.

### SELECTION 132.

*For the internal sense, see Selection 123.*

1. Thou art my portion, | O Je|hovah:
   I have said that | I would | keep thy | words.
2. I entreated thy favor with | all the | heart:
   Be merciful unto me ac|cording | to thy | word.
3. I thought up|on my | ways,
   And turned my | feet · to thy | testi|monies.
4. I made haste, and de|layed | not,
   To | keep | thy com|mandments.
5. The bands of the wicked have | robbed | me:
   I have | not for|gotten thy | law.
6. At midnight I will rise to give | thanks unto | thee,
   Because of the | judgments | of thy | justice.
7. I am a companion of all | them that | fear thee,
   And of | them that | keep thy | precepts.
8. The earth, O Jehovah, is | full · of thy | mercy:
   O | teach thou | me thy | statutes.     Ps cxix. 57.

### SELECTION 133.

*The Lord's confidence that the Father will assist him, 1—5: that he was his from nativity, 6.*

1. In thee, O Jehovah, do I | put my | trust:
   Let me | nev·er be | put · to con|fusion.
2. Deliver me in thy righteousness, and cause me | to es|cape:
   Incline thine | ear unto | me, and | save me.

SELECTIONS AND CHANTS. 107

3. Be thou my strong | habi|tation,
Whereunto I may con|tin·ual|ly re|sort.
4. Thou hast given com|mand·ment to | save me,
For thou art my | rock | and my | fortress.
5. Deliver me, O my God, out of the | hand ·of the | wicked,
Out of the hand of the un|right·eous and | cruel | man :
6. For thou art my hope, O | Lord Je|hovah;
Thou art my | trust | from my | youth.       Ps. lxxi.

CHANT 123. DOUBLE.

SELECTION 134.

For the internal sense, see Selection 123.

1. Thou hast dealt | well ·with thy | servant,
O Jehovah, ac|cording | to thy | word.
2. Teach me good | judg·ment and | knowledge ;
For I have be|lieved | thy com|mandments
3 Before I was afflicted I | went a|stray ;
But now | have I | kept thy | word.
4 Thou art good, and | doest | good ;
O | teach thou | me thy | statutes.
5. The proud have forged a | lie a|gainst me :
I will keep thy | pre·cepts with | all the | heart.
6. Their heart is | gross like | fat :
I de|light | in thy | law.
7. It is good for me that I have | been af|flicted ;
That | I might | learn thy | statutes.
8. The law of thy mouth is better | unto | me.
Than | thou·sands of | gold and | silver.       Ps. cxix. 65.

## SELECTION 135.

*For the Internal sense, see Selection 138.*

1. Thy word is a | lamp · to my | feet,
And a | light un|to my | path.
2. I have sworn, and I | will per|form,
That I will keep the | judgments | of thy | justice.
3. I am afflicted | very | much:
Quicken me, O JEHOVAH, ac|cording | to thy | word.
4. Accept, I beseech thee, the free-will offerings of my mouth | O JE|HOVAH;
And | teach thou | me thy | judgments.
5. My soul is continually | in my | hand:
Yet do I | not for|get thy | law.
6. The wicked have laid a | snare for | me:
Yet I have not | wandered | from thy | precepts.
7. Thy testimonies have I taken as an heri|tage for | ever;
For they are the re|joicing | of my | heart.
8 I have in|clined my | heart,
To perform thy statutes | always, | to the | end.

Ps. cxix. 105

## SELECTION 136.

*For the Internal sense, see Selection 138.*

1. I hate di|vided | thoughts:
But thy | law | do I | love.
2. Thou art my hiding place | and my | shield:
I | hope | in thy | word.

SELECTIONS AND CHANTS.   109

3. Depart from me, ye | evil|doers;
   For I will keep the com|mandments | of my | GOD.
4. Uphold me according to thy word, that | I may | live:
   And let me not | be a|shamed ·of my | hope.
5. Hold thou me up, and I | shall be | safe:
   And I will have respect unto thy | stat·utes con|tin·ual|ly.
6. Thou hast trodden down all that | err· from thy | statutes;
   For | their de|ceit is | falsehood.
7. Thou puttest away all the wicked of the | earth as | dross:
   Therefore I | love thy | testi|monies.
8. My flesh trembleth for | fear of | thee;
   And of thy | judg·ments I | am a|fraid.   Ps. cxix 113.

CHANT 125.

SELECTION 137.

For the internal sense, see Selection 138.

1. My soul fainteth for | thy sal|vation:
   I | hope | in thy | word.
2. Mine eyes | fail· for thy | word,
   Saying, When | wilt thou | comfort | me?
3. For I am become like a bottle | in the | smoke:
   I do | not for|get thy | statutes.
4. How many are the | days· of thy | servant?
   When wilt thou execute judgment on | them that | perse-
       ·cute | me?
5. The proud have digged | pits for | me,
   Which are not ac|cording | to thy | law.
6. All thy commandments are | faithful|ness:
   They persecute me with | falsehood; | help thou | me.
7. They had almost consumed me up|on the | earth;
   But I did | not for|sake thy | precepts.
8. Quicken me according | to thy | mercy;
   And I shall keep the testi|mony | of thy | mouth.
                                    Ps. cxix. 81.

j

### CHANT 126. DOUBLE.

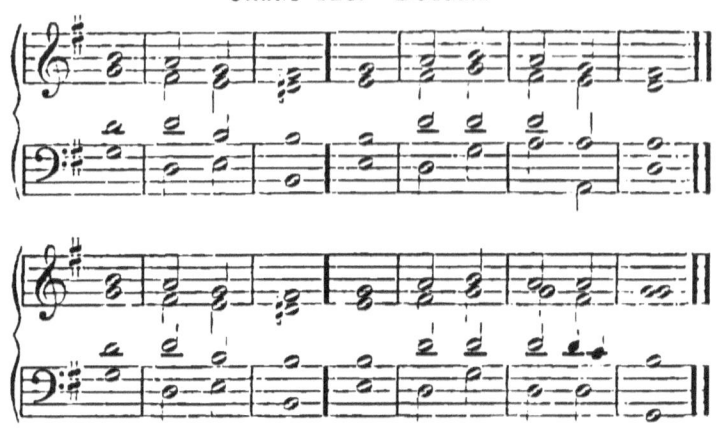

### SELECTION 138.

That the Lord fulfilled the law, or the Word, from the first to the last things of it; and that he was therefore hated, and suffered temptations; and that thus he united the Humanity to his Divinity.

1. I have done | judg·ment and | justice :
Leave me | not to | mine op|pressors.
2. Be surety for thy | ser·vant for | good :
Let | not the | proud op|press me.
3. Mine eyes fail for | thy sal|vation,
And for the | word · of thy | righteous|ness.
4. Deal with thy servant according | to thy | mercy,
And | teach thou | me thy | statutes.
5. I am thy servant; give me | under|standing,
That I may | know thy | testi|monies.
6. It is time for thee, O Je|ho·vah, to | work ;
For they | have made | void thy | law.
7. Therefore I love thy commandments | more than | gold,
And | more than | fine | gold.
8 Therefore all thy precepts concerning all things do | I es·teem | right ;
And every | false way | do I | hate.    Ps. cxix. 121.

### SELECTION 139.

For the internal sense, see Selection, 138.

1. I cried with all the heart ; hear me, | O Je|hovah :
Thy | statutes | will I | keep.

SELECTIONS AND CHANTS.    111

2  I cried unto | thee : O | save me ;
   And I shall | keep thy | testi|monies.
3. I prevented the | dawn, and | cried :
   I | hoped | in thy | word.
4. Mine eyes pre|vent the | watches,
   That I might | medi·tate | in thy | word.
5. Hear my voice according | to thy | mercy :
   O Jehovah, quicken me ac|cording | to thy | judgment.
6. They draw near that | follow | mischief :
   They | are far | from thy | law.
7. Thou art near, | O Je|hovah ;
   And all | thy com|mand·ments are | truth.
8. Concerning thy testimonies, I have | known of | old,
   That thou hast | founded | them for|ever.    Ps. cxix. 145.

CHANT 127.

SELECTION 140.

For the internal sense see Selection 138

1. Behold mine affliction, and de|liver | me :
   For I do | not for|get thy | law.
2. Plead my cause, and re|deem | me :
   Quicken me ac|cording | to thy | word.
3. Salvation is | far·from the | wicked ;
   For they | do not | seek thy | statutes.
4. Great are thy tender mercies, | O Je|hovah :
   Quicken me ac|cording | to thy | judgments.
5. Many are my persecutors and mine | ene|mies :
   I do not de|cline·from thy | testi|monies.
6. I beheld the transgressors | and was | grieved ;
   Because they | did not | keep thy | word.
7. Behold how I | love thy | precepts :
   Quicken me, O Jehovah, ac·cording | to thy | mercy.
8. The sum of thy | word is | truth ;
   And every judgment of thy | jus·tice is | ever|lasting.
                                          Ps. cxix. 153.

### CHANT 128. DOUBLE.

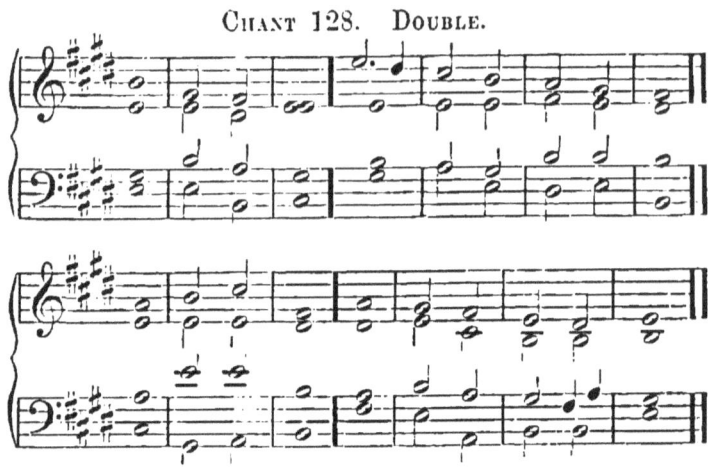

### SELECTION 141.

That the Lord fulfilled the law or the Word from the first to the last things of it, and was therefore hated, and suffered temptations; and that thus he united the Humanity to his Divinity, 1—8.

1. Thy testimonies are | wonder|ful ;
   Therefore | doth my | soul | keep them.
2. The entrance of thy words | giveth | light ;
   It giveth under|standing | to the | simple.
3. I opened my | mouth, and | panted ;
   For I | longed for | thy com|mandments.
4. Look thou upon me, and be merciful | unto | me ;
   As thou usest to do unto | those that | love thy | name.
5. Order my steps | in thy | word :
   And let not any iniquity have do|minion | over | me.
6. Deliver me from the op|pres·sion of | man ;
   So | will I | keep thy | precepts.
7. Make thy face to shine up|on thy | servant ;
   And | teach thou | me thy | statutes.
8. Rivers of waters run | down mine | eyes,
   Because they | do not | keep thy | law.   Ps. cxix. 129

### SELECTION 142.

For the internal sense, see Selection 141.

1. Let my cry come near before thy face, | O Je|hovah
   Make me to understand ac|cording | to thy | word.
2. Let my supplication come be|fore thy | face :
   Deliver me ac|cording | to thy | word.

SELECTIONS AND CHANTS.  113

3. My lips shall | utter | praise,
   When thou hast | taught | me thy | statutes.
4. My tongue shall | speak · of thy | word;
   For all thy com|mand·ments are | righteous|ness.
5. Let thine hand be | for my | help;
   For I have | chosen | thy | precepts.
6. I have longed for thy salvation, | O Je|hovah;
   And thy | law is | my de|light.
7. Let my soul live, and it shall | praise | thee;
   And let thy | judgments | help | me.
8. I have gone astray like a | lost | sheep:
   Seek thy servant, for I do | not for|get · thy com|mandments.
   Ps. cxix. 169.

CHANT 129.

SELECTION 143.

For the internal sense, see Selection 141.

1. Let thy mercies come also unto me, | O Je|hovah;
   Thy salvation, ac|cording | to thy | word.
2. So shall I have wherewith to answer him that re|proacheth | me;
   For I | trust | in thy | word.
3. And take not the word of truth utterly | out · of my | mouth;
   For I have | hoped | in thy | judgments.
4. So shall I keep thy law con|tin·ual|ly,
   For | ever | and | ever.
5. And I will walk at | liber|ty;
   For | I do | seek thy | precepts.
6. I will speak of thy testimonies also be|fore | kings,
   And | will not | be a|shamed.
7. And I will de|light my|self
   In thy com|mand·ments which | I have | loved.
8. My hands also will I lift up unto thy commandments, which | I have | loved;
   And I will | medi·tate | in thy | statutes.    Ps. cxix. 41.

## CHANT 130. TERNARY.

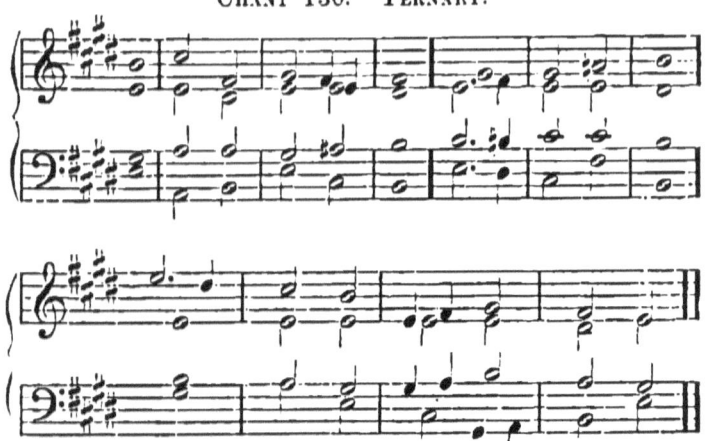

## SELECTION 144.

Celebration of the Lord, that he is to be worshiped from the heart, because he is the former of the church, 1, 2: that they should come to him by the truths of the Word, and confess him, 3, 4.

1. Make a joyful noise unto JE|HOVAH, | all the | earth :
Serve JE|HOVAH with | gladness :
Come be|fore his | face with | singing.
2. Know ye that JE|HOVAH | he is | GOD :
He hath made us, and not | we our|selves,
His people, and the | sheep | of his | pasture.
3. Enter into his | gates with | thanksgiv|ing,
Into his | courts with | praise :
Give thanks unto | him, and | bless his | name.
4. For JE|HO|VAH is | good :
His mercy is | ever|lasting,
And his truth to | all | gener|ations.     Ps. c.

## SELECTION 145.

The Lord's advent is foretold, when the good are to be saved, and the evil will perish, 1—5.

1. Comfort ye, comfort ye my | people, | saith your | GOD :
Speak ye comfortably to Je|rusa|lem ;
And cry unto her, that her | warfare | is ac|complished ;
2 That her in|iqui|ty is | pardoned :
For she hath received from JE|HOVAH's | hand
Double | for | all her | sins.

SELECTIONS AND CHANTS.    115

8. The voice of him that crieth | in the | wilder ness,
   Prepare ye the | way · of Je|hovah,
   Make straight in the desert a | highway | for our | God.
4. Every | val·ley shall | be ex|alted ;
   And every mountain and hill shall | be made | low :
   And the crooked shall be made straight, and the | rough |
      places | plain.
5. And the glory of Je|ho·vah shall | be re|vealed :
   And all flesh shall | see · it to|gether :
   For the mouth of Je|ho·vah hath | spoken | it.    Is. xl

CHANT 131.  TERNARY.

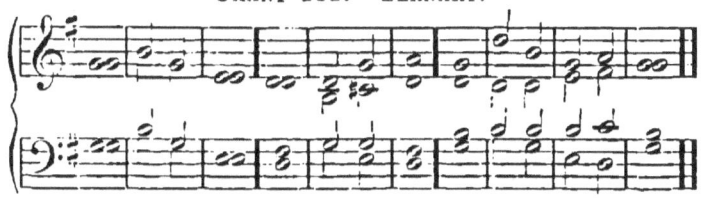

SELECTION 146.

That the Lord comforts himself from his Divinity, from things past, that those have been saved who implored, 1, 2; and that by divine truth he has power, 3—6; and that the church has been preserved, 7.

1. Thy way, O God, is in the | sanctu|ary :
   Who is so great a | god as | God?
   Thou art the | God that | doest | wonders.
2. Thou hast declared thy strength a|mong the | people :
   Thou hast with thine arm re|deemed thy | people,
   The sons of | Joseph | and of | Jacob.
3. The waters | saw · thee, O | God ;
   The waters saw thee ; they | were a|fraid :
   The | depths were | also | troubled.
4. The clouds | poured out | water ;
   The skies sent | out a | sound ;
   Thine arrows | also | went a|broad.
5. The voice of thy thunder was | in the | whirlwind ;
   Thy lightnings | light·ened the | world ;
   The | earth did | tremble and | shake.
6. Thy way is | in the | sea ;
   And thy path in | many | waters ;
   And thy | footsteps | are not | known.
7. Thou didst | lead thy | people,
   Like | un·to a | flock,
   By the hand of | Moses | and of | Aaron.    Ps. lxxvii. 13

### CHANT 132.

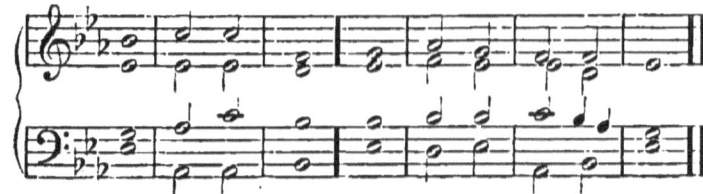

### SELECTION 147.

*That the Divinity is to be worshiped in the Lord, 1—8.*

1. What shall I render | un·to Je|hovah,
   For all his | bene·fits | to·ward | me?
2. I will take the | cup·of sal|vation,
   And call upon the | name | of Je|hovah.
3. I will pay my vows | un·to Je|hovah,
   Now in the | pres·ence of | all his | people.
4. Precious in the | sight·of Je|hovah
   Is the | death | of his | saints.
5. O Jehovah, truly I am thy servant; I | am thy | servant;
   The son of thine handmaid : | thou hast | loosed my | bonds.
6. I will offer to thee the sacrifice of | thanksgiv|ing,
   And will call upon the | name | of Je|hovah.
7. I will pay my vows | un·to Je|hovah,
   Now in the | pres·ence of | all his | people ;
8. In the courts of the | house·of Je|hovah ;
   In the midst of thee, | O Je|rusa|lem.
   Praise ye | Jah.                                Ps. cxvi. 12

### SELECTION 148.

*That there is salvation from the Lord for the humble, and life and protection.*

1. Though Jehovah be high, he hath re|spect·to the | lowly ·
   But the proud he | know·eth a|far |off.
2. Though I walk in the | midst of | trouble,
   Thou | wilt re|vive | me.

## SELECTIONS AND CHANTS. 117

3. Thou wilt stretch | forth thine | hand,
   Against the | wrath · of mine | ene|mies.
4. And thy right | hand shall | save me :
   Jehovah will perfect | that · which con|cerneth | me.
5. Thy mercy, O Jehovah, | is for | ever :
   Forsake not the | works of | thine own | hands.

        Ps. cxxxviii. 6—8

### Chant 133.

### SELECTION 149.

That the Lord will save those that trust in him, 1—5, 8: that heaven and the church are his, 6: that those who do not trust in him are not saved, 7.

1. Jehovah hath been | mindful | of us:
   He | will | bless | us.
2. He will bless the house of | Isra|el:
   He will | bless the | house of | Aaron.
3. He will bless them that | fear Je|hovah,
   The | small | with the | great.
4. Jehovah | shall in|crease you
   More and | more, you | and your | children.
5. Ye are blessed | of Je|hovah,
   Who | made | heaven and | earth.
6. The heavens, the heavens, | are Je|hovah's:
   But the earth hath he given | to the | chil·dren of | men.
7. The dead praise | not Je|hovah,
   Neither any that go | down | into | silence.
8. But we | will bless | Jah,
   From this time | forth · and for | ever | more.

Praise ye | Jah.

        Ps. cxv. 12

## CHANT 134.

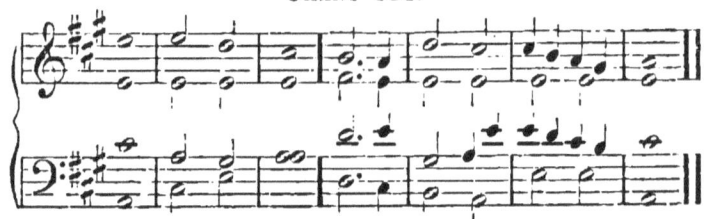

## SELECTION 150.

That the Lord has omnipotence, 1—4: that man is nothing of himself but the falsity of evil, 5—9: that all who are in goods and truths, trust in the Lord, 10—11.

1. Not unto us, O JEHOVAH, | not ⋅ unto | us;
But unto thy name give glory, for thy | mer cy and | for thy ⋅ truth's | sake.
2. Wherefore should the | heathen | say,
Where | is | now their | GOD?
3. But our GOD is | in the | heavens:
He hath done whatso|ever | he hath | pleased.
4. Their idols are | sil·ver and | gold,
The | work ⋅ of the | hands of | man.
5. They have mouths, but they | do not | speak:
Eyes have they, | but they | do not | see.
6. They have ears, but they | do not | hear:
Noses have they, | but they | do not | smell.
7. They have hands, but they | handle | not:
¹ Feet have they, but they | do not | walk:
Neither | speak they | through their | throat.
8. They that make them are | like unto | them:
So is every | one that | trust·eth in | them.
9. O Israel, trust thou | in JE|HOVAH:
He is their | help | and their | shield.
10. O house of Aaron, | trust ⋅ in JE|HOVAH:
He is their | help | and their | shield.
11. Ye that fear JEHOVAH, | trust ⋅ in JE|HOVAH:
He is their | help | and their | shield.    Ps. cxv

## SELECTION 151.

That the church was established by God, and not by men, 1—6.

1. Thou art my | king, O | GOD:
Command de|liv·eran|ces for | Jacob.

2. Through thee will we push down our | ene|mies :
   In thy name will we tread down | them that | rise a|gainst us.
3. For I will not | trust · in my | bow ;
   Neither | shall my | sword save | me.
4. But thou hast saved us from our | ene|mies,
   And hast put them to | shame that | hated | us.
5. In God will we glory | all the | day,
   And we will | praise thy | name for|ever.    Ps. xliv. 4.

CHANT 135.  DOUBLE.

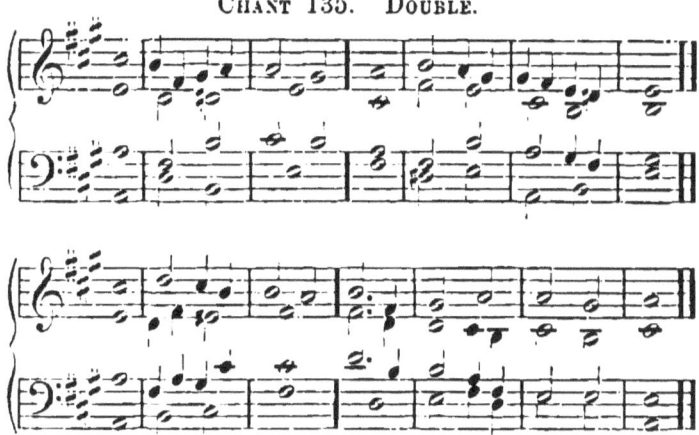

SELECTION 152.

For the internal sense, see Selection 141.

1. Teach me, O Jehovah, the | way · of thy | statutes ;
   And I shall | keep it | unto the | end.
2. Make me to understand, and I shall | keep thy | law ;
   And I shall observe it | with the | whole | heart.
3. Make me to go in the path of | thy com|mandments ;
   For there|in do | I de|light.
4. Incline my heart unto thy | testi|monies,
   And not | unto | cov·etous|ness.
5. Turn away mine eyes from beholding | vani|ty :
   Quicken | thou me | in thy | way.
6. Establish thy word | un·to thy | servant,
   Who is de|voted | to thy | fear.
7. Turn away my reproach | which I | fear ;
   For thy | judgments | are | good.
8. Behold, I have | longed · for thy | precepts :
   Quicken me | in thy | righteous|ness.    Ps. cxix. 33.

## Chant 136. Double.

## SELECTION 153.

*For the internal sense, see Selection 141.*

1. Princes have persecuted me with|out a | cause ;
But my heart doth | tremble | at thy | word.
2. I rejoice | at thy | word,
As one that | findeth | great | spoil.
3. Falsehood do I | hate and ab|hor ;
But thy | law | do I | love.
4. Seven times a day | do I | praise thee,
Because of the | judgments | of thy | justice.
5. Great peace have they who | love thy | law ;
And no | stumbling|block have | they.
6 O Jehovah, I have hoped for | thy sal|vation ;
And thy com|mandments | have I | done.
7 My soul hath kept thy | testi|monies ;
And I do | love them ex|ceeding|ly.
8. I have kept thy precepts and thy | testi|monies ;
For all my | ways | are be|fore thee.    Ps. cxix. 161.

## SELECTION 154.

That the Lord is blasphemed by the evil in the church, notwithstanding his integrity, 1—4: that he endures this for the sake of the Divinity, 5: prayer that the Divinity may assist him, 6.

1. Our heart is | not turned | back,
Neither have our steps de|clined | from thy | way.
2. Though thou hast sorely broken us in the | place of | dragons,
And covered us | with the | shad·ow of | death.

SELECTIONS AND CHANTS.   121

3. If we have forgotten the | name · of our | GOD,
   Or stretched out our | hand · to a | strange | god;
4. Shall not GOD | search this | out?
   For he knoweth the | secrets | of the | heart.
5. Yea, for thy sake are we killed | all the | day:
   We are | count·ed as | sheep · for the | slaughter.
6. Awake; why sleepest | thou, O | LORD?
   Arise; | cast not | off for | ever.       Ps. xliv. 18.

CHANT 137.  DOUBLE.

SELECTION 155.
For the internal sense, see Selection 141.

1. O how I | love thy | law:
   It is my medi|tation | all the | day.
2. Thou hast made me wiser | than mine | enemies,
   Through thy commandments, for | they are | ever | with me.
3. I have more understanding than | all my | teachers;
   For thy testimonies | are my | medi|tation.
4. I understand | more · than the | ancients,
   Be|cause I | keep thy | precepts.
5. I have refrained my feet from every | evil | way,
   That | I might | keep thy | word.
6. I have not departed | from thy | judgments;
   For | thou hast | taught | me.
7. How sweet are thy words | unto my | taste:
   Sweeter than | honey | unto my | mouth.
8. Through thy precepts I get | under|standing;
   Therefore I hate | every | path of | falsehood.  Ps. cxix. 97.

K

## CHANT 138.

## SELECTION 156.

Prayer of the Lord to the Father, that he would assist in temptations, 1—4: because no one knows him but the Father alone, in whom is his trust, 5—8: that he may be delivered from temptations, and come among those who acknowledge him, 8—11.

1. I cried unto JEHOVAH | with my | voice:
   With my voice to JEHOVAH made | I my | suppli|cation.
2. I poured out my com|plaint be|fore him:
   I showed be|fore | him my | trouble.
3. When my spirit was over|whelmed with|in me,
   Then thou | knewest | my | path.
4. In the way where|in I | walked,
   Have they privily | laid a | snare for | me.
5. I looked on my right hand. | and be|held;
   But there was | no one | that would | know me.
6. Refuge | perished | from me:
   No one | sought | af·ter my | soul.
7. I cried to thee, O JEHOVAH; I said, | Thou·art my | refuge,
   My portion | in the | land ·of the | living.
8. Attend | un·to my | cry;
   For I | am brought | very | low.
9. Deliver me from my | perse|cutors;
   For | they are | strong·er than | I.
10. Bring my soul | out of | prison,
    That | I may | praise thy | name.
11. The righteous shall compass | me a|bout;
    For thou shalt deal | bounti|fully | with me.   Ps. cxlii.

## SELECTION 157.

The state of the Lord's temptation, insomuch that he was even in despair whether the Father would assist him.

1. I have considered the | days of | old,
   The | years of | ancient | times.
2. I call to remembrance my | song·in the | night:
   ¹I commune with | mine own | heart:
   And my | spirit made | dil·igent | search.

SELECTIONS AND CHANTS.   123

3. Will the LORD cast | off for | ever?
   And will he be | favor|able no | more?
4. Is his mercy clean | gone for | ever?
   Doth his promise | fail for | ever|more?
5. Hath GOD forgotten | to be | gracious?
   Hath he in anger shut | up his | tender | mercies?
   
   Ps. lxxvii. 5.

CHANT 139.   DOUBLE.

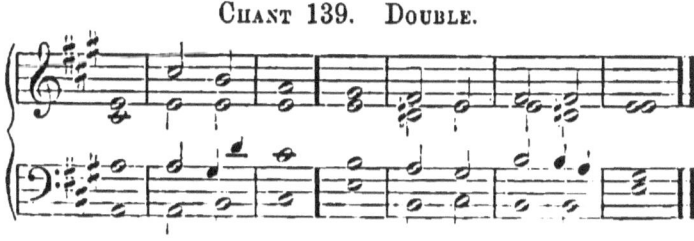

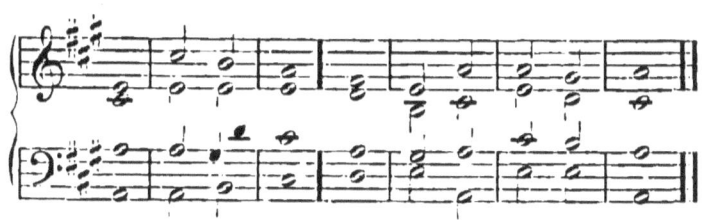

SELECTION 158.

To the Father, that he would preserve, 1—8.

1. I will lift up mine | eyes · to the | mountains,
   From | whence doth | come my | help.
2. My help is | from JE|HOVAH,
   Who made the | heavens | and the | earth.
3. He will not suffer thy | foot · to | be | moved:
   He that doth | keep thee | will not | slumber.
4. Behold, he that keepeth | Isra|el,
   Shall neither | slumber | nor | sleep.
5. JEHOVAH | is thy | keeper:
   JEHOVAH is thy | shade on | thy right | hand.
6. The sun shall not | smite · thee by | day,
   Nei|ther the | moon by | night.
7. JEHOVAH shall keep thee | from all | evil;
   He | shall | keep thy | soul.
8. JEHOVAH shall keep thy going out and thy | coming | in,
   From this time forth, and | e·ven for | ever|more. Ps. cxxi

## CHANT 140. DOUBLE.

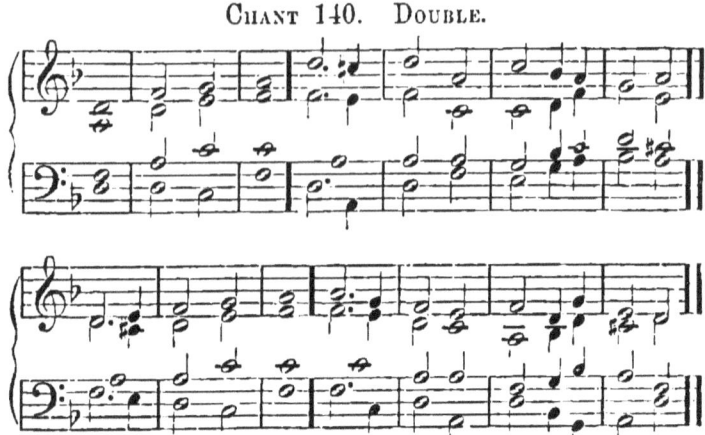

## SELECTION 159.

Prayer of the Lord to the Father that he may be preserved, 1—4: that the coming of the Lord is expected, 5—8.

1. Out of the depths have I cried unto thee, | O Je|hovah:
    O Lord, | hearken | un·to my | voice.
2. Let thine ears | be at|tentive
    Unto the | voice · of my | suppli|cations.
3. If thou, O Jah, shouldst mark in|iqui|ties,
    O | Lord, | who shall | stand?
4. But with | thee · is for|giveness,
    That | thou | mayst be | feared.
5. I wait for Jehovah, my | soul doth | wait;
    And in his | word | do I | hope.
6. My soul waiteth for Jehovah more than watchers | for the
        | morning:
    Than | watchers | for the | morning.
7. Let Israel hope | in Je|hovah;
    For with Je|hovah | there is | mercy:
8. And with him is | plen·teous re|demption;
    And he shall redeem Isra|el from | all · his in|iqui·ties.

Ps. cxxx.

## SELECTION 160.

Celebration of the Father by the Lord, that he knows all of the thought and will, because he is united to them, 1—5; that he has omniscience and omnipotence, 6—10; that from him is illustration in the natural man, 11, 12.

1. O Je|ho|vah,
    Thou hast | searched | me, and | known me.

2. Thou knowest my downsitting and | mine up|rising :
Thou dost under|stand my | thoughts a|far off.
3. Thou compassest my path and my | lying | down,
And art ac|quaint·ed with | all my | ways.
4. For there is not a | word·in my | tongue,
But, lo, O Jehovah, thou | know·est it | alto|gether.
5. Thou hast beset me be|hind·and be|fore,
And hast | laid thine | hand up|on me.
6. Such knowledge is too | won·derful | for me :
It is high ; I | can·not at|tain·unto | it.
7. Whither shall I | go·from thy | Spirit?
Or whither | shall I | flee·from thy | presence?
8. If I ascend up into heaven, | thou art | there :
If I make my bed in | hell, be|hold, thou art | there.
9. If I take the | wings·of the | morning,
And dwell in the | ut·termost | parts·of the | sea ;
10. Even there thy | hand shall | lead me.
And thy | right | hand shall | hold me.
11. If I say, Surely the darkness shall | cover | me ;
Even the | night·shall be | light a|bout me.
12. Yea, the darkness hideth | not from | thee ;
\*But the night shineth | as the | day :
The darkness and the light are | both a|like to | thee.
Ps. cxxxix.

## SELECTION 161.

*That all things of the Father were united with him, 1, 2: that the Lord rejects from himself all evil and falsity, 3—6: that he has integrity, 7—8.*

1. How precious also are thy thoughts unto | me, O | God ;
How | great·is the | sum of | them :
2. If I should count them, they are more in number | than
When I a|wake, I am | still with | thee.     [the | sand :
3. Surely, thou wilt slay the | wick·ed, O | God :
Depart from me, | there·fore, ye | men of | blood.
4. For they speak against thee | wicked||ly ;
And thine enemies | take thy | name in | vain.
5 Do not I hate, O Jehovah, | them·that hate | thee ?
And am I not grieved with | those that | rise·up a|gainst
6. I hate them with | perfect | hatred :     [thee ?
For enemies | have they | been unto | me.
7. Search me, O God, and | know my | heart ;
Try | me, and | know my | thoughts :
8. And see if there be any wicked | way in | me ;
And lead me | in the | way·ever'lasting.   Ps. cxxxix. 17.

K\*

## CHANT 141. DOUBLE.

## SELECTION 162.

That the Lord united the Divinity to his Humanity, 1: they worship him from good and from truth, 2, 3: that it is an eternal truth, that those who worship him are saved, 4—6: that the Lord dwells in his church because he loves it, 7, 8; because it is in truths and goods, 9, 10: that it is thence in power and in light against the falsities of evil, 11, 12.

1. Arise, O Jehovah, | into thy | rest ;
   Thou and the | ark | of thy | strength.
2. Let thy priests be clothed with | righteous|ness ;
   And let thy | saints | shout for | joy.
3. For thy servant | David's | sake,
   Turn not away the | face of | thine an|ointed.
4. Jehovah hath sworn in | truth unto | David ;
   He will not | turn a|way from | it ;
5. Of the fruit of thy body will I set up|on thy | throne :
   If thy children will | keep my | cove|nant,
6. And my testimony that | I shall | teach them,
   Their children shall also sit upon thy | throne for ! ever more.
7. For Jehovah hath | chosen | Zion :
   He hath desired it | for his | habi|tation.
8. This is my | rest for | ever :
   Here will I dwell ; for | I · have de|sired | it.
9. I will abundantly | bless · her pro|vision :
   Her poor will I | satis|fy with | bread.
10. I will also clothe her | priests · with sal|vation ;
    And her saints shall | shout a|loud for | joy.

SELECTIONS AND CHANTS. 127

11. There will I make the horn of | Da·vid to | bud :
    I have ordained a | lamp for | mine an|ointed.
12. His enemies will I | clothe with | shame ;
    But upon him|self his | crown shall | flourish.

Ps. cxxxii. 8.

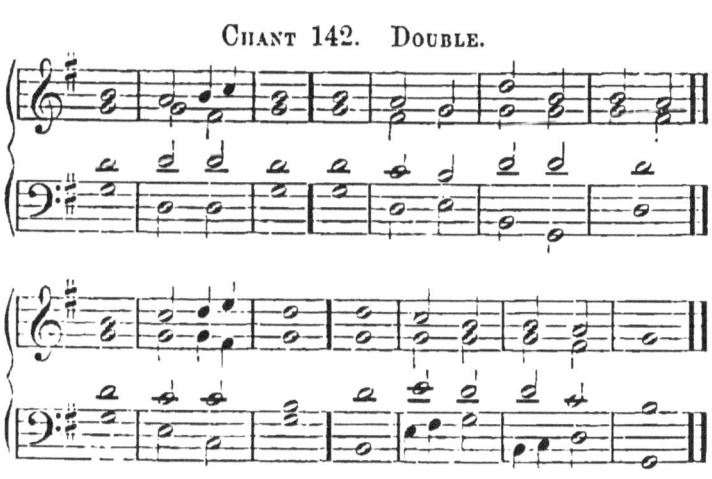

CHANT 142. DOUBLE.

SELECTION 163.

*The joy of the Lord over the new church where he reigns, 1—8.*

1. I was glad when they | said unto | me,
   Let us go unto the | house | of Je|hovah.
2. Our feet shall stand within thy gates, O Je|rusa|lem :
   Jerusalem is built as a city that | is com|pact to|gether.
3. Whither the tribes go up, the | tribes of | Jah ;
   A testimony to Israel, to give | thanks·to the | name·of Je|hovah.
4. For there are set | thrones of | judgment,
   The | thrones·of the | house of | David.
5. Pray for the peace of Je|rusa|lem :
   They shall | prosper | that do | love thee.
6. Peace be with|in thy | walls ;
   Prosperity with|in thy | pala|ces.
7. For my brethren and com|panions' | sakes,
   I will now say, | Peace | be with|in thee.
8. For the sake of the house of Je|ho·vah our | God,
   I | will seek | good to | thee.

Ps. cxxii.

## CHANT 143.

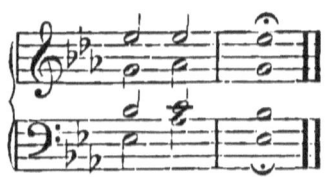

## SELECTION 164.

Celebration of the Lord, that he is omnipotent, 1—5: that he came into the world, 6: that he will save those who shall be of his church, 7—9.

1. Praise ye | JAH.
 Praise, O ye servants | of JE|HOVAH,
 Praise ye the | name | of JE|HOVAH.
2. Blessed be the | name · of JE|HOVAH,
 From this time | forth · and for | ever|more.
3. From the rising of the sun to its | going | down,
 The name of JE|HOVAH | is · to be | praised.
4. JEHOVAH is high a|bove all | nations ;
 And his | glo·ry a|bove the | heavens.
5. Who is like unto JE|HO·VAH our | GOD ?
 Who exalteth him|self to | dwell on | high:
6. Who humbleth him|self to | look
 Upon the heavens | and up|on the | earth.
7. He raiseth up the poor | out · of the | dust ;
 He lifteth the | needy | out · of the | dunghill ;
8. That he may | set · him with | nobles,
 With the | nobles | of his | people.
9. He maketh the barren woman to | dwell · in an house,
 And to be a | joyful | moth·er of | children
 Praise ye | JAH. Ps. cxiii

## Chant 144.

## SELECTION 165.

Celebration of the Lord in his Divine Humanity, 1—3: who instituted the church, 4: and who alone is God, 5: who alone teaches the church external and internal truths, 6—8.

1. Praise ye | Jah.
 Praise ye the | name of Je|hovah ;
 Praise, O ye | servants | of Je|hovah ;
2. Ye that stand in the | house of Je|hovah,
 In the courts of the | house | of our | God.
3. Praise Jehovah, for Je|ho·vah is | good :
 Sing praises to his | name, for | it is | pleasant.
4. For Jah hath chosen Jacob | for him|self,
 Israel for | his pe|culiar | treasure.
5. For I know that Je|ho·vah is | great :
 And that our | Lord · is a|bove all | gods.
6. All that Jehovah | pleased he | did,
 In heaven and in earth, in the | seas and | in all | depths.
7. He causeth the vapors | to as|cend
 From the | ends | of the | earth.
8 He maketh lightnings | for the | rain :
 He bringeth the wind | out of | his store-|houses.
 Praise ye | Jah.        Ps. cxxxv

## SELECTIONS AND CHANTS.

### CHANT 145. DOUBLE.

### SELECTION 166.

That the Lord regenerates the church, 1: that he leads the church, 2: that man's own intelligence does nothing, 3—6: that the spiritual and celestial church worships the Lord, who is the God of the church, 7—9.

1. Praise ye | JAH.
   Thy name, O JEHOVAH, | is for | ever;
   Thy memorial, O JEHOVAH, to | all | gener|ations:
2. For JEHOVAH will | judge his | people;
   And he will repent him|self con|cern ·ing his | servants.
3. The idols of the heathen are | sil·ver and | gold,
   The | work · of the | hands of | men.
4. They have mouths, but they | do not | speak:
   Eyes have they, | but they | do not | see:
5. They have ears, but they | do not | hear;
   Neither is there any | breath | in their | mouths.
6. They that make them are | like unto | them:
   So is every | one that | trust·eth in | them.
7. Bless JEHOVAH, O house of | Isra|el:
   Bless JE|HO·VAH, O | house of | Aaron:
8. Bless JEHOVAH, O | house of | Levi:
   Ye that fear JE|HOVAH, | bless JE|HOVAH.

## SELECTIONS AND CHANTS. 131

9. *Blessed be JEHOVAH | out of | Zion,
Who dwelleth | at Je|rusa|lem.
Praise ye | JAH.  Ps. cxxxv. 13

CHANT 146.

## SELECTION 167.

That the church will worship the Lord, who protects it, and teaches the Word, 1—4: that he removes ignorance thereby, 5—7: that he does these things for his church. 8, 9.

1. Praise JEHOVAH, O Je|rusa|lem :
   Praise | thou thy | GOD, O | Zion.
2. For he hath strengthened the | bars of thy | gates ;
   He hath | blessed thy | chil·dren with|in thee.
3. He maketh thy | border | peace :
   He filleth thee with the | finest | of the | wheat.
4. He sendeth forth his commandment | to the | earth :
   His word | runneth | very | swiftly.
5. He giveth | snow like | wool :
   He scattereth the | hoarfrost | like | ashes.
6. He casteth forth his | ice like | morsels :
   Who can | stand be|fore his | cold ?
7. He sendeth out his word, and | melteth | them :
   He causeth his wind to | blow ; the | waters | flow.
8. He declareth his | word unto | Jacob,
   His statutes and his judgments | unto | Isra|el.
9. He hath not dealt so with | any | nation :
   And his judgments, they | have not | known | them.
   Praise ye | JAH.  Ps. cxlvii. 12.

## SELECTIONS AND CHANTS.

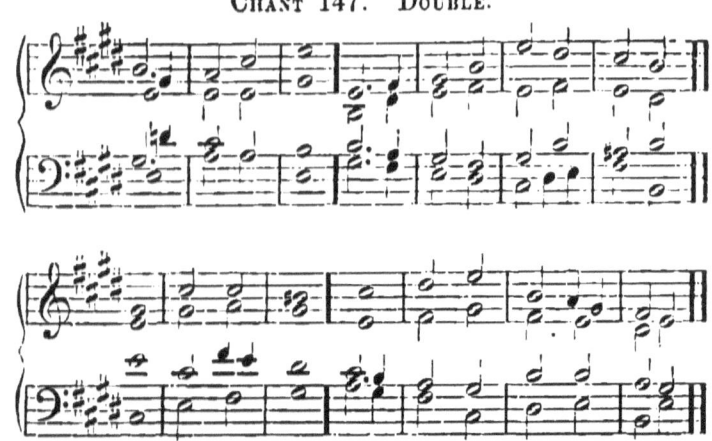

## SELECTION 168.

That they should confess the Lord, who alone is God and Lord, 1—3: who by divine truth formed heaven and the church, 4—6: from whom is all truth of doctrine and good of love, and the knowledge of them, 7—9: who delivers the natural man from the falsities of evil, and there establishes the church, and dissipates evils of every kind, 10—22: celebration and confession of the Lord, who delivers from falsities and evils, and gives truths and goods, 23—26: and this from mercy alone, 1—26.

1. O give thanks unto JEHOVAH; for | he is | good:
   For his | mercy | is for | ever.
2. O give thanks unto the | God of | gods:
   For his | mercy | is for | ever.
3. O give thanks unto the | Lord of | lords:
   For his | mercy | is for | ever.
4. To him who alone | doeth great | wonders:
   For his | mercy | is for | ever.
5. To him that by wisdom | made the | heavens:
   For his | mercy | is for | ever.
6. To him that spread out the earth a|bove the | waters:
   For his | mercy | is for | ever.
7. To him that | made great | lights:
   For his | mercy | is for | ever.
8. The sun to | rule by | day:
   For his | mercy | is for | ever.
9. The moon and stars to | rule by | night:
   For his | mercy | is for | ever.
10. To him that smote Egypt | in their | firstborn:
    For his | mercy | is for | ever.

11. And brought out Israel | from a|mong them :
    For his | mercy | is for | ever.
12. With a strong hand, and with an | outstretched | arm :
    For his | mercy | is for | ever.
13. To him who divided the Red Sea | into | parts :
    For his | mercy | is for | ever.
14. And made Israel to pass through the | midst of | it :
    For his | mercy | is for | ever.
15. But overthrew Pharaoh and his host | in the · Red | Sea :
    For his | mercy | is for | ever.
16. To him who led his people through the | wilder|ness :
    For his | mercy | is for | ever.
17. To him who | smote great | kings :
    For his | mercy | is for | ever.
18. And slew | famous | kings :
    For his | mercy | is for | ever.
19. Sihon king of the | Amor|ites :
    For his | mercy | is for | ever.
20. And Og the | king of | Bashan :
    For his | mercy | is for | ever.
21. And gave their land for an | heri|tage :
    For his | mercy | is for | ever.
22. An heritage to his servant | Isra|el :
    For his | mercy | is for | ever.
23. Who remembered us in our | low es|tate :
    For his | mercy | is for | ever.
24. And hath redeemed us from our | ene|mies :
    For his | mercy | is for | ever.
25. Who giveth food | to all | flesh :
    For his | mercy | is for | ever.
26. O give thanks unto the | GOD of | heaven :
    For his | mercy | is for | ever.            Ps. cxxxvi.

## SELECTION 169.

Celebration of the Lord by those who worship him, when the church is vastated, 1 : let them worship the Lord, who is the God of heaven and the church 2, 8.

1. Behold, bless ye JEHOVAH, all ye servants | of JE|HOVAH,
   Who by night | stand · in the | house · of JE|HOVAH.
2. Lift up your hands in the | sanctu|ary,
   And | bless | JE|HOVAH.
3. *JEHOVAH that made | heaven and | earth
   Bless | thee | out of | Zion.            Ps. cxxxiv.

## CHANT 148. DOUBLE.

## SELECTION 170.

Celebration of the Lord, 1, 2: that man of himself is nothing, 3, 4: that he is blessed who trusts in the Lord, who is the God of heaven and earth, 5, 6: who teaches and leads all who are in falsities from ignorance and desire truth, 7—11: that he reigns to eternity, 12

1. Praise ye | JAH.
Praise JEHOVAH, | O my | soul:
While I | live · will I | praise JE|HOVAH.
2. I will sing praises | un·to my | GOD,
While | I have | any | being.
3. Put not your | trust in | princes,
In the son of man, in | whom there | is no | help.
4. His breath goeth forth; he returneth | to his | earth:
In that very | day his | thoughts do | perish.
5. Happy is he that hath the GOD of Jacob | for his | help,
Whose hope is | in JE|HOVAH his | GOD.
6. Who made | heaven and | earth,
The sea, and | all that | is there|in.
7. Who keepeth | truth for | ever:
Who executeth | judgment | for · the op|pressed:

8 Who giveth | food · to the | hungry :
  Jehovah | loos·eth the | prison|ers :
9. Jehovah openeth the | eyes · of the | blind :
  Jehovah raiseth | them · that are | bowed | down :
10. Jehovah | lov·eth the | righteous :
  Jehovah | doth pre|serve the | strangers :
11. He relieveth the fatherless | and the | widow :
  But the way of the | wick·ed he | maketh | crooked.
12. Jehovah shall | reign for | ever,
  Thy God, O Zion, to | all | gener|ations :
  Praise ye | Jah.                          Ps. cxlvi.

CHANT 149.

## SELECTION 171.

Celebration of the Lord on account of his works and his justice, 1—7.

1. I will extol thee, my | God, O | King ;
  And I will bless thy | name for | ev·er and | ever.
2. Every | day · will I | bless thee ;
  And I will praise thy | name for | ev·er and | ever.
3. Great is Jehovah, and greatly | to be | praised ;
  And un|search·able | is his | greatness.
4. Generation to generation shall | praise thy | works,
  And shall de|clare thy | mighty | acts.
5. I will speak of the glorious honor of thy | majes|ty,
  And | of thy | wondrous | works.
6. And men shall speak of the might of thy | ter·rible | acts :
  And I | will de|clare thy | greatness.
7. The memory of thy great goodness shall | they pro|claim ;
  And shall sing a|loud · of thy | righteous|ness.     Ps. cxlv.

### Chant 150. Double.

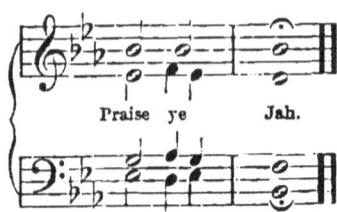

Praise ye    Jah.

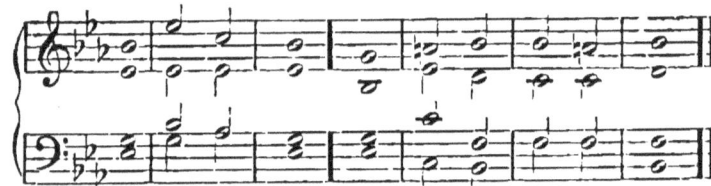

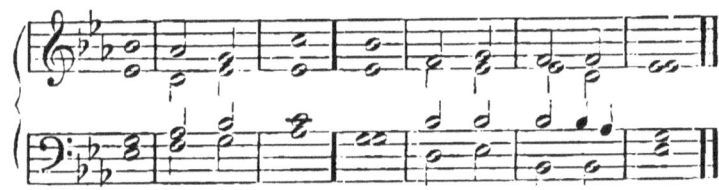

### SELECTION 172.

Celebration of the Lord by his church, 1, 2, 7: who reforms by the knowledges of truth, 3, 4: who alone can do this, 5: who teaches truths to those who are in ignorance, 6, 8—10: that man's own intelligence is not anything, but only that which is from Him, 11, 12.

1. Praise ye | Jah :
 For it is good to sing praises | un·to our | God ;
 For it is | pleas·ant ; and | praise is | comely.
2. Jehovah doth build up Je|rusa|lem :
 He gathereth together the | out·casts of | Isra|el.
3 He healeth the | bro·ken in | heart,
 And | bindeth | up their | wounds.
4 He telleth the number | of the | stars :
 He calleth them | all | by their | names.
5. Great is our Lord, and | great in | power :
 His under|stand·ing is | infi|nite.
6. Jehovah lifteth | up the | meek :
 He casteth the | wicked | down·to the | ground.
7. Sing unto Jehovah with | thanksgiv|ing :
 Sing praise upon the | harp un|to our | God :

SELECTIONS AND CHANTS. 137

8. Who covereth the | heaven with | clouds;
   Who prepareth | rain | for the | earth :
9. Who | mak·eth the | grass
   To | grow up|on the | mountains.
10. He giveth to the | beast his | food,
    To the young of | ravens | which do | cry.
11. He delighteth not in the | strength · of the | horse :
    He taketh not pleasure | in the | legs · of a | man.
12 JEHOVAH taketh pleasure in | them that | fear him,
   In those that | hope | in his | mercy.
   Praise ye | JAH.  Ps. cxlvii.

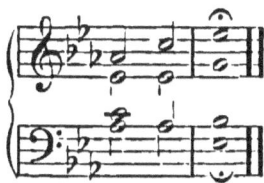

CHANT 151.

SELECTION 173.

That the Lord is not approached by the externals of worship, but by the internals, which are of truth and good.

1. Wherewith shall I | come be|fore JE|HOVAH,
   And bow myself be|fore the | High | GOD ?
2 Shall I come before him | with burnt-|offer|ings,
   With | calves · of a | year | old ?
3 Will JEHOVAH be | pleased with | thou·sands of | rams,
   With ten | thou·sands of | riv·ers of | oil ?
4. Shall I give my | firstborn for | my trans|gression,
   The fruit of my body | for the | sins · of my | soul ?
5. He hath showed thee. | O man, | what is | good ;
   And what doth JE|HO·VAH re|quire of | thee,
6. But to do justly, | and to | love | mercy,
   And to walk | humbly | with thy | GOD ?  Mic. vi. 6.

L.*

## CHANT 152. DOUBLE.

## SELECTION 174.

That all in the heavens and in the earths should worship the Lord from the goods and truths which are from him, 1—6; that all who are in the ultimates of heaven and the church should worship from truths and goods of every kind, 7—10; in general from the understanding and will of truth and good, 11, 12; because salvation is by those things which he gives, 13—16.

1. Praise ye | Jah.
 Praise ye Jehovah | from the | heavens:
 Praise | ye him | in the | heights.
2. Praise ye him, | all his | angels:
 Praise | ye him, | all his | hosts.
3. Praise ye him, | sun and | moon:
 Praise him, | all ye | stars of | light.
4. Praise him, ye | heavens of | heavens;
 And ye waters that | are a|bove the | heavens.
5. Let them praise the | name of Je|hovah;
 For he commanded, | and they | were cre|ated.
6. He hath also established them for | ev·er and | ever:
 He hath made a de|cree, and it | shall not | pass.

7. Praise Jehovah | from the | earth,
 Ye | sea-beasts, | and all | deeps ·

8. Fire and hail, | snow and | vapor,
   Stormy | wind ful|fil·ling his | word.
9. Mountains, | and all | hills;
   Trees of | fruit, | and all | cedars;
10. Wild beasts, | and all | cattle;
    Creeping | things, and | flying | fowl:
11. Kings of the earth, | and all | people;
    Princes, and all | judges | of the | earth:
12. Both young | men, and | maidens;
    Old | men, | with | children :
13. Let them praise the | name · of Je|hovah;
    For his name a|lone | is ex|alted :
14. His | glory | is
    A|bove the | earth and | heavens.
15. He also exalteth the | horn · of his | people,
    The | praise of | all his | saints ;
16. Of the children of | Isra|el,
    A people | near | unto | him.
    Praise ye | Jah.                    Ps. cxlviii.

## SELECTION 175.

That the Lord has overthrown the hells before, 1—4; and that he has established the church before, 5, 6.

1. God is my | king of | old,
   Working salvation | in the | midst · of the | earth.
2. Thou didst divide the | sea · by thy | strength :
   Thou didst break the heads of the | sea-beasts | in the | waters.
3. Thou didst break in pieces the heads of le|via|than,
   And gavest him for meat to the people | of the | wilder|ness.
4. Thou didst cleave the fountain | and the | flood :
   Thou didst dry | up · the un|failing | streams.
5. The day is thine, the night | also is | thine :
   Thou hast pre|pared the | light · and the | sun.
6. Thou hast set all the borders | of the | earth :
   Summer and | winter, | thou hast | made them.   Ps. lxxiv. 12.

## Chant 153.

## SELECTION 176.

That the Lord is to be worshiped from the affection of truth and good, because he loves them, 1—4: because they have divine truth, 5, 6; by which the hells are restrained, 7—9.

1. Praise ye | Jah.
   Sing unto Jehovah a | new | song;
   His praise in the | congre|ga·tion of | saints.
2. Let Israel rejoice in | him that | made him :
   Let the children of Zion be | joyful | in their | king.
3. Let them praise his | name · in the | dance :
   Let them sing praises to | him with | tim·brel and | harp.
4. For Jehovah taketh pleasure | in his | people :
   He will a|dorn the | meek · with sal|vation.
5. Let the saints be | joy·ful in | glory :
   Let them sing a|loud up|on their | beds.
6. Let the high praises of God be | in their | mouth,
   And a | two-edged | sword · in their | hand :
7. To execute vengeance up|on the | heathen,
   And punish|ments up|on the | people :
8. To bind their | kings with | chains,
   And their | no·bles with | fet·ters of | iron :
9. To execute upon them the | judgment | written :
   This | hon·or have | all the | saints.
   Praise ye | Jah.     Ps. cxlix

### Chant 154.

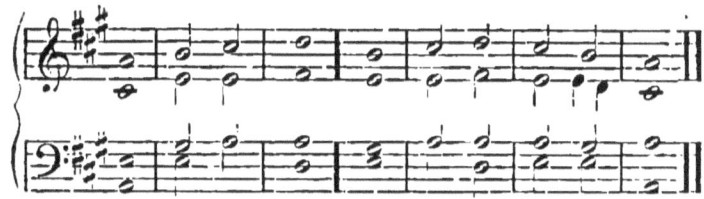

### SELECTION 177.*

That the Lord is to be worshiped, because he is omnipotent, 1, 2: that he is to be worshiped from every affection of good and truth, 3—6.

1. Praise ye | Jah.
Praise God in his | sanctu|ary :
Praise him in the | firmament | of his | power.
2. Praise him for his | mighty | acts :
Praise him according | to his | excellent | greatness.
3. Praise him with the | sound · of the | trumpet :
Praise him with the | psaltery | and the | harp.
4. Praise him with the | timbrel and | dance :
Praise him with stringed | instru|ments and | organs.
5. Praise him upon the | cymbals of | hearing :
Praise him up|on the | cymbals of | shouting.
6 Let | every | thing
That hath | breath | praise | Jah.
**Praise ye** | **Jah**              Ps. cl.

* See p. 210.

142  SELECTIONS AND CHANTS.

### Chant 155. Double.

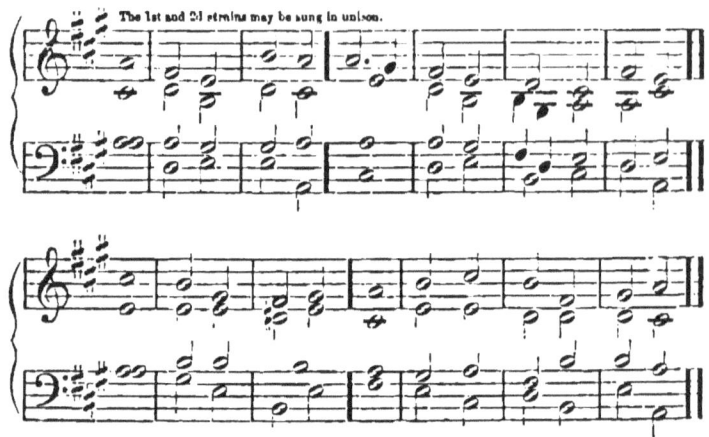

## SELECTION 178.

Concerning the redemption and salvation of those who are in the new church from the Lord, 1, 2: that falsities and evils will not hurt them, 3, 4: that they will come to him from all parts out of every nation, 5—14.

1. But now thus saith Jehovah, that created | thee, O | Jacob;
And he that | formed | thee, O | Israel;
2. Fear not; for | I · have re|deemed thee:
I have called thee by thy | name, | thou art | mine.
3. When thou passest through the waters, | I · will be | with thee;
And through the rivers, they | shall not | over|flow thee:
4. When thou walkest through the fire, thou shalt | not be | burned;
Neither shall the | flame | kin·dle up|on thee.
5. For I am Jeho·vah, thy | God,
The Holy One of | Israel, thy | Savior:
6. I gave Egypt | for thy | ransom,
Ethiopia and | Seba | for thee.
7. Since thou wast precious | in my | sight,
Thou hast been honor|able, and | I have | loved thee:
8. Therefore will I give | men for | thee,
And | people | for thy | life.
9. Fear not thou; for | I am | with thee:
I will bring thy seed from the east, and | gather | thee from the | west:
10. I will say to the | north, Give | up;
And to the | south. | Keep not | back:

SELECTIONS AND CHANTS.   142

11. Bring my sons from far, and my daughters from the | ends of the | earth :
Every one that is | called | by my | name ;
12. For I have created him | for my | glory :
I have | formed him ; | yea, I have | made him.   Is. xliii.

CHANT 156.

SELECTION 179.

That it is the Lord from whom is all salvation, 2—4: that it is the Divine Humanity from the Divinity within Himself, from whom it is, 5—8: that blessed is he who confesses and worships the Lord, 9—12.

1. O give thanks unto JEHOVAH ; for | he is | good :
For his | mercy | is for | ever. . . . .

2. Open to me the gates of | righteous|ness :
I will go into them ; | I will | praise JE|HOVAH.

3. This is the | gate of JE|HOVAH,
The righteous shall | enter | into | it.

4. I will praise thee ; for | thou hast | heard me,
And art be|come | my sal|vation.

5. The stone which the | build·ers re|fused,
Is become the | head-stone | of the | corner.

6. This is | from JE|HOVAH :
It is | mar·vellous | in our | eyes.

7. This is the day which JE|HO·VAH hath | made :
We will re|joice · and be | glad in | it.

8. Save now, I beseech thee, | O JE|HOVAH :
O JEHOVAH, I beseech thee, send | now pros|peri|ty.

9. Blessed be he that cometh in the | name · of JE|HOVAH :
We have blessed you | out · of the | house · of JE|HOVAH.

10. GOD is JEHOVAH, who hath | showed us | light :
Bind the sacrifice with | cords · to the | horns · of the | altar

11. Thou art my GOD, and | I will | praise thee ;
My | GOD, I | will ex|alt thee.

12. O give thanks unto JEHOVAH, for | he is | good :
For his | mercy | is for | ever.   Ps. cxviii. 1, 19—29

## Chant 157.

## SELECTION 180.

*Concerning the coming of the Lord, and a new heaven and a new church thcr*

1. And it shall come to pass | in the · last | days,
   That the mountain of the | house | of Je|hovah
2. Shall be established in the | top · of the | mountains,
   And shall be ex|alt·ed a|bove the | hills.
3. And all nations shall | flow unto | it ;
   And many | peo·ple shall | go, and | say,
4. Come ye, and let us go up to the mountain | of Je|hovah,
   To the | house · of the | God of | Jacob.
5. And he will teach us | of his | ways,
   And we will | walk | in his | paths.
6. For out of Zion shall go | forth the | law,
   And the word of Jehovah | from Je|rusa|lem.
7. And he shall judge a|mong the | nations,
   And shall re|buke | many | people.
8. And they shall beat their | swords into | plough-shares,
   And their | spears into | pruning-|hooks.
9. Nation shall not lift up | sword a·gainst | nation ;
   Neither shall they | learn war | any | more.
10. O house of | Jacob, | come ye,
    And let us | walk · in the | light · of Je|hovah.   Is. ii. 2.

## SELECTION 181.

*The Lord will open truths, and take away blindness, 1—6: confession of Him, 7 8*

1. And in this mountain shall Jehovah of Hosts | make · to all
   | people
   A feast of fat things, a | feast of | wines · on the | lees,
2. Of fat things | full of | marrow,
   Of wines on the | lees | well re|fined.
3. And he will de|stroy · in this | mountain
   The face of the covering | cast | o·ver all | people,
4. And the vail that is spread | o·ver all | nations.
   He will swallow up | death in | victo|ry :

DOUBLE.

5. And the | LORD JE|HOVAH
Will wipe away | tears from | off all | faces:
6. And the rebuke of his people shall he | take a|way
From off all the earth: for JE|HO·VAH hath | spoken | it.
7. And it shall be said in that day, Lo, | this·is our | GOD;
We have waited for | him, and | he will | save us:
8. This is JEHOVAH; we have | waited | for him;
We will be glad and re|joice in | his sal|vation.   Is. xxv. 6.

## SELECTION 182.

That falsity will be everywhere in the church, 1—3; until there be divine truth from the Lord, when there will be truth and good, and protection from falsities, 4—8; falsity will still remain to the end, 9; but not with those who love truth and good, 10.

1. Upon the land of my people shall come up | thorns and | briers;
Yea, upon all the houses of | joy·in the | joyous | city.
2. Because the palaces shall | be for|saken :
The multitudes of the | city | shall be | left.
3. The forts and towers shall be for | dens for | ever :
A joy of wild | ass·es, a | pas·ture of | flocks :
4. Un|til the | Spirit
Be poured up|on us | from on | high ;
5. And the wilderness be a | fruitful | field,
And the fruitful field be | counted | for a | forest.
6. Then judgment shall dwell in the | wilder|ness,
And righteousness re|main·in the | fruitful | field :
7. And the work of righteousness | shall be | peace ;
And the effect of righteousness quietness | and as|sur·ance
for | ever.
8. And my people shall dwell in a peaceable | habi|tation,
And in sure dwellings, and in | quiet | rest·ing | places:
9. When it shall hail, coming | down·on the | forest ;
And the city shall be | low·in a | low | place.
10. Blessed are ye that sow be|side all | waters,
That send forth the | feet·of the | ox·and the | ass.
Is. xxxii. 13

## Chant 82.

### SELECTION 183.

*The state of innocence with those in the heavens who trust in the Lord, 1—6.*

1. The wolf shall | dwell · with the | lamb ;
   And the leopard | shall lie | down with · the | kid ;
2. And the calf, and the young lion, and the | fat·ling to|gether ;
   And a | little | child shall | lead them.
3. And the cow and the | bear shall | feed ;
   ¹Their young ones shall lie | down to|gether ;
   And the lion | shall eat | straw like · the | ox.
4. And the sucking child shall play on the | hole · of the | asp ,
   And the weaned child shall put his hand up|on the | cocka · trice' | den.
5. They shall not | hurt · nor de|stroy,
   In all the mountain | of my | holi|ness :
6. For the earth shall be full of the knowledge | of JE|HOVAH,
   As the | waters | cover the | seas.      Is. xi. 6.

## Chant 158.

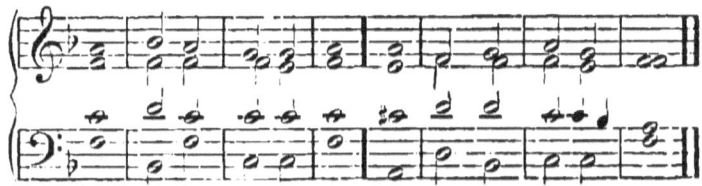

### SELECTION 184.

*Concerning the coming of the Lord, that he will judge from divine wisdom, and save the faithful, and destroy the unfaithful, 1—8.*

1. There shall come forth a Rod | out · of the | stem of | Jesse,
   And a branch shall | grow out | of his | roots.
2. And the Spirit of JE|HO·VAH shall | rest up|on him,
   The Spirit of | wis·dom and | under|standing,

SELECTIONS AND CHANTS.  147

3. The Spirit of | counsel | and of | might,
The Spirit of knowledge and | of the | fear · of JE|HOVAH;
4. And shall make him | quick of | under|standing,
In the | fear · of JE|HO|VAH.
5. And he shall not judge | after the | sight · of his | eyes,
Neither reprove after the | hearing | of his | ears.
6. But with righteousness | shall he | judge the | poor,
And reprove with equity | for the | meek · of the | earth.
7 And he shall smite the | earth · with the | rod · of his | mouth;
And with the breath of his | lips · shall he | slay the | wicked.
8 And righteousness shall be the | girdle | of his | loins,
And faithfulness the | girdle | of his | reins.  Is. xi.

CHANT 69.

SELECTION 185.

The coming of the Lord, and the new church which will receive him, 1, 2: that the Lord will do all things; who is described, and who will protect from falsities and evils, 3--8.

1 The people that | walked in | darkness,
Have | seen a | great | light :
2. They that dwell in the land of the | shad·ow of | death,
Upon them | hath the | light | shined.....
3. For unto us a | CHILD is | born,
Unto | us a | SON is | given :
4. And the government shall be up|on his | shoulder;
And his | name | shall be | called,
5 Wonderful, Counsellor, | GOD, the | Mighty,
FATHER of e|ter·nity, | Prince of | peace.
6 Of the increase of his government and peace there shall | be
no | end,
Upon the throne of David, | and up|on his | kingdom;
7. To order it, and to es|tablish | it,
With | judgment | and with | justice,
8. From henceforth | e·ven for | ever :
The zeal of JEHOVAH of Hosts | will per|form | this.
Is ix. 2, 6, 7

## CHANT 159.

## SELECTION 186.

That when the Lord comes, the things of the church, which have perished, are to be restored, 1, 2; the exteruals of the church, 3; the Interuals of the church, 4, 5; more than ever before, 6, 7: that by their truths and goods there will be conjunction, 8, 9; and they are to be acknowledged, 10, 11.

1. And they shall | build the · old | wastes ;
   They shall raise up the | former | deso|lations :
2. And they shall re|pair the · waste | cities,
   The desolations of | many | gener|ations.
3. And strangers shall stand, and | feed your | flocks ;
   And the sons of the alien shall be your ploughmen | and your | vine-dress|ers.
4. But ye shall be named the | priests · of JE|HOVAH :
   They shall call you the | min·isters | of our | GOD.
5. Ye shall eat of the riches | of the | Gentiles ;
   And in their glory | shall ye | boast your|selves.
6. For your shame ye | shall have | double ;
   And for confusion they | shall re|joice · in their | portion.
7. Therefore in their land they shall pos|sess the | double :
   Everlasting | joy shall | be · unto | them.
8. For I JEHOVAH | love | judgment :
   I hate robbery | for burnt-|offer|ing.
9. And I will direct their | work in | truth ;
   And I will make an everlasting | cove|nant with | them.
10. And their seed shall be known a|mong the | nations,
    And their | off·spring a|mong the | people.
11. All that see them shall ac|knowledge | them,
    That they are the | seed JE|HO·VAH hath | blessed.

Is. lxi. 4

## SELECTION 187. (Cht. 160.)

A new church, which will acknowledge the Lord.

1. Sing, O | daugh·ter of | Zion ;
   Shout, | O | Isra|el :
2. Be glad and rejoice with | all the | heart,
   O daughter | of Je|rusa|lem.

3. Jehovah hath taken a|way thy | judgments ;
He hath cast | out thine | ene|my :
4. The King of Israel, Jehovah, is in the | midst of | thee :
Thou shalt not see | evil | any | more.   Zeph. iii. 14.

CHANT 160. DOUBLE.

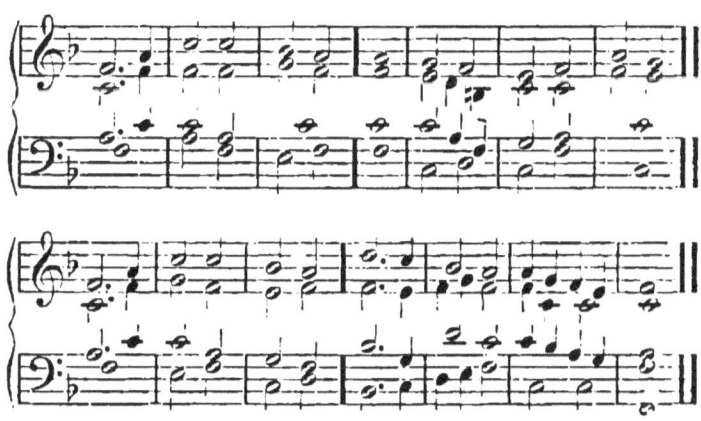

SELECTION 188.

**Confession and celebration of the Lord on account of salvation, 1—10.**

1. And in that day thou shalt say, O Jehovah, | I will | praise
Though | thou wast | angry | with me.   [Lord,
2. Thine anger is | turned a|way,
And | thou hast | comfort·ed | me.
3. Behold, God is | my sal|vation ;
I will | trust, and | not · be a|fraid :
4 For Jah Jehovah is my | strength and | song ;
He also is be|come | my sal|vation.
5. Therefore with joy shall | ye draw | water,
Out of the | wells | of sal|vation.
6 And in that day | shall ye | say,
Praise Jehovah, | call up|on his | name ;
7. Declare his doings a|mong the | people ;
Make mention that his | name | is ex|alted.
8. Sing | un·to Je|hovah ;
For he | hath done | excel·lent | things :
9. This is made known in | all the | earth :
Cry out and shout, thou in|habi|tant of | Zion :
10. For great in the | midst of | thee
Is the Holy | One of | Isra|el.   Is. xii

M*

## CHANT 161.

## SELECTION 189.

That the Lord hears, and can do all things; but that falsities and evils hinder, 1—4: that truths have been falsified by them, whence are evils of life and falsities of doctrine, 5—8.

1. Behold, Jehovah's | hand · is not | shortened,
That it | cannot | save;
2. Neither his | ear | heavy,
That it | cannot | hear.
3. But your iniquities have | sepa|rated
Between | you · and your | God;
4. And your sins have hid his | face from | you,
That he | will not | hear.
5. For your hands are de|filed with | blood,
And your fingers with in|iqui|ty:
6. Your lips have | spoken | lies;
Your tongue hath | mut·tered per|verseness.
7. None | call·eth for | justice,
Nor any | plead·eth for | truth:
8. They trust in vanity, | and speak | lies;
They conceive mischief, and bring forth in|iqui|ty. Is. lix.

## SELECTION 190.

The new church which is to be established, 1, 2: the judgment upon those who have adulterated the goods of the church and profaned its truths, which is Babylon, 3—8.

1. And it shall come to pass | in the | day
That Jehovah shall | give you | rest,
2. From thy sorrow and | from thy | fear,
And from the hard bondage wherein thou wast ¦ made to|
3. That thou shalt take | up this | proverb, [serve,
Against the king of Babylon, | and shalt | say,
4. How hath the op|pressor | ceased,
The golden | city | ceased.
5. Jehovah hath broken the | staff· of the | wicked,
The sceptre | of the | rulers.

DOUBLE.

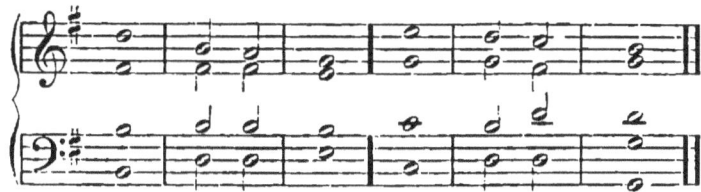

6. He who smote the | peo·ple in | wrath,
   With a con|tin·ual | stroke,
7. He that ruled the | na·tions in | anger,
   Is persecuted, and none | hinder|eth.
8. The whole earth is at | rest, is | quiet:
   They break forth | into | singing.          Is. xiv. 3.

## SELECTION 191.

That the Lord rules the heavens, 1—4: why the church is ignorant of it, 5, 6: that the Lord sustains the church with those who look to him, 7, 8, 11, 12: that those who do not look to him have no power, but fall, 9, 10.

1. To whom then will ye | liken | me,
   Or shall I be equal? saith the | Holy | One.
2. Lift up your eyes round a|bout and | see,
   Who hath cre|ated | these?
3. That bringeth out their | host by | number:
   He calleth them | all by | names:
4. By the greatness | of his | might,
   For that he is strong in power, not | one doth | fail.
5. Why sayest | thou, O | Jacob,
   And speakest, O | Isra|el,
6. My way is | hid·from Je|hovah,
   And my judgment is passed over | from my | God?
7. Hast thou not known? hast | thou not | heard?
   That the everlasting | God, Je|hovah,
8. The creator of the ends of the earth, fainteth not, | nei ther
       is | weary?
   There is no searching of his | under|standing.
9. He giveth power | to the | faint;
   And to them that have no might he in|creaseth | strength.
10. Even the youths shall | faint·and be | weary,
    And the young men shall | ut·terly | fall.
11. But they that wait for Jehovah | shall re·new | strength;
    They shall mount up with | wings as | eagles;
12. They shall run, and | not be | weary;
    They shall walk, | and not | faint.          Is. xl. 25.

### CHANT 162.

## SELECTION 192.

*That they who do good from the Lord will be of his church, and that they will have from the Lord an abundance of all things of truth, 1—7.*

1. Look | upon | Zion,
   The city of | our so|lemni|ties.
2. Thine eyes shall see Jerusalem a quiet | habi|tation,
   A tabernacle that shall | not be | taken | down.
3. Not one of the stakes thereof shall ever | be re|moved,
   Neither shall any of the | cords there|of be | broken.
4. But there the glorious JEHOVAH shall be | unto | us
   A place of | broad | riv·ers and | streams ;
5. Wherein shall go no | gal·ley with | oars,
   Neither shall gallant | ship | pass there|by.
6. For JEHOVAH | is our | Judge,
   JEHOVAH | is our | Lawgiv|er,
7. JEHOVAH | is our | King,
   He | will | save | us.

Is. xxxiii. 20.

### CHANT 163.

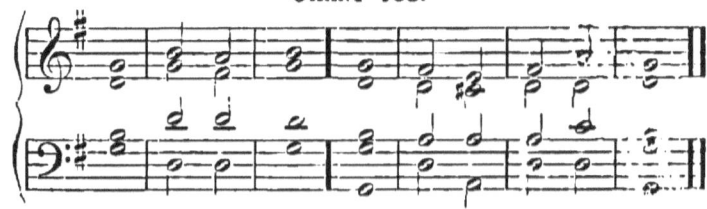

## SELECTION 193.

*A new church, from which the Lord will remove evils and falsities.*

1. Behold, | at that | time,
   I will un|do all | that af|flict thee :
2. And I will save | her that | halteth,
   And gather | her · that was | driven | out:

3. And I will get them | praise and | fame,
In every land where they | have been | put to | shame.
4. At that time | will I | bring you,
Even in the | time · that I | gather | you:
5. For I will make you a | name · and a | praise,
Among all | people | of the | earth;
6 When I turn back your cap|tivi|ty
Before your | eyes, | saith JE|HOVAH.    Zeph. iii. 19.

CHANT 164.   DOUBLE.

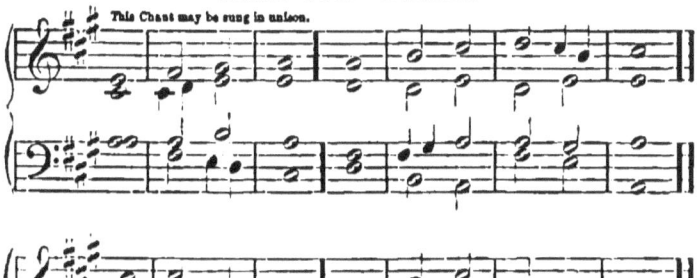

SELECTION 194.

That from the Lord is all good and truth, and in him every nation will trust, 1—4: nothing remains to eternity, except what is from him, 5—8.

1. Hearken unto | me, my | people;
And give ear unto | me, | O my | nation:
2 For a law shall pro|ceed from | me;              [people.
And I will make my judgment to | rest · for a | light · of the
3 My righteousness is near; my salvation | is gone | forth;
And mine | arms shall | judge the | people.
4 The isles shall | wait upon | me,
And on mine | arm | shall they | trust.
5. Lift up your | eyes · to the | heavens,
And look up|on the | earth be|neath:
6. For the heavens shall vanish a|way like | smoke,
And the earth | shall wax | old · like a | garment:
7. And they that | dwell there|in
Shall | die in | like | manner:
8. But my salvation shall | be for | ever,
And my righteousness | shall not | be a|bolished.   Is. li. 4

## CHANT 165.

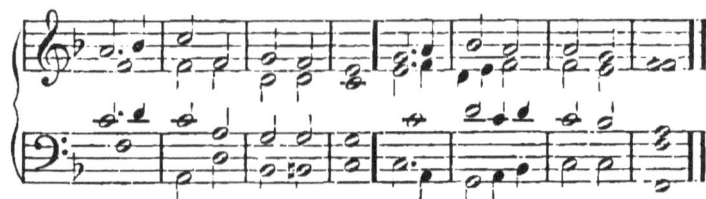

### SELECTION 195.

*A prediction concerning the coming of the Lord, and concerning the salvation of those who receive him, 1—7.*

1. O Zion, that | bringest | good | tidings,
Get thee up | in·to the | high | mountain.
2. O Jerusalem, that | bringest | good | tidings,
Lift | up thy | voice with | strength.
3. Lift it | up, be | not a|fraid :
Say unto the cities of | Ju·dah, Be|hold your | GOD.
4. Behold, the LORD JE|HO·VIH will | come in | strength ;
And his | arm shall | rule for | him.
5. Behold, his re|ward is | with | him,
And his | work be|fore | him.
6. He shall | feed his | flock·like a | shepherd ;
He shall gather the | lambs | with his | arm ;
7. And shall | carry | them·in his | bosom :
And shall gently | lead·those that | are with | young.
Is. xl. 9

### SELECTION 196.

*That a new church will be instituted under the Lord, who will reign over it.*

1. Rejoice greatly, O | daughter | of | Zion ;
Shout, O daughter | of Je|rusa|lem.
2. Behold, thy | King·cometh | unto | thee :
He is | just, and | hav·ing sal|vation ;
3. Lowly, and | rid·ing up|on an | ass ;
And upon a | colt, the | foal·of an | ass.
4. And I will cut off the | chari|ot from | Ephraim,
And the | horse·from Je|rusa|lem.
5. And the battle-|bow shall | be cut | off :
And he shall speak | peace un|to the | heathen.
6. And his dominion shall | be from | sea to | sea,
And from the river | to the | ends·of the | earth. Zech. ix. 9

## CHANT 166.

## SELECTION 197.

*Concerning the Lord in whom is the Divinity, that he will gently lead and teach.*

1. Behold my servant, whom | I up|hold ;
Mine elect, in | whom my | soul de|lighteth.
2. I will put my | Spir·it up|on him :
He shall bring forth | judgment | un·to the | Gentiles.
3. He shall not | cry, nor lift | up ;
Nor cause his | voice · to be | heard · in the | street.
4. A bruised reed shall | he not | break ;
¹And the smoking flax shall | he not | quench :
He shall bring forth | judgment | unto | truth.
5. He shall not fail, nor | be dis|couraged ;
Till he have set | judgment | in the | earth :
²And the isles shall | wait | for his | law.    Is. xlii.

## SELECTION 198.

*That the Lord causes the infernals to perish, when he comes with divine power, 1—4 : that before it was not heard and done, 5, 6 : that thus he saves the faithful, 7.*

1. Oh that thou wouldst rend the heavens, that thou | wouldst come | down,
That the mountains | might flow | down · at thy | presence.
2 As when the melting | fire | burneth,
The fire doth | cause the | wa·ters to | boil :
3 To make thy name known to thine | adver|saries,
That the nations may | tremble | at thy | presence.
4. When thou didst terrible things we | looked not | for,
Thou camest down ; the mountains flowed | down | at thy |
5. For since the beginning | of the | world,    [presence.
They have not | heard · nor per|ceived · by the | ear ;
6. Neither hath the eye seen, O God, a|side from | thee,
What he hath prepared for | him that | waiteth | for him.
7. Thou meetest him that rejoiceth and worketh | righteous|ness,
Those that re|member | thee · in thy | ways.    Is. lxiv

## CHANT 167. DOUBLE.

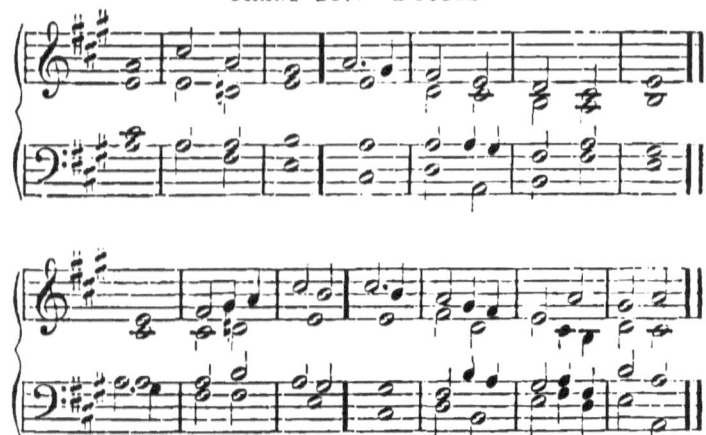

## SELECTION 199.

That man's own intelligence is of no avail, 1—4 : that the Lord has dominion over all things, and that without him all things fail, 5—12.

1. To whom then will ye | liken | God?
   Or what likeness will | ye com|pare unto | him?
2. The workmen melteth a |graven | image,
   And the goldsmith spreadeth it over with gold, and | casteth | silver | chains.
3. He that is so impoverished that he hath | no ob|lation,
   Chooseth a | tree that | will not | rot :
4. He seeketh unto him a | cunning | workman,
   To prepare a graven image | that shall | not be | moved.
5. Have ye not known? have | ye not | heard?
   Hath it not been | told you | from · the be|ginning?
6. Have ye not | under|stood
   From the found|ations | of the | earth?
7. It is he that sitteth upon the circle | of the | earth,
   And the inhabitants there|of · are as | grasshop|pers :
8. That stretcheth out the heavens | as a | curtain,
   And spreadeth them | out · as a | tent to | dwell in :
9. That bringeth the | prin·ces to | nothing :
   He maketh the judges of the | earth as | vani|ty.      sown :
10. Yea, they shall not be planted ; yea, they shall | not be |
    Yea, their stock shall | not take | root · in the | earth.
11. And he shall also blow upon them, and | they shall | wither ;
    And the whirlwind shall | take · them a|way as | stubble.

SELECTIONS AND CHANTS. 157

12. To whom then will ye | liken | me,
Or shall I be equal? | saith the | HOLY | ONE.  Is. xl. 18.

CHANT 168. DOUBLE.

SELECTION 200.

That those who are out of the church, who have not the Word, are to be accepted, that they may become the church; and that all things of heaven are to be given to them, 1—6: that the Lord will protect and deliver them from the infernals, 7—10.

1. The wilderness and the | barren | place
   Shall | be | glad for | them ;
2. And the desert | shall re|joice,
   And | blossom | as the | rose.
3. It shall blossom a|bundant|ly,
   And rejoice | e·ven with | joy and | singing.
4. The glory of Lebanon shall be | giv·en to | it,
   The excellency of | Carmel | and of | Sharon.
5. They shall see the glory | of JE|HOVAH,
   The excel|lency | of our | GOD.
6. Strengthen ye the | weak | hands, ·
   And con|firm the | feeble | knees.
7. Say to them of | fearful | heart,
   Be | strong, | fear | not.
8. Behold, your GOD will | come with | vengeance,
   GOD with a recompense; | he will | come and | save you.
9. Then the eyes of the | blind·shall be | opened,
   And the ears of the | deaf shall | be un|stopped.
10. Then shall the lame | leap·as an | hart,
    And the | tongue·of the | dumb shall | sing.  Is. xxxv

## CHANT 169.

## SELECTION 201.

That the Lord will fight against the hells, which he will conquer, and destroy their power, 1—6: that those who are in ignorance are then to be illustrated, 7—9.

1. JEHOVAH shall go forth as a | mighty | man:
   He shall stir up jealousy like a | man of | war:
2. He shall | cry, yea, | roar:
   He shall prevail against his | ene|mies.
3. I have long time | hold·on my | peace:
   I have been still, and have re|frained my|self.
4. I will cry like a | trav·ailing | woman:
   I will destroy and de|vour at | once.
5. I will make waste | moun·tains and | hills;
   And will dry up | all their | herbs:
6. And I will make their | rivers | islands;
   And I will dry | up their | pools.
7. And I will bring the blind by a | way they | knew not;
   I will lead them in paths they | have not | known.
8. I will make darkness | light be|fore them;
   And crooked things | into | straightness.
9. These things will I | do unto | them,
   ⁴And will not for|sake | them.  Is. xlii. 13.

## SELECTION 202.

That the worshipers of God look to the Lord from whom, and to the church by which, they live, 1—4; because,the Lord will fill them with intelligence, and make them blessed, 5—7.

1. Hearken to me, ye that follow after | righteous|ness,
   Ye that | seek JE|HOVAH:
2. Look unto the rock whence | ye are | hewn,
   And to the hole of the pit whence | ye are | digged.
3. Look unto Abra|ham your | father,
   And unto Sarah that | bare | you:
4. For I called | him a|lone,
   And blessed him, | and in|creased him.

## DOUBLE.

5 For JEHOVAH shall | comfort | Zion :
 He will comfort all her | waste | places:
6. And he will make her wilder|ness like | Eden,
 And her desert like the garden | of JE|HOVAH.
7. Joy and gladness shall be | found there|in ;
 \*Thanksgiving, and the voice of | melo|dy.  Is. li.

## SELECTION 203.

To the new church : that the Lord alone is the God of heaven and earth, 1—3 : that the Lord rejects those that cause falsity to appear as truth and evil as good, because from their own intelligence they are insane, 4, 5 ; when he reëstablishes his church, 6—8 ; and destroys the old, 9 : that this is from the Lord by the Divine Humanity, which is here Cyrus, 10.

1. Thus saith JEHOVAH, | thy Re|deemer,
 And he that formed thee | from the | womb ;
2. I am JEHOVAH, that | mak·eth all | things ;
 \*That stretcheth forth the | heavens a|lone ;
 That spreadeth abroad the | earth · by my|self :
3. That frustrateth the tokens | of the | liars,
 And maketh di|viners | mad :
4. That turneth | wise men | backward,
 And maketh their | knowledge | foolish :
5. That confirmeth the | word · of his | servant,
 And performeth the counsel of his | messen|gers :
6 That saith to Jerusalem, Thou shalt be in|habit|ed ;
 \*And to the cities of Judah, Ye | shall be | built :
 And I will raise up the decayed | places there|of :
7 That saith to the | deep, Be | dry ;
 And I will dry | up thy | rivers :
8 That saith of Cyrus, | He · is my | shepherd ;
 And shall perform | all my | pleasure :
9. Even saying to Je|rusa|lem,
 Thou | shalt be | built ;
10. And | to the | temple,
 Thy foundations | shall be | laid.  Is. xliv. 24.

## CHANT 170. DOUBLE.

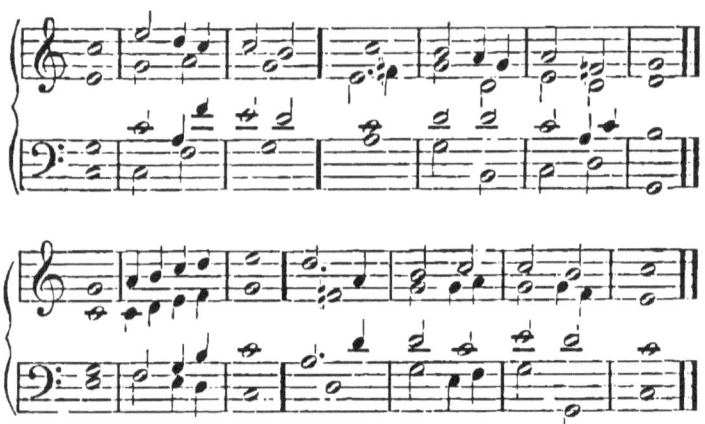

## SELECTION 204.

To the new church : that the doctrine of truth will be enlarged, lest falsities break in, 1, 2; and that it may reject the falsities, 3, 4; by which they have been taken captive, and from which they will be delivered, 5; because they were imbued with knowledges of falsity confirmed by reasonings, 6; therefore evil and ignorance of God, 7, 8: but they shall know their God, when he comes into the world, 9, 10.

1. Awake, awake, put on thy | strength, O | Zion ;   [city :
Put on thy beautiful garments, O Jerusa|lem, the | Holy |
2. For henceforth there shall no more | come · into | thee
The uncircum|cised and | the un|clean.
3. Shake thyself | from the | dust :
Arise, sit down, | O Je|rusa|lem.
4. Loose thyself from the | bands · of thy | neck,
O | captive | daugh·ter of | Zion.
5. For thus saith Jehovah, Ye have sold your|selves for |
And ye shall | be re|deemed · without | money :   [nought ;
6. For thus saith the Lord Jehovah, my people went down
aforetime into Egypt to | sojourn | there ;
And the Assyrian op|pressed · them with|out a | cause.
7 Now therefore, what have I here, | saith Je|hovah,
That my people is | ta·ken a|way for | nought ?
8. They that rule over them make them to howl, | saith Je-|
hovah ;
And my name continually | ev·ery | day · is blas|phemed.
9. Therefore my people shall | know my | name :
Therefore | shall they | know · in that | day,
10. That I am | he · that doth | speak ;
Be|hold, | it is | I.                    Is. lii

## Chant 171.

## SELECTION 205.

Glorification of the Lord on account of truth from him, which they will receive and confess, 1—4: that the old church, being utterly destroyed, is rejected, 5—7: wherefore there is then expectation of the coming of the Lord, 8—12: that the impious will not receive him, 13—14.

1. We have a | strong | city :
   Salvation will he ap|point for | walls and | bulwarks.
2. Open | ye the | gates,
   That the righteous nation which | keepeth | truth may | enter.
3. Thou wilt keep the stayed | mind in | peace,
   In peace be|cause · it hath | trust·ed in | thee.
4. Trust ye in Je|ho·vah for|ever ;
   For in Jah Jehovah | is the | Rock of | ages.
5. For he bringeth down them that | dwell on | high :
   The lofty city, | he doth | lay it | low ;
6. He layeth it low, even | to the | ground ;
   He bringeth | it un|to the | dust.
7. The foot shall | tread it | down,
   The feet of the | poor, the | steps · of the | needy.
8. The way of the just is | upright|ness ;
   Thou, Most Upright, dost | weigh the | path · of the | just.
9. Yea, in the | way · of thy | judgments,
   O Jehovah, | I have | waited | for thee :
10. The desire of our soul is | unto thy | name,
    And to the re|mem|brance of | thee.
11. With my soul have I desired thee | in the | night ;
    Yea, with my spirit within me | will I | seek the | early :
12. For when thy judgments are | in the | earth,
    The inhabitants of the world will | learn | righteous|ness.
13. Let favor be | showed · to the | wicked,
    Yet will he not | learn | righteous·|ness
14. In the land of uprightness will he | deal un|justly,
    And will not behold the | maj·esty | of Je|hovah. Is. xxvi

N*

## CHANT 172.

## SELECTION 206.

They shall know their God when he comes into the world, 1—3: when he will restore the church, 4—7; and will manifest himself, 8, 9.

1. How beautiful up|on the | mountains
Are the feet of | him that | bringeth good | tidings,
2. That pro|claimeth | peace,
That | bringeth good | tidings of | good,
3. ⁸That pro|claimeth sal|vation ;
That saith to | Zion, | Thy God | reigneth.
4. Thy watchmen shall lift | up the | voice :
With the voice to|gether | shall they | sing.
5. For they shall see | eye to | eye,
When Jehovah shall | bring a|gain | Zion.
6. Break forth | into | joy ;
Sing together, ye waste places | of Je|rusa|lem :
7. For Jehovah hath comfort|ed his | people ;
He hath re|deemed Je|rusa|lem.
8. Jehovah hath made bare his | holy | arm,
In the | eyes of | all the | nations ;
9. And all the | ends · of the | earth
Shall see the sal|vation | of our | God.    Is. lii. 7.

## SELECTION 207.

Grief that there is nothing more of the church, 1—3: that those who in heart acknowledge the Lord will be saved, 4—6.

1. Although the fig-tree | shall not | blossom,
And there shall be no | fruit | in the | vines ;
2. The produce of the | ol·ive shall | fail,
And the | fields shall | yield no | food ;
3. The flock shall be cut | off · from the | fold ;
And there shall be no | herd | in the | stalls ;
4. Yet will I re|joice · in Je|hovah,
I will joy in the | God of | my sal|vation.

DOUBLE.

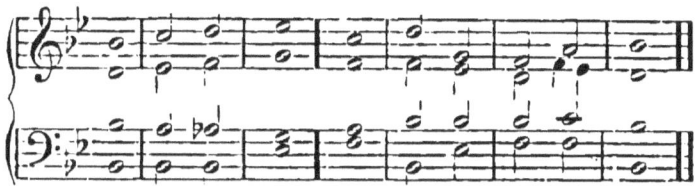

5. The LORD JEHOVIH | is my | strength,
And he will | make my | feet like | hinds';
6. And he will | make · me to | walk
Up|on mine | high | places.  Hab. iii. 17.

## SELECTION 208.

1. Blessed be the LORD GOD of | Isra|el ;
For he hath visited | and re|deemed his | people ;
2. And hath raised up an horn of sal|vation | for us,
In the | house · of his | servant | David.
3. As he spake by the mouth of his | holy | prophets,
Who have been | since the | world be|gan ;
4. That we should be saved from our | ene|mies,
And from the | hand of | all that | hate us.
5. To perform the mercy promised | to our | fathers,
And to remember his | holy | cove|nant ;
6. The oath which he sware to our father | Abra|ham,
That he would | grant | unto | us ;
7. That we, being delivered from the hand our | ene|mies,
Might | serve him | without | fear,
8. In holiness and in | righteous|ness,
All the | days | of our | life.

9. And thou, child, shalt be called the prophet | of the |
HIGHEST;
For thou shalt go before the face of the | LORD · to pre'pare
his | ways;
10. To give knowledge of salvation | to his | people,
By the re|mission | of their | sins :
11. Through the tender mercies | of our | GOD,
Whereby the dayspring from on | high hath | vis·ited | us :
12. To give light to them that sit in darkness and the | shad·ow
of | death,
To guide our feet | in·to the | way of | peace.  Luke i. 68.

164  SELECTIONS AND CHANTS.

### CHANT 173.

### SELECTION 209.

That the Lord will appear in humility, 1—3: that then those who are in goods and truths will come, 4, 5. The appearance of the Lord in a state of humiliation: that it is scarcely believed that the omnipotence of God is in the Lord, 6; because he will appear as vile, and therefore to be despised, 7—10; and that he appeared as if the Divinity were not in him, 11, 12; when yet thereby is salvation, 13, 14: that he endured all things, even to the passion of the cross, 15—20; and that he subdued the hells, 21, 22: that by the passion of the cross a new church would exist, 23—25; and because he endured such things, that he will come forth a conquerer, 26—30.

1. Behold, my servant shall deal | prudent|ly,
   He shall be ex|alted | and ex|tolled;
2. And shall be | very | high;
   As many | were as|tonished | at thee:
3. His visage was so marred, more than | any | man,
   And his form | more · than the | sons of | men:
4. So shall he sprinkle | many | nations;
   The kings shall | shut their | mouths at | him:
5. For that which had not been told them | shall they | see;
   And that which they had not | heard shall | they con|sider.
6. Who hath believed | our re|port?
   And to whom is the arm of JE|HO|VAH re|vealed?
7. For he shall grow up before him as a | tender | plant,
   And as a | root out | of a · dry | ground.
8. He hath no form nor | comeli|ness:
   ¹ And when | we shall | see him,
   There is no beauty that we | should de|sire | him.
9. He is despised and re|ject·ed of | men;
   A man of sorrows, and ac|quaint|ed with | grief.
10. And we hid as it were our | faces | from him:
    He was despised, and | we es|teemed him | not.
11. Surely he hath | borne our | griefs,
    And | carried | our | sorrows.
12. Yet we did es|teem him | stricken;
    Smitten of | GOD, | and af|flicted.
13. But he was wounded for | our trans|gressions,
    He was bruised for | our in|iqui|ties

### Chant 174.

14. The chastisement of our peace | was upon | him;
    And with his | stripes | we are | healed.
15. All we like sheep have | gone a|stray;
    We have turned every | one to | his own | way:
16. And JEHOVAH hath | laid on | him
    The in|i·quity | of us | all.
17. He was oppressed, and he | was af|flicted,
    Yet he | opened | not his | mouth.
18. He is brought as a | lamb · to the | slaughter;
    ¹And as a sheep before her | shear·ers is | dumb,
    So he | ope·neth | not his | mouth.
19. He was taken from prison | and from | judgment:
    And who shall de|clare his | gener|ation.
20. For he was cut off out of the | land · of the | living:
    For the transgression of my | people | was he | stricken.
21. And he made his | grave · with the | wicked,
    And with the | rich | in his | death:
22. Because he had done no | vio|lence;
    Neither was de|ceit | in his | mouth.
23. Yet it pleased JEHOVAH to | bruise | him:
    He hath | put | him to | grief.
24. When thou shalt make his soul a trespass-|offer|ing,
    He shall see his seed, he | shall pro|long his | days;
25. And the pleasure | of JE|HOVAH
    Shall | prosper | in his | hand.
26. He shall see of the travail | of his | soul,
    And | shall be | satis|fied.
27. By his knowledge shall my just servant | justi·fy | many,
    For he shall | bear · their in|iqui|ties.
28. Therefore will I divide him a portion | with the | great;
    And he shall divide the | spoil | with the | strong:
29. Because he hath poured out his | soul unto | death;
    And he was | numbered | with · the trans'|gressors:
30. And he bare the | sin of | many,
    And made inter|cession | for · the trans·gressors.

Is. lii. 13—15, and liii.

### CHANT 175.

### SELECTION 210.

That the Lord will be the God of the church, 1, 2: that for some time they were as without God, 3, 4: that this was the case when there was no church, but that it is to be restored by the Lord, 5, 6; when there is no truth, although afterwards it will not fail, 7—10.

1. For thy Maker | is thine | husband ,
   Je|ho·vah of | Hosts · is his | name :
2. And thy Redeemer, the Holy One of | Isra|el ;
   The God of the whole | earth shall | he be | called.
3. For Jehovah hath | called | thee,
   As a woman for|sa·ken and | grieved in | spirit,
4. And a | wife of | youth,
   When thou wast re|fused, | saith thy | God.
5. For a small moment have I for|saken | thee ;
   But with great mercies | will I | gather | thee.
6. In a little wrath I hid my face from thee | for a | moment ;
   But with everlasting kindness will I have mercy on thee,
   saith Je|hovah | thy Re|deemer.
7. For this is as the waters of Noah | unto | me :
   For as I have sworn that the waters of Noah should no |
8. So | have I | sworn [more go | o·ver the | earth ;
   That I would not be | wroth with | thee, nor re|buke thee.
9. For the mountains shall depart, and the | hills · be re|moved ;
   But my kindness shall | not de|part from | thee,
10. Neither shall the covenant of my | peace · be re | moved,
    Saith Jehovah | that hath | mer·cy up|on thee. Is. liv. 5.

### SELECTION 211.

That doctrines will be full of spiritual and celestial truths from the Lord, 1—4 : they will no longer be afraid of falsities from hell, 5—8 : that those who from them are against the church will be cast into hell, 9—12.

1. O | thou af|flicted,
   Tossed with tempest, | and not | comfort|ed,
2. Behold, I will lay thy | stones · with fair | colors,
   And | lay · thy foun|da·tions with | sapphires.

SELECTIONS AND CHANTS. 167

DOUBLE.

3. And I will make thy windows of agates, and thy gates of |
 And all thy | bor·ders of | precious | stones. [carbun|cles,
4. And all thy children shall be | taught · of JE|HOVAH ;
 And great shall | be the | peace · of thy | children.
5. In righteousness shalt thou | be es|tablished :
 Thou | shalt be | far · from op|pression,
6. For thou | shalt not | fear ;
 And from terror, for | it shall | not come | near thee.
7. Behold, they shall surely | gath·er to|gether,
 But | not | by | me :
8. Whosoever shall gather to|geth·er a|gainst thee,
 Shall | fall | for thy | sake.
9. Behold, I have cre|a·ted the | smith,
 That bloweth the | coals | in the | fire,
10. And that bringeth forth an instrument | for his | work ;
 And I have created the | waster | to de|stroy.
11. No weapon that is formed against | thee shall | prosper ;
 And every tongue that shall rise against thee in | judg·ment
  thou | shalt con|demn.
12. This is the heritage of the servants | of JE|HOVAH ;
 And their righteousness | is of | me, saith JE|HOVAH. 11.

SELECTION 212.

*That the Lord will teach truths and remove falsities with the humble in heart,*
*1—3 : that he cannot do it for those who are wise from themselves, 4, 5.*

1. For thus saith the High and | Lofty | One,
 That inhabiteth eternity, | and whose | name is | holy ;
2. I dwell in the high and | holy | place ;
 With him also that is of a | con·trite and | humble | spirit :
3. *To revive the spirit | of the | humble,
 And to revive the | heart · of the | contrite | ones.
4. For I will not con|tend for | ever,
 Neither will | I be | always | wroth :
5. For the spirit should | fail be|fore me,
 And the | souls which | I have | made.  Is. lvii. 15.

## CHANT 176. PECULIAR.

## SELECTION 213.

That they will receive truths from the Lord freely, 1, 2; that they will reject such things as have in them no spiritual life, 3, 4; that truth in which is life, and by which is conjunction, will be given by the Lord, 5—7; that those will come to the Lord, who knew him not before, 8, 9.

1. Ho, every one that thirsteth, come | ye · to the | waters ;
And he that hath no | money, | come ye, | buy and | eat.
2. Yea, come, buy | wine and | milk,
Without | money, | and with|out | price.
3. Wherefore do ye spend money for that which | is not | bread ?
And your labor for | that which | satis|fieth | not ?
4. Hearken diligently unto me, and eat ye | that · which is | good ;
And let your | soul de|light it|self in | fatness.
5. Incline your ear, and | come · unto |me :
Hear, | and your | soul | shall | live.
6. And I will make an everlasting | cov·enant | with you,
Even the | sure | mer cies of | Da|vid.
7. Behold, I have given him for a witness | to the | people,
A leader | and com|mander | to the | people.
8. Behold, thou shalt call a nation that thou | knowest | not ;
And nations that | know not | thee shall | run unto | thee :
9. Because of Je|ho·vah thy | God ; ·
And for the Holy One of Israel ; for | he hath | glori|fied |
thee.                                                    Is. lv.

## SELECTION 214.

Concerning repentance, 1—4; that they know not the way by which salvation is wrought, 5, 6; that it is by the coming of the Lord, 7—10; that by that only is heavenly happiness, 11, 12; and instead of evil and falsity, good and truth to eternity, 13, 14.

1. Seek ye Jehovah, while he | may be | found ;
Call ye up|on him, | while | he is | near.
2. Let the wicked for|sake his | way.
And | the un|righteous| man his | thoughts :

3. And let him return | un·to Je|hovah,
   And he | will have | mer·cy up|on | him;
4. And | un·to our | God,
   For he | will a|bun·dantly | par|don.
5. For my thoughts are | not your | thoughts,
   Neither are my ways | your ways, | saith Je|ho|vah.
6. For as the heavens are higher | than the | earth,
   So are my ways higher than | your · ways, and | my thoughts | than your | thoughts.
7. For as the rain cometh down, and the | snow from | heaven,
   And returneth not | thith·er, but | water|eth the | earth;
8. And maketh it bring | forth and | bud,
   That it may give | seed · to the | sow·er, and | bread · to the | eater:
9. So shall my word be, that goeth forth | out · of my | mouth:
   It shall | not re|turn unto | me | void;
10. But it shall accomplish | that · which I | please,
    And it shall prosper in the | thing where|to I | sent | it.
11. For ye shall go | out with | joy,
    And | shall be | led | forth with | peace.
12. The mountains and the hills shall break forth before you | into | singing;
    And all the | trees · of the | field shall | clap their | hands.
13. Instead of the thorn shall come | up the | fir-tree;
    And instead of the brier | shall come | up the | myrtle-|tree:
14. And it shall be to Jehovah | for a | name;
    For an everlasting | sign that | shall not | be cut | off.
    Is. lv. 6.

## SELECTION 215.

1. Blessed | are the | dead,
   Who | die · in the | Lord from | hence|forth.
2. Yea, saith the Spirit; that they may | rest · from their | labors;
   And their | works do | follow | with | them.   Rev. xiv. 13.
3. Blessed and holy is he that hath part in the | first · resur-·
   rection:
   Upon such the | second | death hath | no | power.
4. But they shall be priests of | God · and of | Christ,
   And shall | reign with | him a | thousand | years.   xx. 6.

Dox. Amen: Blessing, and | glo·ry, and | wisdom,
     And thanks|giv·ing, and | hon·or, and | power, and | might,
     Be | un·to our | God,
     For | ev·er and | ever: | A|men.   Rev. vii. 12.

### CHANT 177.

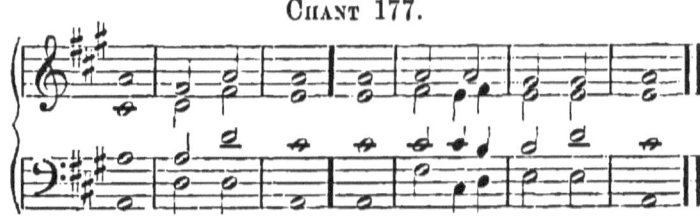

### SELECTION 216.

Concerning the iniquity of the old church, that it is to be disclosed, 1, 2; they are as those who love truth, 3—5; and as those who convert themselves, 6, 7; but they convert themselves from an evil motive, 8, 9; that conversion is not to speak devoutly, but to shun evils, 10—14; and to exercise charity, 15, 16: then they will have truths in abundance, and the Lord will be with them, 17—24: thus the church will be with them, and they will restore all things of the church, 25, 26: that if they esteem the union of the Lord with the church holy, they will come into heaven, 27–31.

1. Cry a|loud, spare | not ;
   Lift | up thy | voice · like a | trumpet ;
2. And show my people | their trans|gression,
   And the | house of | Ja·cob their | sins.
3. Yet they | seek me | daily,
   And de|light to | know my | ways ;
4. As a nation that did | righteous|ness,
   And forsook not the | or·dinance | of their | GOD.
5. They ask of me the ordinances of | righteous|ness ;
   They take delight in ap|proaching | unto | GOD.

6. Wherefore have we fasted, and thou | seest | not ?
   Have afflicted our soul, and | thou dost | take no | knowl‐
       edge ?
7. Behold, in the day of your | fast · ye find | pleasure,
   And ex|act | all your | labors.
8. Behold, ye fast for | strife · and de|bate,
   And to smite with the | fist of | wicked|ness.

9. Ye shall not fast as ye | do this | day,
   To make your | voice · to be | heard on | high.
10. Is it such a fast that | I have | chosen ?
    A day for a | man · to af|flict his | soul ?
11. To bow down his | head · as a | bulrush,
    And to | spread sack|cloth and | ashes ?
12. Wilt thou call | this a | fast,
    And an acceptable | day un|to JE|HOVAH ?

13. Is not this the fast that | I have | chosen ?
    To loose the | bands of | wicked|ness ;

14. To undo the heavy burdens, and to let the op|pressed | go free ;
    And that ye | break | every | yoke ?
15. Is it not to deal thy | bread·to the | hungry,
    And that thou bring the poor that are cast | out un¦to thy | house ?
16. When thou seest the naked that thou | cover | him,
    And that thou hide not thy|self from | thine own | flesh ?
17. Then shall thy light break | forth·as the | morning,
    And thine health shall | spring forth | speedi|ly :
18. And thy righteousness shall | go be|fore thee :
    The glory of Jehovah shall | be thy | rear|ward.
19. Then shalt thou call, and Je|hovah shall | answer :
    Thou shalt cry, and he shall | say, | Here I | am.

20. If thou take away from the midst of | thee the | yoke,
    The putting forth of the finger, and | speaking | vani|ty ;
21. And if thou draw out thy | soul·to the | hungry,
    And satisfy | the af|flicted | soul ;
22. Then shall thy light rise in ob|scuri|ty,
    And thy darkness | shall be | as the | noonday.
23. And Jehovah shall guide thee con|tin·ual|ly,
    And satisfy thy soul in | drought, and make | fat thy | bones.
24. And thou shalt be like a | watered | garden ;
    And like a spring of water, whose | waters | do not | fail.
25. And they that shall be of thee shall build the | old waste | places :
    Thou shalt raise up the foundations of | many | gener|ations.
26. And thou shalt be called, the repairer | of the | breach,
    The re|stor·er of | paths to | dwell in.

27. If thou turn away thy | foot·from the | sabbath,
    From doing thy pleasure | on my | holy | day ;
28. And call the sabbath | a de|light,
    The holy of Je|hovah, | honor|able ;
29. And shalt honor him, not doing | thine own | ways,
    Nor finding thine own pleasure, nor | speaking | thine own | words ;
30. Then shalt thou delight thy|self·in Je|hovah ;
    And I will cause thee to ride upon the high | places | of the | earth ;
31. And feed thee with the heritage of | Jacob thy | father :
    For the mouth of Je|hovah hath | spoken | it.

Is. lviii

## CHANT 178. DOUBLE.

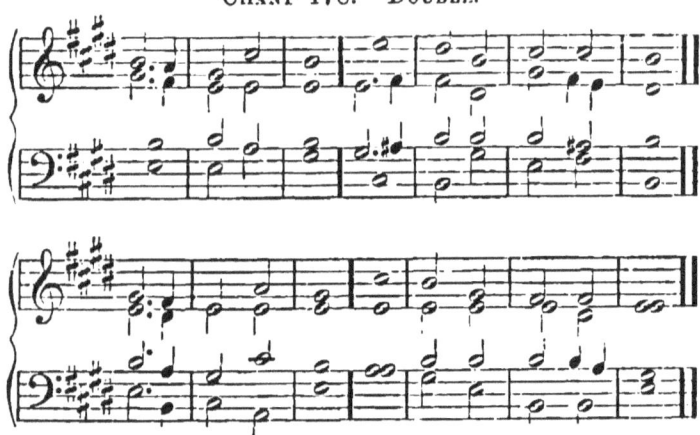

## SELECTION 217.

The coming of the Lord with divine truth, when there is nothing but falsity and the evil of falsity, 1—3: that the Divinity is only in the Lord, 3: that they will come to him from all parts in great numbers, even those who are external, 4—8; who will worship the Lord from good and truth. 9—12.

1. Arise, shine, for thy | light is | come;
 And the glory of Je|ho·vah is | ris·en up|on thee:
2. For, behold, darkness shall | cov·er the | earth,
 And | gross | dark·ness the | people.
3. But Jehovah shall a|rise up|on thee;
 And his glory | shall be | seen up|on thee.
4. And the Gentiles shall | come · to thy | light,
 And kings to the | brightness | of thy | rising.
5. Lift up thine eyes round a|bout, and | see:
 All they gather themselves to|geth·er, they | come to | thee.
6. Thy sons shall | come from | far,
 And thy daughters shall be | nursed | at thy | side
7. Then thou shalt see, and | flow to|gether;
 And thy heart shall | fear, and | be en|larged: [thee ;
8. Because the abundance of the sea shall be converted | unto |
 The forces of the Gentiles | shall come | unto | thee.
9. The multitude of camels shall | cover | thee,
 The dromedaries of | Mid·ian | and of | Ephah.
10. All they from Sheba shall come; they shall bring | gold and | incense;
 And they shall show forth the | praises | of Je|hovah.
11 All the flocks of Kedar shall be gathered | unto | thee;
 The rams of Nebaioth shall | minis·ter | unto | thee.

12. They shall come up with acceptance | on mine | altar;
And I will glorify the | house | of my | glory.   Is. lx.

## SELECTION 218.

That those will come to the Lord who are in the shade of truth, 1: that the truths of the church and the church itself will be with them, 2—6: that there will be a continual accession for the sake of salvation, 7—10.

1. Who are these that | fly · as a | cloud?
And as the | doves | to their | windows?
2. Surely the isles shall | wait for | me,
And the | ships of | Tarshish | first;
3. To bring thy | sons from | far,
Their silver | and their | gold with | them,
4. Unto the name of Je|hovah thy | God,       [thee.
And to the Holy One of Israel; for | he hath | glori·fied |
5. And the sons of strangers shall build | up thy | walls;
And their kings shall | minis·ter | unto | thee:
6. For in my | wrath I | smote thee;
But in my favor have | I had | mercy | on thee.
7. Therefore thy gates shall be open con|tin·ual|ly;
They shall not be | shut | day nor | night:
8. That they may bring the forces | of the | Gentiles;
And that their | kings | may be | brought.
9. For the | na·tion and | kingdom
That will not | serve | thee shall | perish:
10. Yea, | those | nations
Shall | utter|ly be | wasted.           Is. lx. 8.

## SELECTION 219.

That the spiritual moral will come to the Lord, 1, 2; also those who have not known Him before, 3—6.

1. The glory of Lebanon shall | come unto | thee,
The fir-tree, the pine-tree, | and the | box to|gether;
2. To beautify the place of my | sanctu|ary:
And I will make the place of my | feet | glori|ous.
3. The sons also of them that af|flicted | thee,
Shall come | bending | unto | thee:
4. And all they that des|pised | thee,
Shall bow themselves down at the | soles | of thy | feet.
5. And they shall | call | thee,
The | city | of Je|hovah,
6. The | Zi|on
Of the Holy | One of | Isra|el.       Is. lx 13.

## Chant 179.

## SELECTION 220.

That those who have not known the Lord will come to him, who will learn spiritual truths from him, 1—4: that there will no longer be perversion of truth and good, 5, 6.

1. Whereas thou hast been for|sak·en and | hated,
   So that no | man went | through thee ;
2. I will make thee an eternal | excel|lency,
   A joy of many | gener|ations.
3. Thou shalt also suck the | milk · of the | Gentiles,
   And shalt suck the | breast of | kings.
4. And thou shalt know that I JEHOVAH | am thy | Savior ;
   And thy Redeemer, the MIGHTY | ONE of | Jacob.
5. For brass I will bring gold ; and for iron I | will bring | sil-
   And for wood, brass ; and for | stones, | iron :       [ver ;
6. I will also make thine | offi·cers | peace,
   And thine exactors | righteous|ness.           Is. lx. 15.

## SELECTION 221.

That there will no longer be perversion of truth and good, 1, 2 ; nor the love of falsity, but the love of the Lord, 3, 4 ; and this to eternity, 5, 6 ; in heaven with increasing intelligence, 7—10 : these things when the Lord comes, 9, 10.

1. Violence shall no more be | heard · in thy | land,
   Wasting nor destruction with|in thy | borders :
2. But thou shalt call thy | walls, Sal|vation,
   And thy | gates, | Praise.
3. The sun shall be no more thy | light by | day ;
   Neither for brightness shall the moon give | light unto | thee :
4. But JEHOVAH shall be unto thee an ever|lasting | light,
   And thy | GOD thy | glory.
5. Thy sun shall no ! more go | down ;
   Neither shall thy moon with|draw it|self :
6. For JEHOVAH shall be thine ever|lasting | light ;
   And the days of thy mourning | shall be | ended.
7. Thy people also shall | be all | righteous :
   They shall inherit the | land for|ever :

SELECTIONS AND CHANTS. 175

DOUBLE.

8. The branch | of my | planting,
   The work of my hands, that I may be | glori|fied.
9. A little one shall be|come a | thousand,
   And a small one a | strong | nation :
10. I Je|ho|vah
    Will hasten it | in his | time.  Is. lx. 18.

SELECTION 222.

*That those with whom the church was not before, will have many truths of the church, and be multiplied, 1—6: that former falsities will not be remembered, because the Lord will be God of the church, 7—10.*

1. Sing, O barren, thou that | didst not | bear ;
   Break forth into singing, and cry aloud, thou that didst not | trav·ail with | child ;
2. For more are the children of the | deso|late,
   Than the children of the married wife, | saith Je|hovah.
3. Enlarge the | place · of thy | tent,
   And let them stretch forth the curtains of thine | habilta-tions :
4. Spare not ; | length·en thy | cords,
   And | strength·en thy | stakes.
5. For thou | shalt break | forth,
   On the right hand and | on the | left :
6. And thy seed shall in|her·it the | Gentiles,
   And make the desolate cities to be in|habit|ed.
7. Fear not ; for thou shalt not | be a|shamed :
   Neither be thou confounded ; for thou shalt not be | put to | shame :
8. For thou shalt forget the | shame · of thy | youth,
   And shalt not remember the reproach of thy widowhood | any | more.
9. For thy Maker | is thy | husband ;
   Jehovah of Hosts | is his | name ;
10. And thy Redeemer the Holy One of | Isra|el ;
    The God of the whole earth shall | he be | called.  Is. liv.

## CHANT 180.

### SELECTION 223.

That the Lord will teach the faithful all the truths of salvation, 1—8; that those who were removed from truths will draw near, 9, 10: wherefore they have joy, 11, 12: they should not believe that the Lord does not remember them; he always does, 13–16.

1. Thus saith JEHOVAH, In an accep|table time | have I | heard
And in a day of sal|vation | have I | helped thee. [thee;
2. And I | will pre|serve thee,
And give thee for a | cov·enant | of the | people;
3. To es|tab·lish the | earth,
To cause to inherit the | des·olate | heri|tages:
4. That thou mayst say to the prisoners, | Go ye | forth;
To them that are in | darkness, | Show your|selves.
5. They shall | feed·in the | ways;
And their pastures shall | be in | all high | places.
6. They shall not | hun·ger nor | thirst;
Neither shall the | heat nor | sun | smite them:
7. For he that hath mercy | on·them shall | lead them;
Even by the springs of | water | shall he | guide them.
8. And I will make all my | moun·tains a | way,
And my high|ways shall | be ex|alted.
9. Behold, these shall | come from | far;
And, lo, | these | from the | north,
10. And | from the | west;
And these | from the | land of | Sinim.
11. Sing, O heavens; and be | joyful, O | earth;
And break forth into | singing, | O | mountains:
12. For JEHOVAH hath comfort|ed his | people,
And will have | mercy | on·his af|flicted.
13. But Zion said, JEHOVAH hath for|saken | me,
And the LORD | hath for|gotten | me.
14. Can a woman forget her | sucking | child,
That she should not have compassion | on the | son·of her |
15. Yea, they | may for|get; [womb?
Yet will I | not for|get | thee.
16. Behold, I have graven thee upon the | palms·of my | hands;
Thy walls are con|tin·ual|ly be|fore me.     Is. xlix. 8.

### CHANT 181. DOUBLE.

## SELECTION 224.

*That in the midst of the infernals the gentiles are to be protected and saved, 1-10: the church is from them, and that they will have the good of the church, 11, 12*

1. Then shall the eyes of the | blind be | opened,
And the ears of the | deaf shall | be un|stopped.
2. Then shall the lame | leap · as an | hart,
And the | tongue · of the | dumb shall | sing.
3. For in the wilderness shall | wa·ters break | out,
And | streams | in the | desert :
4. And the parched ground shall be|come a | pool,
And the thirsty | land | springs of | water.
5. In the habitation of dragons, | where each | lay,
Shall be | grass with | reeds and | rushes.
6. And an highway shall be | there, and a | way;
And it shall be | called the | way of | holi·ness:
7 The unclean shall not pass | over | it,
But | it shall | be for | those :
8 The way· faring | men,
Though | fools, | shall not | err.
9 No lion | shall be | there,
Nor any ravenous | beast · shall go | up there|on :
10. It shall not be | found | there ;
But the re|deemed shall | walk | there. [Zion,
11. And the ransomed of Jehovah shall return, and | come to |
With songs, and everlasting | joy up|on their | heads.
12. They shall obtain | joy and | gladness,
And sorrow and | sigh·ing shall | flee a|way. Is. xxxv 5

## CHANT 182.

This Chant may be sung in unison.

## SELECTION 225.

*That the goods and truths of the church will exist when the Lord comes, 1—5.*

1. I will greatly re|joice · in JE|HOVAH ;
  My soul shall be | joyful | in my | GOD :
2. For he hath clothed me with the garments | of sal|vation ;
  He hath covered me | with the | robe of | righteous·ness :
3. ⁸ As a bridegroom putteth | on a | mitre,
  And as a bride a|dorn·eth her|self · with her | jewels.
4. For as the earth bringeth | forth her | bud, [| forth ;
  And as the garden causeth the things | sown · in it | to spring
5. So the LORD JEHOVAH | will cause | righteous·ness
  And praise to spring | forth be|fore · all the | nations.

Is. lxi. 10.

## SELECTION 226.

*The Lord's coming, and the church then : that it will acknowledge Him, and will be in the very truth of heaven, and more than before, 1—5 : that they will not be separated from Him, but conjoined with Him, 6—10.*

1. For Zion's sake will I not | hold my | peace,
  And for Jerusalem's | sake I | will not | rest ;
2. Until the righteousness thereof go | forth as | brightness,
  And the salvation there|of · as a | lamp that | burneth.
3. And the Gentiles shall | see thy | righteous·ness,
  And | all | kings thy | glory :
4. And thou shalt be called by a | new | name,
  Which the mouth of JE|HO|VAH shall | name.
5. Thou shalt be a crown of glory in the | hand · of JE|HOVAH,
  And a royal diadem in the | hand | of thy | GOD.
6. Thou shalt no more be | termed, For|saken ;
  Neither shall thy land any | more be | termed, | Deso·late.
7. But thou shalt be called, My de|light is | in her ;
  And | thy | land, the | Married :
8. For JEHOVAH de|lighteth | in thee ;
  And thy | land | shall be | married.
9. For as a young man doth | mar·ry a | virgin,
  So shall thy | sons | marry | thee :

SELECTIONS AND CHANTS. 179

### DOUBLE.

10. And as the bridegroom rejoiceth | o ver the | bride,
So shall thy GOD re|joice | over | thee.　　　　Is. lxii.

### SELECTION 227.

That the Lord's coming will be preached until it takes place, 1—3; that then the truths of the Word will not be for those who falsify them, but for those who receive them, 4—8; that a preparation will be made, 9, 10; and it will be announced that the Lord is about to come, 9—12; and that the church will be from him, 13, 14.

1. I have set watchmen upon thy walls, | O Je|rusa·lem,
Who shall never hold their | peace | day nor | night:
2. Ye that make mention | of JE|HOVAH,
Keep not silence, and | give | him no | rest;
3. Till | he es|tablish,
And till he make Jerusa|lem a | praise·in the | earth.
4. JEHOVAH hath sworn by | his right | hand,
And by the | arm | of his | strength;
5. Surely I will no more | give thy | corn
To be | meat | for thine | ene·mies:
6. And the sons of the stranger shall not | drink thy | wine,
For the | which | thou hast | labored.
7. But they that have | gathered | it,
Shall | eat·it, and | praise JE|HOVAH;
8. And they that have | brought·it to|gether,
Shall drink it in the | courts | of my | holi·ness.
9. Go through, go | through the | gates;
Prepare | ye the | way·of the | people:
10. Cast up, cast up the highway; gather | out the | stones;
Lift up a | standard | for the | people.　　　[world,
11. Behold, JEHOVAH hath proclaimed to the | end·of the
Say ye to the daughter of Zion. Behold, | thy sal|vation
12. Behold, his re|ward is | with him,　　　　　　[cometh:
And | his | work be!fore him.
13. And they shall call them, The | holy | people,
The re|deemed | of JE|HOVAH:
14. And thou shalt be | called, Sought | out,
A | city | not for|saken.　　　　　　　　Is. lxii. 6.

### CHANT 183. TERNARY.

### SELECTION 228.

Concerning the coming of the Lord, to save those who are in ignorance of truth and in the desire of it, and when a judgment is to take place, 1—5.

1. The Spirit of the LORD JEHOVIH | is up|on me ;
   Because JEHOVAH hath an|ointed | me,
   To preach glad | tidings | to the | meek.
2. He hath sent me to bind up the | broken-|hearted,
   To proclaim liberty | to the | captives,
   And the opening of the | prison | to the | bound :
3. To proclaim the acceptable | year · of JE|HOVAH,
   And the day of vengeance | of our | GOD :
   To | comfort | all that | mourn :
4. To appoint unto them that | mourn in | Zion ;
   To give unto them | beau·ty for | ashes,
   The | oil of | joy for | mourning :
5. The garment of praise for the | spir·it of | heavi·ness ;
   That they may be called | trees of | righteous·ness ;
   The planting of JEHOVAH, that he | might be | glori|fied.
   
   Is. lxi.

### CHANT 184.

### SELECTION 229.

A new church : that the divine mercy will be therein.

1. Who is a GOD | like to | thee,
   That pardoneth in|iqui|ty,

SELECTIONS AND CHANTS.        181

2. And passeth | by · the trans|gression
   Of the remnant of his | heri|tage?
3. He retaineth not his | an·ger for | ever ;
   Because he de|light·eth in | mercy.
4. He will | turn a|gain ;
   He will have com|pas·sion up|on us:
5. He will subdue our in|iqui|ties :
   And thou wilt cast all their sins into the | depths · of the | sea.
6. Thou wilt perform the | truth unto | Jacob,
   The mercy unto | Abra|ham,
7. Which thou hast sworn | un·to our | fathers,
   From the | days of | old.                Mic. vii. 18.

CHANT 185.

SELECTION 230.

Prayer to the Lord that he would have pity, because he alone has redeemed, 1—4 : that otherwise they would have perished, and hell would have ruled, 5—7: that there will be power when the Lord comes, 8.

1. Look down from heaven, | and be|hold,
   From the habitation of thy | ho·liness | and thy | glory.
2. Where is thy | zeal · and thy | strength,
   The sounding of thy bowels and of thy mercies | tow'rd ·
   me ? | are · they re|strained ?
3. Doubtless, thou | art our | Father,
   Though Abraham be ignorant of us, and Isra|el ac|knowl-
   ·edge us | not.
4. Thou, O JEHOVAH, | art our | Father,
   Our Redeemer; thy | name · is from | ever|lasting.
5. O JEHOVAH, why hast thou made us to | err · from thy | ways,
   And hardened our | heart | from thy | fear ?
6. Return for thy | servants' | sake,
   The tribes of | thine in|heri|tance.              [while :
7. The people of thy holiness have possessed it but a | little ¹
   Our adversaries have trodden | down thy | sanctu|ary.
8. We are thine : thou never barest | rule over | them ;
   They were not | called | by thy | name.         Is. lxiii. 15

P

### Chant 186.

### SELECTION 231.

*That the new church will not perish, 1—5: that the Lord will teach, 6: that falsities and evils will no longer destroy, 7, 8.*

1. And they shall build | houses, | and in|habit;
 They shall plant vineyards, and eat the|fruit of | them.
2. They shall not | build, and an|oth·er in|habit;
 They shall not plant, and an|other | eat.
3. For as the days of a | tree · are the | days · of my | people;
 And mine elect shall long enjoy the | work · of their | hands.
4. They | shall not | la·bor in | vain,
 Nor bring | forth for | trouble:
5. For they are the seed of the | blessed | of Je|hovah,
 And their | offspring | with them.
6. And it shall come to pass, that be|fore they | call, I will |
  answer;
 And while they are yet speaking, | I will | hear.
7. The wolf and the | lamb shall | feed to|gether;
 And the lion shall eat | straw · like the | bullock;
8. And dust shall | be the | serpent's | meat:
 They shall not hurt nor destroy in all my holy mountain, |
  saith Je|hovah.  Is. lxv. 21.

### SELECTION 232.

*That those who trust in the Lord shall not fail, 1, 2: that they will have truths and goods in all abundance, 3—8.*

1. The poor and needy seek | water, | and · there is | none;
 And their tongue doth | fail for | thirst:
2. I Je|hovah | will hear | them;
 I the God of Israel will | not for|sake them.
3. I will open | rivers | in high | places,
 And fountains in the | midst · of the | valleys:
4. I will make the | des·ert a | pool of | water,
 And the dry land | springs of | water.

DOUBLE.

5  I will plant in the wilderness the | ce·dar, the | shittah-|tree,
   And the myrtle, | and the | oil-tree ;
6. I will set | in the | des·ert the | fir-tree,
   The pine, and the | box-·tree to|gether :
7. That | they may | see and | know,
   And consider, and under|stand to|gether,
8. That the hand of JE|HOVAH | hath done | this,
   And the HOLY ONE of Israel hath cre|ated | it. Is. xli. 17.

SELECTION 233.

Those that love good should look to the Lord, and not regard the oppositions of men, because these will perish from falsities and evils, 1—4 : they should look to the Lord, because he has divine power to act, and because he is able to remove the hells, so that they may joyfully pass through them without hurt, 5—10.

1. Hearken unto me, ye that | know | righteous|ness ;
   The people in whose | heart·is my | law :
2. Fear ye | not · the re|proach of | men,
   Neither be ye afraid of | their re|vilings.
3. For the moth shall | eat them | up·like a | garment,
   And the worm shall eat them | up like | wool.
4. But my righteousness | shall en|dure for | ever,
   And my salvation from generation to | gener|ation.
5. Awake, a|wake, | put on | strength,
   O | arm ·of JE|HOVAH :
6. Awake as | in the | ancient | days,
   In the gener|a·tions of | old.
7. Art thou not | it·that hath | dried the | sea,
   The waters of the | great | deep ?
8. That hath made the | depths·of the | sea a | way
   For the ransomed to | pass | over ?
9. Therefore the redeemed of JEHOVAH shall re|turn, and
      come to | Zion,
   With singing, and everlasting joy up|on their | head :
10. They shall ob|tain | glad·ness and | joy ;
    And sorrow and mourning shall | flee a|way.      Is. li 7

## CHANT 187.

## SELECTION 234.

*Concerning those who will acknowledge the Lord, that they shall receive the Holy Spirit, 1—6: that it is Jehovah who foretold that he himself would do it, 7—10.*

1. Yet now hear, O | Ja·cob, my | servant;
And Israel, whom | I have | chosen:
2. Thus saith JEHOVAH, that | made | thee,
And formed thee from the womb; | who will | help thee:
3. Fear not, O | Ja·cob, my | servant;
And thou, Jesurun, whom | I have | chosen:
4. For I will pour water upon | him · that is | thirsty,
And floods up|on the · dry | ground.
5. I will pour my Spirit up|on thy | seed,
And my blessing up|on thine | offspring:
6. And they shall spring up as a|mong the | grass,
As willows by the | water-|courses.
7. One shall say, I | am JE|HOVAH'S;
And another shall call himself by the | name of | Jacob:
8. And another shall subscribe with his | hand · to JE|HOVAH,
And surname himself by the name of | Isra|el.
9. Thus saith JEHOVAH, the King of | Isra|el;
And his Redeemer, JE|HO·VAH of | Hosts;
10. I am the First, and | I the | Last;
And beside me there | is no | GOD.           Is. xliv.

## SELECTION 235.

*That the Lord will establish a new church, 1—4; in which will be all goods and truths, thus all things of heaven, 5—8.*

1. For behold, | I cre|ate
New heavens and a | new | earth:
2. And the former shall not | be re|membered,
Nor come up|on the | heart.
3. But be ye glad, and re|joice for | ever,
In that which | I cre|ate:
4. For, behold, I create Jerusalem | a re|joicing,
And her | peo·ple a | joy.

DOUBLE.

5  And I will rejoice in Je|rusa|lem,
   And joy | in my | people.
6. And the voice of weeping shall no more be | heard in | her,
   Nor the | voice of | crying.
7. There shall be no more thence an | in·fant of | days,
   Nor an old man that hath not | filled his | days:
8. For the child shall die an | hun·dred years | old;
   But the sinner an hundred years old shall | be ac|cursed.
                                                            Is. lxv. 17

## SELECTION 236.

1. And I saw a | new | heaven
   And a | new | earth :
2. For the first heaven and the first earth were | passed a|way;
   And there was | no more | sea.
3. And I saw the holy city, New Je|rusa|lem,
   Descending out of | heaven from | God,
4. Prepared | as a | bride
   Adorned | for her | husband.
5. And I heard a great voice out of | heaven, | saying,
   Behold, the tabernacle of | God·is with | men ;      [ple :
6. And he will dwell with them; and they shall | be his | peo-
   And God himself shall be | with them, their | God.
7. And he shall wipe away all | tears·from their | eyes ;
   And death shall | be no | more ;
8  Neither sorrow, nor crying, nor | pain·shall be | more :
   For the former things are | passed a|way.
9. And he that sat up|on the·throne | said,
   Behold, I make | all things | new.
10. And he said | unto me, | Write ;
    For these words are | true and | faithful.
11. And he said unto me, | It is | done :
    I am the Alpha and the Omega, the Beginning | and the
12. I will give to | him that | thirsteth,             [End
    Of the fountain of the water of | life | freely.   Rev. xxi

### Chant 188. Double.

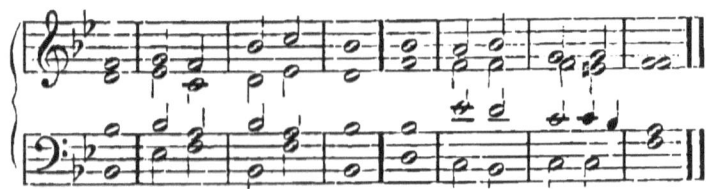

### SELECTION 237.

That they will come to the Lord from all parts, 1; of every religion, 2, 3: they will be in every truth of the doctrine of the church, 4—7; and in its good, 8: that whatever is of heaven and the church will abide with them, 9, 10: that they will continually worship the Lord, 11, 12.

1. It shall come that I will | gath·er all | na·tions and | tongues;
 And they shall | come and | see my | glory.
2. And I will | set a | sign a|mong them;
 And I will send those that es|cape · of them | to the | nations, . . . .
3. That have not heard my | fame, nor | seen my | glory:
 And they shall declare my | glo·ry a|mong the | Gentiles.
4. And they shall | bring | all your | brethren,
 An offering unto JE|HOVAH, | out · of all | nations;
5. Upon horses, | and in | chari|ots,
 And in | litters, | and upon | mules,
6. And | upon | swift | beasts,
 To my holy mountain, Je|ru·salem, | saith JE|HOVAH:
7. As the children of Israel | bring an | offer|ing,
 In a clean vessel into the | house | of JE|HOVAH.
8. And I will | also | take of | them,
 For priests and for | Levites, | saith JE|HOVAH.
9. For | as the | new | heavens,
 And the new | earth, which | I will | make,
10. Shall remain be|fore me, | saith JE|HOVAH;
 So shall your | seed · and your | name re|main.

SELECTIONS AND CHANTS. 187

11. And | it shall | come to | pass,
That from | one new | moon · to an|other,
12. And from one | sabbath | to an|other,
Shall all flesh come to worship be|fore me, | saith JE|HOVAH.
Is. lxvi. 18.

CHANT 189.

SELECTION 238.

That all are in sins, and none can be saved unless the Lord comes, 1—4: when yet all were created by him, 5: that therefore he would regard them, 6, 7; when all things of the church are vastated, 7—10: this the Lord cannot suffer, 11.

1. But we are | all · as an | unclean | thing ;
And all our righteousnesses | are as | filthy | rags :
2. And we | all do | fade · as a | leaf ;
And our iniquities, like the winds, have | taken | us a|way.
3. And there is none that | call·eth up|on thy | name,
That stirreth up him|self · to take | hold on | thee :
4. For thou hast | hid thy | face from | us ;
And hast consumed us, because of | our in|iqui|ties.
5. But now, O JE|HOVAH, | thou · art our | Father :
¹We are the | clay, and | thou our | potter ;
And we all are the | work of | thine | hand.
6 Be not wroth very | sorely, | O JE|HOVAH ;
Neither remember in|iqui|ty for | ever.
7 Behold, see, we beseech thee, | we are | all thy | people :
Thy holy cities | are a | wilder|ness ;
8 Zion | is a | wilder|ness ;
Jerusa|lem a | deso|lation.
9. Our holy | and our | beau·tiful | house,
Where our | fathers | praised | thee,
10. Is | burned | up with | fire ;
And all our pleas·ant | things are | laid | waste.
11. Wilt thou refrain thyself for | these things, | O JE|HOVAH ?
Wilt thou hold thy peace, and af|flict us | very | sore ?
Is. lxiv. 6—12.

### CHANT 190. DOUBLE.

### SELECTION 239.

*A prophecy concerning the combats of the Lord with the hells, concerning his most grievous temptations then, and concerning his state then.*

1. I cried by reason of | mine af|fliction,
 Unto Je|hovah, | and he | heard me :
2. Out of the belly of | hell cried | I,
 And | thou didst | hear my | voice.
3. For thou hadst cast me | in·to the | deep,
 In the | midst | of the | seas :
4. And the floods compassed | me a|bout :
 All thy billows and thy | waves passed | over | me,
5. Then I said, I am cast | out · of thy | sight ;
 Yet I will look again | toward · thy | holy | temple.
6. The waters compassed me a|bout · to the | soul :
 The depth closed me around ; the weeds were | wrapped a|bout my | head.
7. I went down to the bottoms | of the | mountains :
 The earth with her | bars · was a|bout · me for | ever:
8. Yet hast thou brought | up my | life
 From corruption, | O Je|ho·vah, my | God.
9. When my soul did | faint with|in me,
 I re|mem·bered Je|ho|vah ;
10. And my prayer came | in · unto | thee,
 Into the temple | of thy | holi|ness.
11. They that observe lying vanities for|sake · their own | mercy ;      [giv|ing :
 But I will sacrifice unto thee with the | voice of | thanks

SELECTIONS AND CHANTS. 189

12. I will pay that | I have | vowed.
Salvation is | of Je|ho|vah. Jonah ii. 2.

CHANT 191. TERNARY.

SELECTION 240.

An exhortation to the church adulterating the goods and profaning the truths of the Word, that they should desist: that it was given them to be a church, and to acknowledge the Lord, but in vain, 1—3: that they were averted, which was shown them, 4: that if they had obeyed the Lord, they would have had the goods and truths of the church in all abundance, 5—7.

1. Hear ye this, O | house of | Jacob,
That are called by the name of | Isra|el,
And are come forth | out of the | waters of | Judah:

2. Who swear by the | name of Je|hovah,
And make mention of the God of | Isra|el;
But not in truth, | nor in | righteous|ness.

3. For they call themselves of the | holy | city,
And stay themselves upon the God of | Isra|el:
Jehovah of | Hosts | is his | name.

4. I have declared the former things | from the be|ginning;
And they went out of my mouth, | and I | showed them:
I did them suddenly, | and they | came to | pass.....

5 Thus saith Jehovah, thy Redeemer, the HOLY ONE of
Isra|el;
I am Jehovah thy God, who teacheth | thee to | profit,
Who leadeth thee by the | way that | thou shouldst | go.

6 O that thou hadst hearkened to | my com|mandments;
Then had thy peace | been as a | river.
And thy righteousness | as the | waves of the | sea.

7. Thy seed also had | been as the | sand,
And the offspring of thy bowels as the | grav|el there|of:
His name should not have been cut | off nor de|stroyed
from be|fore me. Is. xlviii. 1—3, 17—19

## SELECTIONS AND CHANTS.

### Chant 192. Double.

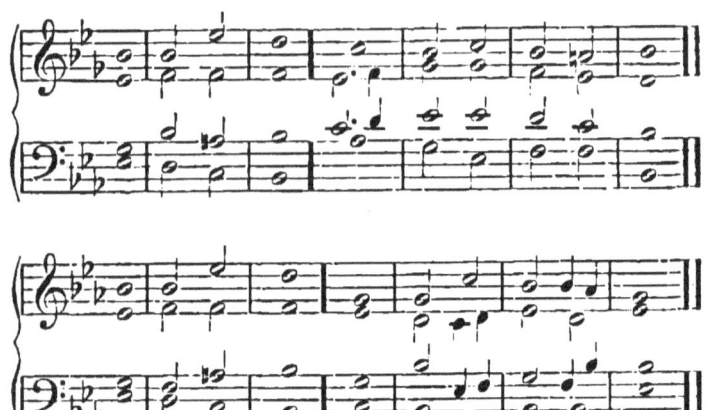

### SELECTION 241.

That a new church will be established by the Lord when he comes into the world, and it will be from the Gentiles, 1—6: that there will be therein no more falsities and evils, but truths and goods, 7—11; under the Lord, 12, 13.

1. And in the last days it shall | come to | pass,
That the mountain of the | house | of Je|hovah
2. Shall be established in the | top · of the | mountains,
And it shall be ex|alt·ed a|bove the | hills :
3. ⁸And people shall | flow unto | it ;
And many | na·tions shall | come, and | say,

4. Come, and let us go up to the mountain | of Je|hovah,
To the | house · of the | God of | Jacob.
5. And he will teach us | of his | ways ;
And we will | walk | in his | paths.
6. For the law shall go | forth of | Zion,
And the word of Jehovah | from Je|rusa|lem.
7. And he shall judge among | many | people,
And rebuke strong | nations | to a|far.
8. And they shall beat their | swords into | ploughshares,
And their | spears into | pruning-|hooks.
9. Nation shall not lift up a | sword a·gainst | nation,
Neither shall they | learn war | any | more.
10. But they shall sit, | eve·ry | man,
Under his | vine and | un·der his | fig-tree :
11. And none shall | make a|fraid :
For the mouth of Jehovah of | Hosts hath | spoken | it

SELECTIONS AND CHANTS. 191

12. For all | people will | walk,
Every one in the | name | of his | god:
13 But we will | walk·in the | name
Of Jehovah our | God for | ev·er and | ever    Mic. iv.

CHANT 193.

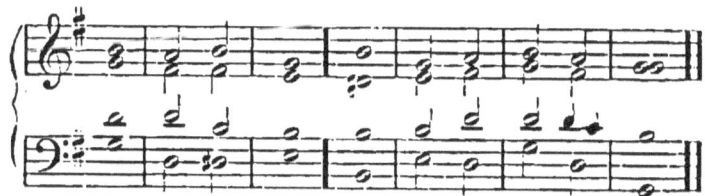

SELECTION 242.

When the Lord shall reign by divine truth, 1; then there will be truth received, and the understanding of truth, 2—5; and simulation will cease, 6: then the false-speaker will speak falsities, and the malevolent do evils, 7—11; and the reverse, 12.

1. Behold, a king shall reign in | righteous|ness,
   And | prin·ces shall | rule in | judgment.
2. And a man shall be as an hiding place | from the | wind,
   And a | covert | from the | tempest:
3. As rivers of waters | in a·dry | place,
   As the shadow of a great | rock·in a | weary | land.
4. And the eyes of them that see shall | not be | dim,
   And the ears of | them that | hear shall | hearken.
5. The heart also of the rash shall | under·stand | knowledge;
   And the tongue of the stammerers shall be | read·y to |
   speak | plainly.
6 The vile person shall no more be called | liber|al,
   Nor the churl be | said·to be | bounti|ful.
7. For the vile person | will speak | vileness,
   And his heart will | work in|iqui|ty;
8 To practise hy|pocri|sy,
   And to utter | er·ror a|gainst Je|hovah;
9 To make empty the | soul·of the | hungry;
   And he will cause the | drink·of the | thirs·ty to | fail.
10. The instruments also of the | churl are | evil:
    He de|viseth | wick·ed de|vices;
11. To destroy the poor with | lying | words,
    Even when the | needy | speaketh | right.
12. But the liberal deviseth | lib·eral | things,
    And by liberal | things | shall he | stand.    Is. xxxii

## 192 SELECTIONS AND CHANTS.

CHANT 194. DOUBLE.

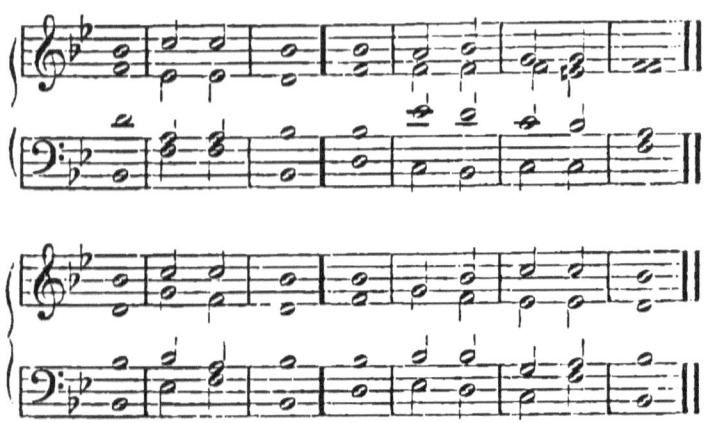

### SELECTION 243.

*A prediction that the Lord will come into the world, who has divine truth and good, 1—5: that he will survey the church, that there is none, 6—9: that by his divine truth he will dissipate the falsities of evil, 10—13.*

1. O JEHOVAH, I have heard thy speech, I | was a|fraid :
   O JEHOVAH, revive thy | work · in the | midst · of the | years;
2. In the midst of the | years make | known ;
   In | wrath re|member | mercy.
3. GOD | came from | Teman,
   And the HOLY | ONE from | mount | Paran.
4. His glory | cov·ered the | heavens ;
   And the | earth was | full · of his | praise.
5. And his brightness was | as the | light :
   ¹He had horns | out · of his | hand ;
   And there was the | hiding | of his | power.
6. Before him went the | pesti|lence ;
   And burning | coals went | forth · at his | feet.
7. He stood and | meas·ured the | earth :
   He beheld, and | drove a|sun·der the | nations.
8. And the everlasting | moun·tains were | scattered ;
   The perpetual hills did bow: his | ways are ¦ ever|lasting
9. I saw the tents of Cushan | in af|fliction :
   ⁴The curtains of the land of | Midi|an did | tremble.
10. Was JEHOVAH displeased a|gainst the | rivers ?
    Was thine | an·ger a|gainst the | rivers ?

SELECTIONS AND CHANTS. 193

11. Was thy wrath against the sea, that | thou didst | ride
Upon thy horses, thy | char·iots | of sal|vation?....

12. Thou didst march through the land in | indig|nation:
Thou didst | thresh the | hea·then in | anger.

13. Thou wentest forth for the salvation | of thy | people;
For sal|va·tion with | thine an|ointed.        Hab. iii.

CHANT 195.

SELECTION 244.

That the Lord is omnipotent and omniscient, 1—5: that all against him are of no avail, 6—10.

1. Who hath measured the waters in the | hollow | of his | hand?
   And meted out | heaven | with a | span?
2. And comprehended the dust of the | earth | in a | measure?
   And weighed the mountains in | scales, and the | hills · in a | balance?
3. Who hath directed the | Spirit | of JE|HOVAH?
   Or, being his | counsel|lor, hath | taught him?
4. With whom took he counsel, and | who in|structed | him?
   And taught him | in the | path of | judgment?
5. And | taught him | know|ledge?
   And showed unto him the | way of | under|standing?
6. Behold, the nations are as a | drop | of a | bucket;
   And are counted as the | small dust | of the | balance.
7. Behold, he | taketh | up the | isles,
   As a | very | little | thing:
8. And Lebanon is | not suf|ficient to | burn,
   Nor the beasts thereof sufficient | for · a burnt-|offer|ing.
9. All nations be|fore him | are as | nothing;
   And they are counted to him less than | noth·ing, and vani|ty.
10. To whom then | will ye | liken | GOD?
    Or what likeness will | ye com|pare unto | him?   Is. xl. 12

Q

### CHANT 196.

### SELECTION 245.

*Celebration of the Lord, that, after he glorified his Humanity, he cast down into the hells the evil who infested the good in the other life, and elevated into heaven the good who were infested.*

1. I will sing unto JEHOVAH, for he hath triumphed | glo·ri-ous|ly :
 The horse and his rider hath | he cast | in·to the | sea.
2. JAH is my | strength and | song,
 And he | has been | my sal|vation.
3. He is my GOD, and I will prepare him an | habi|tation ;
 My father's | GOD, and I | will ex|alt him.
4. JEHOVAH is a | man of | war :
 JE|HOVAH | is his | name.
5. Pharaoh's chariots and his host hath he cast | in·to the | sea :
 His chosen captains also are | drowned | in the · Red | Sea.
6. The depths have | covered | them :
 They sank into the | bottom | as a | stone.
7. Thy right hand, O JEHOVAH, is become glori|ous in | power :
 Thy right hand, O JEHOVAH, hath dashed in | pie·ces the | ene|my.
8 And in the greatness of thine | excel|lency,
 Thou hast overthrown | them that ' rose · up a|gainst thee
9. Thou sentest | forth thy | wrath ;
 It con|sumed | them as | stubble.
10 And with the | blast · of thy | nostrils,
 Were the | waters | gath·ered to|gether.
11. The floods stood upright | as an | heap ;
 The depths were con|gealed · in the | heart · of the | sea.
12. The enemy said, I | will pur|sue,
 I will overtake, I | will di|vide the | spoil :
13. My lust shall be satis|fied up|on them ;
 I will draw my | sword, my | hand · shall de|stroy them.

## SELECTIONS AND CHANTS.

**DOUBLE.**

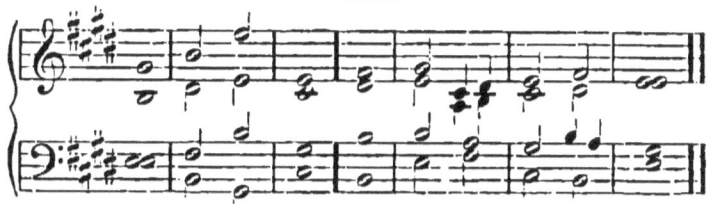

14. Thou didst blow with thy wind, the sea | covered | them :
 They sank as | lead · in the | mighty | waters.
15. Who is like unto thee, O JEHOVAH, a|mong the | gods ?
 Who is like thee, glorious in holiness, fearful in | praises,
 doing | wonders?
16. Thou stretchedst out | thy right | hand ;
 The | earth did | swallow | them.            [deemed ;
17. Thou in thy mercy hast led forth the people thou | hast re-|
 Thou hast guided them in thy strength to thy | holy | habi-
 |tation.
18. The people shall hear, and | be a|fraid :
 Sorrow shall take hold on the inhabitants | of Phi|listi|a.
19. Then the dukes of Edom shall | be a|mazed,
 The | mighty | men of | Moab ;
20. Trembling shall take | hold up|on them ;
 All the inhabitants of | Ca·naan shall | melt a|way.
21. Fear and dread shall | fall up|on them :
 By the greatness of thine arm they | shall be | still · as a |
22. Till thy people pass over, | O JE|HOVAH ;          [stone :
 Till the people pass | o·ver, which | thou hast | purchased.
23. Thou shalt | bring them | in,
 And plant them in the mountain of | thine in|heri|tance ;
24 The place, O JEHOVAH, thou hast wrought for | thee to |
 dwell in,
 The sanctuary, O | LORD, thy | hands · have pre|pared.
25. JEHOVAH shall reign for ever and ever.   Ex. xv. 1—18.

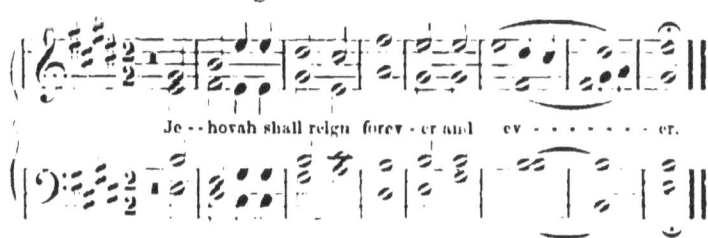

Je- -hovah shall reign for ev - er and    ev - - - - - - - er.

## CHANT 188.

## SELECTION 246.

1. God is not a | man, that | he should | lie ;
   Neither the son of | man, that | he ·should re|pent :
2. Hath he | said, and | shall·he not | do ?
   Or hath he spoken, and | shall·he not | make it | good ?
3. Behold, I have re|ceived com|mand to | bless ;
   And he hath blessed, and | I can|not re|verse it.
4. He hath not beheld in|iqui|ty in | Jacob ;
   Neither hath he seen per|verse·ness in | Isra|el.
5. Jehovah his | God is | with | him,
   And the shout of a | king | is a|mong them.
6. God | brought them | out of | Egypt :
   He hath as it were the | strength·of an | uni|corn.
7. Surely there is no en|chant·ment a|gainst | Jacob ;
   Neither is there any divination a|gainst | Isra|el.
8. According to this time it | shall be | said of | Jacob,
   And of Israel, | What hath | God | wrought ?
9. Behold, the people shall rise | up·as a | great | lion,
   And lift up him|self·as a | young | lion.
10. He shall not lie down un|til he | eat·of the | prey,
    And drink the | blood | of the | slain.    Num. xxiii. 19

## SELECTION 247.

1. How goodly | are thy | tents, O | Jacob ;
   Thy tabern|a·cles, O | Isra|el.
2. ¹As the valleys | are they | spread | forth,
   As gardens | by the | river's | side,
3. As the trees of lign aloes | which Je|ho·vah hath | planted,
   As cedar | trees be|side the | waters.
4. He shall pour the | water | out·of his | buckets ;
   And his seed shall | be in | many | waters :
5. And his king | shall be | high·er than | Agag ;
   And his | king·dom shall | be ex|alted.

SELECTIONS AND CHANTS. 197

DOUBLE.

6. God brought him | forth | out of | Egypt:
He hath as it were the | strength · of an | uni|corn.
7. He shall eat up the | na·tions his | ene|mies;
And break their bones, and | pierce them | with his | arrows.
8. He couched, he | lay down | as a | lion,
And as a great lion; | who shall | stir him | up?
9. Blessed is | he that | blesseth | thee;
And cursed is | he that | curseth | thee.   Num. xxiv. 5.

SELECTION 248.

1. He hath said, who | heard the | words of | God,
And knew the | knowledge | of the · Most | High,
2. Who saw the | vision | of · the Al|mighty,
Falling, but | hav·ing his | eyes | open:
3. I shall | see him, | but not | now;
I shall be|hold him, | but not | nigh:
4. There shall | come a | Star · out of | Jacob;
And a Sceptre shall | rise · out of | Isra|el;
5. And shall | smite the | cor·ners of | Moab,
And shall destroy | all the | child·ren of | Sheth.
6. And Edom shall be a possession, Seir also shall be a posses-
sion | for his | ene|mies;
And Israel | shall do | valiant|ly.
7.*Out of Jacob shall come | he · that shall | have do|minion,
And shall destroy him that re|maineth | of the | city.
  Num. xxiv. 16.

SELECTION 249.

1. From the | top · of the | rocks I | see him,
And from the | hills do | I be|hold him.
2. Lo, the | peo·ple shall | dwell a|lone,
And shall not be | reck·oned a|mong the | nations.
3. Who can | count the | dust of | Jacob,
And the number of the | fourth of | Isra|el?
4. Let me | die the | death · of the | righteous,
And let my | last end | be like | his.   Num. xxiii. 9.

### CHANT 197.

### SELECTION 250.

1. Behold, Je|ho·vah our | God
Hath showed us his | glory | and his | greatness:
2. And we have | heard his | voice
Out | of the | midst · of the | fire.
3. We have | seen this | day,
That God doth | talk with | man · and he | liveth.

Deut. v. 24

### SELECTION 251. (Cht. 198.)

1. Give ear, O ye heavens, and | I will | speak;
And hear, O | earth, the | words · of my | mouth.
2. My doctrine shall | drop · as the | rain;
My speech | shall dis|til · as the | dew;
3. As the small rain upon the | tender | herb,
And as the | show·ers up|on the | grass:
4. Because I will publish the | name · of Je|hovah:
Ascribe ye | greatness | to our | God.
5. He is the Rock, his | work is | perfect;
For | all his | ways are | judgment:
6. A God of truth, and without in|iqui|ty;
Both | just and | right is | he.
7. They have cor|rupt·ed them|selves:
Their spot is | not the | spot · of his | children:
8. They | are · a per|verse
And a | crooked | gener|ation.
9. Do ye thus re|quite Je|hovah,
O foolish | people | and un|wise?
10. Is not he thy father | that hath | bought thee?
Hath he not made thee, | and es|tablished | thee?
11. Remember the | days of | old;
Consider the years of | many | gener|ations:
12. Ask thy father, and | he will | show thee;
Thy elders, and | they will | tell | thee.

Deut xxxii

## Chant 198. Double.

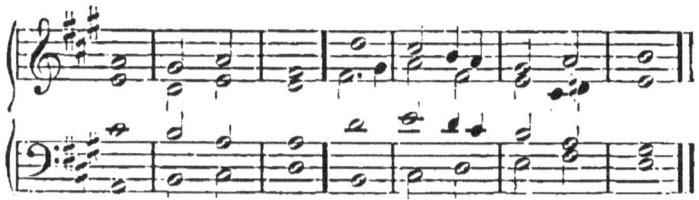

## SELECTION 252.

1. When the Most High divided to the nations their in|heri-|tance,
   When he sepa|rat·ed the | sons of | Adam,
2. He set the | bounds · of the | people,
   According to the number of the | sons of | Isra|el.
3. For Jehovah's portion | is his | people;
   Jacob is the lot of | his in|heri|tance.
4. He found him in a | desert | land,
   And in the waste | howling | wilder|ness.
5. He led him about, he in|structed | him,
   He kept him as the | apple | of his | eye.
6. As an eagle stirreth | up her | nest,
   Fluttereth | over | her | young,
7. Spreadeth a|broad her | wings,
   Taketh them, | beareth them | on her | wings;
8. So Jehovah a|lone did | lead him,
   And there was | no strange | god with | him.
9. He made him ride on the high places | of the | earth,
   That he might eat the | increase | of the | fields;
10. And he made him to suck honey | out · of the | rock,
    And oil | out · of the | flinty | rock:
11. Butter of kine, and milk of sheep, with | fat of | lambs,
    And rams of the | breed of | Bashan, and | goats,
12. With the fat of | kid·neys of | wheat;
    And thou didst drink the | pure | blood · of the | grape.

Deut. xxxii. 8

## CHANT 199. DOUBLE.

## SELECTION 253.

1. My heart rejoiceth | in Je|hovah;
   Mine horn is ex|alted | in Je|hovah:
2. My mouth is enlarged over mine | ene|mies;
   Because I re|joice in | thy sal|vation.
3. None is holy as Jehovah; for there is | none like | thee;
   Neither is there any | rock like | unto our | God.
4. Talk no more so ex|ceeding | proudly;
   Let not arrogancy | come out | of your | mouth:
5. For Jehovah is a | God of | knowledge,
   And by | him are | actions | weighed.
6. The bows of the mighty | men are | broken,
   And they that stumbled | are be|girt with | strength.
7. The full have hired out them|selves for | bread;
   And the | hungry | they have | ceased:
8. So that the barren | hath borne | seven;
   And she that hath many | children | is waxed | feeble.

1 Sam. ii

## SELECTION 254.

1. Jehovah killeth, and | maketh a|live:
   He bringeth down to the | grave, and | bringeth | up.
2. Jehovah maketh poor, and | maketh | rich:
   He bringeth | low, and | lifteth | up.
3. He raiseth up the poor | out · of the | dust,
   And lifteth up the | beggar | from the | dunghill;

SELECTIONS AND CHANTS. 201

4. To set | them a·mong | princes,
And to make them in|her·it the | throne of | glory.
5. ³For the pillars of the earth | are Je|hovah's,
And he hath | set the | world up|on them.
6. He will keep the | feet · of his | saints;
And the wicked | shall be | si·lent in | darkness:
7. For by strength shall no | man pre|vail:
The adversaries of Jehovah | shall be | bro·ken in | pieces
8. Out of heaven shall he | thun·der up|on them:
Jehovah shall | judge the | ends · of the | earth:
9 And he shall give | strength · to his | king,
And exalt the | horn of | his an|ointed.    1 Sam. ii. 6.

### Chant 200.

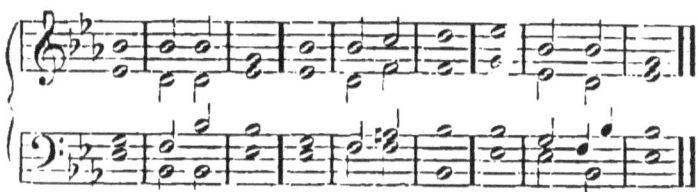

### SELECTION 255.

1. I will heal | their back|sliding;
I will | love them | freely:
For mine anger is turned a|way from | him.
2. I will be as the dew unto | Isra|el:
He shall | grow · as the | lily,
And cast forth his roots as | Leba|non.
3. His branches | shall | spread,
And his beauty shall be as the | olive-|tree,
And his smell shall be as | Leba|non.
4. They that dwell under his shadow | shall re|turn;
They shall revive as the corn, and | grow · as the | vine;
The scent thereof shall be as the wine of | Leba|non.....
5. Who|so is | wise,
And he shall under|stand these | things;
Prudent, and | he shall | know them.
6. For the ways of Je|ho·vah are | right;
And the just shall | walk in | them:
But the transgressors shall | fall there|in.
                         Hos. xiv. 4—7, 9.

## CHANT 201. DOUBLE.

### SELECTION 256.

1. My soul doth magni|fy the | Lord,
   And my spirit hath re|joiced in | God my | Savior:
2. For he hath regarded the low es|tate of his | handmaid;
   For, behold, from henceforth all gener|a·tions shall | call me | blessed.
3. ⁸For he that is mighty hath done to | me great | things,
   And | holy | is his | name.
4. And his mercy is on | them that | fear him,
   To gener|a·tions of | gener|ations.
5. He hath showed | strength·with his | arm;     [heart.
   He hath scattered the proud in the imagin|ation | of their |
6. He hath put down the mighty | from their | seats,
   And exalted | them of | low de|gree.
7. He hath filled the hungry | with good | things.
   And the rich he hath | sent | emp·ty a|way.
8. He hath holpen his servant | Isra|el,
   In re|membrance | of his | mercy:
9. As he spake | to our | fathers,
   To Abraham, and | to his | seed for | ever.      Luke i. 46.

### SELECTION 257. (Cht. 151.)

1. In that day, | saith Je|hovah,
   Will I as|semble | her that | halteth:
2. And I will gather | her·that is | driven | out,
   And | her·that I | have af|flicted.

SELECTIONS AND CHANTS. 203

3. And I will make | her · that did | halt a | remnant,
And her that was cast | off a | strong | nation.
4. And JEHOVAH shall reign | over · them | in mount | Zion,
From | henceforth, | e·ven for | ever.
5. And thou, | O tower | of the | flock,
The strong | hold · of the | daugh·ter of | Zion,
6. Unto thee shall it come, | even the | first do|minion ;
The kingdom shall come to the daughter | of Je|rusa||lem.
Mic. iv. 6.

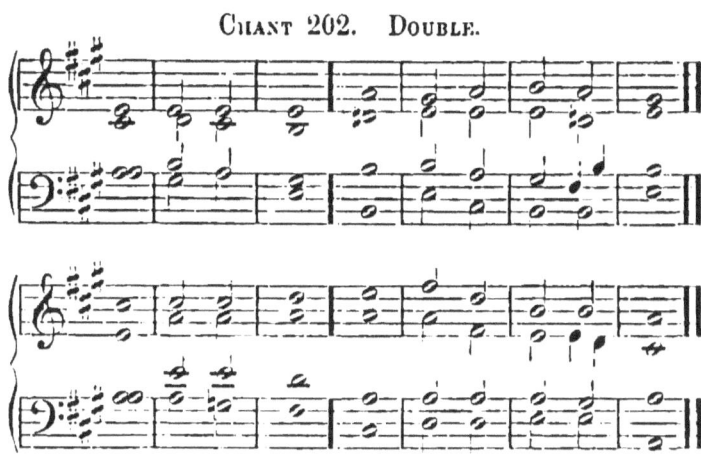

CHANT 202. DOUBLE.

SELECTION 258.

1. And in the same country were shepherds abiding | in the |
Keeping watch | o·ver their | flock by | night.   [field,
2 And, lo, the angel of the LORD | came up|on them,
And the glory of the | LORD shone | round a|bout them.
3. And they were | sore a̦fraid :
And the angel | said unto | them, Fear | not :
4. For, behold, I | bring you · good | tidings
Of great joy, which | shall be | to all | people.
5. For to you in the city of David is | born this | day
A Savior, | who is | CHRIST the | LORD.
6. And this shall be a | sign unto | you :
Ye shall find the Babe, wrapped in swaddling clothes, | lying
| in a | manger.
7. And suddenly there | was · with the | angel
A multitude of the heavenly host, | prai·sing | GOD, and | say·
8. Glory to | GOD · in the | highest :                [ing,
And on earth | peace ; among | men good | will.  Luke ii. 8.

### Chant 203.

### SELECTION 259.

1. The bread of God is he that cometh | down from | heaven,
And giveth | life un|to the | world....
2. He that cometh to me shall | never | hunger,
And he that believeth on | me shall | never | thirst.....
3. This is the bread that cometh | down from | heaven,
That one may | eat there|of, and not | die.
4. I am the living bread that came | down from | heaven:
If any one eat of this | bread, he shall | live for | ever.
5. And the bread that I will give | is my | flesh,
Which I will give | for the | life of the | world.
6. And the Spirit and the | Bride say, | Come:
And let him that | heareth | say, | Come:
7. And let him that | thirsteth | come:
And let him that willeth take | wa·ter of | life | freely.
John vi. 33, 35, 50, 51 : Rev. xxii. 17.

### SELECTION 260.

1. Unto him that | loved | us,
And washed us from our | sins in | his own | blood,
2. And hath made us kings and priests unto | God · and his | Father.
To him be glory and dominion for | ever and | ever : A|men
3. Behold, he cometh | with the | clouds;
And every eye shall see him, and | they who | pierced | him.
4. And all the tribes of the | earth shall | wail
Because of him : | even | so ; A|men.
5. I am the Alpha | and · the O|mega,
The Beginning and the | End, | saith the | Lord ;
6. Who is, and who was, and who | is to | come ;
The | Al|migh|ty.                      Rev. i. 5—8

SELECTIONS AND CHANTS. 205

CHANT 204.

SELECTION 261.

1. Holy, Holy, Holy, Lord | God Al|mighty,
Who was, and who | is, and who | is to | come.   Rev. iv. 8.
2. Thou art | worthy, O | Lord,
To receive | glo·ry, and | hon·or, and | power :
3. For thou hast cre|ated all | things;
And for thy pleasure they | are, and | were cre|ated.   11.

SELECTION 262.

1. Great and marvellous are thy works, Lord | God Al|mighty;
Just and true are thy | ways, thou | king of | saints.
2. Who shall not fear | thee, O | Lord,
And glorify thy name? for |thou a|lone art | holy.
3. For all nations shall come and | wor·ship be|fore thee;
For thy judgments | are made | mani|fest.   Rev. xv. 3, 4.

SELECTION 263.

1. The kingdoms of this world are become our | Lord's and
his | Christ's ;
And he shall | reign for | ev·er and | ever. ...
2. We give thee thanks, O Lord | God Al|mighty.
Who art, and who | wast, and who | art to | come;
3. Because thou hast taken | unto | thee
Thy great | power, | and hast | reigned.   Rev. xi. 15, 17.

SELECTION 264.

1. Salvation | to our | God,
Who sitteth upon the | throne, and | to the | Lamb.
   Rev. vii. 10.
Dox.  Amen : Blessing, and | glo·ry, and | wisdom,
And thanksgiving, and | hon·or, and | power, and | might,
Be | unto our | God,
For | ever and | ever : Amen.   Rev. vii. 12

### CHANT 205.

### SELECTION 265.

1. Now is come the salvation, | and the | strength,
And the kingdom of our God, and the | power | of his | Christ:
2. For the accuser of our brethren | is cast | down,
Who accused them be|fore our | God · day and | night.
3. And they overcame him by the blood of the Lamb, and by the word of their | testi|mony :
And they loved | not their | lives · unto | death.
4. Therefore rejoice, | O ye | heavens,
And | ye that | dwell in | them. Rev. xii 10—12.

Dox. Amen : Blessing, and | glo·ry, and | wisdom,
And thanksgiving, and | honor, and | power, and | might,
Be | un·to our | God,
For | ever and | ever : A|men. Rev. vii. 12.

### CHANT 206.

### SELECTION 266.

Confession of the Lord, 1, 2; after all things of the church had utterly perished, 3, 4: that then, lest those who are out of the church should perish, they shall come and be protected from those who would infest them, 5—10.

1. O Jehovah, thou | art my | God ;
I will exalt thee, | I will | praise thy | name :
2. For thou hast done | won·derful | things ;
Thy counsels of old are | faithful|ness and | truth.

3. For thou hast made of a | ci·ty an | heap ;
   Of a de|fenced | ci·ty a | ruin ;
4. A palace of strangers to | be no | city ;
   It | never | shall be | built.
5. Therefore shall the strong people | glori|fy thee ;
   The city of the terrible | nations | shall | fear thee.
6. For thou hast been a | strength·to the | poor,
   A strength to the | need·y in | his dis|tress ;
7. A refuge | from the | storm,
   A | shadow | from the | heat ;
8. When the blast of the | ter·rible | ones
   Is as a | storm a|gainst the | wall.
9. Thou shalt bring down the | noise of | strangers,
   As the | heat·in a | dry | place ;
10. The heat with the shadow | of a | cloud :
    The branch of terrible ones | shall be | brought | low.
    Is. xxv.

CHANT 207.

SELECTION 267.    (Or CHT. 203.)

1. Alle|lu|ia :
   For the LORD | GOD om|nip·otent | reigneth.
2. Let us be | glad, and re|joice,
   And give the | glory | unto | him :
3. For the marriage of the | LAMB is | come ;
   And his | Wife hath | made·herself | ready.
4. And to her was granted that she should | be ar|rayed
   In fine | linen | bright and | clean :
5. For the | fine | linen
   Is the | righteous|ness of | saints.
6. Blessed are | they·that are | called
   Unto the marriage | supper | of the | LAMB.    Rev. xix. 6.

Dox. Amen : Blessing, and | glo·ry, and | | wisdom,
     And thanksgiving, and | hon·or, and | power, and | might,
     Be | unto our | God,
     For | ev·er and | ever : A m·n.    Rev. vii. 12.

### Chant 179. Double.

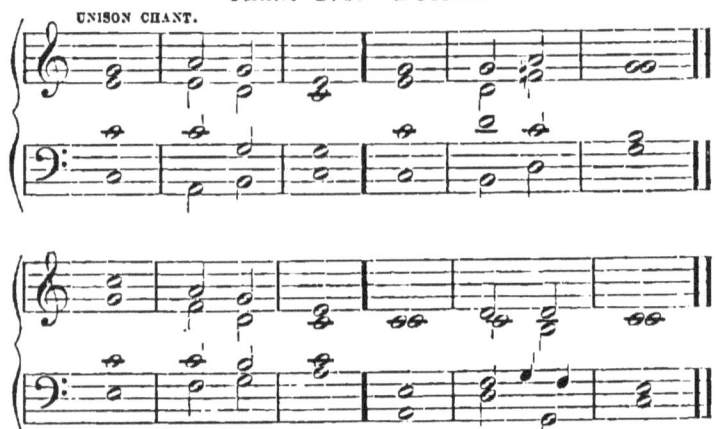

### SELECTION 268.

1. And he showed me the city, Holy Je|rusa|lem,
   Descending | out of | heaven from | God..... [tal,
2. And he showed me a river of water of life, | clear as | crys-
   Proceeding out of the throne of | God and | of the | Lamb.
3. In the midst of the street of it, and | of the | river,
   On this side and on that, | was the | tree of | life,
4. Bearing twelve fruits, yielding its fruit | every | month :
   And the leaves of the tree were for the | healing | of the ᵢ
5. And there shall be | no more | curse : [nations.
   But the throne of God and of the | Lamb shall | be in | it ;
6. And his servants shall | serve | him :
   And they shall see his face ; and his | name shall | be · in
7. And night shall | not be | there : [their | foreheads.
   And they have no need of a | lamp and | light · of the | sun :
8. For the Lord God giveth | light up|on them ;
   And they shall | reign for | ev·er and | ever.
9. And he said unto me, These words are | faith·ful and | true :
   And the Lord God of the holy | prophets | sent his ; angel,
10 To show | unto his | servants
   The things | which must | short·ly be | done.....
11. And the Spirit and the | Bride say, | Come :
    And let | him that | heareth say, | Come :
12. And let him that | thirsteth | come :
    And whosoever will, let him take | wa·ter of | life | freely..
13. He that testifieth | these | things,
    Saith, | Surely | I come | quickly ;

SELECTIONS AND CHANTS.    209

14. A|-----|men :
    Even | so, | come, LORD | JESUS.    Rev. xxii.

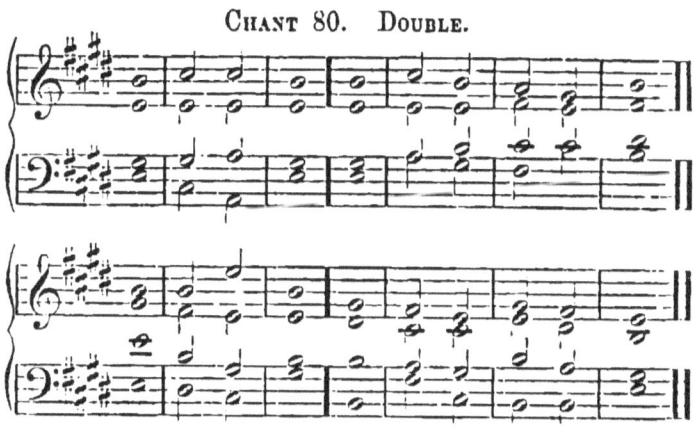

CHANT 80. DOUBLE.

SELECTION 269.

1. And he carried me a|way · in the | spirit,
   Upon a | mountain | great and | high,
2. And showed me the city, Holy Je|rusa|lem,
   Descending | out of | heaven from | GOD :
3. Having the | glo ry of | GOD.
   And I | saw no | temple there|in :
4. For the LORD | GOD Al|mighty,
   And the LAMB, | are the | temple | of it.
5. And the city had no | need · of the | sun,
   Neither of the | moon, to | shine in | it :
6. For the glory of GOD did | lighten | it,
   And the | lamp there|of · is the | LAMB.
7. And the nations of | them · that are | saved,
   Shall | walk · in the | light of | it :
8. And the kings of the | earth do | bring
   Their glory and | honor | into | it.
9. And the gates of it shall not be shut at | all by | day ;
   For | night shall | not be | there.
10. And | they shall | bring
    The glory and honor of the | nations | into | it.
11. And there shall in no wise enter | into | it
    Any | thing that | doth de|file,
12. Neither doeth abomination | or a | lie ;
    But they that are written in the | LAMB's | book of | life.

R*                                              Rev xxi.

## SELECTION 177. (p. 141.)

1. Praise ye | Jah.
Praise God in his | sanctuary:
Praise him in the firmament of his | power.
2. Praise him for his mighty | acts:
Praise him according to his | ex·cellent | greatness.
3. Praise him with the sound of the | trumpet:
Praise him with the psaltery | and the | harp.
4. Praise him with the | tim·brel and | dance:
Praise him with | stringed instru|ments and | organs.
5. Praise him upon the cymbals of | hearing:
Praise him upon the | cym·bals of | shouting.
6. Let every thing that hath breath praise | Jah.
Hallelujah: Praise ye Jah.     Ps. cl.

### Chant 208.

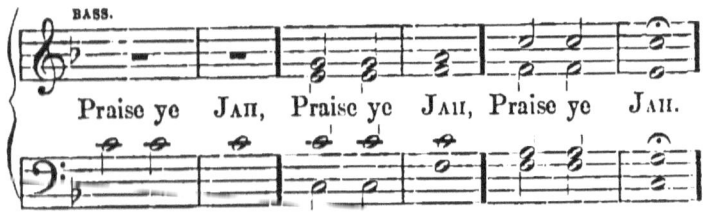

Praise ye Jah, Praise ye Jah, Praise ye Jah.

## DOXOLOGY.

*[ The Doxology on page 23 of the Order of Worship may be sung to any suitable Chant, or as here set.]*

*Minister.* To JESUS CHRIST be glory and dominion for ever and ever.

*People.* He is the Alpha and the O-mega, the Beginning and the End, the First and the Last: Who is, and who was, and who is to come; The Al - - - - - migh - ty.

The Al - - - mighty

## BENEDICTION.*

The grace of our | LORD | JESUS | CHRIST Be | with you | all : A|men.   Rev. xxii. 21.

*This may be sung at the close of the last Selection, when the services are not conducted by a minister.

# ANTHEMS.

## ANTHEM 1.

#### HE THAT HATH AN EAR, LET HIM HEAR.

These things saith the First and the Last, who was dead, and is alive; I know thy works, and tribulation, and poverty. Fear none of those things which thou shalt suffer. Be thou faithful unto death, and I will give thee a crown of life.

He that hath an ear, let him hear what the Spirit saith unto the churches. He that overcometh shall not be hurt of the second death.

## ANTHEM 2

#### AND THE GLORY OF JEHOVAH

Prepare ye the way of JEHOVAH; make straight in the desert a highway for our GOD. Every valley shall be exalted, and every mountain and hill shall be made low: and the crooked shall be made straight, and the rough places plain. And the glory of JEHOVAH shall be revealed, and all flesh shall see it together: for the mouth of JEHOVAH hath spoken it.

ANTHEM 3.

## ANTHEM 3.

#### THOU ART MY GOD.

Blessed be he that cometh in the name of JEHOVAH:
We have blessed you out of the house of JEHOVAH.
Thou art my GOD, and I will praise thee:
My GOD, I will exalt thee.
O give thanks to JEHOVAH; for he is good:
For his mercy is forever.

## ANTHEM 4.

#### HIS DOMINION.

I saw in the night visions, and, behold, one like the Son of Man came with the clouds of heaven, and came to the Ancient of Days, and they brought him near before him. And there was given him dominion, and glory, and a kingdom; that all people, nations, and languages should serve him. His dominion is an everlasting dominion, which shall not pass away; and his kingdom that which shall not be destroyed.—Dan. vii. 13.

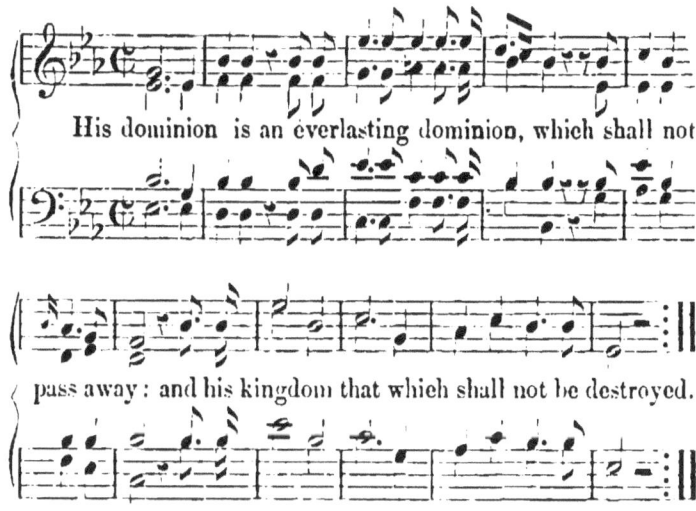

His dominion is an everlasting dominion, which shall not pass away: and his kingdom that which shall not be destroyed.

## ANTHEM 5.

#### UNTO US A CHILD IS BORN.

Unto us a Child is born,
Unto us a Son is given:
And the government shall be upon his shoulder:
And his name shall be called
Wonderful, Counsellor, God, Mighty,
Father of Eternity, Prince of Peace.
Of the increase of his government and peace there shall be no end,
Upon the throne of David and upon his kingdom;
To order it, and to establish it,
With judgment and with justice,
From henceforth, even for ever:
The zeal of Jehovah of Hosts will perform this.   Is. ix. 6

218 ANTHEMS

## ANTHEM 5.

### Anthem 5.

## ANTHEM 6.

#### NOW IS COME THE SALVATION.

And I heard a loud voice saying in heaven, Now is come the salvation, and the strength, and the kingdom of our God, and the power of his Christ. For this rejoice, O ye heavens, and ye that dwell in them. Who shall not fear thee, O Lord, and glorify thy name? for thou alone art holy. Just and true are thy ways, thou King of saints.

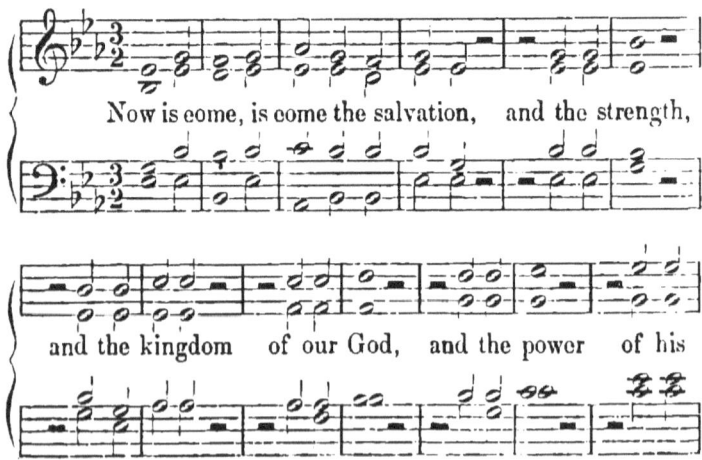

## ANTHEM 7.

#### GLORY TO GOD IN THE HIGHEST.

And in the same country were shepherds abiding in the field, keeping watch over their flock by night. And lo, the angel of the LORD came upon them; and the glory of the LORD shone round about them: and they were sore afraid. And the angel said unto them, Fear not: for behold I bring you good tidings of great joy, which shall be to all people: For unto you, in the city of David, is born this day a Savior, who is CHRIST the LORD. And this shall be a sign unto you: ye shall find the Babe wrapped in swaddling clothes, lying in a manger. And suddenly there was with the angel a multitude of the heavenly host, praising GOD, and saying, Glory to GOD in the highest; and on earth peace; among men good will.

## ANTHEM 8.

### HOSANNA.

Tell ye the daughter of Zion, Behold, thy King cometh unto thee, meek, and riding upon an ass, and upon a colt the foal of an ass. And the multitudes that went before, and that followed, cried, saying, Hosanna! Blessed is he that cometh in the name of the LORD! Hosanna in the highest!

## ANTHEM 8.

He, that cometh in the name, in the name of the Lord. Ho-san - - - na, Ho-san - - - - na, Ho-san - - - - - - na, Hosanna in the highest, Hosanna in the highest, in the high - - est.

## ANTHEM 9.

### WORTHY IS THE LAMB.

Worthy is the LAMB that was slain, to receive power, and riches, and wisdom, and might, and honor, and glory, and blessing. Blessing, and honor, and glory, and strength be unto Him that sitteth upon the throne, and unto the LAMB, for ever and ever. Amen.

## ANTHEM 10.

**BLESSED BE JEHOVAH.**

Bless JEHOVAH, O my soul;
And all that is within me, bless his holy name.
Bless JEHOVAH, O my soul,
And forget not all his benefits. . . .
Blessed be JEHOVAH forevermore: Amen, and Amen.

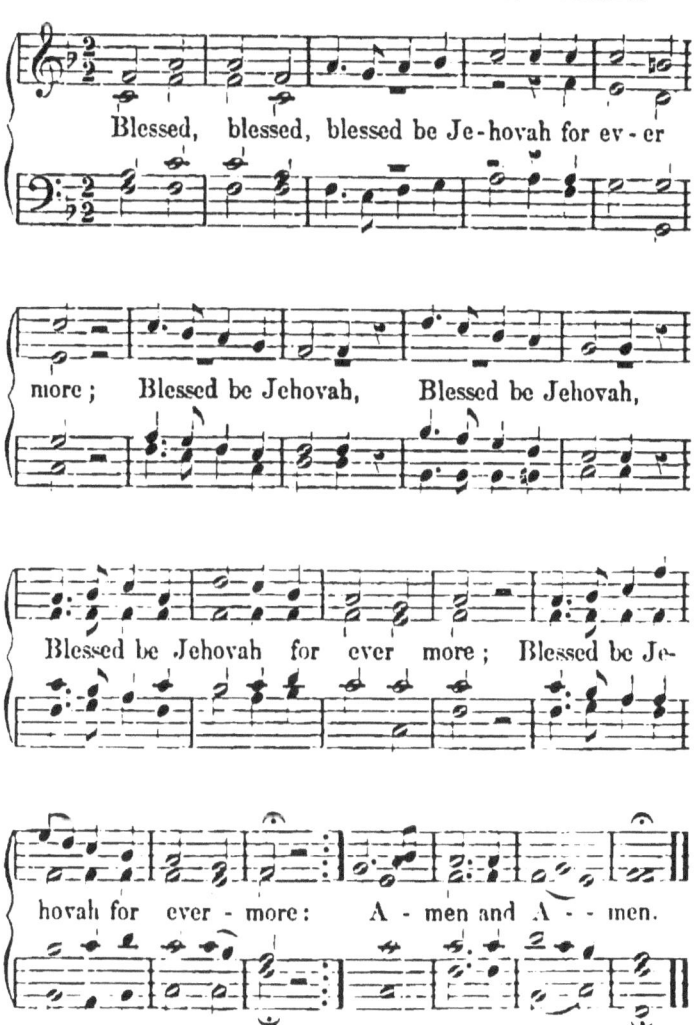

## ANTHEM 11.

#### BEHOLD HOW GOOD AND HOW PLEASANT.

Behold, how good and how pleasant it is,
For brethren to dwell together in unity.
It is like the dew of Hermon,
That descended upon the mountains of Zion:
For there JEHOVAH commanded the blessing,
Life forevermore.

ANTHEM 12.

### ANTHEM 12. BEHOLD, I COME QUICKLY.

Behold, I come quickly; and my reward is with me, to give to every one as his work shall be. I am Alpha and Omega, the Beginning and the End, the First and the Last. And the Spirit and the Bride say, Come! And let him that heareth, say, Come! And let him that thirsteth come; And let him that willeth take water of life freely. He who testifieth these things saith, Surely I come quickly. Amen: Yea, come, LORD JESUS.

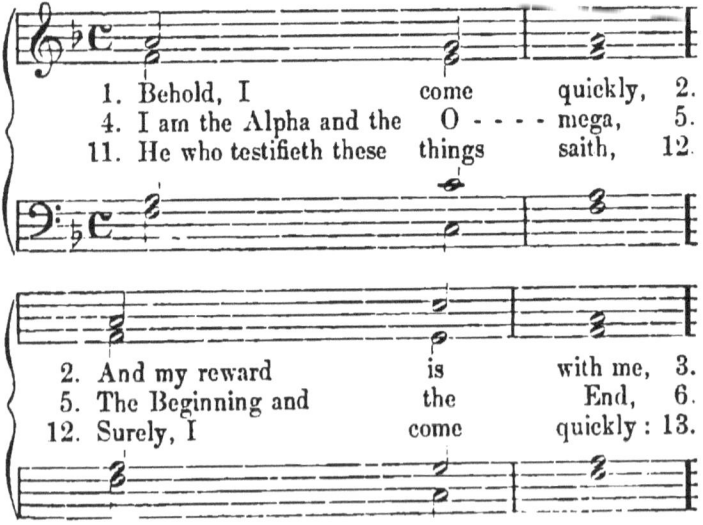

## ANTHEM 13.

### SING, O HEAVENS.

Sing, O heavens; and be joyful, O earth:
Break forth into singing, O mountains:
JEHOVAH hath comforted his people;
He will have mercy on his afflicted.
But Zion said, JEHOVAH hath forsaken me,
And my LORD hath forgotten me.
Behold, I have graven thee upon the palms of my hands;
Thy walls are continually before me.

## ANTHEM 14.

**THOU WILT SHOW ME THE PATH OF LIFE**

I set JEHOVAH always before me:
Because he is at my right hand, I shall not be moved.
Thou wilt show me the path of life:
In thy presence is fulness of joy;
And at thy right hand there are pleasures forevermore.

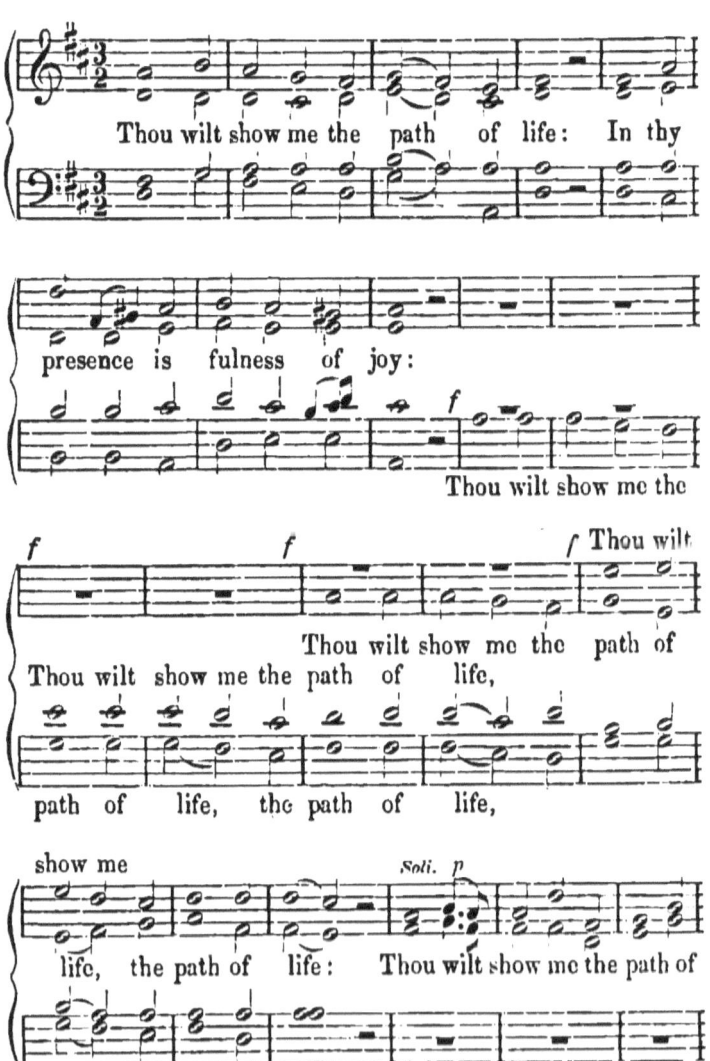

# CHANTS

## SUITABLE FOR RESPONSIVE SERVICES.

In chanting Responsive Selections, any suitable *division* or part of a chant may be used, either among the following or the foregoing, provided it terminate with a final cadence.

CHANTS. 241

# CHANTING.

THE LORD is Love and Wisdom, or Goodness and Truth; and the doctrines of the New Church teach that these two not only make one in him, but are always found united in his Word. It is on this account that in the Scriptures subjects so often occur in pairs; and it is for the same reason that in the Psalms the verses are generally made up of two clauses or lines, composing a couplet, called by scholars a *parallelism*. The same is the case in the Prophets, except that the verses often contain two or more couplets. This feature in the Scriptures is the origin of the common Chant.

A Chant is a short musical composition, consisting of two divisions, for singing the two lines of a couplet or verse. The first note of each division is called the *chanting note:* it has no time, but is longer or shorter according to the number of words sung to it. The remainder of each division is called the *cadence*, and must be sung in strict time. To the chanting note of the first division are sung the words of the first line, except so many syllables as are necessary to sing the notes of the cadence; and the second line is sung to the second division in the same manner. This is the Single Chant. A Double Chant consists of four divisions, and sings two verses. Verses are sometimes found having three lines, as in Sel. 38, ver. 7 - 10; Sel. 255: these require a Chant of three divisions, called a Ternary Chant.

In this work, the words are marked for application to the music, measure for measure. The lines are divided by perpendicular *dashes*, which correspond to the bars of the music. The words, therefore, which precede the first dash, are to be sung to the *chanting note;* and the words or syllables between the dashes, and after the last dash, are to be sung to corresponding measures of the cadence.

The simplest form of division is where the accents of the words admit of giving *one syllable* to *each note* of the cadence; as in Sel. 59, verse 1. But the accents of the words often render it necessary to leave but *one* syllable in a measure, or to put *three* into a measure, or to give *two* to the last note: and all these may be found in the same line; as in Sel. 217, ver. 2, line 2.

When *one* syllable fills a measure, it is to be sung to *all the notes* of that measure; as in Sel. 59, ver. 5, line 2. When *three* syllables are found in a measure, the middle of the measure is indicated by a *dot;* and the *two syllables* which fall on either side of the dot are to be sung as *two quarter-notes;* Sel. 59, ver. 4 and 5. There are two classes of cases in which the dot is dispensed with. *First*, when *any mark of punctuation* falls among *the three syllables*, it serves the purpose of the dot; as in Sel. 59, ver. 3, line 2: unless it be contradicted by a *dot*, as in Sel. 195, ver. 3, line 2. *Secondly*, when *two* of the three syllables belong to the *same word*, the space between the words divides the measure; as in Sel. 59, ver. 2, line 2; also Sel. 92, ver. 3, line 2: unless contradicted by a dot, as in Sel. 59, ver. 4, line 2, and ver. 5, line 1. When *two syllables* are given to the last note of the chant, they are to be sung as *two half-notes*.

A small figure [1], [2], [3], or [4], placed before a line, as in Sel. 58, ver. 9 and 10, indicates that that line is to be sung to the *first*, *second*, *third*, or *fourth* division of the chant.

Words ending in *ed*, in which by common usage the *ed* is not pronounced as a distinct syllable, as *bowed*, *cried*, *hoped*, *nursed*, &c., are sometimes found in situations in which the chanting will be facilitated by making the *ed* a separate syllable; as in Sel. 217, ver. 6, line 2; Sel. 6, ver. 2, line 2.

In singing the words to the chanting note, the *utterance*, *pronunciation*, *accent*, *emphasis*, *inflection*, *pauses*, and *expression*, should be the same as when reading very deliberately to an audience, only more marked. In reading or speaking, unimportant, unemphatic, and unaccented words and syllables occupy much less time, and are uttered with much less force, than important, emphatic, and accented ones; and in singing the words to the chanting note, the same relative time, and force of utterance, should not only be carefully maintained, but the force and time of accented and emphatic words and syllables should be increased, and the unaccented and unimportant should be passed over lightly.

This rule for singing the words to the *chanting note* ceases when we come to the *cadence;* for the cadence must always "be given in correct time, the beat of which can be felt." Still, however, as much of the expression and emphasis of good reading or speaking should be given to the words of the cadence, as is consistent with correct time.

If there be a *passing note* in the chanting measure, (Chts. 26, 60, 166,) the last syllable before the dash is sung to it, if it be an unaccented syllable; but if accented or important, it should be commenced on the chanting note, and then pass to the quarter note, as in Sel. 61, ver. 1, line 1, and ver. 5, line 1. To do this properly and readily requires practice and careful attention.

Some of the most simple Selections for applying these rules are Sel. 16, 27, 34, 59, 91, 125, 197, 259.

The words which we chant are taken from the Word of the LORD, who is himself the Word. Singing is the expression of affection, and the object in chanting is first to feel, and then to express the proper affection which belongs to the words. In chanting portions of the Word, therefore, the more we love it, and the more fully we are filled with the sense and feeling of its divinity, and of the LORD as flowing into us through it; the more fully shall we be able to express these affections, and to heighten them in ourselves and others; and the better shall we chant.

Those Chants which consist of six measures, from Chant 218 to Chant 248 inclusive, are composed on the basis of the ancient ecclesiastical modes.

U *

# INDEX

OF

## RESPONSIVE SELECTIONS.

These are additional to the Responsive Selections on pages 34 to 38 of the Order of Worship, and may be used at any time. The Minister should read the first line of each verse, and the people may either read or sing the second line. When a verse has three lines, if read, the Minister and people may read the third line together; but, if sung, the people may sing the second and third lines.

And it shall come to pass in the last days, (ver. 4–10,)............Sel. 180
Arise, O Jehovah, into thy rest, (ver. 1, 2, 7–12,)....................162
Behold mine affliction, and deliver me...................................140
Behold my servant shall deal prudently, (any after ver. 5,)............209
Blessed be the Lord God of Israel..........................................208
Bless Jehovah, O my soul....................................................115
Create in me a clean heart, O God, (8 verses,)............................67
Good and upright is Jehovah....................................................4
How goodly are thy tents, O Jacob........................................247
How lovely are thy tabernacles, O Jehovah of Hosts......................80
I cried with all the heart; hear me, O Jehovah...........................139
I hate divided thoughts, but thy law do I love............................136
I have done judgment and justice..........................................138
I was glad when they said unto me........................................163
I will extol thee, my God O King...........................................171
Jehovah is full of compassion and gracious..............................110
Jehovah reigneth, he is clothed with majesty..............................90
Jehovah upholdeth all that fall.............................................125
Let my cry come near before thy face, O Jehovah........................142
Make a joyful noise unto Jehovah, all the earth..........................144
My soul cleaveth unto the dust.............................................130
My soul fainteth for thy salvation..........................................137
O clap your hands, all ye people..............................................60
O come, let us sing to Jehovah, (7 verses,)................................101
O give thanks unto Jehovah, for he is good...............................168
O how I love thy law........................................................155
O sing unto Jehovah a new song, (9 verses,)...............................96
Praise ye Jah: Praise Jehovah, O my soul..................................170
Princes have persecuted me without a cause..............................153
Remember the word unto thy servant.......................................131
Righteous art thou, O Jehovah................................................92
The earth is Jehovah's, and the fulness thereof............................38
The law of Jehovah is perfect, converting the soul........................27
Thou art my portion, O Jehovah............................................132
Thou hast been favorable, O Jehovah, to thy land.........................16
Thou hast dealt bountifully with thy servant..............................134
Thy hands have made me and fashioned me...................................6
Turn us again, O God of Hosts; and cause thy face to shine..............81
Wherewith shall a young man cleanse his way.............................128
Wherewith shall I come before Jehovah...................................173

# INDEX

### OF THE

### FIRST LINES OF THE SELECTIONS.

A little that a righteous man hath..........................Sel. 46
Alleluia; for the Lord God omnipotent reigneth......................267
Although the fig-tree shall not blossom.............................207
And he carried me away in the spirit upon a mountain................269
And he showed me the city, holy Jerusalem...........................268
And in that day thou shalt say, O Jehovah, I will praise thee.......188
And in the last days it shall come to pass, that the mountain.......241
And in the same country were shepherds abiding in the field.........258
And in this mountain shall Jehovah of hosts make unto all people....181
And I saw a new heaven and a new earth..............................236
And it shall come to pass in the day that Jehovah shall give you rest...190
And it shall come to pass in the last days..........................180
And they shall build houses, and inhabit............................231
And they shall build the old wastes.................................186
Arise, O Jehovah, into thy rest.....................................162
Arise, shine, for thy light is come.................................217
As the hart panteth for the brooks of water..........................7
Awake, awake, put on thy strength, O Zion...........................204

Because thou hast made Jehovah, my refuge...........................79
Behold, a king shall reign in righteousness.........................242
Behold, at that time I will undo all that afflict thee..............193
Behold, bless ye Jehovah, all ye servants of Jehovah................169
Behold, how good and how pleasant it is, for brethren...............122
Behold, I create new heavens and a new earth........................235
Behold, Jehovah our God hath showed us his glory....................250
Behold, Jehovah's hand is not shortened, that it cannot save........189
Behold mine affliction, and deliver me..............................140
Behold, my servant shall deal prudently.............................209
Behold my servant, whom I uphold....................................197
Behold the man whose name is The Branch.............................73
Blessed are the dead, who die in the Lord...........................215
Blessed are the perfect in the way..................................123
Blessed be Jehovah, because he hath heard the voice of my supplications..13
Blessed be the Lord God of Israel...................................208
Blessed is he that doth consider the poor...........................56
Blessed is the man that walketh not in the counsel of the ungodly...1
Blessed is the man whom thou dost chasten, O Jah....................94
Blessed is the nation whose God is Jehovah..........................45
Bless Jehovah, O my soul, and all that is within me bless his holy name..31
Bless Jehovah, O my soul: O Jehovah, my God, thou art very great...115
Bow down thine ear, O Jehovah; hear me..............................82
But thus saith Jehovah, that created thee, O Jacob..................175
But we are all as an unclean thing..................................234

## FIRST LINES OF THE SELECTIONS.

Come, and let us return to Jehovah............................Sel. 105
Come, ye children, hearken unto me..................................46
Comfort ye, comfort ye my people, saith your God...................145
Create in me a clean heart, O God...................................67
Cry aloud, spare not...............................................210

Deal bountifully with thy servant, that I may live.................127

Fools, from the way of their transgressions.........................29
For ever, O Jehovah, thy word is established in the heavens........124
For thus saith the High and Lofty One..............................212
For thy Maker is thine husband.....................................210
For Zion's sake will I not hold my peace...........................226
Fret not thyself because of evil-doers..............................48
From the top of the rocks I see him................................249

Give ear, O ye heavens, and I will speak...........................251
Give ear to my prayer, O God; and hide not thyself..................64
Give ear to my words, O Jehovah; consider my complaint..............5
Give the king thy judgments, O God..................................76
Give unto Jehovah, O ye sons of God; give glory and strength........41
God be merciful unto us, and bless us...............................75
God is my king of old, working salvation...........................175
God is not a man that he should lie................................246
God is our refuge and strength......................................58
Good and upright is Jehovah..........................................4
Great and marvellous are thy works, Lord God Almighty..............262
Great is Jehovah, and greatly to be praised.........................61

Have mercy upon me, O God, according to thy loving kindness.........65
Hearken to me, ye that follow after righteousness..................202
Hearken unto me, my people.........................................194
Hearken unto me, ye that know righteousness........................233
Hear me speedily, O Jehovah; my spirit faileth......................88
Hear me when I call, O God of my righteousness.......................3
Hear my cry, O God; attend to my prayer.............................68
Hear my prayer, O Jehovah; give ear unto my supplications...........55
Hear, O Jehovah; I cry with my voice...............................111
Hear the right, O Jehovah; attend unto my cry.......................54
Hear ye this, O house of Jacob.....................................240
He hath said, who heard the words of God...........................248
He made darkness his secret place...................................22
He sendeth forth springs into brooks...............................100
He sent a man before them, Joseph..................................114
He that dwelleth in the secret place of the Most High...............93
He weakened my strength in the way; he shortened my days...........104
Ho, every one that thirsteth, come ye to the waters................213
Holy, holy, holy, Lord God Almighty................................261
How beautiful upon the mountains are the feet of him...............206
How goodly are thy tents, O Jacob..................................217
How great is thy goodness, which thou hast laid up..................43
How long wilt thou forget me, O Jehovah? for ever?..................23
How lovely are thy tabernacles, O Jehovah of Hosts..................80
How manifold are thy works, O Jehovah..............................109
How precious also are thy thoughts unto me, O God..................161

I cried by reason of mine affliction...............................239
I cried unto Jehovah with my voice.................................158
I cried with all the heart; hear me, O Jehovah.....................130
I hate divided thoughts, but thy law do I love.....................136
I have considered the days of old..................................157
I have done judgment and justice...................................137

# FIRST LINES OF THE SELECTIONS.

I have set watchmen upon thy walls, O Jerusalem...............Sel. 227
I love Jehovah, because he hath heard my voice.....................117
In God will I praise his word.........................................59
In Judah is God known................................................72
In that day, saith Jehovah, will I assemble her that halteth.........257
In thee, O Jehovah, do I put my trust; let me never be ashamed.......42
In thee, O Jehovah, do I put my trust; let me never be put to confusion.133
It is a good thing to give thanks unto Jehovah........................89
It is God that girdeth me with strength...............................20
It shall come that I will gather all nations and tongues.............237
I waited patiently for Jehovah........................................51
I was glad when they said unto me....................................163
I will bless Jehovah at all times.....................................36
I will declare thy name to my brethren................................26
I will extol thee, my God, O King; and I will bless thy name.........171
I will greatly rejoice in Jehovah....................................225
I will heal their backsliding; I will love them freely...............255
I will hear what Jehovah God will speak...............................91
I will lift up mine eyes to the mountains............................158
I will love thee, O Jehovah, my strength..............................19
I will praise thee, O Jehovah, with all the heart......................9
I will praise thee with all the heart................................129
I will praise the name of God with a song.............................74
I will sing of mercy and judgment....................................112
I will sing of the mercies of Jehovah for ever........................84
I will sing to Jehovah, for he hath triumphed gloriously.............245

Jehovah hath been mindful of us, he will bless us....................149
Jehovah hath prepared his throne in the heavens.......................37
Jehovah hear thee in the day of trouble...............................24
Jehovah is full of compassion and gracious...........................110
Jehovah is gracious and full of compassion............................32
Jehovah is my light and my salvation..................................40
Jehovah is my Shepherd; I shall not want..............................17
Jehovah is the portion of my part, and of my cup......................30
Jehovah killeth, and maketh alive....................................254
Jehovah reigneth, he is clothed with majesty..........................90
Jehovah reigneth, let the earth rejoice..............................108
Jehovah reigneth, let the people tremble..............................97
Jehovah rewarded me according to my righteousness.....................21
Jehovah shall go forth as a mighty man...............................201
Jehovah upholdeth all that fall......................................125
Judge me, O God, and plead my cause...................................57
Judge me, O Jehovah; for I have walked in mine integrity..............39

Let my cry come near before thy face, O Jehovah......................142
Let them exalt him in the congregation of the people.................116
Let thy mercies come also unto me, O Jehovah.........................143
Look down from heaven, and behold....................................230
Look upon Zion, the city of our solemnities..........................102

Make a joyful noise unto God, all the earth..........................107
Make a joyful noise unto Jehovah, all the earth......................144
Many, O Jehovah, my God, are thy wonderful works......................52
Mine eyes are ever toward Jehovah.....................................15
My days are like a shadow that declineth..............................98
My heart rejoiceth in Jehovah........................................253
My soul cleaveth unto the dust.......................................130
My soul doth magnify the Lord........................................256
My soul fainteth for thy salvation...................................137
My soul, wait thou only upon God......................................69

Not unto us, O Jehovah, not unto us..........................Sel. 150
Now is come the salvation, and the strength.........................265

O clap your hands, all ye people..............................60
O come let us sing to Jehovah, let us make a joyful noise..............101
O give thanks to Jehovah, for he is good: Fools, from the way..........29
O give thanks to Jehovah, for he is good: Let Israel now say..........120
O give thanks to Jehovah, for he is good: Those that sit in darkness....102
O give thanks to Jehovah, for he is good: Thus shall the redeemed......103
O give thanks to Jehovah, for he is good: Who can utter the mighty acts..31
O give thanks unto Jehovah, call upon his name......................113
O give thanks unto Jehovah, for he is good: All nations compassed me..121
O give thanks unto Jehovah, for he is good: They that go down to the sea..99
O give thanks unto Jehovah: Open to me the gates of righteousness....179
O give thanks unto Jehovah: unto the God of gods..................108
O God, my heart is fixed..........................................28
O God, thou art my God; early will I seek thee.....................77
O how I love thy law.............................................155
O Jehovah, how are they increased that trouble me....................2
O Jehovah, I have heard thy speech, I was afraid...................245
O Jehovah, our Lord, how excellent is thy name in all the earth........11
O Jehovah, rebuke me not in thine anger............................8
O Jehovah, thou art my God; I will exalt thee.....................266
O Jehovah, thou hast searched me, and known me..................160
O Jehovah, who shall abide in thy tabernacle.......................25
O praise Jehovah, all ye nations; praise him, all ye people............86
O sing unto Jehovah a new song, for he hath done marvellous things.....95
O sing unto Jehovah a new song; sing unto Jehovah, all the earth......96
O that thou wouldst rend the heavens, that thou wouldst come down,..198
O thou afflicted, tossed with tempest, and not comforted.............211
Our heart is not turned back.....................................154
Out of the depths have I cried unto thee, O Jehovah................159
O Zion, that bringest good tidings...............................195

Praise Jehovah, O Jerusalem; praise thou thy God, O Zion............167
Praise waiteth for thee, O God, in Zion............................70
Praise ye Jah: Blessed is the man that feareth Jehovah..............119
Praise ye Jah: For it is good to sing praises unto our God............172
Praise ye Jah: I will praise Jehovah with all the heart..............118
Praise ye Jah: O give thanks to Jehovah, for he is good..............81
Praise ye Jah: Praise God in his sanctuary..............(also p. 210) 177
Praise ye Jah: Praise Jehovah, O my soul..........................170
Praise ye Jah: Praise, O ye servants of Jehovah....................164
Praise ye Jah: Praise ye Jehovah from the heavens..................174
Praise ye Jah: Praise ye the name of Jehovah......................165
Praise ye Jah: Sing unto Jehovah a new song, his praise.............176
Praise ye Jah: Thy name, O Jehovah, is for ever...................166
Princes have persecuted me without a cause.......................153

Rejoice greatly, O daughter of Zion...............................196
Rejoice in Jehovah, O ye righteous.................................44
Remember the word unto thy servant...............................131
Righteous art thou, O Jehovah.....................................92

Salvation to our God, who sitteth upon the throne..................264
Save me, O God, by thy name; and judge me by thy strength..........35
Seek ye Jehovah, while he may be found...........................214
Sing a new song unto Jehovah, his praise from the end of the earth....126
Sing, O barren, thou that didst not bear..........................222
Sing, O daughter of Zion; shout, O Israel........................187

Teach me, O Jehovah, the way of thy statutes.....................152

# FIRST LINES OF THE SELECTIONS. 251

Teach me thy way, O Jehovah: I will walk in thy truth..............Sel. 83
The bread of God is he that cometh down from heaven.................259
The earth is Jehovah's, and the fulness thereof.......................38
The glory of Lebanon shall come unto thee............................219
The heavens are thine, the earth is also thine........................85
The heavens declare the glory of God..................................10
The kingdoms of this world are become our Lord's and His Christ's....262
The king shall joy in thy strength, O Jehovah........................32
The law of Jehovah is perfect, converting the soul...................27
The mighty God, Jehovah, hath spoken, and called the earth...........63
Then shall the eyes of the blind be opened..........................221
Then thou spakest in vision to thine Holy One........................87
The people that walked in darkness have seen a great light..........185
The poor and needy seek water, and there is none....................232
There shall come forth a Rod out of the stem of Jesse...............144
The Spirit of the Lord Jehovih is upon me...........................228
The wicked doth watch the righteous..................................50
The wilderness and the barren place shall be glad for them..........200
The wolf shall dwell with the lamb..................................183
Thou art my king, O God..............................................151
Thou art my portion, O Jehovah.......................................132
Thou dost visit the earth, and water it...............................18
Though Jehovah be high, he hath respect to the lowly................148
Thou hast been favorable, O Jehovah, to thy land.....................16
Thou hast dealt well with thy servant, O Jehovah....................134
Thou hast delivered me from the strivings of the people..............14
Thou, O God, hast proved us; thou hast tried us as silver is tried...71
Thus saith Jehovah, In an acceptable time have I heard thee.........223
Thus saith Jehovah, thy Redeemer, and he that formed thee...........203
Thy hands have made me and fashioned me...............................6
Thy mercy, O Jehovah, is in the heavens..............................47
Thy testimonies are wonderful.......................................141
Thy way, O God, is in the sanctuary.................................146
Thy word is a lamp to my feet.......................................135
To whom then will ye liken God......................................199
To whom then will ye liken me, or shall I be equal..................191
Turn us again, O God; and cause thy face to shine....................66
Turn us again, O God of Hosts; and cause thy face to shine...........81

Unto him that loved us..............................................260
Unto thee, O Jehovah, do I lift up my soul...........................12
Upon the land of my people shall come up thorns and briers..........182

Violence shall no more be heard in thy land.........................221

We have a strong city...............................................205
We have thought of thy kindness, O God...............................62
What shall I render to Jehovah, for all his benefits................147
When Israel went out of Egypt.......................................106
When the Most High divided to the nations their inheritance.........252
Wherefore thou hast been forsaken and hated.........................220
Wherewith shall a young man cleanse his way.........................128
Wherewith shall I come before Jehovah...............................173
Who are these that fly as a cloud, and as the doves.................218
Who hath measured the waters in the hollow of his hand..............244
Who is a God like to thee, that pardoneth iniquity..................229
Withhold thou not thy mercy from me, O Jehovah.......................53

Yea, all kings shall bow down to him.................................78
Yet now hear, O Jacob, my servant...................................234

# INDEX OF THE ANTHEMS.

| TITLE | PAGE. | AUTHOR. |
|---|---|---|
| 1. He that hath an ear let him hear | 213 | Kent. |
| 2. And the glory of Jehovah | 214 | G. J. Webb. |
| 3. Thou art my God | 215 | Dr. Clarke. |
| 4. His Dominion | 217 | Dr. G. K. Jackson. |
| 5. Unto us a child is born | 217 | G. J. Webb. |
| 6. Now is come the salvation | 220 | Kent. |
| 7. Glory to God in the highest | 222 | G. J. Webb. |
| 8. Hosanna | 224 | G. J. Webb. |
| 9. Worthy is the Lamb | 225 | G. J. Webb. |
| 10. Blessed be Jehovah | 229 | Anon. |
| 11. Behold, how good and how pleasant | 230 | G. J. Webb. |
| 12. Behold, I come quickly | 232 | G. J. Webb. |
| 13. Sing, O heavens | 234 | Kent. |
| 14. Thou wilt show me the path of life | 236 | Anon. |
| 15. I will lay me down in peace | 238 | Neukomm. |
| 16. Holy, holy, holy, Jehovah of Hosts | 238 | R. Taylor. |
| 17. Psalm 150 | 210 | G. J. Webb. |
| 18. Doxology | 212 | G. J. Webb. |

# INDEX OF SELECTIONS

## FOR OCCASIONAL SERVICES.

Baptism of Infants and Children. 13, 17, 46, 123, 125, 158, 178, 188, 208.
Baptism of Adults. 17, 34, 40, 59, 92, 123, 125, 128, 158, 183, 188, 213.
Confirmation. 17, 34, 40, 79, 80, 123, 155, 158, 183, 188, 213, 222, 223, 224, 226
The Holy Supper. 91, 181, 182, 183, 188, 192, 198, 221, 222, 223, 259, 267.
Marriage. 17, 27, 30, 91, 125, 158, 178; 45, ver. 7, 9–11; Anthem 14.
Funerals. 17, 105, 110, 125, 158, 215.
Ordination. 40, 155, 162, 195, 197, 206, 213, 214, 226, 227, 228.
Consecration. 87, 162, 179, 195, 197, 206, 226, 227, 228, 236, 268, 269.
Dedication. 38, 60, 80, 144, 162, 195, 196, 217, 223, 224, 226, 227, 236, 268, 269.
Institution of Societies. 61, 62, 80, 122, 163, 192, 217, 218, 222, 236, 268, 269.
Institution of Associations. 61, 62, 122, 163, 180, 183, 192, 217, 218, 236, 268, 269.

# INDEX

OF

PASSAGES OF SCRIPTURE FOUND IN THE SELECTIONS, ANTHEMS, ETC.

THE first column gives the chapter, the second the verse, of the passage, in the Bible and the third shows where it is to be found in this work. If the number in the third column has no letter prefixed, it indicates a *Selection*. A. prefixed means *Anthem*, B. *Benediction*, and D. *Doxology*. If *p.* is prefixed, the number indicates the page.

| | EXODUS. | | xxv. | 1—7. | 12 | lxix. | 30—36. | 74 |
|---|---|---|---|---|---|---|---|---|
| xv. | 1—18. | 245 | " | 8—14. | 2 | lxxi. | 1—5. | 183 |
| | | | " | 15—22. | 15 | lxxii | 1—12. | 76 |
| | NUMBERS. | | xxvi. | 1—12. | 89 | " | 11—19. | 78 |
| xxiii. | 19—24. | 246 | xxvii. | 1—6. | 40 | lxxiv. | 12—17. | 175 |
| " | 9, 10. | 249 | " | 7—11. | 111 | lxxvi. | 1—12. | 72 |
| xxiv. | 5—9. | 247 | xxviii. | 6—9. | 13 | lxxvii. | 5—9. | 157 |
| " | 16—19. | 248 | xxix. | 1—11. | 41 | " | 13—20. | 146 |
| | | | xxxi. | 1—8. | 42 | lxxx. | 3—7. | 66 |
| | DEUTERONOMY. | | " | 19—24. | 43 | " | 7—19. | 81 |
| v. | 24. | 250 | xxxiii. | 1—12. | 44 | lxxxiv. | 1—12. | 80 |
| xxxii. | 1—7. | 251 | " | 12—22. | 45 | lxxxv. | 1—7. | 16 |
| " | 8—14. | 252 | xxxiv. | 1—10. | 36 | " | 8—13. | 91 |
| | | | " | 11—22. | 46 | lxxxvi. | 1—12. | 82 |
| | 1 SAMUEL. | | xxxvi. | 5—12. | 47 | " | 11—17 | 83 |
| ii. | 1—5. | 253 | xxxvii. | 1—16. | 48 | lxxxix. | 1—10. | 84 |
| " | 6—10. | 254 | " | 16—31. | 49 | " | 11—18. | 85 |
| | | | " | 32—40. | 50 | " | 19—37. | 87 |
| | PSALMS. | | xl. | 1—4. | 51 | " | 52. | A. 10 |
| i. | 1—6. | 1 | " | 5—10 | 52 | xci. | 1—8. | 98 |
| iii. | 1—8. | 3 | " | 11—17. | 53 | " | 9—16. | 79 |
| " | 8. | D. p. 61 | xli. | 1—4, 11—13. | 56 | xcii. | 1—15. | 89 |
| iv. | 1—8. | 4 | xlii. | 1—5. | 7 | xciii. | 1—5. | 90 |
| " | 8. | A. 15 | xliii. | 1—5. | 57 | xciv. | 12—23. | 94 |
| v. | 1—8. | 5 | xliv. | 4—8. | 151 | xcv. | 1—11. | 101 |
| vi. | 1—10. | 8 | " | 18—23. | 154 | xcvi. | 1—13. | 96 |
| viii. | 1—9. | 11 | xlvi. | 1—11. | 58 | xcvii. | 1—12. | 108 |
| ix. | 1—10. | 9 | xlvii. | 1—9. | 60 | xcviii. | 1—9. | 95 |
| xiii. | 1—6. | 23 | xlviii. | 1—10. | 61 | xcix. | 1—9. | 97 |
| xv. | 1—5. | 25 | " | 9—14. | 62 | c. | 1—5. | 144 |
| xvi. | 5—11. | 80 | l. | 1—6 | 68 | ci. | 1—8. | 112 |
| " | 11. | A. 14 | li. | 1—9. | 65 | cii. | 11—22. | 98 |
| xvii. | 1—5. | 54 | " | 10—19. | 67 | " | 23—28. | 104 |
| xviii. | 1—10. | 19 | liv. | 1—7. | 85 | ciii. | 1—7. | 84 |
| " | 11—19. | 22 | lv. | 1—8. | 64 | " | 8—18. | 110 |
| " | 20—31. | 21 | lvi. | 10—13. | 59 | " | 19—22. | 87 |
| " | 32—42. | 20 | lxi. | 1—8. | 63 | civ. | 1—9. | 115 |
| " | 43—50. | 14 | lxii. | 5—8, 11, 12. | 69 | " | 10—23. | 100 |
| xix. | 1—6. | 10 | lxiii. | 1—11. | 77 | " | 24—35. | 109 |
| " | 7—14. | 27 | lxv. | 1—8. | 70 | cv. | 1—8. | 113 |
| xx. | 1—9. | 24 | " | 9—13. | 18 | " | 17—22. | 114 |
| xxi. | 1—7, 13. | 83 | lxvi. | 1—9. | 107 | cvi. | 1—5. | 81 |
| xxii. | 22—31. | 26 | " | 8, 9. D. pp. 33, 95 | cvii. | 1—9. | 103 |
| xxiii. | 1—6. | 17 | " | 10—20. | 71 | " | 10—16. | 102 |
| xxiv. | 1—10. | 33 | lxvii. | 1—7. | 75 | " | 17—22. | 29 |

| | | | | | | | | |
|---|---|---|---|---|---|---|---|---|
| cvii. | 28—31. | 99 | | ISAIAH. | | | DANIEL. | |
| " | 32—43. | 116 | ii. | 2—5. | 180 | vii. | 14. | A. 4 |
| cviii. | 1—6. | 28 | vi. | 3. | A. 16 | | | |
| cxi. | 1—10. | 118 | " | 8. | p. 211 | | HOSEA. | |
| cxii. | 1—10. | 119 | ix. | 2, 6, 7. | 185 | vi. | 1—8. | 105 |
| cxiii. | 1—9. | 164 | " | 6. | A. 5 | xiv. | 4—7, 9. | 255 |
| cxiv. | 1—8. | 106 | xi. | 1—5. | 164 | | | |
| cxv. | 1—11. | 150 | " | 6—9. | 183 | | JONAH. | |
| " | 12—18. | 149 | xii. | 1—6. | 188 | ii. | 2—9. | 239 |
| cxvi. | 1—9. | 117 | xiv. | 8—7. | 190 | | | |
| " | 12—19. | 147 | xxv. | 1—5. | 206 | | MICAH. | |
| cxvii. | 1, 2. | 86 | " | 6—9. | 181 | iv. | 1—5. | 241 |
| cxviii. | 1—9, 29 | 120 | xxvi. | 1—10. | 205 | " | 6—8. | 257 |
| " | 1, 10—18, 20. | 121 | xxxii. | 1—8. | 242 | vi. | 6—8. | 173 |
| " | 1, 19—29. | 179 | " | 13—20. | 182 | vii. | 18—20. | 229 |
| " | 28. | A. 3 | xxxiii. | 20—22. | 192 | | | |
| cxix. | 1—8. | 123 | xxxv. | 1—6. | 200 | | HABAKKUK. | |
| " | 9—16. | 128 | " | 5—10. | 224 | iii. | 2—8, 12, 13. | 243 |
| " | 17—24. | 127 | xl. | 1—5. | 145 | " | 17—19. | 207 |
| " | 25—32. | 130 | " | 5. | A. 2 | | | |
| " | 33—40. | 152 | " | 9—11. | 195 | | ZEPHANIAH. | |
| " | 41—48. | 143 | " | 12—19. | 244 | iii. | 14, 15. | 187 |
| " | 49—56. | 131 | " | 18—25. | 199 | " | 19, 20. | 193 |
| " | 57—64. | 132 | " | 25—31. | 191 | | | |
| " | 65—72. | 134 | xli. | 17—20. | 232 | | ZECHARIAH. | |
| " | 73—80. | 6 | xlii. | 1—4. | 197 | vi. | 12, 13. | 73 |
| " | 81—88. | 187 | " | 10—12. | 126 | ix. | 9, 10. | 196 |
| " | 89—96. | 124 | " | 13—16. | 201 | | | |
| " | 97—104. | 155 | xliii. | 1—7. | 178 | | MATTHEW. | |
| " | 105—112. | 135 | xliv. | 1—6. | 234 | xxi. | 9. | A. 8 |
| " | 113—120. | 136 | " | 24—28. | 203 | | | |
| " | 121—128. | 138 | xlviii. | 1—3, 17—19. | 240 | | LUKE. | |
| " | 129—136. | 141 | xlix. | 8—16. | 223 | i. | 46—55. | 256 |
| " | 137—144. | 92 | " | 13. | A. 13 | " | 68—79. | 208 |
| " | 145—152. | 139 | li. | 1—8. | 202 | ii. | 8—14. | 258 |
| " | 153—160. | 140 | " | 4—6. | 194 | " | 14. | A. 7 |
| " | 161—168. | 153 | " | 7—11. | 233 | | | |
| " | 169—176. | 142 | iii. | 1—6. | 204 | | JOHN. | |
| cxxi. | 1—8. | 158 | " | 17—10. | 206 | vi. | 33, 35, 50, 51. | 259 |
| cxxii. | 1—9. | 163 | " | 8—15. | 209 | | | |
| cxxx. | 1—8. | 159 | liii. | 1—12. | 209 | | REVELATION. | |
| cxxxii. | 8—18. | 162 | liv. | 1—6. | 222 | i. | 5—8. | 260 |
| cxxxiii. | 1—3. | 122 | " | 5—10. | 210 | " | 6, 8. | D. p. 212 |
| " | 1, 3. | A. 11 | " | 11—17. | 211 | ii. | 11. | A. 1 |
| cxxxiv. | 1—8. | 169 | iv. | 1—5. | 213 | iv. | 8, 11. | 261 |
| cxxxv. | 1—7. | 165 | " | 6—13. | 214 | v. | 12, 13, 14. | A. 9 |
| " | 13—21. | 166 | lvii. | 15, 16. | 212 | vii. | 10. | 264 |
| cxxxvi. | 1—26. | 168 | lviii. | 1—14. | 216 | " | 12. D. pp. 169, 205, |
| cxxxviii. | 1—5. | 129 | lix. | 1—4. | 189 | | | [206, 207 |
| " | 6—8. | 148 | lx. | 1—7. | 217 | xi. | 15, 17. | 263 |
| cxxxix. | 1—12. | 160 | " | 8—12. | 218 | xii. | 10—12. | 265 |
| " | 17—24. | 161 | " | 13, 14. | 219 | " | 10, 12. | A. 6 |
| cxliii. | 1—7. | 156 | " | 15—17. | 220 | xiv. | 13. | 215 |
| cxlv. | 1—6. | 55 | " | 18—22. | 221 | xv. | 3, 4. | 262 |
| " | 7—12. | 88 | lxi. | 1—8. | 228 | " | 4. | A. 6 |
| cxlv. | 1—7. | 171 | " | 4—9. | 186 | xix. | 6—9. | 267 |
| " | 8—13. | 32 | " | 10, 11. | 225 | " | 6. | 215 |
| " | 14—21. | 125 | lxii. | 1—5. | 226 | xx. | 1—6. | 236 |
| cxlvi. | 1—10. | 170 | " | 6—12. | 227 | xxi. | 10, 11, 22—27. | 269 |
| cxlvii. | 1—11. | 172 | lxiii. | 15—19. | 230 | xxii. | 1—6, 17, 20. | 268 |
| " | 12—20. | 167 | lxiv. | 1—5. | 198 | " | 12, 13, 17, 20. A. 5 |
| cxlviii. | 1—14. | 174 | " | 6—12. | 238 | " | 17. | 259 |
| cxlix. | 1—9. | 176 | lxv. | 17—20. | 235 | " | 21. B. p. 212 |
| cl. | 1—6. | 177 | " | 21—25. | 231 | | | |
| " | 1—6. | p. 210 | lxvi. | 18—23. | 237 | | | |

# TE DOMINUM:

## A HYMN OF GLORIFICATION TO THE LORD JESUS CHRIST.

Chant 196. Double.

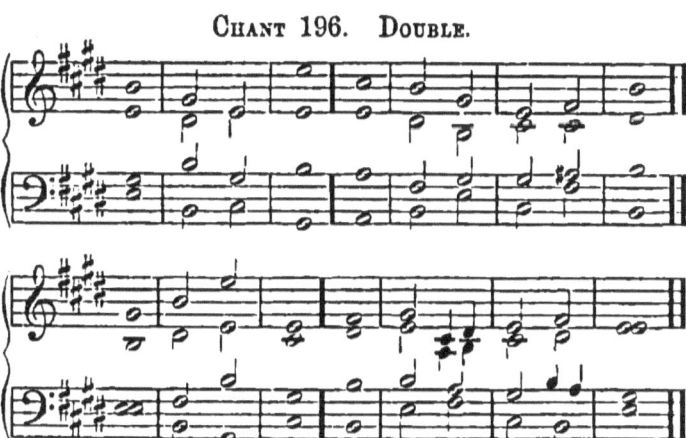

1. We praise Thee, O Lord; we magnify thy | holy | name:
 The heavens and earth praise Thee, the sea, and | all that |
2. By thy Word were the | heavens | made, [is there|in.
 And all the host of them | by the | breath · of thy | mouth.
3. All thy works praise Thee, | and thy · saints | bless Thee :
 Thy church doth worship and ac|knowledge | Thee a|lone ;
4. The Father eternal, the Word incarnate, the Holy Spirit the | Comfort|er :
 In essence and in person One; Je|hovah, | Jesus, | Lord.
5  To Thee cherubim and | seraph|im,
 Angels and blessed spirits lift | up their | voic·es, and | say
6. Holy, holy, holy, Lord | God Al|mighty :
 Heaven and | earth are | full · of thy | glory.
7. Thousand thousands minister | unto | Thee :
 Ten thousand times ten | thousand | stand be|fore Thee.
8. They do thy commandments, hearkening to the | voice of· thy | Word ;
 And with one consent celebrate the | wonders | of thy | love.
9. Thou didst bow the heavens, and come down for | our sal|vation :
 Thou didst clothe thyself with our nature, and be|camest | God with | us

10. Thou didst gird on thy sword as a mighty | Man of | war,
And thine own arm brought sal|vation | unto | Thee.
11. Thou didst overcome and put to flight all the legions | of the
| enemy:
Thou didst bring | down their | strength · to the | earth.
12. In thy love and in thy pity thou | didst re|deem us:
And the chastisement of our | peace was | upon | Thee.
13. Thou didst pass through the bitterness of suffering | and
tempt|ation:
Thou didst humble thyself even to the | passion | of the |
14. Thou didst sanctify and glori|fy Thy|self, [cross
By uniting thy Human | Essence | with · the Di|vine.
15. Thou didst burst asunder all the | bonds of | death:
Thou didst rise in Divine | majes|ty and | glory.
16. Thou didst ascend on high; thou didst lead cap|tivi·ty |
captive:
The everlasting doors were | opened | to re|ceive Thee.
17. High above all the heavens didst thou | set thy | throne,
Clothed with light inaccessible, girt with om|nipo|tence and
| love.
18. Thy kingdom is an ever|lasting | kingdom,
And thy dominion from gener|a·tion to | gener|ation.
19. Righteous and true are thy ways, Thou | King of | saints:
Who shall not fear Thee, O LORD, and | glori|fy thy | name?
20. Thou art the Alpha and the Omega, the Beginning and the
End, the | First · and the | Last;
Who wast, and who art, and who | art to | come, the Al|-
21. From everlasting to | ever|lasting, [mighty.
Thou alone art | GOD of | heaven and | earth.
22. Thou art the | King of | glory:
Thou | art JE|HO·VAH OF | HOSTS.
23. Day unto day will we exalt Thee, O | LORD our | GOD;
And worship at thy footstool, for | Thou a|lone art | Holy.
24. We will praise Thee; | we will | bless Thee;
And magnify thy | name for|ev·er and | ever.
Hallelujah: Amen.

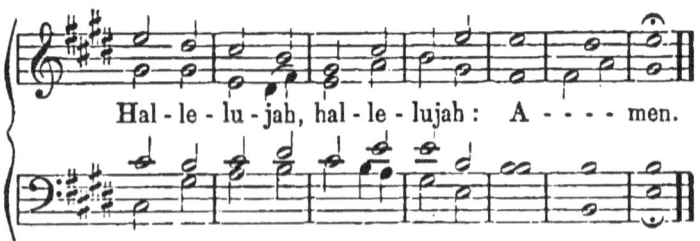

Hal - le - lu - jah, hal - le - lujah : A - - - - men.

# HYMNS.

### HYMN 1. L. M.
#### THANKSGIVING AND PRAISE TO THE LORD
*Enter into his gates with thanksgiving,
And into his courts with praise.*

1 WITH one consent, let all the earth
   To GOD their cheerful voices raise;
   Glad homage pay, with hallowed mirth,
   And sing before him songs of praise.

2 The LORD is GOD; the LORD alone
   Doth life, and breath, and being give.
   We are his work, and not our own,
   The sheep that on his pastures live

3 Enter his gates with songs of joy,
   With praises to his courts repair;
   And make it your divine employ,
   To pay your thanks and honors there.

4 For he's the LORD, supremely good;
   His mercy is for ever sure;
   His truth, which always firmly stood,
   To endless ages shall endure.

### HYMN 2. 11's and 8's.
*Make a joyful noise unto GOD, all ye lands.*

1 BE joyful in GOD, all ye lands of the earth;
   O serve him with gladness and fear:
   Exult in his presence with music and mirth,
   With love and devotion draw near.

2 The LORD, he is GOD, and JEHOVAH, alone;
   Creator, and ruler o'er all:

1*

And we are his people, his sceptre we own;
His sheep, and we follow his call.

3 O enter his gates with thanksgiving and song,
Your vows in his temple proclaim;
His praise with melodious accordance prolong,
And bless his adorable name.

4 For good is the LORD, inexpressibly good;
And we are the work of his hand:
His mercy and truth from eternity stood,
And shall to eternity stand.

## HYMN 3. L. M.

*Jehovah reigneth; let the people tremble:
He sitteth between the cherubims; let the earth be moved.*

1 BEFORE JEHOVAH'S holy throne,
Ye nations, worship and adore:
Know that the LORD is GOD alone;
He can create, and he restore.

2 His sovereign power, without our aid,
Called us to life, and formed us men;
And when, like wandering sheep, we strayed,
He brought us to his fold again.

3 We are his people, we his care;
Our souls, and all our mortal frame:
What lasting honors shall we rear,
O LORD our Maker, to thy name.

4 We'll crowd thy gates with thankful songs;
High as the heavens our voices raise:
And earth, with her ten thousand tongues,
Shall fill thy courts with sounding praise.

5 Wide as the world is thy command;
Vast as eternity thy love:
Firm as a rock thy truth shall stand,
While rolling years unceasing move.

## HYMN 4. L. M.

*Be thou exalted, O God, above the heavens;
And thy glory above all the earth.*

1 BE thou, O GOD, exalted high;
And as thy glory fills the sky,
So let it be on earth displayed,
Till thou art here, as there, obeyed.

2 Thy praises, LORD, we will resound
  To all the listening nations round:
  Thy mercy highest heaven transcends;
  Thy truth beyond the clouds extends.

3 Be thou, O GOD, exalted high;
  And as thy glory fills the sky,
  So let it be on earth displayed,
  Till thou art here, as there, obeyed.

## HYMN 5. L. M.

*Give unto JEHOVAH the glory due unto his name*

1 GIVE to the LORD immortal praise:
  Mercy and truth are all his ways:
  Wonders of grace to him belong:
  Repeat his mercies in your song.

2 He formed the sun to cheer the ground,
  And make its varied fruits abound:
  He bids the clouds, with plenteous rain,
  Refresh the thirsty earth again.

3 'Tis to his care we owe our breath,
  And all our near escapes from death:
  Safety and health to GOD belong;
  He heals the weak, and guards the strong.

4 Give to the LORD of lords renown;
  The KING of kings with glory crown;
  Who pours his blessings from the skies,
  And every needful gift supplies.

## HYMN 6. L. M.

*O give thanks unto JEHOVAH; for he is good·
For his mercy endureth forever.*

1 O RENDER thanks to GOD above,
  The Fountain of eternal love;
  Whose mercy, firm, through ages past,
  Hath stood, and shall for ever last.

2 Who can recount His wondrous deeds,
  Whose greatness all our thought exceeds?
  What mortal eloquence can raise
  A tribute equal to his praise?

3 Happy are they, and only they,
Who from his precepts never stray;
Who know what's right, nor only so,
But always practise what they know.

## HYMN 7. L. M.

*O that men would praise JEHOVAH for his goodness,
And for his wonderful works to the children of men.*

1 GIVE thanks to GOD; he reigns above:
Kind are his thoughts; his name is love:
His mercy ages past have known,
And ages long to come shall own.

2 He feeds and clothes us all the way;
He guides our footsteps, lest we stray;
He guards us with a powerful hand,
And brings us to the heavenly land.

3 Then let us all with joy record
The truth and goodness of the LORD:
How great his works; how kind his ways:
Let every tongue pronounce his praise.

## HYMN 8. C. M.

*I will sing unto JEHOVAH as long as I live:
I will sing praise unto my GOD, while I have any being.*

1 LONG as I live, I'll bless thy name,
  My King, my GOD of love;
My work and joy shall be the same,
  In brighter worlds above.

2 Great is the LORD, his power unknown;
  O let his praise be great:
I'll sing the honors of thy throne,
  Thy works of grace repeat.

3 Thy love shall dwell upon my tongue;
  And while my lips rejoice,
The men who hear my sacred song,
  Shall join their cheerful voice.

4 Fathers to sons shall tell thy name,
  And children learn thy ways;
Ages to come thy truth proclaim,
  And nations sound thy praise.

PRAISE TO THE LORD.

5 The world is governed by thy hand,
Thy saints are ruled by love;
Eternal does thy kingdom stand,
Though rocks and hills remove.

HYMN 9. C. P. M.
Let every thing that hath breath praise Jah.

1 BEGIN, my soul, the exalted lay;
Let each enraptured thought obey,
  And praise the Almighty's name:
Lo, heaven, and earth, and seas, and skies,
In one melodious concert rise,
  To swell the inspiring theme.

2 Thou heaven of heavens, his vast abode,
Ye clouds, proclaim your maker, GOD;
  Ye thunders, speak his power:
Lo, on the lightning's fiery wing,
In triumph, walks the eternal King;
  The astonished worlds adore.

3 Ye deeps, with roaring billows rise,
To join the thunders of the skies;
  Praise him who bids you roll:
His praise in softer notes declare,
Each whispering breeze of yielding air,
  And breathe it to the soul.

4 Wake, all ye soaring throngs, and sing;
Ye feathered warblers of the spring,
  Harmonious anthems raise
To him, who shaped your finer mould,
Who tipped your glittering wings with gold,
  And tuned your voice to praise.

5 Let man, by nobler passions swayed,
Let man, in GOD's own image made,
  His breath in praise employ;
Spread wide his Maker's name around,
Till heaven shall echo back the sound,
  In songs of holy joy.

HYMN 10. L. M.
The heavens declare the glory of GOD,
And the firmament showeth the work of his hands.

1 THE spacious firmament on high,
With all the blue ethereal sky,

And spangled heavens, a shining frame,
Their great Original proclaim.

2 The unwearied sun, from day to day,
Does his Creator's power display,
And publishes to every land
The work of an almighty hand.

3 Soon as the evening shades prevail,
The moon takes up the wondrous tale,
And nightly, to the listening earth,
Repeats the story of her birth.

4 While all the stars that round her burn,
And all the planets in their turn,
Confirm the tidings, as they roll,
And spread the truth from pole to pole.

5 What though, in solemn silence, all
Move round this dark terrestrial ball?
What though no real voice, nor sound,
Amid their radiant orbs be found?

6 In reason's ear they all rejoice,
And utter forth a glorious voice;
For ever singing, as they shine,
"The hand that made us is divine."

## HYMN 11. L. M.

His name shall endure forever:
His name shall be continued as long as the sun.

1 From all that dwell below the skies,
Let the Creator's praise arise:
Let the Redeemer's name be sung,
Through every land, by every tongue.

2 Eternal are thy mercies, Lord;
Eternal truth dwells in thy word:
Thy praise shall sound from shore to shore,
Till suns shall rise and set no more.

## HYMN 12. L. M.

### CONFIDENCE IN THE LORD.

God is our Refuge and Strength,
A very present help in trouble.

1 God is the refuge of his saints,
When storms of sharp distress invade;

CONFIDENCE IN THE LORD.

Ere we can offer our complaints,
Behold him present with his aid.

2 Loud may the troubled ocean roar;
In sacred peace our souls abide;
While every nation, every shore,
Trembles, and dreads the swelling tide.

3 There is a stream, whose gentle flow
Supplies the city of our God:
Life, love, and joy still gliding through,
And watering our divine abode.

4 That sacred stream, thine holy Word,
Supports our faith, our fear controls:
Sweet peace thy promises afford,
And give new strength to fainting souls.

5 Zion enjoys her Savior's love,
Secure against a threatening hour;
Nor can her firm foundation move,
Built on his truth, and armed with power.

HYMN 13. C. M.

Rest in Jehovah, and wait patiently for him.

1 God moves in a mysterious way
His wonders to perform;
He plants his footsteps on the sea,
And rides upon the storm.

2 Deep in unfathomable mines
Of never-failing skill,
He treasures up his bright designs,
And works his gracious will.

3 Ye fearful souls, fresh courage take
The clouds you so much dread,
Are big with mercy, and shall break
In blessings on your head.

4 Judge not the Lord by feeble sense,
But trust his constant grace:
Behind a frowning providence
He hides a smiling face.

5 His purposes will ripen fast,
Unfolding every hour;

The bud may have a bitter taste,
    But sweet will be the flower.

6 Blind unbelief is sure to err,
    And scan his work in vain:
God is his own interpreter,
    And he will make it plain.

## HYMN 14. C. M.

*Lord, thou hast been our dwelling place in all generations.*

1 O Lord, our help in ages past,
    Our hope for years to come;
Our shelter from the stormy blast,
    And our eternal home:

2 Beneath the shadow of thy throne,
    Thy people dwell secure;
Sufficient is thine arm alone,
    And our defence is sure.

3 Before the hills in order stood,
    Or earth received her frame,
From everlasting thou art God,
    To endless years the same.

4 O Lord, our help in ages past,
    Our hope for years to come,
Be thou our guard, while troubles last,
    And our eternal home.

## HYMN 15. C. M.

*God is the strength of my heart, and my portion forever.*

1 God, my supporter, and my hope,
    My help forever near,
Thine arm of mercy held me up,
    When sinking in despair.

2 Thy counsels, Lord, shall guide my feet,
    Through this dark wilderness;
Thine hand conduct me near thy seat,
    To dwell before thy face.

3 Then to draw near to thee, my God,
    Shall be my sweet employ;
My tongue shall sound thy works abroad,
    And tell the world my joy.

CONFIDENCE IN THE LORD.

HYMN 16. S. M.
*Jehovah is my Shepherd, I shall not want.*

1 THE LORD my Shepherd is;
  I shall be well supplied:
Since he is mine, and I am his,
  What can I want beside?

2 He leads me to the place
  Where heavenly pasture grows,
Where living waters gently pass,
  And full salvation flows.

3 If e'er I go astray,
  He doth my soul reclaim,
And guides me, in his own right way,
  For his most holy name.

4 While he affords his aid,
  I cannot yield to fear;
Though I should walk through death's dark shade,
  My Shepherd's with me there.

HYMN 17. L. M. 6 lines.
*He maketh me to lie down in green pastures:
He leadeth me beside the still waters.*

1 THE LORD my pasture shall prepare,
And feed me with a Shepherd's care;
His presence shall my wants supply,
And guard me with a watchful eye:
My noon-day walks he shall attend,
And all my midnight hours defend.

2 When in the sultry glebe I faint,
Or on the thirsty mountain pant,
To fertile vales, and dewy meads
My weary, wandering steps he leads;
Where peaceful rivers, soft and slow,
Amid the verdant landscape flow.

3 Though in the paths of death I tread,
With gloomy horrors overspread,
My steadfast heart shall fear no ill,
For thou, O LORD, art with me still:
Thy friendly rod shall give me aid,
And guide me through the dreadful shade.

### HYMN 18. C. M.

*I will extol thee, my God, O King;
And I will bless thy name for ever and ever.*

1 SWEET is the memory of thy grace,
  My GOD, my heavenly King;
  Let age to age thy righteousness
  In songs of glory sing.

2 GOD reigns on high, but ne'er confines
  His goodness to the skies;
  Through all the earth his bounty shines
  And every want supplies.

3 How kind are thy compassions, LORD!
  How slow thine anger moves!
  How soon he sends his pardoning word,
  To cheer the souls he loves.

4 Sweet is the memory of thy grace,
  My GOD, my heavenly King;
  Let age to age thy righteousness
  In songs of glory sing.

### HYMN 19. S. M.

*I will abide in thy tabernacle for ever:
I will trust in the covert of thy wings.*

1 WHEN, overwhelmed with grief,
    My heart within me dies,
  Helpless, and far from all relief,
    To heaven I lift mine eyes.

2 O lead me to the Rock
    That's high above my head;
  And make the covert of thy wings
    My shelter and my shade.

3 Within thy presence, LORD,
    Forever I'll abide:
  Thou art the tower of my defence,
    The refuge where I hide.

### HYMN 20. S. M.

*As far as the east is from the west,
So far hath He removed our transgressions from us.*

1 MY soul, repeat his praise,
    Whose mercies are so great;

Whose anger is so slow to rise,
  So ready to abate.

2 His grace subdues our sins,
  And his forgiving love,
  Far as the east is from the west,
  Doth all our guilt remove.

3 High as the heavens are raised
  Above the ground we tread,
  So far the riches of his grace
  Our highest thoughts exceed.

## HYMN 21. C. M.

*Whom have I in heaven but thee?
And there is none on earth that I desire beside thee.*

1 Whom have we, Lord, in heaven but thee,
  And whom on earth beside?
  Where else for succor can we flee,
  Or in whose strength confide?

2 Thou art our portion here below,
  Our promised bliss above;
  Ne'er may our souls an object know
  So precious as thy love.

3 Thou, Lord, wilt be our guide through life,
  And help and strength supply;
  Sustain us in death's fearful strife,
  And welcome us on high.

## HYMN 22. S. M.

*They that trust in Jehovah shall be as Mount Zion,
Which cannot be moved, but abideth for ever.*

1 Firm and unmoved are they,
  Who rest their souls on God;
  Firm as the mount where David dwelt,
  Or where the ark abode.

2 As mountains stood to guard
  The city's sacred ground,
  So God, and his upholding love
  Embrace his people round.

3 Deal gently, LORD, with those,
  Whose faith and holy fear,
  Whose hope, and trust, and life of love,
  Proclaim their hearts sincere.

### HYMN 23. S. M.

*Return unto thy rest, O my soul:
For JEHOVAH hath dealt bountifully with thee.*

1 O cease, my wandering soul,
  On restless wing to roam;
  All this wide world, to either pole,
  Has not for thee a home.

2 Behold the ark of GOD;
  Behold the open door:
  O, haste to gain that dear abode,
  And rove, my soul, no more.

3 There, safe thou shalt abide,
  There, sweet shall be thy rest,
  And every longing satisfied,
  With full salvation blest.

### HYMN 24. C. M.
#### INCARNATION OF THE LORD.

*And they sang as it were a new song before the throne:
And no one could learn that song, but those who were redeemed from the earth*

1 FATHER, how wide thy glory shines!
  How high thy wonders rise!
  Known through the earth by myriad signs,
  By myriads through the skies.

2 But when we view thy vast design,
  To save our fallen race;
  Where wisdom, love, and power combine
  Thy justice and thy grace:

3 Our thoughts are lost in sacred awe;
  We wonder and adore:
  The highest angels never saw
  So much of GOD before.

4 O may I bear some humble part,
  In that immortal song:
  Wonder and joy shall tune my heart,
  And love command my tongue.

INCARNATION OF THE LORD. 17

### HYMN 25. C. M.

*Jehovah is my strength, and my song;
And he is become my salvation.*

1 Hark, the glad sound; Jehovah comes,
   The Savior promised long:
   Let every heart prepare a throne,
   And every voice a song.

2 He comes, the prisoners to release,
   In Satan's bondage held:
   The gates of brass before him burst,
   The iron fetters yield.

3 He comes, the broken heart to bind,
   The wounded soul to cure;
   And with the treasures of his love
   To bless the humble poor.

4 Our glad hosannas, Prince of peace,
   Thy welcome shall proclaim;
   And heaven's eternal arches ring
   With thy beloved name.

### HYMN 26. C. M.

*Glory to God in the highest; and on earth peace; good will toward men.*

1 Mortals, awake, with angels join,
   And chant the solemn lay;
   Joy, love, and gratitude, combine
   To hail the auspicious day.

2 In heaven the rapturous song began;
   And sweet seraphic fire
   Through all the shining legions ran,
   And strung, and tuned the lyre.

3 Swift through the vast expanse it flew,
   And loud the echo rolled;
   The theme, the song, the joy was new,
   'Twas more than heaven could hold.

4 Down through the portals of the sky
   The impetuous torrent ran;
   And angels flew, with eager joy,
   To bear the news to man.

## INCARNATION OF THE LORD.

5 Hark! the angelic armies shout;
"Glory to God" they sing:
With "Peace on earth, good will to men."
The heavenly arches ring.

### HYMN 27. C. M.

*He bowed the heavens also and came down;
And darkness was under his feet.*

1 The Lord descended from above,
And bowed the heavens most high;
And underneath his feet he cast
The darkness of the sky.

2 He sat serene upon the floods,
Their fury to restrain;
And he, as sovereign Lord and King,
For evermore shall reign.

### HYMN 28. C. M.

*Salvation belongeth to Jehovah:
Thy blessing is upon thy people.*

1 Salvation! O, the joyful sound!
'Tis pleasure to our ears;
A sovereign balm for every wound,
A cordial for our fears.

2 Buried in sorrow and in sin,
At hell's dark door we lay,
But we arise by grace divine,
To see a heavenly day.

3 Salvation! — let the echo fly
The spacious earth around;
While all the armies of the sky
Conspire to raise the sound.

### HYMN 29. L. M.

*Blessed is he that cometh in the name of the Lord:
Hosanna in the highest.*

1 Now to the Lord a noble song!
Awake, my soul; awake, my tongue:
Hosanna to the Savior's name,
And all his boundless love proclaim.

2 Grace! — 'tis a sweet, a charming theme;
My thoughts rejoice at Jesus' name:

Ye angels, dwell upon the sound;
Ye heavens, reflect it to the ground.

3 O, may I reach that happy place,
Where he unveils his lovely face;
Where all his glories you behold,
And sing his name to harps of gold

## HYMN 30. S. M.
*Jesus wept.*

1 BEHOLD, the SAVIOR weeps!
And shall our cheeks be dry?
Let floods of penitential grief
Burst forth from every eye.

2 The SAVIOR GOD in tears
Angels with wonder see:
Be thou astonished, O my soul!
He shed those tears for thee.

3 He wept, that we might weep;
'Tis sin demands the tear:
In heaven alone no grief is found,
Because no sin is there.

4 O SAVIOR, GOD above,
Repentance true impart;
Bestow that precious gift of thine,
The humble, contrite heart.

## HYMN 31. S. M.
*Occupy till I come.*

1 A CHARGE to keep I have,
A GOD to glorify;
A never-dying soul to save,
And fit it for the sky.

2 To serve the present age,
My calling to fulfil:
O may it all my powers engage,
To do my Master's will.

3 Help me to watch and pray,
And on thyself rely,
Assured, if I my trust betray,
I shall for ever die.

INCARNATION OF THE LORD.

### HYMN 32. C. M.

*I am the Way, the Truth, and the Life.*

1 THE LORD our Savior is the Way
  To purity and peace;
By doctrine from his Word, he leads
  To everlasting bliss.

2 The LORD our Savior is the Truth,
  The inward, shining Light,
That reason guides, and gives to faith
  The evidence of sight.

3 The LORD our Savior is the Life
  Of every soul that lives;
And everlasting life, to those
  Who keep his Word, he gives.

4 JESUS, my Way, my Truth, my Life,
  My GOD, my All in all;
At thy blest feet, in humble love,
  And lowly fear, I fall.

### HYMN 33. C. M.

*Come unto me, all ye that labor, and are heavy laden; and I will give you rest.*

1 Come hither, all ye weary souls;
  Ye heavy laden sinners, come;
I'll give you rest from all your toils,
  And raise you to my heavenly home.

2 They shall find rest, who learn of me:
  I'm of a meek and lowly mind:
But passion rages like the sea;
  And pride is restless as the wind.

3 Blest is the man, whose shoulders take
  My yoke, and bear it with delight;
My yoke is easy to the neck,
  My grace shall make the burden light.

### HYMN 34. 7's.

*Incline your ear, and come unto me:
Hear, and your soul shall live.*

1 COME, said JESUS' sacred voice,
Come, and make my paths your choice:

I will guide you to your home ;
Weary pilgrims, hither come.

2 Hither come, for here is found
Balm for every bleeding wound ;
Peace, which ever shall endure;
Rest, eternal, sacred, sure.

## HYMN 35. 7s.

*Praise our God, all ye his servants,
And ye that fear him, both small and great.*

1 ANGELS, roll the rock away ;
Death, yield up thy mighty prey :
See, he rises from the tomb,
Rises with immortal bloom.

2 'Tis the SAVIOR ; angels, raise
Your triumphant songs of praise ;
Let the earth's remotest bound
Hear the joy-inspiring sound.

3 O ye people, lift your eyes ;
High in glory see him rise :
Hosts of angels on the road
Hail and sing the incarnate GOD

4 Praise him, all ye heavenly choirs,
Praise, and sweep your golden lyres ;
Praise him in the noblest songs,
Praise him from ten thousand tongues.

## HYMN 36. C. M.

*Worthy is the Lamb that was slain.*

1 COME, let us join our cheerful songs,
　With angels round the throne ;
Ten thousand thousand are their tongues,
　But all their joys are one.

3 " Worthy the LAMB that died," they cry,
　" To be exalted thus : "
" Worthy the LAMB," our lips reply,
　" For he was slain for us."

2 JESUS is worthy to receive
　Honor and power divine ;
And blessings, more than we can give,
　Be, LORD, forever thine.

4 The whole creation join in one
　To bless the sacred name
　Of him who sits upon the throne,
　And to adore the LAMB.

### HYMN 37. C. M.

*And he had on his vesture and on his thigh a name written, KING OF KINGS, and LORD OF LORDS.*

1 ALL hail the great IMMANUEL's name!
　Let seraphs prostrate fall;
　Bring forth the royal diadem,
　And crown him LORD of all.

2 Let countless angels strike the lyre,
　And low before Him fall,
　Who tune to love their holy choir,
　And crown him LORD of all.

3 Let every tribe, of every tongue,
　All creatures, great and small,
　Loud swell this universal song,
　And crown him LORD of all.

4 Our Heavenly Father, JESUS, LORD,
　Whom King of kings we call;
　We worship thee, Incarnate Word,
　And crown thee LORD of all.

### HYMN 38. 8's and 7's.

*Thou art worthy, O LORD, to receive glory, and honor, and power: For thou hast created all things.*

1 JESUS, LORD of all creation,
　Pure, unbounded love thou art:
　Visit us with thy salvation;
　Enter every waiting heart.

2 Breathe, O breathe thy Holy Spirit
　Into every troubled breast:
　Let us all thy grace inherit;
　Let us find the promised rest.

3 Finish, now, thy new creation;
　From our sins O set us free:
　May we find thy great salvation
　Come, with healing power, from thee.

4 Lord, we would on earth adore thee,
   Till in heaven we take our place;
   Till we cast our crowns before thee,
   Lost in wonder, love, and praise.

## HYMN 39. L. M.

*Who shall not fear thee, O Lord, and glorify thy name?
For thou alone art holy.*

1 Jesus, in thee our hopes shall rest,
   Fountain of peace, and joy, and love,
   Be thy great name on earth confessed,
   As by the hosts of heaven above.

2 Thine is all wisdom, thine alone:
   Mercy and truth before thee stand:
   Justice and judgment form thy throne;
   And love divine impels thy hand.

3 No other can thy honors claim,
   Or join in thy redeeming care;
   No rival bear thy sacred name;
   No equal in thy glory share.

4 Worship to thee alone belongs;
   Worship to thee alone we give:
   Thine be our hearts, and thine our songs,
   O Lord, in whom alone we live.

## HYMN 40. S. M.

*Bless Jehovah, O my soul:
And all that is within me, bless his holy name.*

1 O bless the Lord, my soul;
      Let all within me join,
   And aid my tongue to bless his name,
      Whose favors are divine.

2 The Lord forgives thy sins,
      The Lord relieves thy pain,
   The Lord doth heal thy sicknesses,
      And give thee strength again.

3 He crowns thy life with love,
      When ransomed from the grave:
   He, who redeemed my soul from hell,
      Hath sovereign power to save.

4 O bless the LORD, my soul;
    Let all within me join,
  And aid my tongue to bless his name,
    Whose favors are divine.

### HYMN 41. 7's.

*Thou hast been my defence and refuge in the day of trouble.*

1 JESUS, Refuge of my soul,
    Let me to thy bosom fly,
  While the angry billows roll,
    While the tempest still is high.

2 Hide me, O my Savior, hide,
    Till the storm of life is past:
  Safe into the haven guide;
    O receive my soul at last.

### HYMN 42. S. M.

*He that dwelleth in the secret place of the Most High,
Shall abide under the shadow of the Almighty.*

1   WHILE my Redeemer's near,
      My shepherd, and my guide,
    I bid farewell to every fear;
      My wants are all supplied.

2   To ever fragrant meads,
      Where rich abundance grows,
    His gracious hand indulgent leads,
      And guards my sweet repose.

3   Dear Shepherd, if I stray,
      My wandering feet restore;
    And guard me with thy watchful eye,
      And let me rove no more.

### HYMN 43. C. M.

*Behold, GOD is mine helper:
JEHOVAH is with them that uphold my soul.*

1 FOREVER blessed be the LORD,
    My Savior, and my shield;
  He sends the Spirit of his Word,
    To arm me for the field.

2 When sin and hell their force unite,
    He makes my soul his care;

Instructs me in the heavenly fight,
And guards me through the war.

3 A friend and helper so divine
My fainting hope shall raise;
He makes the glorious victory mine,
And his shall be the praise.

HYMN 44. C. M.

*Glory to God in the highest; and on earth peace; good will toward men*

1 CALM on the listening ear of night
Come heaven's melodious strains,
Where wild Judea stretches far
Her silver-mantled plains.

2 Celestial choirs, from courts above,
Shed sacred glories there;
And angels, with their sparkling lyres,
Make music on the air.

3 The answering hills of Palestine
Send back the glad reply;
And greet, from all their sacred heights,
The day-spring from on high.

4 O'er the blue depths of Galilee
There comes a holier calm;
And Sharon waves, in solemn praise,
Her silent groves of palm.

5 "Glory to God!" the sounding skies
Loud with their anthems ring:
"Peace to the earth, good will to men,
From heaven's Eternal King!"

6 Light on thy hills, Jerusalem!
The Savior now is born;
And bright on Bethlehem's joyous plains
Breaks the first Christmas morn.

HYMN 45. C. M.

THE WORD.

*Forever, O Jehovah, thy word is settled in heaven.*

1 WHAT glory gilds the sacred page,
Majestic, like the sun:
It gives a light to every age;
It gives, but borrows none.

2 The power that gave it still supplies
   The gracious light and heat:
   Its truths upon the nations rise;
   They rise, no more to set.

3 Let everlasting thanks be thine
   For such a bright display,
   As makes a world of darkness shine
   With beams of heavenly day.

4 My soul rejoices to pursue
   The steps of him I love,
   Till glory break upon my view
   In brighter worlds above.

### HYMN 46. C. M.

*Wherewith shall a young man cleanse his way?
By taking heed according to thy Word.*

1 How shall the young secure their hearts,
   And guard their lives from sin?
   Thy Word the choicest rules imparts
   To keep the conscience clean.

2 'Tis like the sun, a heavenly light,
   That guides us all the day;
   And, through the dangers of the night,
   A lamp to lead our way.

3 Thy Word is everlasting truth;
   How pure is every page!
   That holy book shall guide our youth,
   And well support our age.

### HYMN 47. C. M.

*Thy Word is a lamp unto my feet,
And a light unto my path.*

1 How precious is the book divine,
   By inspiration given!
   Bright as a lamp its doctrines shine,
   To guide our souls to heaven.

2 It sweetly cheers our drooping hearts,
   In this dark vale of tears;
   Life, light, and joy it still imparts,
   And quells our rising fears.

3 This lamp, through all the tedious night
   Of life, shall guide our way;
   Till we behold the clearer light
   Of an eternal day.

### HYMN 48. C. M.

*The light of the moon shall be as the light of the sun: And the light of the sun sevenfold, as the light of seven days.*

1 How shall we celebrate thy love,
   Thou ever-blessed LORD,
   For all thy mercies from above,
   But chiefly for thy Word.

2 Goodness and truth are now display'd
   In their own heavenly light:
   Thy Holy Word is open laid
   To our astonished sight.

3 'Tis ours to walk in light divine,
   Through all our happy road:
   The beams of truth around us shine,
   And lead to thine abode.

4 Blest day of heavenly light and heat,
   Of sacred truth and love!
   Now we may run, with cheerful feet,
   To realms of bliss above.

### HYMN 49. L. P. M.

*O how I love thy law: it is my meditation all the day.*

1 I LOVE the volume of thy Word;
   What light and joy those leaves afford
      To souls benighted and distressed!
   Thy precepts guide my doubtful way;
   Thy fear forbids my feet to stray;
      Thy promise leads my heart to rest.

2 Who knows the errors of his thoughts?
   O LORD, forgive my secret faults,
      And from presumptuous sins restrain:
   Accept my words of prayer, O LORD,
   My meditations on thy Word;
      Nor let me read its truths in vain.

## HYMN 50. C. M.

*And on either side of the river was the Tree of life*

1 FATHER of mercies, in thy Word,
  What grace and glory shine!
Forever be thy name adored
  For wisdom so divine.

2 The tree of life here fruitful grows,
  Adorned with healing leaves:
Sublimer sweets than nature knows
  The hungry soul receives.

3 O may these heavenly pages be
  My ever dear delight;
And still new beauties may I see,
  And still increasing light.

4 Divine Instructor, gracious LORD,
  Be thou forever near;
Teach me to love thy holy Word,
  And view thy glory there.

## HYMN 51. C. M.

*O that my ways were directed to keep thy statutes!*

1 O THAT the LORD would guide my ways
  To keep his statutes still!
O that my GOD would grant me grace
  To know and do his will!

2 O send thy Spirit down, to write
  Thy law upon my heart!
Nor let my tongue indulge deceit,
  Nor act the liar's part.

3 From vanity turn off mine eyes;
  Let no corrupt design,
Nor covetous desires, arise
  Within this soul of mine.

4 Order my footsteps by thy Word,
  And make my heart sincere;
Let sin have no dominion, LORD,
  But keep my conscience clear.

5 Make me to walk in thy commands;
  'Tis a delightful road:

Nor let my head, nor heart, nor hands,
Offend against my God.

## HYMN 52. L. M.
### THE LORD'S UNIVERSAL PROVIDENCE.
*O Jehovah, thou hast searched me, and known me.*

1 Lord, Thou hast searched and seen me through;
Thine eye commands, with piercing view,
My rising and my resting hours,
My inmost heart, and all my powers.

2 My thoughts, before they are my own,
Are to the Lord distinctly known:
He knows the words I mean to speak,
Ere from my opening lips they break.

3 Within thy circling power I stand;
On every side I find thy hand;
Awake, asleep, at home, abroad,
Still present with me is my God.

4 O may these thoughts possess my breast,
Where'er I rove, where'er I rest!
Nor let my weaker passions dare
Consent to sin, for God is there.

## HYMN 53. C. M.
*For there is not a word in my tongue,
But lo, O Jehovah, thou knowest it altogether.*

1 In all my vast concerns with thee,
In vain my soul would try
To shun thy presence, Lord, or flee
The notice of thine eye.

2 Thine all-surrounding sight surveys
My rising and my rest,
My public walks, my private ways,
And secrets of my breast.

3 My thoughts lie open to the Lord,
Before they're formed within;
And ere my lips pronounce the word,
He knows the sense I mean.

4 O, wondrous knowledge, deep and high!
Where can a creature hide?

Within thy circling arms I lie,
Enclosed on every side.

5 So let thy grace surround me still,
And like a bulwark prove,
To guard my soul from every ill,
Secured by sovereign love.

## HYMN 54. L. M.

*The darkness and the light are both alike to thee.*

1 O THOU, to whose all-searching sight
The darkness shineth as the light,
Search, prove my heart; it pants for thee:
O burst these bonds, and set it free.

2 While in this darksome wild I stray,
Be thou my light, be thou my way:
No foes, no violence, I fear;
No harm, if thou, O LORD, art near.

3 When rising floods my soul o'erflow,
When sinks my heart in waves of woe,
O LORD, thy timely aid impart,
And raise my head, and cheer my heart.

4 If rough and thorny be the way,
My strength proportion to my day;
Till toil, and grief, and pain, shall cease,
Where all is calm, and joy, and peace.

## HYMN 55. C. M.

*Jehovah is good to all:*
*And his tender mercies are over all his works.*

1 WHEN all thy mercies, gracious LORD,
My rising soul surveys,
Transported with the view I'm lost
In wonder, love, and praise.

2 Thy Providence my life sustained,
And all my wants redressed,
When in the silent womb I lay,
Or hung upon the breast.

3 Unnumbered comforts on my soul
Thy tender care bestowed,
Before my infant heart conceived
From whom those comforts flowed.

4 While in the slippery paths of youth,
With heedless steps, I ran,
Thine arm, unseen, conveyed me safe,
From childhood up to man.

5 Through every period of my life
Thy goodness I'll pursue;
And after death, in happier worlds,
The glorious theme renew.

### HYMN 56. P. M.
#### THE TEMPLE WORSHIP.
Jehovah is in his holy temple.

1 The Lord is in his holy temple,
In his house of prayer below;
There his faithful ones assemble,
And before his footstool bow.
Behold, he's present with us ever,
When assembled in his name,
Aiding every good endeavor,
Guiding every humble aim.

2 The Lord is in his holy temple,
In the church he calls his own,
In the city where assemble
All who worship him alone.
The New Jerusalem, all glorious,
Is the city of our God;
There Immanuel reigns victorious,
There he makes his loved abode.

3 The Lord is in his holy temple,
In the heavenly world above,
Where the saints in light assemble,
Who are perfected in love.
And there eternal songs ascending
From celestial voices flow;
Joys supreme, and never ending,
Crown the toils endured below.

### HYMN 57. C. M.
God is greatly to be feared in the assembly of the saints:
And to be had in reverence by all that are about him.

1 With reverence let us all appear,
And bow before the Lord;

His high commands with reverence hear,
And tremble at his word.

2 How terrible thy glories be!
How bright thy precepts shine!
Where is the power that vies with thee?
Or truth compared with thine?

3 Thy words the raging winds control,
And rule the boisterous deep;
Thou mak'st the sleeping billows roll,
The rolling billows sleep.

4 Justice and judgment are thy throne,
Yet wondrous is thy grace;
While truth and mercy, joined in one,
Invite us near thy face.

### HYMN 58. C. M.
*O come, let us worship and bow down;
Let us kneel before the face of JEHOVAH our Maker.*

1 SING to the LORD JEHOVAH'S name,
And in his strength rejoice;
When his salvation is our theme,
Exalted be our voice.

2 Come, and with humble souls adore;
Come, kneel before his face:
O may the creatures of his power
Be children of his grace!

### HYMN 59. S. M.
*I will worship toward thy holy temple.*

1 LORD, at thy sacred feet
Joyful we now appear;
Within thy earthly temple meet,
To see thy glory here.

2 We come to worship thee,
For thou art GOD alone;
In humble prayer to bend the knee,
Before thy holy throne.

3 Thy Word is our delight;
Thy truth will make us free:
'Tis from thyself, a heavenly light;
It leads our souls to thee.

THE TEMPLE WORSHIP.

4  Thy goodness we behold,
    While, in thy presence, LORD,
    Thou dost thy truth and love unfold,
    The treasures of thy Word.

### HYMN 60. S. M.
*O come, let us sing unto JEHOVAH.*

1  COME, sound his praise abroad,
    And hymns of glory sing:
    JEHOVAH is the sovereign GOD,
    The universal King.

2  Come, worship at his throne;
    Come, bow before the LORD:
    We are his work, and not our own;
    He formed us by his Word.

3  Come, and obey his voice;
    Come, and receive his grace,
    Come, like the people of his choice,
    And seek your Father's face.

### HYMN 61. H. M.
*How lovely are thy tabernacles, O JEHOVAH OF HOSTS*

1  LORD of the heavens above,
        How pleasant and how fair
    The dwellings of thy love,
        Thine earthly temples, are!
            To thine abode
    My heart aspires, with warm desires
            To see my GOD.

2  O happy souls that pray
        Where GOD appoints to hear!
    O happy men that pay
        Their constant service there!
            They praise thee still:
    And happy they, who find the way
            To Zion's hill.

3  They go from strength to strength,
        Through this dark vale of tears;
    Till each arrives at length,
        Till each in heaven appears.
            There shall we meet,
    When GOD our King shall thither bring
            Our willing feet.

## HYMN 62. L. M.

*And there shall be no more death, neither sorrow nor crying: Neither shall there be any more pain.*

1 Thine earthly Sabbaths, Lord, we love;
But there's a nobler rest above:
To that our longing souls aspire,
With cheerful hope, and strong desire.

2 No more fatigue, no more distress,
Nor sin, nor death shall reach the place;
No groans shall mingle with the songs,
Which warble from immortal tongues.

3 No rude alarms of raging foes;
No cares to break the long repose;
No midnight shade, no clouded sun;
But sacred, high, eternal noon.

4 Thine earthly Sabbaths, Lord, we love;
But there's a nobler rest above:
To that our longing souls aspire,
With cheerful hope, and strong desire.

## HYMN 63. L. M.

BAPTISM OF A CHILD.

*Suffer the little children to come unto Me, and forbid them not; for of such is the kingdom of heaven.*

1 O Lord of grace and purity,
We dedicate this child to thee:
Shield *him* from sin and threatening wrong,
And let thy love *his* life prolong.

2 O, may thy spirit gently draw
*His* willing soul to keep thy law:
May virtue, piety, and truth
Dawn even with *his* dawning youth.

3 Grant that, with true and faithful heart,
We, too, may act the Christian's part;
Cheered by each promise thou hast given,
And striving for the life of heaven.

## HYMN 64. C. M.

BAPTISM OF AN ADULT.

1 Thy servant, gracious Lord, receive,
And give *his* soul a place

Among thy children who believe
On thee, and know thy grace.

2 Baptized in thy most holy name,
May *he* thy Word obey;
And with an ardent, constant flame,
Pursue the heavenly way.

3 O may *he* live to thee alone,
In truth and goodness shine;
Thy heavenly laws and doctrines own,
And be forever thine.

## HYMN 65. L. M.
### BAPTISM OF A FAMILY.

1 FATHER of every holy tie,
Which forms the happiness of home,
To crave thy blessing from on high,
Thy servants now before thee come.

2 Let the dear pledges of their love
Like tender plants around them grow;
Thy present grace, and joys above,
Upon their little ones bestow.

3 Receive, at their believing hand,
The charge which they devote as thine
Obedient to their LORD's command;
And seal, with power, the right divine.

4 Smile on this waiting family,
Whose prayers in unison ascend;
To every member of this house
Thy grace impart, thy love extend.

## HYMN 66. 7's.
### THE HOLY SUPPER.
Do this in remembrance of Me.

1 AT thy table, LORD of life,
May our souls find peace and rest;
On the Savior may we lean,
Safe repose upon his breast.

2 He invites us to this feast,
He hath said, "Remember me;"

May we come with trustful hearts,
Hearts devoted, LORD, to thee.

3 May thy grace our souls awake;
Make them glow with holy love:
While we take the bread and cup,
Set our hearts on things above.

### HYMN 67. 8's, 7's, and 4's.

*Thou wilt guide me with thy counsel;
And afterward receive me to glory.*

1 GUIDE me, O thou great JEHOVAH,
Pilgrim through this barren land:
I am weak, but thou art mighty;
Hold me with thy powerful hand:
Bread of heaven,
Feed me now and evermore.

2 Open, LORD, the crystal fountain,
Whence the living waters flow;
Let the fiery, cloudy pillar
Guide me all my journey through:
Strong Deliverer,
Be thou still my Strength and Shield.

3 When I tread the verge of Jordan,
Bid my anxious fears subside;
Bear me through the swelling current;
Land me safe on Canaan's side:
Songs of praises
I will ever give to thee.

### HYMN 68. C. M.

#### MARRIAGE.

*They are no more twain, but one flesh.*

1 NOT for the summer hour alone.
When skies resplendent shine,
And youth and pleasure fill the throne,
Our hearts and hands we join;

2 But for those stern and wintry days
Of sorrow, pain, and fear,
When Heaven's wise discipline doth make
Our earthly journey drear.

3 Not for this span of life alone,
    Which like a blast doth fly,
And, as the transient flowers of grass,
    Just blossom, droop, and die;

4 But for a being without end
    This vow of love we take;
Grant us, O LORD, one home at last,
    For thy great mercy's sake.

## HYMN 69. C. M.
### CONFIRMATION.
*What shall I render unto the Lord for all his benefits toward me?*

1 WHAT shall I render to my GOD
    For all his kindness shown?
My feet shall visit thine abode,
    My songs address thy throne.

2 Among the saints that fill thine house,
    My offering shall be paid;
There shall my zeal perform the vows
    My soul, repentant, made.

3 How happy all thy servants are!
    How great thy love to me!
My life, which thou hast made thy care,
    LORD, I devote to thee.

4 Now I am thine, forever thine,
    Nor shall my purpose move;
Thy hand has loosed my chains of sin,
    And bound me with thy love

## HYMN 70. L. M.
*I will pay my vows unto Jehovah now in the presence of his people.*

1 O HAPPY day, that fixed my choice
    On thee, my Savior and my LORD!
Well may this glowing heart rejoice,
    And tell its raptures all abroad.

2 O happy bond, that seals my vows
    To Him who merits all my love!
Let cheerful anthems fill the house,
    While to his altar now I move.

3 Now rest, my long-divided heart;
   Fixed on the Rock of ages, rest;
   Here have I found a nobler part;
   Here heavenly pleasures fill my breast.

4 High Heaven, that hears the solemn vow,
   That vow renewed shall daily hear:
   Till in life's latest hour I bow,
   And bless in death a bond so dear.

### HYMN 71.  8's, 7's, and 4's.

#### CLOSE OF WORSHIP.

*If thy presence go not with us, carry us not up hence*

1 LORD, dismiss us with thy blessing,
   Fill our hearts with joy and peace;
   Let us each, thy love possessing,
   Triumph in redeeming grace:
      O refresh us,
   Travelling through this wilderness.

2 Thanks we give, and adoration,
   For the gospel's joyful sound;
   May the fruits of thy salvation
   In our hearts and lives abound:
      May thy presence
   With us evermore be found.

### HYMN 72.  C. M.

#### SUBMISSION TO THE LORD.

*Your Heavenly Father knoweth that ye have need of all these things.*

1 FATHER, whate'er of earthly bliss
   Thy sovereign will denies,
   Accepted at thy throne of grace
   Let this petition rise:

2 "Give me a calm, a thankful heart,
   From every murmur free;
   The blessings of thy love impart,
   And make me live to thee.

3 O let the hope that thou art mine
   My life and death attend;
   Thy presence through my journey shine,
   And crown my journey's end."

SUBMISSION TO THE LORD.

## HYMN 73. 8's and 6's.
*Thy will be done.*

1 O Lord, my Father, while I stray
Far from my home on life's rough way,
O teach me from my heart to say,
"Thy will, O Lord, be done."

2 Though dark my path, and sad my lot,
Let me be still, and murmur not,
And breathe the prayer divinely taught,
"Thy will, O Lord, be done."

3 Should pining sickness waste away
My life in premature decay,
In life or death teach me to say,
"Thy will, O Lord, be done."

4 Renew my will from day to day,
Blend it with thine, and take away
Whate'er now makes it hard to say,
"Thy will, O Lord, be done."

## HYMN 74. C. M.
*Thou art my Refuge and my Portion in the land of the living.*

1 While thee I seek, protecting Power,
Be my vain wishes stilled;
And may this consecrated hour
With better hopes be filled.

2 Thy love the power of thought bestowed;
To thee my thoughts would soar:
Thy mercy o'er my life has flowed;
That mercy I adore.

3 In each event of life, how clear
Thy ruling hand I see!
Each blessing to my soul more dear,
Because conferred by thee.

4 In every joy that crowns my days,
In every pain I bear,
My heart shall find delight in praise,
Or seek relief in prayer.

5 When gladness wings my favored hour,
Thy love my thoughts shall fill;

Resigned, when storms of sorrow lower,
My soul shall meet thy will.

6 My lifted eye, without a tear,
The gathering storm shall see:
My steadfast heart shall know no fear;
That heart shall rest on thee.

## HYMN 75. 8's and 4's.
*Thy will be done.*

1 "Thy will be done!" In devious way
The hurrying stream of life may run,
Yet still our grateful hearts shall say,
  "Thy will be done."

2 "Thy will be done!" If o'er us shine
A gladdening and a prosperous sun,
This prayer will make it more divine,
  "Thy will be done."

3 "Thy will be done!" Though shrouded o'er
Our path with gloom, one comfort — one
Is ours; — to breathe, while we adore,
  "Thy will be done."

## HYMN 76. S. M.
*Surely goodness and mercy shall follow me all the days of my life.*

1 How gentle God's commands!
  How kind his precepts are!
Come, cast your burdens on the Lord,
  And trust his constant care.

2 His bounty will provide;
  His people safely dwell:
That hand which bears creation up,
  Shall guard his children well.

3 Why should this anxious load
  Press down your weary mind?
O seek your heavenly Father's throne,
  And peace and comfort find.

4 His goodness stands approved,
  Unchanged from day to day:
I'll drop my burden at his feet,
  And bear a song away.

## HYMN 77. C. M.

**THE WORLD TO COME.**

*In my Father's house are many mansions.*

1 There is a land of pure delight,
  Where saints immortal reign;
  Eternal day excludes the night,
  And pleasures banish pain.

2 There everlasting spring abides,
  And never-withering flowers:
  Death, like a narrow sea, divides
  That heavenly land from ours.

3 Sweet fields, beyond the swelling flood,
  Stand drest in living green;
  So to the Jews their Canaan stood,
  While Jordan rolled between.

4 But timorous mortals start, and shrink
  To cross this narrow sea;
  And linger, shivering on the brink;
  And fear to launch away.

5 O could we climb where Moses stood,
  And view the landscape o'er,
  Not Jordan's stream, nor death's cold flood,
  Should fright us from the shore.

## HYMN 78. C. M.

*In thy presence is fulness of joy:
At thy right hand are pleasures for evermore*

1 Eternal Source of life and light,
  Supremely good and wise,
  To thee we bring our grateful vows;
  Accept our sacrifice.

2 Our dark and erring minds illume
  With truth's celestial rays:
  Inspire our hearts with heavenly love,
  And tune our lips to praise.

3 Safely conduct us, by thy truth,
  Through life's perplexing road;
  And bring us, when our journey's o'er,
  Lord, to thine own abode.

4 For in thy presence e'er abounds
    Fulness of purest joy;
At thy right hand unceasing flow
    Pleasures without alloy.

## HYMN 79. C. M.

*They that dwell in the land of the shadow of death,
Upon them hath the light shined.*

1 On Jordan's stormy banks I stand,
    And cast a wishful eye
To Canaan's fair and happy land,
    Where my possessions lie.

2 O the transporting, rapturous scene,
    That rises to my sight!
Sweet fields arrayed in living green,
    And rivers of delight.

3 No chilling winds, nor poisonous breath,
    Can reach that healthful shore;
Sickness and sorrow, pain and death,
    Are felt and feared no more.

4 When shall I reach that happy place,
    And be forever blest?
When shall I see my Father's face,
    And in his mansions rest?

## HYMN 80. 7's.

*He brought them out of darkness and the shadow of death:
And brake their bands in sunder.*

1 High, in yonder realms of light,
    Dwell the ransomed hosts above.
Far beyond our feeble sight,
    Happy in Immanuel's love.

2 Pilgrims in this vale of tears,
    Once they knew, like us below,
Gloomy doubts, distressing fears,
    Torturing pain, and heavy woe.

3 Happy spirits, ye are fled
    Where no grief can entrance find;
Lulled to rest the aching head,
    Soothed the anguish of the mind.

4 'Mid the chorus of the skies,
   'Mid the angelic lyres above,
   Hark! their songs melodious rise,
   Songs of praise to JESUS' love.

## HYMN 81. L. M.
### MORNING AND EVENING.
*Thou makest the out-goings of the morning and evening to rejoice*

1 GOD of the morning, at thy voice
    The cheerful sun makes haste to rise,
    And like a giant doth rejoice
    To run his journey through the skies.

2 O like the sun may I fulfil
    The appointed duties of the day;
    With ready mind and active will
    March on, and keep my heavenly way.

3 LORD, thy commands are clean and pure,
    Enlightening our beclouded eyes;
    Thy judgments just, thy promise sure;
    Thy gospel makes the simple wise.

4 Give me thy counsels for my guide,
    And then receive me to thy bliss;
    All my desires and hopes beside
    Are faint and cold compared with this.

## HYMN 82. L. M.
*JEHOVAH will command his loving kindness in the day time;
And in the night his song shall be with me.*

1 SWEET is the work, my GOD, my King,
    To praise thy name, give thanks, and sing,
    To show thy love by morning light,
    And talk of all thy truth at night.

2 My heart shall triumph in my LORD,
    And bless his works, and bless his word:
    Thy works of grace, how bright they shine!
    How deep thy counsels, how divine!

3 Soon shall I see, and hear, and know
    All I desired, or wished below;
    And every power find sweet employ,
    In that eternal world of joy.

## HYMN 83. L. M.

*How excellent is thy loving kindness, O God:
Therefore the children of men put their trust under the shadow of thy wings.*

1 O LORD, how boundless is thy love!
  Thy gifts are every evening new;
  And morning mercies from above
  Gently distil like early dew.

2 Thou spread'st the curtains of the night,
  Great Guardian of my sleeping hours;
  Thy sovereign word restores the light,
  And quickens all my drowsy powers.

3 I yield my powers to thy command,
  To thee I consecrate my days;
  Perpetual blessings from thine hand
  Demand perpetual songs of praise.

## HYMN 84. L. M.

*The Angel of JEHOVAH encampeth round about them that fear him, and delivereth them.*

1 GLORY to thee, my GOD, this night,
  For all the blessings of the light:
  Keep me, O keep me, King of kings,
  Beneath the shadow of thy wings.

2 O let my soul on thee repose,
  And may sweet sleep mine eyelids close;
  Sleep, which shall me more vigorous make,
  To serve the LORD when I awake.

3 Be thou my guardian, while I sleep;
  Thy watchful station near me keep;
  My heart with love celestial fill,
  And guard me from approaching ill.

4 LORD, let my soul forever share
  The bliss of thy paternal care:
  'Tis heaven on earth, 'tis heaven above,
  To see thy face, and feel thy love.

## HYMN 85. C. M.

*I remember thee upon my bed:
I meditate upon thee in the night-watches.*

1 'TWAS in the watches of the night,
  I thought upon thy power;

I kept thy lovely face in sight,
Amid the darkest hour.

2 While I lay resting on my bed,
My soul arose on high:
O LORD, my life, my hope, I said,
Bring thy salvation nigh.

3 I strive to mount thy holy hill,
And walk the heavenly road:
Thy glories all my spirit fill,
While I commune with GOD.

4 Thy mercy stretches o'er my head
The shadow of thy wing;
My heart rejoices in thine aid,
And I thy praises sing.

## HYMN 86. L. M.
### THE SEASONS.

*Thou crownest the year with thy goodness;
And thy paths drop fatness.*

1 ETERNAL Source of every joy,
Well may thy praise our lips employ,
While in thy presence we appear,
Whose goodness crowns the circling year.

2 Wide as the wheels of nature roll,
Thy hand supports and guides the whole:
The sun is taught by thee to rise,
And darkness when to vail the skies.

3 Seasons and months, and weeks and days,
Demand successive songs of praise:
Then be the grateful homage paid,
With morning light, and evening shade.

4 LORD, in thy house let incense rise,
And circling Sabbaths bless our eyes,
Till to those lofty heights we soar,
Where days and years revolve no more.

## HYMN 87. 7's.

*It is a good thing to give thanks unto JEHOVAH:
And to sing praises unto thy name, O Most High.*

1 PRAISE to GOD, immortal praise,
For the love that crowns our days:

Bounteous Source of every joy,
Let thy praise our tongues employ.

2 All that Spring, with lavish hand,
Scatters o'er the smiling land;
All that liberal Autumn pours
From her rich, o'erflowing stores:

3 These to thee, O Lord, we owe,
Source whence all our blessings flow;
And for these our souls shall raise
Grateful vows, and solemn praise.

4 But, if such thy will divine,
All these gifts will we resign;
And, when earthly hopes are flown,
Love thee for thyself alone.

## HYMN 88. C. M.
### PRAYER.
*Whatsoever ye shall ask in my name, that will I do.*

1 Prayer is the simplest form of speech
  That infant lips can try;
  Prayer the sublimest strains that reach
  The Majesty on high.

2 Prayer is the contrite sinner's voice,
  Returning from his ways;
  While angels in their songs rejoice,
  And cry, " Behold, he prays!"

3 Prayer is the Christian's vital breath,
  The Christian's native air,
  The watchword at the gates of death;
  He enters heaven with prayer.

## HYMN 89. C. M.
### EARLY RELIGION.
*My Father, thou art the guide of my youth*

1 By cool Siloam's shady rill
  How fair the lily grows!
  How sweet the breath, beneath the hill,
  Of Sharon's dewy rose!

2 Lo, such the child whose early feet
  The paths of peace have trod;

Whose secret heart, with influence sweet,
Is upward drawn to GOD.

3 By cool Siloam's shady rill
The lily must decay;
The rose, that blooms beneath the hill,
Must shortly fade away.

4 And soon, too soon, the wintry hour
Of man's maturer age
Will shake the soul with sorrow's power
And stormy passion's rage.

5 O Thou, who givest life and breath,
We seek thy grace alone,
In childhood, manhood, age, and death,
To keep us still thine own.

HYMN 90. S. M.
THE NEW JERUSALEM.

*And I saw the holy city, New Jerusalem, coming down from God out of heaven,*

1   Built by JEHOVAH's hand,
    The holy city see:
  Its happy gates wide open stand:
    To enter, all are free.

2   One bright, eternal day
    Shall in the city reign;
  Darkness and death are fled away,
    Ne'er to return again.

3   O blessed, happy state!
    O LORD, we thankful come;
  Low at thy footstool humbly wait,
    And make thy church our home.

4   Jerusalem shall be
    Our peaceful, blest abode:
  Here will we love and worship thee,
    Our SAVIOR and our GOD.

HYMN 91. S. M.
DEDICATION OF A TEMPLE.

*Jehovah hath chosen Zion:
He hath desired it for his habitation.*

1   JEHOVAH, LORD of heaven,
    By men on earth adored,

This temple now to thee is given;
Accept the offering, LORD.

2 Here may thy glory rest;
Here may thy truth be known;
Be thou by every heart confess'd,
As LORD and GOD alone.

3 Here, LORD, thyself reveal,
Thy Love Divine impart;
The doctrines of thy kingdom seal
On every humble heart.

4 May peace, within these walls,
A constant guest be found;
With plenty and prosperity,
These palaces be crowned.

## HYMN 92. L. M.
### MISCELLANEOUS.
*He shall have dominion from sea to sea.*

1 JESUS shall reign where'er the sun
Does his successive journeys run;
His kingdom stretch from shore to shore,
Till moons shall wax and wane no more.

2 To him shall endless prayer be made,
And praises throng to crown his head;
His name, like sweet perfume, shall rise
With every morning sacrifice.

3 People, and realms, of every tongue,
Dwell on his love with sweetest song;
And infant voices shall proclaim
Their early blessings on his name.

4 Blessings abound where'er he reigns;
The prisoner leaps to lose his chains.
The weary find eternal rest,
And all the sons of want are blest.

5 Let every creature rise and bring
Peculiar honors to our King;
Angels descend with songs again,
And earth repeat the loud Amen.

## HYMN 93. 8's and 7's.

*O continue thy loving kindness unto them that know thee:
And thy righteousness to the upright in heart.*

1 Love Divine, all love excelling,
   Joy of heaven, to earth come down,
Fix in us thy humble dwelling;
   All thy faithful mercies crown.

2 Jesus, thou art all compassion,
   Pure, unbounded love thou art;
Visit us with thy salvation,
   Enter every trembling heart.

3 Breathe, O Lord, thy Holy Spirit
   Into every troubled breast;
Let us all thy grace inherit,
   Let us find thy promised rest.

4 Take away the love of sinning,
   Take our load of guilt away;
End the work of thy beginning,
   Bring us to eternal day.

## HYMN 94. S. M.

*Blessed are the pure in heart: for they shall see God.*

1   Blest are the pure in heart,
    For they shall see our God:
The secret of the Lord is theirs;
    Their soul is His abode.

2   Still to the lowly soul
    God doth Himself impart,
And for His temple and his throne
    Doth choose the pure in heart.

## HYMN 95. 8's and 7's.

*Peace I leave with you: my peace I give unto you.*

Peace of God, which knows no measure,
   Heavenly sunlight of the soul,
Peace beyond all earthly treasure,
   Come, and all our hearts control.
Come, almighty to deliver!
   Nought shall make us then afraid;
We will trust in thee forever,
   Thou on whom our hope is stayed.

MISCELLANEOUS.

### HYMN 96. 7's.

*As the hart panteth for the brooks of water,
So panteth my soul for thee, O God.*

1 As the hart, with eager looks,
Panteth for the water-brooks,
So my soul, athirst for Thee,
Pants the living God to see;
When, O when, without a fear,
Lord, shall I to Thee draw near?

2 Why art thou cast down, my soul?
God, thy God, shall make thee whole;
Why art thou disquieted?
God shall raise thy fallen head,
And His countenance benign
Be the saving health of thine.

### HYMN 97. 7's.

*Ask, and it shall be given you.*

1 Suppliant, lo, thy children bend,
Father, for thy blessing now;
Thou canst teach us, guide, defend;
We are weak, almighty thou!

2 With the peace thy Word imparts
Be the taught and teacher blessed;
In our lives and in our hearts,
Father, be thy laws impressed.

3 Pour into each longing mind,
Light and knowledge from above,
Charity for all mankind,
Trusting faith, enduring love.

### HYMN 98. C. M.

*Turn you to the strong hold, ye prisoners of hope*

1 Return, O wanderer, now return,
And wipe the falling tear:
Thy Father calls; no longer mourn
'Tis love invites thee near.

2 Return, O wanderer, now return;
He hears thy humble sigh:
He sees thy softened spirit mourn,
When no one else is nigh.

3 Return, O wanderer, now return;
Thy SAVIOR bids thee live:
Go to his feet, and grateful learn
How freely he'll forgive.

HYMN 99. 7's.

*Whoso eateth my flesh, and drinketh my blood, dwelleth in me, and I in him.*

1 BREAD of heaven, on thee we feed,
For thy flesh is meat indeed;
Ever let our souls be fed
With this true and living bread.

2 Vine of heaven, thy blood supplies
This blest cup of sacrifice:
LORD, thy wounds our healing give;
To thy cross we look and live.

3 Day by day with strength supplied,
Through the life of him who died,
LORD of life, O let us be
Rooted, grafted, built on thee.

HYMN 100. C. M.

*They are no more twain, but one flesh.*

1 WE join to pray, with wishes kind,
A blessing, LORD, from Thee,
On those who now the bands have twined,
Which ne'er may broken be.

2 We know that scenes not always bright
Must unto them be given;
But over all give Thou the light
Of love, and truth, and heaven.

3 Still hand in hand, their journey through,
Joint pilgrims may they go;
Mingling their joys as helpers true,
And sharing every woe.

4 May each in each still feed the flame
Of pure and holy love;
In faith, and trust, and heart, the same,
The same their home above.

## HYMN 101. C. M.

*Suffer little children to come unto Me.*

1 Lo, Israel's gentle Shepherd stands
With all-engaging charms:
Hark, how he calls the tender lambs,
And folds them in his arms.

2 "Suffer the little ones," he says,
"Forbid them not to come:
Of such is heaven; and souls like these
Shall find in heaven their home."

3 We bring them, Lord, with thankful hearts,
And yield them up to Thee;
Joyful that we ourselves are Thine,
Thine let our offspring be.

## HYMN 102. C. M.

*Guide our feet into the way of peace.*

1 Through Thee as we together came,
In singleness of heart,
And met, Lord Jesus, in thy name,
So in thy name we part.

2 Nearer to Thee our spirits lead,
And still thy love bestow,
Till Thou hast made us free indeed,
And spotless, here below.

3 When to the right or left we stray,
Leave us not comfortless,
But guide our feet into the way
Of everlasting peace.

## HYMN 103. L. M.

*He that hath ears to hear, let him hear.*

1 Ere to the world again we go,
Its pleasures, cares, and idle show,
Thy grace once more, O Lord, we crave,
From folly and from sin to save.

2 May the great truths we here have heard,
The lessons of thy holy Word,
Dwell in our inmost bosoms deep,
And all our souls from error keep.

3 O may the influence of this day
Long as our memory with us stay,
And as an angel guardian prove,
To guide us to our home above.

### HYMN 104. L. M.
*The sower soweth the Word.*

1 O Thou, at whose divine command
Good seed is sown in every land,
Thy Holy Spirit now impart,
And for thy Word prepare each heart.

2 Not 'mid the thorns of worldly thought,
Nor soon by passing plunderers caught,
Nor lacking depth the root to feed,
May we receive thy Spirit's seed.

3 But may it, where thy sowers toil,
Fall in a good and honest soil;
And springing up from firmest root,
Through patience, bear abundant fruit.

### HYMN 105. L. M.
*The kingdom of God is within you.*

1 Heaven is a state of rest from sin;
But all who hope to enter there,
Must here that course of life begin,
Which shall their souls for heaven prepare.

2 Clean hearts, O God, in us create;
Right spirits, Lord, in us renew;
Commence we now that higher state,
To do thy will as angels do.

3 In Jesus' footsteps may we tread,
Learn every lesson of his love;
And by his grace and truth be led,
From life below to heaven above.

### HYMN 106. 7's
*Thou shalt be pleased with the sacrifices of righteousness.*

1 Lord, what offering shall we bring,
At thine altars when we bow?
Hearts, the pure, unsullied spring,
Whence the kind affections flow:

2 Willing hands, to lead the blind,
Heal the wounded, feed the poor;
Love, embracing all our kind;
Charity, with liberal store.

3 Teach us, O thou Heavenly King,
Thus to show our grateful mind,
Thus the accepted offering bring,
Love to Thee and all mankind.

### HYMN 107. S. M.

*A new Commandment I give unto you, that ye love one another.*

1 THAT blessed law of thine,
   Father, to me impart—
The Spirit's law of life divine,
   O write it in my heart.

2 Implant it deep within,
   Whence it may ne'er remove—
The law of liberty from sin,
   The perfect law of love.

3 Thy nature be my law,
   Thy spotless sanctity;
And nearer every moment draw
   My trusting soul to Thee.

### HYMN 108. C. M.

*Give, and it shall be given unto you.*

1 Pour forth the oil; pour freely forth;
   It will not fail, until
Thou failest vessels to provide,
   Which it may largely fill.

2 Make channels for the streams of love,
   Where they may broadly run;
And love has overflowing streams,
   To fill them every one.

3 But if at any time we cease
   Such channels to provide,
The very founts of love for us
   Will soon be parched and dried.

4 For we must share, if we would keep
   That blessing from above:

Ceasing to give, we cease to have:
Such is the law of love.

## HYMN 109. 7's.

*As ye would that men should do to you, do ye also to them.*

1 Thus said Jesus : "Go and do
As thou wouldst be done unto:"
Here thy perfect duty see,
All that God requires of thee.

2 Wouldst thou, when thy faults are known,
Wish that pardon should be shown?
Be forgiving, then, and do
As thou wouldst be done unto.

3 Shouldst thou helpless be and poor,
Wouldst thou not for aid implore?
Think of others, then, and be
What thou wouldst they should to thee.

4 For compassion if thou call,
Be compassionate to all:
If thou wouldst affection find,
Be affectionate and kind.

5 If thou wouldst obtain the love
Of thy gracious Lord above,
Then to all His children be
What thou wouldst they should to thee.

## HYMN 110. L. M.

*The grass withereth, the flower fadeth:
But the Word of our God shall stand forever.*

1 The morning flowers display their sweets,
And gay their silken leaves unfold,
As careless of the noontide heats,
As fearless of the evening cold.

2 Nipped by the wind's untimely blast,
Parched by the sun's directer ray,
The momentary glories waste,
The short-lived beauties die away.

3 So blooms the human face divine,
When youth its pride of beauty shows;
Fairer than spring the colors shine,
And sweeter than the opening rose.

4 But worn by slowly rolling years,
   Or broke by sickness in a day,
   The fading glory disappears,
   The short-lived beauties die away.

5 But inward beauties pass the tomb:
   With lustre brighter far they shine,
   In human form, with youthful bloom,
   Safe from diseases and decline.

6 Let sickness blast, let death devour,
   If heavenly life support our pains:
   Perish the grass, and fade the flower,
   For firm the love of GOD remains.

### HYMN 111. S. M.

*And they heard a voice from heaven, saying unto them, Come up hither.*

1 COME to the land of peace,
   From shadows come away;
   Where all the sounds of weeping cease,
   And storms no more have sway.

2 Fear hath no dwelling here;
   But pure repose and love
   Breathe through the bright, celestial air
   The spirit of the dove.

3 Come to the bright and blest,
   Gathered from every land;
   For here thy soul shall find its rest,
   Amidst the shining band.

4 In this divine abode
   Change leaves no saddening trace;
   Come, trusting spirit, to thy GOD,
   Thy holy resting-place.

### HYMN 112. S. M.

*And the Spirit and the Bride say, Come.*

1 THE Spirit in our hearts
   Is whispering, "Wanderer, come."
   The Bride, the church of CHRIST, proclaims
   To all his children, "Come."

2 Let him that heareth say
   To all about him, "Come."

Let him that thirsts for righteousness,
To CHRIST, the fountain, come.

3 Yes, whosoever will,
O let him freely come,
And freely drink the stream of life;
'Tis JESUS bids you come.

4 Lo, JESUS, who invites,
Declares, "I quickly come."
LORD, even so; I wait thine hour;
JESUS, my Savior, come.

HYMN 113. 7's.

*He shall give His angels charge over thee.*

1 THEY, who on the LORD rely,
Safely dwell, though danger's nigh;
Lo, His sheltering wings are spread
O'er each faithful servant's head.

2 Vain temptation's wily snare;
They shall be their Father's care:
Harmless flies the shaft by day,
Or in darkness wings its way.

3 When they wake, or when they sleep,
Angel guards their vigils keep:
Death and danger may be near;
Faith and love can never fear.

HYMN 114. L. M.

*Awake, awake, put on thy strength, O Zion.*

1 TRIUMPHANT Zion, lift thy head
From dust, and darkness, and the dead:
Though humbled long, awake at length,
And gird thee with thy SAVIOR's strength.

2 Put all thy beauteous garments on,
And let thine excellence be known:
Decked in the robes of righteousness,
Thy glories shall the world confess.

3 No more shall foes unclean invade,
And fill thy hallowed walls with dread:
No more shall sin's insulting host
Their victory and thy sorrows boast.

4 The LORD on high has heard thy prayer;
His hand thy ruin shall repair;
Nor will thy watchful monarch cease
To guard thee in eternal peace.

## HYMN 115. C. M.

*Put on thy beautiful garments O Jerusalem, the holy city*

1 DAUGHTER of Zion, from the dust
  Lift up thy fallen head:
  Again in thy Redeemer trust;
  He calls thee from the dead.

2 Awake, awake, put on thy strength,
  Thy beautiful array;
  The day of freedom dawns at length,
  The LORD's appointed day.

3 Rebuild thy walls, thy bounds enlarge,
  And send thy heralds forth;
  Say to the south, "Give up thy charge,
  And keep not back, O north."

4 They come, they come: thine exiled bands,
  Where'er they rest or roam,
  Have heard thy voice in distant lands,
  And hasten to their home.

## HYMN 116. 7's.

*Jehovah shall keep thy going out and thy coming in.*

1 Now the shades of night are gone;
  Now the morning light is come:
  LORD, may we be thine to-day;
  Drive the shades of sin away.

2 Fill our souls with heavenly light;
  Banish doubt, and clear our sight:
  In thy service, LORD, to-day,
  May we stand, and watch, and pray

3 Keep our evil passions bound;
  Save us from our foes around;
  Going out and coming in,
  Keep us safe from every sin.

# INDEX TO THE HYMNS.

| TITLE. | AUTHOR. | PAGE. |
|---|---|---|
| A charge to keep I have | C. Wesley | 19 |
| All hail the great Immanuel's name | Perronet | 22 |
| Angels, roll the rock away | T. Scott, altered | 21 |
| As the hart, with eager looks | Montgomery | 50 |
| At thy table, Lord of life | Anonymous | 35 |
| Before Jehovah's holy throne | Watts, altered | 6 |
| Begin, my soul, the exalted lay | Ogilvie | 9 |
| Behold, the Savior weeps | Conference Hymns | 19 |
| Be joyful in God, all ye lands of the earth | Montgomery | 5 |
| Be thou, O God, exalted high | Tate and Brady | 6 |
| Blest are the pure in heart | Keble | 49 |
| Bread of heaven, on thee we feed | Pratt's Coll. | 51 |
| Built by Jehovah's hand | Conference Hymns | 47 |
| By cool Siloam's shady rill | Heber | 46 |
| Calm on the listening ear of night | E. H. Sears | 25 |
| Come hither, all ye weary souls | Watts | 20 |
| Come, let us join our cheerful songs | Watts | 21 |
| Come, said Jesus' sacred voice | Barbauld | 20 |
| Come, sound his praise abroad | Watts | 33 |
| Come to the land of peace | Briggs's Coll | 56 |
| Daughter of Zion, from the dust | Montgomery | 58 |
| Ere to the world again we go | Univ. Coll. | 52 |
| Eternal source of every joy | Doddridge | 45 |
| Eternal source of life and light | Cappe's Sel., altered | 41 |
| Father, how wide thy glory shines | Watts, altered | 16 |
| Father of every holy tie | Anonymous, altered | 35 |
| Father of mercies, in thy Word | Steele | 28 |
| Father, whate'er of earthly bliss | Steele | 38 |
| Firm and unmoved are they | Watts, altered | 15 |
| Forever blessed be the Lord | Watts | 24 |
| From all that dwell below the skies | Watts | 10 |
| Give thanks to God, he reigns above | Watts | 8 |
| Give to the Lord immortal praise | Watts | 7 |
| Glory to thee, my God, this night | Kenn, altered | 44 |
| God is the refuge of his saints | Watts | 10 |
| God moves in a mysterious way | Cowper | 11 |
| God, my supporter, and my hope | Watts | 12 |
| God of the morning, at thy voice | Watts | 43 |
| Guide me, O thou great Jehovah | Oliver | 36 |
| Hark, the glad sound; Jehovah comes | Doddridge, altered | 17 |
| Heaven is a state of rest from sin | Montgomery, altered | 53 |
| High, in yonder realms of light | Raffles | 42 |
| How gentle God's commands | Doddridge | 40 |
| How precious is the book divine | Fawcett | 26 |
| How shall the young secure their hearts | Watts | 26 |
| How shall we celebrate thy love | Conference Hymns | 27 |
| I love the volume of thy Word | Watts, altered | 27 |
| In all my vast concerns with thee | Watts | 29 |
| Jehovah, Lord of heaven | Conference Hymns | 47 |
| Jesus, in thee our hopes shall rest | Conference Hymns | 23 |
| Jesus, Lord of all creation | Conference Hymns | 22 |
| Jesus, refuge of my soul | C. Wesley, altered | 24 |
| Jesus shall reign where'er the sun | Watts | 48 |
| Lo, Israel's gentle Shepherd stands | Flint's Coll., altered | 52 |
| Long as I live, I'll bless thy name | Watts | 8 |

# INDEX TO THE HYMNS.

| TITLE. | AUTHOR | PAGE. |
|---|---|---|
| Lord, at thy sacred feet | Conference Hymns | 32 |
| Lord, dismiss us with thy blessing | Burder | 38 |
| Lord of the heavens above | Watts, altered | 33 |
| Lord, thou hast searched and seen me through | Watts | 29 |
| Lord, what offering shall we bring | J. Taylor | 53 |
| Love divine, all love excelling | C. Wesley | 49 |
| Mortals, awake, with angels join | Medley, altered | 17 |
| My soul, repeat his praise | Watts | 14 |
| Not for the summer hour alone | Mrs. Sigourney | 36 |
| Now the shades of night are gone | Episcopal Coll. | 58 |
| Now to the Lord a noble song | Watts | 18 |
| O bless the Lord, my soul | Watts | 23 |
| O cease, my wandering soul | Episcopal Coll. | 16 |
| O happy day, that fixed my choice | Doddridge, altered | 37 |
| O Lord, how boundless is thy love | Watts, altered | 44 |
| O Lord, my Father, while I stray | Anonymous | 39 |
| O Lord of grace and purity | West Boston Coll., alt. | 34 |
| O Lord, our help in ages past | Watts | 12 |
| On Jordan's stormy banks I stand | S. Stennett | 42 |
| O render thanks to God above | Tate and Brady | 7 |
| O that the Lord would guide my ways | Watts | 28 |
| O thou, at whose divine command | Alford | 53 |
| O thou, to whose all-searching sight | J. Wesley, altered | 30 |
| Peace of God, which knows no measure | Anonymous | 49 |
| Pour forth the oil; pour freely forth | Trench | 54 |
| Praise to God, immortal praise | Barbauld | 45 |
| Prayer is the simplest form of speech | Montgomery | 46 |
| Return, O wanderer, now return | Collyer, altered | 50 |
| Salvation, O the joyful sound | Watts | 18 |
| Sing to the Lord Jehovah's name | Watts | 32 |
| Suppliant, lo, thy children bend | Gray | 50 |
| Sweet is the memory of thy grace | Watts | 14 |
| Sweet is the work, my God, my King | Watts | 43 |
| That blessed law of thine | C. Wesley | 54 |
| The Lord descended from above | Sternhold | 18 |
| The Lord is in his holy temple | Conference Hymns, alt. | 31 |
| The Lord my pasture shall prepare | Addison | 13 |
| The Lord my Shepherd is | Watts | 13 |
| The Lord our Savior is the Way | Conference Hymns | 20 |
| The morning flowers display their sweets | S. Wesley, altered | 55 |
| The spacious firmament on high | Addison | 9 |
| The Spirit in our hearts | Anonymous | 56 |
| There is a land of pure delight | Watts | 41 |
| They who on the Lord rely | Spirit of the Psalms | 57 |
| Thine earthly sabbaths, Lord, we love | Doddridge | 34 |
| Through thee as we together came | Anonymous | 52 |
| Thus said Jesus, Go and do | W. Roscoe | 55 |
| Thy servant, gracious Lord, receive | Conference Hymns | 34 |
| Thy will be done: In devious way | Bowring | 40 |
| Triumphant Zion, lift thy head | Anonymous | 57 |
| 'Twas in the watches of the night | Watts | 44 |
| We join to pray, with wishes kind | Gaskell, altered | 51 |
| What glory gilds the sacred page | Cowper | 25 |
| What shall I render to my God | Watts | 37 |
| When all thy mercies, gracious Lord | Addison, altered | 30 |
| When, overwhelmed with grief | Watts | 14 |
| While my Redeemer's near | Steele | 24 |
| While thee I seek, protecting Power | H. M. Williams | 39 |
| Whom have we, Lord, in heaven but thee | Anonymous | 15 |
| With one consent, let all the earth | Tate and Brady | 5 |
| With reverence let us all appear | Watts, altered | 31 |

www.ingramcontent.com/pod-product-compliance
Lightning Source LLC
Chambersburg PA
CBHW022106300426
44117CB00007B/614